A LIBERAL THEORY OF PROPERTY

Property enhances autonomy for most people, but not for all. Because it both empowers and disables, property requires constant vigilance. *A Liberal Theory of Property* addresses key questions: How can property be justified? What core values should property law advance, and how do those values interrelate? How is a liberal state obligated to act when shaping property law? In a liberal polity, the primary commitment to individual autonomy dominates the justification of property, founding it on three pillars: carefully delineated private authority, structural (but not value) pluralism, and relational justice. A genuinely liberal property law meets the legitimacy challenge confronting property by expanding people's opportunities for individual and collective self-determination while carefully restricting their options of interpersonal domination. The book shows how the three pillars of liberal property account for core features of existing property systems, provide a normative vocabulary for evaluating central doctrines, and offer directions for urgent reforms.

Hanoch Dagan is the Stewart and Judy Colton Professor of Legal Theory and Innovation and Director of the Edmond J. Safra Center for Ethics at Tel Aviv University. Dagan has written seven books across the landscape of core private law topics, including *Property: Values and Institutions* (2011) and *The Choice Theory of Contracts* (2017), and has published more than eighty articles in major law reviews and journals. He has been a visiting professor at Yale University, Columbia University, the University of Michigan, Cornell University, the University of California, Los Angeles, and the University of Toronto law schools.

A Liberal Theory of Property

Hanoch Dagan
Tel Aviv University

CAMBRIDGE
UNIVERSITY PRESS

University Printing House, Cambridge CB2 8BS, United Kingdom

One Liberty Plaza, 20th Floor, New York, NY 10006, USA

477 Williamstown Road, Port Melbourne, VIC 3207, Australia

314–321, 3rd Floor, Plot 3, Splendor Forum, Jasola District Centre, New Delhi – 110025, India

79 Anson Road, #06–04/06, Singapore 079906

Cambridge University Press is part of the University of Cambridge.

It furthers the University's mission by disseminating knowledge in the pursuit of education, learning, and research at the highest international levels of excellence.

www.cambridge.org
Information on this title: www.cambridge.org/9781108418546
DOI: 10.1017/9781108290340

© Cambridge University Press 2021

This publication is in copyright. Subject to statutory exception and to the provisions of relevant collective licensing agreements, no reproduction of any part may take place without the written permission of Cambridge University Press.

First published 2021

A catalogue record for this publication is available from the British Library.

Library of Congress Cataloging-in-Publication Data
Names: Dagan, Ḥanokh, author.
Title: A liberal theory of property / Hanoch Dagan, Tel Aviv University Faculty of Law.
Description: Cambridge ; New York, NY : Cambridge University Press, 2021. | Includes bibliographical references and index.
Identifiers: LCCN 2020016003 (print) | LCCN 2020016004 (ebook) | ISBN 9781108418546 (hardback) | ISBN 9781108407533 (paperback) | ISBN 9781108290340 (epub)
Subjects: LCSH: Property–Philosophy. | Property–Political aspects. | Liberalism.
Classification: LCC HB701 .D37 2021 (print) | LCC HB701 (ebook) | DDC 330.1/7–dc23
LC record available at https://lccn.loc.gov/2020016003
LC ebook record available at https://lccn.loc.gov/2020016004

ISBN 978-1-108-41854-6 Hardback
ISBN 978-1-108-40753-3 Paperback

Cambridge University Press has no responsibility for the persistence or accuracy of URLs for external or third-party internet websites referred to in this publication and does not guarantee that any content on such websites is, or will remain, accurate or appropriate.

For Noa, Maya, and Tomer

CONTENTS

Preface . . . . *page* xi

1 **Liberal Property** 1
   From Autonomy to Property 1
   Carefully Delineated Private Authority 4
   Structural Pluralism 6
   Relational Justice 7
   Against the Current 9
   A Brief Roadmap 10

2 **Some Basics** 13
   Property Theory As Legal Theory 13
   Property Theory As Interpretive Theory 16
   Property and Property Types 19
   Property As a Category of Thinking 23
   Property and Contract 25
   Resources and Relations 26
   Form and Substance 31
   Liberal Polity 35

3 **Autonomy and Private Authority** 41
   From Independence to Self-Determination 42
   Property and the Promotion of Autonomy 44
   Ultimate, Intrinsic, and Instrumental Values 46
   Personhood 50
   Community 51
   Utility 55
   Autonomy As Side Constraint 58
   The Powers of Property 60
   Justifying Property 62

	Risking Panglossianism?	67
	Inherent Limitations of Property's Power	68
	Autonomy and Distribution	71
	Challenge of Neutrality	75
4	**Property's Structural Pluralism**	**79**
	Variety of Property	79
	Property Governance	82
	Commons Property	84
	Multiplicity and Autonomy	89
	Nozick's Utopia	93
	Law's Role	96
	Blackstonian Ownership	100
	Developing an Adequate Range of Types	102
	Missing Types	106
	Numerus Clausus	110
5	**Property's Relational Justice**	**114**
	Kantian Property	115
	Mission Impossible	118
	Mission Undesirable	122
	Relational Justice	126
	Relationally Just Private Authority	128
	Public Accommodations	131
	Fair Housing	135
	Owners' Responsibilities	139
	Unjust Property Types	142
6	**Making Property Law**	**148**
	Property's Core and the Institutional Question	149
	Performance	151
	Legitimacy	155
	Both Legislatures and Courts	158
	Property and the Rule of Law	159
	Guidance	161
	The Birth of Common-Interest Communities	163
	Structural Pluralism and Rules	165
	Informative Standards	166
	Constraint	168
	Revisiting *Shelley v. Kraemer*	170

Contents

	Liberal Property and the Rule of Law	172
	The Human Right to Property	173
	The Global Land Rush	176
7	**Just Markets**	**179**
	What Is a Market?	180
	Property and Markets	183
	Autonomy-Based Markets?	185
	Two Roles	189
	Structural Pluralism	193
	Relational Justice	195
	Changing Plans	200
	Incomplete Commodification	203
	Markets and Labor	207
8	**Property Transitions**	**210**
	Property and Time	210
	Vulnerability and Stability across Time	210
	The Transition Intuition	212
	Lucas's Compact	214
	Rule of Change	217
	Two Unacceptable Pacts	220
	Limits to the Libertarian Pact	223
	Limits to the Progressive Pact	225
	The Liberal Pact	227
	Boundaries to the Liberal Pact	231
	Reconstructing Takings Law	236
9	**Afterword**	**243**
	Notes	249
	Index	319

PREFACE

In my work on property over many years, I developed two themes. One is that rather than revolving around a Blackstonian core of "sole and despotic dominion," property law is structurally pluralistic, meaning it assumes many diverse forms, each with its own internal regime of property governance. The other is that property at times implies – from within rather than as an external constraint – limitations to exclusion and even some rights to inclusion.

In recent years, I have come to realize that many of my earlier discussions of both these themes (pluralism and inclusion) as presented in *Property: Values and Institutions* (Oxford University Press, 2011) are incomplete because all begin from the middle. *A Liberal Theory of Property* solves this problem by developing a missing fundamental premise – the ultimate justification of both themes. It thus places them on firmer ground, thereby refining, extending, and, to some extent, also revising my earlier understanding of property. Its ambition, however, aims higher.

This book argues that property's structural pluralism and the significance of the right to be included – or, more generally, property's compliance with relational justice – are two necessary pillars of a genuinely liberal conception of property, founded on the ultimate value of personal self-determination. *A Liberal Theory of Property* returns the analysis to the mainstream twentieth-century political philosophy of liberalism – a tradition enhancing self-determination that is almost absent from property theory today. As such, it offers a coherent and robust vision of property in a liberal society. (I use the terms "liberal" and "liberalism" in their denotation in political philosophy rather than in that common in American or European public discourse, where they are respectively associated – confusingly enough – with the political left and the political right.)

Property should be understood in structurally pluralistic terms because only in those terms can it be conducive to autonomy. We should cultivate the heterogeneity of our existing property law because the multiplicity of property types facilitates the rich diversity of interpersonal relationships needed for adequate self-determination. A repertoire of property types creates a menu of viable opportunities for both individual and collective self-determination. Facilitating this autonomy-enhancing pluralism through law is crucial because collective action problems, bounded rationality, and cognitive failures undermine many types of interactions and, consequently, people's ability to pursue their own conception of the good.

A similar analysis applies to the right to be included, which I now understand as one aspect of the prescription of relational justice, namely, reciprocal respect for self-determination. Thus, fair housing rules that prohibit discrimination in the sale or rental of residential dwellings, for example, are not external to property law. Interpersonal discriminatory practices are objectionable per se, regardless of whether the state takes care of its obligations of distributive justice and democratic citizenship. Refusing to consider a potential house buyer merely because of her skin color, for example, fails to respect the individual on her own terms.

Property law must not (and genuinely liberal property does not) authorize social relationships that reject the equal autonomy of the person subject to discrimination. The limits that property law sets on an owner's right to exclude – as well as the burdens and obligations that accompany ownership in other contexts – reflect liberal property's underlying commitment to reciprocal respect for self-determination.

I will argue that, in order to be legitimate, property is to be premised on a fundamental commitment to autonomy as self-determination or self-authorship. This commitment explains and justifies both the private authority that characterizes all property types and their inherent limitations: whereas property *simpliciter* is private authority, the private authority of liberal property is carefully delineated and circumscribed by its service to owners' autonomy. The commitment to self-determination also explains why a genuinely liberal property law must be both structurally pluralistic and committed to relational justice.

This autonomy-based theory, in which property is founded on the three pillars of *carefully delineated private authority, structural pluralism,* and *relational justice,* is different from some orthodox liberal understandings of property. And yet, as I hope to show in these pages, it is also firmly grounded in liberalism's most fundamental commitments. Finally, this autonomy-based theory of property also turns out to be more faithful to the practice of property than its counterparts.

This book does not attempt to offer a sustained critique of these alternative theories, some of which I have discussed at length elsewhere. Rather, my ambition is to offer a concise articulation and defense of the autonomy-based theory of property I have just sketched. In order to accomplish this mission, I explore the implications that the conception of autonomy as self-determination entails for property. I also address some important challenges confronting an autonomy-enhancing conception of property. Some of these challenges are built into this conception: insufficient or unjust property types are blemishes in the law that the theory helps to highlight, as are property types legally granting authority to owners beyond the scope required for their self-determination. Other challenges emerge once we recognize the complex role that law plays in the ideal of the liberal conception of property and as we try to situate this ideal within the dynamic market-based environment typical of modern societies.

This book shows how property law can enhance individual autonomy while also facing these challenges. Like other interpretive theories of law, it offers a perspective for presenting existing law in its best light, which, as usual, can be helpful in improving understanding, application, and refinement of the actual law. It also generates some proposals for reforming the law to bring it closer to its implicit (autonomy-enhancing) ideals.

Some sections of this book draw on my previous writings, though at times with significant revisions, and I gratefully acknowledge permission for including here from *Pluralism and Perfectionism in Private Law,* 112 COLUM. L. REV. 1409 (2012); *Doctrinal Categories, Legal Realism, and The Rule of Law,* 163 U. PA. L. REV. 1889 (2015); *Inside Property,* 63 U. TORONTO L.J. 1 (2013); *Property's Structural Pluralism: On Autonomy, the Rule of Law, and the Role of Blackstonian Ownership,* 3 BRIGHAM-KANNER PROP. RTS. CONF. J. 27 (2014); *The*

Utopian Promise of Private Law, 65 U. TORONTO L.J. 392 (2016); *The Public Dimension of Private Property*, 24 KING'S L.J. 260 (2013); *The Human Right to Private Property*, 18 THEORETICAL INQ. L. 391 (2017) (with Avihay Dorfman); *Just Relationships*, 116 COLUM. L. REV. 1395 (2016) (with Avihay Dorfman); *Liberalism and the Private Law of Property*, 1 CRIT. ANAL. L. 268 (2014); *The Challenges of Private Law*, in PRIVATE LAW IN THE TWENTY-FIRST CENTURY 67 (Kit Barker et al. eds., 2017); *Judges and Property*, in INTELLECTUAL PROPERTY AND THE COMMON LAW 17 (Shyamkrishna Balganesh ed., 2013); *Private Law Pluralism and the Rule of Law*, in PRIVATE LAW AND THE RULE OF LAW 158 (Lisa Austin & Dennis Klimchuk eds., 2014); *Markets for Self-Authorship*, 28 CORNELL J.L. & PUB. POL'Y 577 (2018); *Why Markets? Welfare, Autonomy, and the Just Society*, 117 MICH. L. REV. 1289 (2019); *Liberalism and the Commons*, 29 CORNELL J.L. & PUB. POL'Y 527 (2020).

These papers benefited from comments by many colleagues as well as by participants at the Cecil A. Wright Memorial Lecture at the University of Toronto Faculty of Law; the conference on "Moral Values in Private Law" at King's College London; the conference on "Private Law Theory" at Villa Vigoni, Lake Como; the conference on "Private Law and the Basic Structure of Society" at the University of Amsterdam; the symposium on "Sovereignty and Property" at the Columbia Law School; the symposium on "The New Doctrinalism" at the University of Pennsylvania Law School; the conference on "The Public/Private Interface in Property" at King's College London; the conference on "The Core of Property" in Frankfurt; the workshop on "Private Law and Public Order" at the Yale Law School; the symposium on "Intellectual Property and the Common Law" at the University of Pennsylvania Law School; the conference on "Private Law and The Rule of Law" at the University of Toronto Faculty of Law; the conference on "The Ethical Challenges of the Market" at the Cornell Law School; the symposium on "The Core Principles of Expropriation Law" in The Hague; and workshops in Amsterdam, Bar-Ilan, Boston, Cardozo, Columbia, Connecticut, Cornell, Fordham, Georgetown, Harvard, Hebrew, IDC, Maryland, Northeastern, NYU, Ramat-Gan, Seton Hall, Tel Aviv, Trento, UCLA, Utrecht, William & Mary, and Yale Law Schools.

Preface

For very helpful comments on this manuscript or parts of it, I am very grateful to Gregory Alexander, Lisa Austin, Aditi Bagchi, Stuart Banner, Itzik Benbaji, Mitch Berman, Nick Blomley, Andrew Botterell, Alan Brudner, Peter Cane, Chiara Cordelli, Nestor Davidson, Avihay Dorfman, Oran Doyle, Neil Duxbury, David Dyzenhaus, Fabrizio Esposito, Chris Essert, Bill Ewald, Lee Fennell, Tali Fisher, Dalit Flaiszhaker, Sheila Foster, Rachel Friedman, Chaim Ganz, Maytal Gilboa, Andrew Gold, David Grewal, Mateusz Grochowski, Andrew Halpin, Sarah Hamill, Ori Herstein, Lisa Herzog, Martijn Hesselink, Sonia Katyal, Larissa Katz, Dennis Klimchuk, Roy Kreitner, Tami Kricheli-Katz, Yael Lifshitz, Adam MacLeod, Menny Mautner, Colin Mayer, Åsbjørn Melkevik, Tom Merrill, Paul Miller, Attila Mráz, Guy Mundlak, Szymon Osmola, Eduardo Peñalver, James Penner, Stephen Perry, Katharina Pistor, David Posen, Robert Post, Aloke Prabhu, Arthur Ripstein, Carol Rose, Arie Rosen, Itamar Rosensweig, Kineret Sadeh, Irit Samet, Amy Sepinwall, Chris Serkin, Molly Shaffer Van Houweling, Assaf Sharon, Joe Singer, Henry Smith, Ohad Somech, Theodosia Stavroulaki, Shai Stern, Simon Stern, Giacomo Tagiuri, Sabine Tsuruda, Laura Underkuffler, Konstanze von Schütz, Ernie Weinrib, Leif Wenar, Katrina Wyman, Mikhaïl Xifaras, Tal Zarsky, Lorenzo Zucca, and participants at the Singapore Symposium in Legal Theory; the Private Law Group's Annual Public Lecture at Trinity College Dublin; the conference on "Property Rights and Human Rights: New Possibilities in an Age of Inequality" at Monash University; the conference on "Property Works in Progress" at Boston University; the International Summer School of The Centre for the Study of European Contract Law; the workshop of the Institute for Law and Philosophy at the University of Pennsylvania; the Legal Theory Workshop at the University of Toronto Faculty of Law; and a joint session of the Advanced Property and Trusts Seminar and the Property Law Discussion Group at the University of Oxford Faculty of Law.

Particular thanks go to my longtime coauthors Michael Heller and Avihay Dorfman, whose contributions to this book are evident in many of its pages. Whereas only Chapter 8 is officially coauthored with Michael, a few other core sections in Chapters 2–4 rely on our previous joint work on both *The Choice Theory of Contracts* (Cambridge University Press, 2017) and on the articles *The Liberal Commons* and *Conflicts in Property*. Avihay's fingerprints are no less conspicuous. Most of Chapter 5 draws heavily on our articles on relational justice (notably *Just Relationships*), and a few important sections in both Chapters 3 and 6 follow our *Human Right to Private Property* piece. Coauthorship is a subtle enterprise and I feel particularly thankful for having had Michael and Avihay in this role. I am deeply indebted to both of them for sharing with me their wisdom, insights, and good judgment, and for numerous exchanges of both ideas and drafts that were essential for refining the thesis of this book.

Finally, warm thanks to Batya Stein for exceptional editorial assistance and to my editor Matt Gallaway for shepherding this project from proposal to publication.

1 LIBERAL PROPERTY

A long tradition in Western political thought connects property and liberalism. John Locke is probably the most familiar liberal theorist to give property a place of honor in his account of the state. But Locke, whose property theory is fraught with difficulties,[1] is certainly not the only one. The right to property is often understood as one of the necessary implications of the status of individual natural persons as free and equal, which may explain its inclusion in the Universal Declaration of Human Rights.[2]

But what do we mean when we invoke liberalism's core commitments to freedom and equality as property's normative premise, and how do these underpinnings impact property law? This introductory chapter provides a short (and necessarily partial and sketchy) synopsis of my answer to this question, which the following chapters elaborate, refine, and defend.

FROM AUTONOMY TO PROPERTY

The core claim of this book is that an analysis of property needs to start from the mainstream liberal tradition of the past century, that is, with a concern for individual autonomy, self-determination, and self-authorship, ensuring to all of us as free and equal individuals the possibility of writing and rewriting our own life stories. This deep and widely shared commitment to people's most fundamental right to self-determination appropriately dominates the central political, legal, and philosophical debates. In more recent times, however, this tradition has, surprisingly, almost disappeared from works on private law generally and on property law specifically.[3]

Property is not the most crucial precondition of personal self-determination; health, education, and means of subsistence are surely more basic. Nonetheless, property does play a distinctive and irreducible role in empowering people. It provides them some temporally extended control over tangible and intangible resources, which they need in order to carry out their projects and advance their plans. The authority that property confers on owners facilitates their ability to determine and pursue their own goals.

Appreciation of property's contribution to autonomy highlights the most fundamental failure of the prevalent view that property is a means for the maximization of welfare. If the private authority of owners serves as a significant self-determination resource, property law cannot be solely dependent on its contribution to the social good. Some sphere of private ownership is imperative in a liberal law even if – say, due to technological advances – eliminating ownership would be welfare-maximizing.

Property's contribution to self-determination is also vital for an understanding of law's requirement that others respect an owner's authority, which is by no means obvious. Quite the contrary. Without suitable justification, law's demand (or even expectation) that non-owners – whose right to self-determination is equally important – defer to owners' authority regarding what to do with an object seems arbitrary and unjust.

The class of nonowners, like that of owners, encompasses everyone: After all, everyone is an owner of *something*. But this truism does not imply that property is always justified or that all property systems are equally justified. Rather, the privileged authority invested in owners through property – the normative power they have over others – implies that property law needs to be answerable to these others – the subjects of this authority. The interpersonal vulnerability generated by property suggests that this justificatory standard is quite onerous. While not everyone needs to accept every individual claim to every particular resource, showing that everyone should accept some abstract idea of property is not enough either. For a property system to be justified, its *animating principles* must be acceptable.[4]

Because the private authority of owners plays a key role in ensuring individual autonomy, property *can* be justified if property law not only

From Autonomy to Property

relies upon but is also guided by our foundational duty to respect each other's self-determination. Thus, while property writ large is private authority *simpliciter*, *liberal* property conceives of that authority as a means of self-determination. In other words, whereas property systems assign private authority over resources in numerous ways, property law can face its formidable justificatory challenge only if it carefully follows property's autonomy-enhancing function. Accordingly, liberal property conceptualizes property as an empowering device in the service of people's self-determination. It understands this contribution to self-determination as property's *telos*.

Property systems vary widely in the way they allocate normative powers to people and cannot be expected to perform uniformly concerning human empowerment. Some of these differences reflect varying environmental, economic, social, cultural, and technological circumstances. But the justifiability of any particular property system is still a function of its performance in light of these circumstances vis-à-vis property's *telos*, namely, its *support* for people's autonomy. In this book, I unpack this proposition and study its implications, but one essential clarification is required at the outset: Performing this function, though necessary, may not be sufficient.

Property cannot be adequately justified simply by reference to the benefits by definition common to all, which derive from the *potential* of being an owner in a property system that, as a whole, is autonomy-enhancing. Instead, in a liberal polity, people have a right to the effective realization of property's autonomy-enhancing potential.[5] This requirement implies that property must rely on a robust background regime that guarantees the material, social, and intellectual preconditions of self-authorship to everyone, together with the authority typical of full private ownership.

Specifying the details of such a background regime exceeds the scope of this book – a theory of liberal property is neither a blueprint nor a full-blown theory of justice. The significance of a liberal theory of property, however, goes beyond the intricacies of property law. Property is a keystone of our economic, social, and political system, and the impact of how we shape it and understand it is therefore far-reaching, as my discussion of markets, especially labor markets, will clearly show.

Consequently, the commitment to individual autonomy in a liberal polity dominates not only the justification of property but also its constitution and thus its most fundamental legal features. Private authority cannot possibly exhaust the idea of liberal property because a genuinely liberal property law proactively expands people's opportunities for both individual and collective self-determination, while carefully restricting their opportunities for interpersonal domination.

A liberal property system thus needs more than one form of property, offering prospective owners (and other property right holders) a choice of options for both individual and communal self-determination, while constantly remaining attentive to the concerns of nonowners. These concerns are intrinsic to property because the instantiation or expansion of property necessarily limits nonowners' liberty. Hence, liberal law should ensure both that no private authority can be claimed in excess of what is required for owners' self-determination, and that such authority is consistent with the self-determination of others.

In a genuinely liberal polity, then, law must be made to rest on the three pillars of the autonomy-enhancing conception of property:

1. Circumscription of owners' private authority to ensure that it follows property's contribution to self-determination
2. Creation of a structurally pluralistic inventory of property types offering people real choice
3. Compliance of owners' powers with relational justice to verify that property does not offend the principle of reciprocal respect for self-determination substantiating its legitimacy

A liberal theory of property highlights its autonomy-enhancing *telos* and studies its implications in order to push property law toward the fulfillment of this implicit promise. I have made that my mission in this book.

CAREFULLY DELINEATED PRIVATE AUTHORITY

Self-determination involves planning. Although people can obviously change their plans and autonomous persons should be entitled to do so, planning is intrinsic to the right to self-determination.[6] In turn, the ability to plan requires some horizon of action, which is facilitated by the temporally extended private authority over resources that property typifies. Thus, property is conducive to people's ability to pursue meaningful projects and goals, be it on their own or with the cooperation of others.

Insofar as property's private authority advances the autonomy of owners along these lines, they can justifiably expect others to respect it and the law rightly vindicates this expectation. Property's private authority – the interpersonal power it generates – is thus justified by reference to its potential contribution to the owners' self-determination. The private authority established by any given type of property, therefore, needs to be adjusted to this contribution. Carefully delineated private authority is the first pillar of liberal property.

Certain types of property contribute to self-determination only indirectly, and a liberal property law needs to structure these types to prevent them from involving an exacting private authority. Circumscribing the private authority that these property types instantiate, then, does not rely on public requirements from owners to support state responsibilities but follows directly from the liberal justification of property. Property's private authority should be delineated so that owners' interpersonal power is indeed necessary for their self-determination.

The paramount outcome of this principle is that the private authority attached to commercial property types – notably to ownership of means of production – must be narrowly circumscribed. A liberal theory of property should not belittle the instrumental role of these resources' ownership as a means for satisfying people's preferences and promoting their welfare, but cannot ignore that private authority over these resources has no freestanding value either. Hence, given that private authority equals interpersonal power, an autonomy-enhancing property law must be particularly vigilant in circumscribing this power. This conclusion dramatically affects the scope of managerial authority, and thus of workers' rights, shaping the liberal idea of a just labor market.

Finally, the combination of property's immanent justificatory challenge and the truisms of changing circumstances and new needs and opportunities implies that liberal property must pay careful attention to the requirement of dynamic changes in the configuration and distribution of property rights.[7] As a result, liberal property needs to be closely aware of property transitions that will invariably upset owners' plans. The temporal dimension of property's autonomy-enhancing *telos* and its ability to face up to its burdensome justificatory challenge is, as I show toward the end of this book, vitally significant to the liberal "property pact" underlying a liberal regime of property transitions.

STRUCTURAL PLURALISM

Property manifests itself in law in a nuanced, contextualized, and multifaceted fashion. The profound heterogeneity of property types causes difficulties for monistic theories that look for *the* structural core of property. From an autonomy-based standpoint, however, this multiplicity is a virtue rather than a concern since it ensures an inventory of alternatives from which people can choose. Structural pluralism is thus a constitutive feature of a liberal property law, the second pillar of a liberal conception of property.

Property law *should* be heterogeneous because there are many ways in which property can support our self-determination, either on our own or – quite often – with others. The internal life of property is accordingly structured through sophisticated governance mechanisms that facilitate various forms of interpersonal relationships, which would not be possible without an enabling legal infrastructure. Think of condos, co-ops, common-interest communities, joint tenancies, leaseholds, and trusts as examples of the existing inventory of land-ownership.

Awareness of property's contribution to autonomy, then, implies celebrating the pluralistic architecture of property law and its many options. Instead of overemphasizing the common denominator of these diverse types or marginalizing certain types as peripheral exceptions to some stipulated core – say, the right to exclude – property is better understood as an umbrella for a limited set of types. These types serve as default frameworks of interpersonal interaction regarding various resources. They thus need to be properly standardized and their interpretation and evaluation should, by and large, look to their specific "local" animating principles.

At its best, this plurality of types enables property law to offer varying balances between the different (intrinsic and instrumental) values that property can serve – independence, personhood, community, and utility – in diverse social settings and respecting a variety of resources. Each of these property types constitutes a distinctive framework of private authority; each offers its own recipe for some temporally extended control that people can have over a resource, either as individuals or as members of a community of owners. When the law's menu of property types is sufficiently rich for each major sphere of human action, it offers people a range of meaningful choices for resource governance and co-governance that supports self-determination.

The obligation of the liberal state to facilitate meaningful choices in important spheres of life implies enabling people's autonomy by ensuring this *intra-sphere multiplicity*, namely, by actively shaping distinct property types that function as *partial functional substitutes*. This obligation is not a matter of strict demand-driven analysis, as an efficiency-based account would have prescribed. Rather, property plays a crucial role in delivering on the liberal promise of self-determination. The state can betray this mission not only by having bad or too much property law. The absence of law, or an attempt to limit property's heterogeneity, will have the same effect. The law's architects, then, are required to develop more types of property, especially in the contexts of housing and the workplace.

RELATIONAL JUSTICE

If property is indeed premised on our foundational duty of mutual respect for self-determination, this duty must apply not only to non-owners but also to owners. Law needs to be attuned to property's effect on self-determination in various contexts of people's interactions as nonowners. The impact of interpersonal contacts on self-determination affirms and vindicates the claims of people – owners and nonowners alike – to mutual respect for self-determination, that is, to relational justice, the third pillar of liberal property.

Relational justice is a conception of interpersonal rather than distributive justice that is notably different from corrective justice, which stands for reciprocal respect for independence. Relational justice focuses on the self-determination of nonowners, but need not, should not, and indeed does not, override the self-determination of owners, an outcome that would have been self-defeating. Relational justice does not undermine the autonomy-enhancing private authority that property creates. Homeowners, for example, are rightly shielded from legal scrutiny of their invitation policy.

By contrast, systemically hierarchical property regimes – such as feudalism, where even tenants under so-called free tenures are obliged to perform services for their lords – represent clear violations of relational justice. Condemning feudalism and similarly repressive property regimes is of course not very controversial and few property theories would celebrate them.[8] But grounding the objection to these regimes on relational justice hints at the breadth and depth of the critical implications ensuing from liberal property's earnest commitment to it. Relational justice limits owners' authority and, at times, also entails burdens and obligations.

Thus, the owners' power of refusal to sell or lease, or to prevent nonowners from entering their land or using their resources, must be – and indeed is – constrained. Common-interest communities law, landlord–tenant law, and the law of public accommodations, all recognize nonowners' claims to access and, more broadly, to respect. Instances of discriminatory exclusion deny nonowners an equal right to self-determination and should thus be viewed (at least prima facie) as *ultra vires*, abusing the institution of property for a purpose that contravenes its *telos*.

Similarly, the commitment of property law to relational justice also explains and justifies some responsibilities incumbent on property rights holders, such as specific burdens of mitigating accidental mistakes by nonowners. Neither the anti-discrimination prescription nor these affirmative obligations depend on any kind of aggregate cost–benefit analysis or on the balance between the right to property and any other conflicting right. Relational justice is not a regulatory or constitutional imposition and its prescriptions immediately follow from the meaning of liberal property itself.

AGAINST THE CURRENT

These propositions, which I attempt to establish in these pages, challenge some conventional views about the nature of property and its liberal foundation. After the bundle-of-sticks picture of property endorsed in the Restatement of Property had for decades been regarded as the conventional wisdom,[9] Blackstone's conception of property as "sole and despotic dominion"[10] has been resurrected as the regulative idea of private property.[11] To be sure, no one seriously thinks any longer that property always entails unqualified dominion. (Blackstone himself did not think so either,[12] even though this view of property is by now intimately connected with his name.) Some theorists, however, again argue that the right to exclude (or its cognates) is the most defining feature of property. The Blackstonian conception seems to be ingrained in the narrative of property,[13] almost inviting the claim that "the differentiating feature of a system of property [is] the right of the owner to act as the exclusive gatekeeper of the owned thing."[14]

This dominion conception of property is closely related to the Kantian understanding of property's normative task. Property, in this view, constrains others because it comprises the external means that a person uses in setting and pursuing purposes, which implies that "if someone interferes with your property, he thereby interferes with your purposiveness."[15] In other words, if people are to be allowed "to exercise their freedom by controlling external objects of choice," the objects are to be subjected to the sole discretion of the choosing party so that all others are bound by the owner's will.[16]

As the preceding preview indicates and the following chapters flesh out, this (renewed) orthodoxy of property as a stronghold of interpersonal independence fails both descriptively and normatively. Descriptively, the dominion understanding of property unduly disregards property's structural pluralism and property's compliance with relational justice. These features of property are particularly conspicuous in contemporary society, where people live more closely together, especially in urban environments. But they are also constitutive of liberal property. The dominion conception of property obscures these features as well as the inherent limitations of private authority in its liberal rendition. Therefore, it is normatively disappointing as well.

Only by grounding property in liberalism's fundamental commitment to individual autonomy can we secure its legitimacy. Property can, should, and in many respects already does enhance our autonomy, namely, the freedom to determine our own life in the context of living with others. A liberal conception of property both justifies and refines the (carefully delineated) private authority property instantiates. Moreover, for liberal property, structural pluralism and relational justice are neither discretionary additions to the private authority of property nor external limitations to it. By founding property on people's right to self-determination, a genuinely liberal law insists on property resting on the three pillars of carefully delineated private authority, structural pluralism, and relational justice.

A BRIEF ROADMAP

A liberal theory of property shows how a foundational commitment to autonomy justifies and shapes property law in a liberal polity, offering (1) a *legal theory* for (2) *property law* in (3) a *liberal polity*. Chapter 2 refines this mission by elaborating on these three components. Having done so, I turn in the next three chapters to my main task: exploring the three pillars of a genuinely liberal property law – carefully delineated private authority, structural pluralism, and relational justice. Some readers may find that following this sequence is helpful, while others may prefer turning to Chapter 2 only after reading Chapters 3–5.

Chapter 3 conceptualizes property as an empowering device crucial to people's self-determination. Property is a power-conferring institution that can only be legitimate if and insofar as the authority it confers, which enables the instantiation of its intrinsic and instrumental values, empowers us in our ultimate right to self-determination. Chapter 3 refines this formidable justificatory challenge and its important implications for the architecture of property and for the background

A Brief Roadmap

regime necessary for its legitimacy. It also explains why grounding property on self-determination is neither perfectionistic nor offensive to the principle of neutrality.

Chapter 4 focuses on structural pluralism, arguing that property's heterogeneity is both irreducible and constructive in a property system centered on enhancing autonomy. This plurality of property types is profound as well as a matter of principle. It is profound in that it reflects fundamental differences between the core values animating these property types and it is a matter of principle in that it serves the liberal commitment to autonomy-enhancing pluralism. In conclusion, Chapter 4 shows that this understanding of property's plurality provides opportunities for reform through support for innovative types and rejection of the *numerus clausus* principle's canonical understanding.

Chapter 5 turns to the third pillar of liberal property: its commitment to relational justice based on reciprocal respect for self-determination. Rejecting the conventional division of labor between public and private law, it argues that people's interdependence and their personal differences imply that the liberal commitment to self-determination, and thus also to substantive equality, cannot be left out of their interpersonal interactions. It then argues that liberal property systems can accommodate commitments to both private authority and relational justice.

Having set in place the three pillars of a liberal property theory, my focus will shift to the theory's institutional dimension. (The significance of this dimension is clarified in Chapter 2.) Chapter 6 argues that both the legislature and the judiciary should be responsible for developing property law. It further maintains that, notwithstanding its multiplicity and dynamism, a liberal conception of property is likely to comply with the two core aspects of the rule of law: providing guidance and restraining the power of officials. Finally, I claim that the autonomy-based foundation of property also implies that (liberal) property is a human right that bounds the power of judges and legislators and provides standing against governments and private parties.

Whereas Chapter 6 deals with the institutional context involved in the creation of property types, Chapters 7 and 8 direct attention, respectively, to the context they subsist in and to that of their transformation and extinction. Thus, Chapter 7 focuses on the market that, given the central role of alienability in liberal property, is its typical setting. Markets appear in different variations and an autonomy-enhancing market, I argue, must assume a specific form. Some of its characteristics echo the (by now familiar) features of liberal property: guarantees that contract law (and not only property law) is structurally pluralistic and complies with relational justice, and commitment to a supporting background regime that ensures everyone's autonomy. Markets also raise additional challenges dealing mostly with the autonomy of the future self and the risk that alienability might turn into alienation, which a liberal conception of the market is required to confront.

Finally, the core claim of Chapter 8 is that a liberal property law endorses a principled bifurcation of the universe of property transitions. Sudden dramatic changes undermine the contribution of property to people's ability to plan and should thus be treated as compensable takings. Moderate and gradual regulatory changes, by contrast, can be seamlessly accommodated since they do not threaten property's autonomy-enhancing function and are necessary for property to face its ongoing justificatory challenge. Chapter 8 develops and defends this "liberal property pact," traces its legacy in both common law tradition and Supreme Court jurisprudence, and investigates both its boundaries and its potential contribution to the tortuous doctrine of regulatory takings.

★ ★ ★

A liberal theory of property does not provide a description of prevailing property law in any specific jurisdiction or a set of detailed blueprints. Its aim is to face property's legitimacy challenge by developing the best justification for property and offering guidance as to its proper constitution. This account of the liberal idea of property hopes to open a conversation, inviting critics to refine it and revise it. Readers who find the theory developed in these pages persuasive, will, in turn, be able to use it in the critical assessment of specific property regimes and in developing suitably contextualized schemes for their reform.

2 SOME BASICS

PROPERTY THEORY AS LEGAL THEORY

1. *Property and Law*. A credible theory of property needs to be a *legal* theory. Readers who subscribe to Jeremy Bentham's assertion that "[p]roperty and law are born together, and die together,"[1] may find the truth of this proposition trivial. Although not a natural right, however, property is not contingent in this strong Benthamite sense either. As I maintain in Chapter 6, property is a convention that, all else being equal, any autonomy-seeking polity is obligated to adopt.

This claim implies that the moral underpinnings of property do *not* eliminate the constitutive role of law or of a law-like set of social norms. By instantiating property rights, law goes beyond protecting people from actual or potential threats that others may pose to their bodily integrity. Property law *proactively* empowers people, expanding their ability to act and interact in the world.

Property, then, imposes duties but, above all, confers power (see Chapter 3). The normative powers that property confers are conducive to its autonomy-enhancing *telos*. The respect that property commands from other individuals and from the government, as well as the various forms of co-governance that property types enable, are pivotal in a liberal polity. Property's duties, by contrast, are conceptually and normatively secondary to its empowering role and, while important, they derive from and are intelligible by reference to its powers.[2]

Property's powers may be justified insofar as it is justified to expect nonowners to submit to the authority of owners given its autonomy-enhancing potential. The legitimacy of any property regime thus depends, as noted, on how well it enhances autonomy. But the implication is not that only the consequences of property's normative powers matter or that the relational structure of these powers is irrelevant. Indeed, liberal property's relational justice derives precisely from this relational structure. Nonetheless, the fact that property is essentially power-conferring does imply that a proper investigation of property's legitimacy also necessitates an *ex ante* discussion about the ways that property law can and should enhance people's autonomy.

The evaluation of property's success in achieving its autonomy-enhancing end is qualitative rather than quantitative. It is not about maximizing the extent of autonomy in the world but is nonetheless teleological, searching for a system of property law intrinsically appropriate to an autonomy-friendly society.[3] Hence, given that property theory must investigate competing systems of property *law* (since law can establish different inventories of property types and fine-tune the rights of owners and nonowners in each type in different ways), property theory is a species of legal theory.

2. *Legal Theory*. Legal theory focuses on the work of society's coercive normative institutions. It studies their traditions and the crafts typical of their members while, at the same time, continuously challenging their outputs by demonstrating their contingency and testing their desirability. In performing some of these tasks, legal theory absorbs lessons from law's neighboring disciplines. But legal theory is more than a sophisticated synthesis of relevant insights from these friendly neighbors because it also focuses on classic jurisprudential questions about the nature of law, such as the relationship between law's normativity and its coerciveness and the implications of its institutional and structural characteristics.[4]

This understanding of legal theory explains my extensive discussion of property's justificatory challenge that, in turn, (1) explicates the need for careful delineation of property's private authority; (2) grounds property's pillars of structural pluralism and relational justice; (3) shapes the law governing property transitions as encapsulated in "the liberal property pact" (the topic of Chapter 8).

Appreciating the irreducible role of law in property theory also directs attention to the institutional dimension of property at the focus of Chapter 6. This chapter investigates the proper division of labor between legislatures and courts in developing property law, and asks

Property Theory As Legal Theory 15

whether the autonomy-enhancing conception of property – notably its structural pluralism – threatens the rule of law. My answer is that it does not. Rather the reverse: by offering relatively narrow, and thus stable and internally coherent doctrinal categories, a structurally pluralistic property law actually provides effective guidance to the law's addressees, thus also effectively constraining the ability of officials to exercise power.

Finally, engaging with the justification of property and with its nuanced legal manifestations implies that, in this book, I need to draw away from the overly abstract views of philosophers and of many social scientists dealing with property, and from the more specific doctrinal focus typical of legal scholarship, including mine.[5] This explains both my use of many doctrinal examples and their relatively brief treatment.

3. *Justification and Design.* The need to account for the intricacies of current property law and explore potential avenues for its interpretation and development is not merely a constraint on legal theorists, which other academics theorizing about property have typically ignored. Taking seriously the existing and potential legal doctrine helps to refine an understanding of property more nuanced and normatively appealing than the conventional (read dominion) one presumed in many extra-legal accounts of it.[6]

One lesson of this book, then, is that just as legal theory benefits from intellectual openness to law's neighboring disciplines, legal theory can – and in many contexts indeed should – provide these disciplines with significant theoretical insights.[7] Property theory is a prominent example of this broad lesson, given property's crucial role in many nonlegal theories and analyses of both the market and the state. The failure to take law seriously is particularly troublesome when manifest in the most fundamental discussions of property, dealing with its legitimacy. As I hope to demonstrate here, in order to critically interrogate property's legitimacy, whether to celebrate it or condemn it, theorists need to appreciate the richness and variability to be yielded from its legal underpinnings. In other words, they must acknowledge property theory as a legal theory.

The inverse conclusion is just as important: engaging with property's justificatory challenge must be a core feature of any acceptable exercise of property design. This lesson explains my quarrel with many functional accounts of property. These accounts presume that the challenge of property's justification has been met once and for all and property theory can now set it aside to focus on the pragmatic task of optimizing its operation, which typically invokes a utilitarian or some other form of welfarist benchmark.[8]

These pragmatic concerns are appropriate and the functional analyses that address them are accordingly valuable. As I explain in Chapter 3, I do not downplay the significance of satisfying people's preferences or of aggregate social welfare. But I do insist that, however important, they are means to an end and, therefore, the system's performance must chiefly be assessed against this end. A liberal polity aware of property's onerous justificatory challenge is expected to be particularly rigorous in ensuring that its property law is indeed founded on the commitment to people's autonomy.

In some limited contexts, this means that autonomy must function as a constraint that trumps any other goals property could potentially promote. A property system that undermines its own *telos* and justificatory premise may thus become illegitimate. (Chapter 6 studies some of the implications of perceiving such a system as violating property.) But a view of autonomy as the linchpin of property's legitimacy implies that its role cannot be limited to gatekeeping. In a genuinely liberal property law, autonomy must also play a major, albeit not an exclusive, role in assessing the performance of existing doctrine and in guiding its future development.[9] As shown below, accommodating other concerns, including functional ones, is not an unduly onerous task for an autonomy-based theory of property, given its basic facilitative attitude.

PROPERTY THEORY AS INTERPRETIVE THEORY

There are various types of legal theories and thus various types of property theories. This book offers an *interpretive* theory of property. It distills a theoretical framework for existing property law in liberal societies, which presents its doctrines in their best light. An interpretive theory of law neither aims to unearth the historical roots of our existing

Property Theory As Interpretive Theory

practices nor to supplant them with wholly innovative ways of organizing society.

An interpretive legal theory is situated between discovery and invention.[10] It builds on existing practices and thus reaffirms much of existing law. An interpretive theory of property, however, is not a descriptive exercise and thus cannot be expected to explain every extant feature of property law. An interpretive theory provides an account of our legal practices that suggests a new perspective on the law and, in turn, inevitably upsets some conventional wisdom by pointing to feasible improvements of the law and, at times, even to urgent reforms necessary to ensure its legitimacy. It also highlights new questions that make up a research agenda for future reformers and scholars.

In other words, although interpretive legal theories should be falsifiable, making them so is usually not an easy task, and that is a virtue rather than a vice.[11] Thus, the liberal theory of property offered in this book is falsifiable in the sense that one can imagine systems wherein one or more of the three pillars of liberal property – carefully delineated private authority, structural pluralism, and relational justice – is clearly missing. (Feudalism, as noted, is a good example.) But the liberal theory of property is not easily falsifiable because interpretation implies reconstruction, which necessarily involves marginalization and demarginalization of various features of the system.[12] Finally, the fact that the theory is not easily falsifiable is a virtue – it can then serve as the normative ideal, or as the compass that offers internal resources of critique to lawyers loyal to their responsibility to push the law to strengthen compliance with its duties of justice.[13]

I do not claim that a legal theory – certainly not one that transcends any specific jurisdiction – can or should generate a fine-grained blueprint for every doctrinal detail. The prescriptions of legal theories, both where they affirm existing law and where they point to its necessary reform, cannot be fully determinate. They leave, as they should, some space for culturally specific considerations and for pragmatic concerns, both local and contextual. And yet, although they cannot be fully specified here, the lessons of the liberal theory of property have practical significance.

Existing property law manifests the three pillars of the liberal conception of property. But its compliance with these maxims is not flawless, even if we ignore the more threatening gap between the legal doctrine of property and its prevalent practice, which reflects the inadequacy of law's background regimes in most liberal polities.[14] In some spheres of human interaction, current property law scarcely offers enough alternatives, and some of the forms it does supply can hardly be described as autonomy-enhancing. Property law also often confers on owners an authority exceeding what the pertinent property type requires for their autonomy and, at times, fails to meet the demands of relational justice. These flaws, rather than undermining the liberal theory of property, highlight its significance as a source of *internal* critique that can help push property law to abide more successfully by its autonomy-enhancing premise.

Thus, as I claim in Chapter 4, structural pluralism requires the carriers of property law to expand the repertoire of property types with sufficiently distinctive options, offering meaningful choices in *all* major spheres of social activity. It also requires them to refine the *numerus clausus* principle so that, alongside this inventory of state-sponsored property types, property law will also include a residual property type that can be privately designed (while properly ensuring the interest of third parties to not be subject to non-transparent arrangements).

Similarly, as Chapter 5 shows, although significant sections of property law already comply with the demands of relational justice, some do not. Architects of property law should thus carefully scrutinize prevailing law to identify property types that deviate from this obligation and then decide – considering the substantive good or goods that such a property type arguably exemplifies and promotes – whether it should be abolished, reformed, or reinstated, this deficiency notwithstanding.

Other implications of the autonomy-based *telos* of property, probably more controversial but no less important, come up in the context of labor markets and in transnational settings. As I argue in Chapter 7, liberal labor markets must constrain the authority of the means of production owners, as well as guard against excessive commodification of people's work, proscribing unwarranted impositions on their future self and ensuring that their interactions do not fall below an acceptable threshold of relational justice. In turn, as I claim in Chapter 6, appreciating the freestanding dimension of relational justice implies that it is relevant across borders, even if many of our other obligations are state bound.

PROPERTY AND PROPERTY TYPES

1. *Limits to Property Monism.* Having discussed what I mean by legal theory, I now turn to consider what I mean by property law. A legal theory of property naturally aims to elucidate one animating notion, either a single value (or a particular balance of values) or a single design principle that shapes property's entire terrain. A prominent monistic understanding of property – property's Blackstonian conception – refers to the owner's sole and despotic dominion as property's regulative principle. This book, by contrast, offers a dramatically different understanding of property: while its normative foundation is monistic – the (one) ultimate value underlying liberal property is autonomy – it celebrates the multiplicity of property types with their diverse normative DNAs, and thus the structural pluralism of property law.

Admittedly, structurally monistic legal theories seem appealing. By conceptualizing an entire legal field as revolving around one idea, they tend to be simple and elegant, thus satisfying an important demand of the practice of theorizing. They also avoid the seemingly intractable difficulties of pluralistic theories in addressing contextual conflicts of values. Finally, the broad coherence that typifies monistic theories means the law speaks in one voice, a feature that some view as a prerequisite for law's demand of obedience.

But monistic theories of property, and particularly the Blackstonian one, can hardly account for property's vast heterogeneity. Property can be understood as sole and despotic dominion only if, somewhat arbitrarily, we set aside large parts of what constitutes property law, at least according to the conventional understanding found in the case law, the Restatements, and the academic commentary.

As Chapter 4 demonstrates, property law is divided into various types, reflecting distinct frameworks of human interaction with respect to different categories of resources. Some property types, such as the fee simple absolute, vindicate people's independence and are thus generally structured along the lines of the Blackstonian conception of property. (Zoning laws and other rules do often circumscribe owners' dominion, so it is more accurate to say that the fee simple absolute is the property type closest to the Blackstonian conception.) Other property types, such as marital property, deal with intimate relationships and are dominated by a much more communitarian view of property, where ownership is a locus of sharing. Finally, many other property types governing relationships between people who are neither strangers nor intimates, such as landlords and tenants, neighbors, co-owners, and members of the same local community, lie somewhere along the spectrum between these poles. In these cases, both independence and community are implicated, and ownership thus implies a complex hybrid of rights and responsibilities.

All these property types also mediate the relationship between owner(s) and nonowners regarding a resource. In all property types, owners enjoy some measure of private authority, which typically implies some rights to exclude others.[15] This common denominator derives from the constitutive function of independence in securing people's self-determination. Its varying significance in different property types derives both from its differing contribution to self-determination in each one of them and from differences among nonowners' claims to relational justice across these types. Beside independence, other values – notably personhood, community, and utility – also play crucial roles in shaping property types. Property types thus offer different configurations of entitlements that constitute the contents of an owner's rights vis-à-vis others, or a certain type of others, with respect to a given resource.

The multiplicity of property types, then, does not simply reflect the truism that the proper application of abstract principles requires their careful adjustment to their context. Property's heterogeneity is profound, pointing to fundamental differences between its distinct types and suggesting that they are better explained by reference to divergent animating principles.

Property and Property Types

2. Three Monistic Approaches. Monistic theorists confronting such deep heterogeneity face rather unappealing choices. They can redefine their subjects marginalizing the (potentially important) sections that do not respond well to the animating principle they advocate. The common strategies adopted by advocates of the dominion view of property is to rename the significant portions of property law dealing with property governance as "contract" and refer to those that vindicate nonowners' claims of relational justice as "regulation."[16] These strategies exclude significant subsets of property law from property's domain. The former also misleadingly ignores the fact that law also protects contract – and not only property – from certain external interferences,[17] while the latter disturbingly obscures both property's inherent limitations and the property-based rationale of relational justice claims.[18]

Both strategies end up threatening to undermine property's legitimacy because they dilute the normative constraints of property's liberal foundation.[19] A liberal property law must, as I argue in Chapter 3, shape property as a means to enhance people's autonomy. It should thus circumscribe owners' authority to its autonomy-enhancing function and ensure that everyone has property. It must also secure property's structural pluralism rather than treat it as a discretionary add-on, and guarantee its compliance with relational justice as an inherent implication of the idea of property rather than a regulatory or constitutional imposition.

A second possible approach of monistic theorists is to discard any pretense to account for existing law and present their theory as reformist and as advocating a significant legal change, thereby rendering property law as solely guided by their favorite animating principle. This strategy may well offer valuable insights on law as, for example, in some lawyer-economists' analyses of doctrines that are unresponsive to efficiency. But its distance from existing law often implies that it can no longer yield an interpretive legal theory.

Finally, monistic theorists can resort to a third approach and offer an animating principle sufficiently abstract and capacious so as to encompass the heterogeneous legal materials they theorize about. This approach – think of conceptual analyses of wholesale categories that shy away from any specific prescription – is unobjectionable per se.

But this strategy nonetheless requires caution because it implies that such theories cannot – and thus must not purport to – perform the prescriptive function for which they are at times recruited.

The common denominator of the wide terrain of legal doctrines covered by wholesale legal categories, such as property, tends to be so thin that it can hardly be determinative enough to provide significant guidance as to the evaluation or development of the doctrines at hand.[20] Property writ large, as mentioned at the outset, is private authority. But this conceptual truism, in and of itself, lacks the prescriptive power for which it is too often invoked. Its only (substantial, for sure) lesson is to highlight the significant justificatory challenge that property necessarily encounters.

3. *The Pluralistic Alternative.* Fortunately, monism is not the only available option for theorizing about a broad and diverse legal category. A structurally pluralistic account of property, such as the one developed in this book, rejects the notion that any single principle suffices for liberal property law. It challenges property monism and relocates much of the normative and doctrinal discussion to the analysis of property types.

An autonomy-based understanding of property should embrace structural pluralism and resist the temptation to impose a uniform understanding of property on the diverse set of property types. Such a straitjacket is not only misleading but also unfortunate because property's structural pluralism enables diverse forms of the good to flourish. Only a sufficiently heterogeneous property law, alongside an attendant commitment to freedom of contract regarding property rules, facilitates the coexistence of a diverse set of social institutions crucial for our autonomy.

Liberal property should thus emphasize the multiplicity of property law and guide its expansion to include a repertoire of sufficiently distinct types in all relevant spheres of human activity. As long as the boundaries between these multiple property types are open and as long as (nonabusive[21]) navigation within this diverse system is a matter of individual choice, commitment to personal autonomy does not necessitate the hegemony of the fee simple absolute, reflected in the dominion conception of property. Nor does this commitment undermine the value of other, more communitarian or utilitarian, property types (say, respectively, cooperatives and patents).

The eradication or marginalization of the fee simple absolute might entail an excessive restriction of liberty and privacy because it erases the option of private sovereignty and thus the option of retreat into one's own safe haven. But as long as this or a similar property type remains a viable alternative, the availability of several different but equally valuable and attainable proprietary frameworks of interpersonal interaction makes autonomy more, not less, meaningful. An autonomy-enhancing property law cannot be content with the fee simple absolute property type and, in each important area of human action and interaction, must also facilitate choice from among diverse and normatively attractive property types (i.e., property types that comply with the prescriptions of carefully delineated private authority and relational justice). Free people are partly defined by the alternatives they reject, not just those they select.[22]

PROPERTY AS A CATEGORY OF THINKING

At first glance, this spotlight on plurality raises a methodological conundrum. If the differences among property types are as significant as I claim, does it follow that "property" is not a meaningful category, in turn implying that no theory of property is actually possible?

The answer is no. A theory of property is possible if we keep in mind the distinction between categories for *deciding* and categories for *thinking*.[23] An autonomy-based theory of property that appreciates the significance of property's deep heterogeneity does imply that the normative concerns underlying property types are so diverse that simply labeling something as "property" is not enough to justify any concrete decision, result, or reform consequence. In other words, we cannot justify treating property as a *category for deciding*. But this does not eliminate the significance of property as a doctrinal category because, while types differ in their normative concerns, there are enough similarities between them to justify viewing "property" as a useful *category for thinking*.

A broad heterogeneous doctrinal category qualifies as a category of thinking if bundling together its subcategories facilitates learning and mutual enrichment. Such a capacious legal category is typically valuable when its subcategories raise similar questions. Similar questions imply some overlap in the pertinent values or normative concerns underlying the subcategories, or in the type of (or constraints on) the means informing the answers to these questions across these subcategories. These overlaps, in turn, promise some cross-fertilization, a typical feature of categories of thinking.[24]

Property is a perfect example of a category of thinking. The similarities among the various property types – all being forms of private authority – justify studying them together. At the very least, the question about the appropriate scope of owners' authority persists across all these different property types.[25] Furthermore, because many of these property types involve more than one stakeholder, the need to prescribe a governance regime befitting the property type at hand is also a recurring concern.

Furthermore, the underlying values animating diverse (liberal) property types do overlap. They all aim at facilitating the intrinsic and instrumental goods of property – primarily independence, personhood, community, and utility – while securing autonomy, always as the ultimate value and sometimes as a side-constraint (distinctions I set out in Chapter 3). This overlap ensures that reflecting on the variety of property types is likely to lead to a constructive exchange, further justifying treating them as a topic of unified scholarly analysis.

Finally, appreciating the common function of all property types in the service of people's autonomy is crucial because it helps us to evaluate the performance of property law as a whole. First and foremost, it invites social scientists to assess the performance of diverse property systems in terms of people's self-determination rather than only of their welfarist consequences. Moreover, highlighting the autonomy-enhancing function of property's structural pluralism implies that, for every sphere of human activity and interaction, law should provide a robust menu of choices. It thus requires us to assess the quality of the repertoire of property types in every such sphere, that is, to ensure that property law's doctrinal divisions track the autonomy-enhancing role that multiplicity should play in a liberal regime. It also implies that, rather than being content with the current understanding of the *numerus clausus* principle, a liberal state should develop a residual category of private arrangements for people who prefer to reject property law's favored types.

PROPERTY AND CONTRACT

The last points (discussed in Chapter 4) highlight the facilitative role of property law, thus also anticipating my support for freedom of contract within property types and hinting at notable continuities between property and contract. Drawing this lesson is problematic for those who insist that property and contract are sharply and qualitatively distinct categories.[26] But such continuity need not threaten a more modest view, which justifies the distinction between property and contract as categories of thinking by reference to the relative abundance and indefiniteness of property's duty-holders.[27]

The continuity between property and contract is not only innocuous but, indeed, to be expected. Contract, like property, is a power-conferring institution and, in a liberal polity, both are premised on the same autonomy-enhancing *telos*. Michael Heller and I have discussed these propositions and their implications at some length elsewhere,[28] so a (very) brief summary should do here.

Contract law offers people a new power: to make credible commitments that can induce others to assist them in realizing their ends. This normative power enhances people's ability to be the authors of their own lives by expanding the available repertoire of secure interpersonal engagements beyond the realm of gift-based and similarly close-knit interactions. Contract enables people to legitimately recruit others to advance their own goals, purposes, and projects, both material and social.

The word "legitimately" is key. Contract, like property, is a convention that offers this service of autonomy-enhancement, and law is justified in enforcing contracts thanks to its important contribution to people's self-authorship. Frustrating a promisee's expectations undermines his or her ability to employ contract in line with its autonomy-enhancing functions because the right to expect, rather than the right to merely rely, is core to the idea of planning and thus to the ideal of self-determination.[29] To be sure, reneging on a wholly executory but yet-to-be-relied contract may not harm the promisee. This means that contract enforcement would have generated a legitimacy crisis if our interpersonal obligations were exhausted by the maxim of reciprocal respect for independence. Contract is nonetheless legitimate because, in a liberal polity, our interpersonal relationships are governed by a reciprocal duty to respect each other's right of self-determination.

Thus, at least in their best (most liberal) light, both property and contract are autonomy-enhancing institutions. A liberal law constructs both property and contract as frameworks of respectful interaction conducive to self-determination. Both property and contract participate in the core liberal challenge of offering a structurally pluralistic legal infrastructure for our interpersonal relationships. Not only does the intra-sphere multiplicity of contract types serve the same role as the parallel multiplicity of property types; at times – think of the sharing economy – contract types and property types can serve as partial functional substitutes to each other.

None of these observations collapses contract into property. While property facilitates planning by securing stability as per people's authority over resources, contract does so by allowing them to count on the future contribution of others. This difference explains why, even when a temporal horizon of action could be secured either way, liberal law should seek to include in its repertoire a minimal number of both property types and contract types. More importantly, it accounts for some of the limitations on the enforcement of contractual obligations that typify liberal contract law, which vindicate its commitment to promisors' future selves.[30] These limitations will inform my account of just labor markets in Chapter 7.

RESOURCES AND RELATIONS

1. *A Hohfeldian Starting Point.* While the previous sections highlighted property's multiplicity and its continuity with contract, we have

not yet addressed what exactly is property to begin with. Property, declares the Restatement of Property, constitutes a set of "legal relations between persons with respect to a thing."[31] This proposition adopts Wesley Hohfeld's insight that, as a species of "jural relations," property rights imply rights vis-à-vis people, not things.[32]

Both the division between *in personam* and *in rem* and the literal meaning of the Latin phrase *in rem*, Hohfeld argued, misleadingly suggest that "a right *in rem* must be a right that is *not against* a *person*, but *against* a *thing*." But this understanding of property rights is "crude and fallacious." People may certainly "sustain close and beneficial *physical* relations to a given *physical thing*," but "physical relations are wholly distinct from jural relations." Jural relations "take significance from the law; and, since the purpose of the law is to regulate the conduct of human beings, all jural relations must... be predicated on such human beings."[33]

The autonomy-based conception of property shares Hohfeld's insistence, which goes even further back to Kant's doctrine of private rights,[34] that property is relational through and through. This proposition has recently come under attack with the invocation of approaches urging a conception of property as first and foremost the law of things.

2. *Smith on Things*. Henry Smith, who is the reporter for the Fourth Restatement of Property, has argued that property law is "the law of modular things," and that "the thing is the linchpin of property." Property law, in his view, "organizes the world into lumpy packages of legal relations – legal things – by setting boundaries around useful attributes that tend to be strong complements," thus encapsulating them "from other modules and outside the world generally."[35]

When Smith emphasizes "the key role of the thing itself in delineating the right," and the "nature of that thing [that] goes a long way toward determining what kinds of rights one can have and how they work,"[36] he may be interpreted as resurrecting the physicalist view of property.[37] Smith, however, explicitly treats intellectual property as property,[38] which explains why he is careful to refer to *legal* things. But once the idea that the (physical) nature of the actual thing itself determines or delineates property rights is not strictly adhered to, it is no longer clear that Smith's claims regarding "the importance of the thing in property"[39] challenges property's relationality.

Smith's proposition – that "[w]hile rights in property, like all other rights, avail between right holders and duty bearers, in property they are typically mediated by the thing"[40] – is already incorporated into the existing Restatement's relational definition of property. Therefore, Smith's most important insights can, and indeed should be embraced by the liberal theory of property.

Thus, Smith is correct when emphasizing the lumpiness of property rights and when claiming that property law typically "carve[s] the world into modular things and associate[s] them with people." As he explains, "[t]he legal thing defined over the actual thing ... allows property rights to be simple enough and impersonal enough to reach an *in rem* set of duty bearers and to be more easily transferable from one party to another."[41]

Property's lumpiness is not only functionally significant[42] but also conducive to its liberal *telos*. In order for people to benefit from a property right as a "writing instrument" necessary for self-authorship, they must enjoy a sufficiently robust measure of private authority with regard to the pertinent object of that right. Sheer wealth or access to things is not enough and there need to be some objects – not necessarily material – that people should be able to form plans about and thus to self-determine.

As long as this standardization of property types (discussed in Chapter 4) revolves around *legal* things, it does not threaten the more fundamental relationality of property. Some "legal things" subject to people's private authority in the service of autonomy are necessary, but the objects of property may change across time and space and may be both technologically and culturally dependent.[43] (The liberal theory of property, in other words, by no means implies a demand to either shrink or refrain from expanding the public domain.[44])

Saying that the role of the *actual* thing is secondary does not imply that it is insignificant. As Smith claims, "the nature of the thing in the world *helps* determine what kind of legal thing it can correspond to," so that the "different qualities" of land, cars, water, and inventions affect "what it means to have property in them."[45] Furthermore, at times certain "collections of attributes" seem to "go together," as in the case of "someone with the right to determine how soil nutrients are used [who] might need control over the moisture level."[46]

The nature of the resources subject to property rights does make a difference. To take another example, the fact that information consumption is generally non-rivalrous implies that, when the resource at hand is information, use may not always necessitate exclusion.[47] Nevertheless, and despite the relevance of the resources' nature to the constitution of property types, they do not challenge the primacy of property's relationality.[48]

3. *The Hegelian Challenge.* By contrast, Alan Brudner's Hegelian theory of property does pose a direct challenge to the primacy of property's relationality. Ownership, Brudner argues, "is a relation between a human being and a thing through which that human being becomes validly the master or end of the thing," that is, "someone for whom that thing is rightfully a means." One becomes "master of an object" after attaining "the power to perform upon it all tokens of the action-types that are necessary and jointly sufficient to display mastery," namely, "excluding, using, and alienating." More pertinent to the current discussion, "the thing's subservience to the person" is in this view "direct" and, therefore, "prior" to any "relation among persons" it "validates." Brudner suggests that we understand this Blackstonian conception of ownership "as the realization of the self-related person's project to confirm itself as the end of things."[49]

This agency-validation account makes absolute sovereignty an inherent feature of ownership because unowned things "challenge" the person's claim of final worth. This challenge makes unilateral acquisition "a moral necessity" since only unqualified ownership, which puts "objects into a relation of subservience" to a person, can "confirm the end-status of that person vis-à-vis the world of things." Conceptualizing acquisition's "intellectual significance" as validating "the person's end-status vis-à-vis the thing" requires that we understand property as the law of things, because it is prior to any interpersonal relations.[50]

The Hegelian account, which assumes the priority of things to relations, remains valid even though it is later embedded in a social framework that limits owners' authority.[51] Its justification, however, is unclear: Why should the sheer existence of an unowned thing challenge the end-status of human beings? And why should the final worth of persons imply their complete mastery over all that is nonhuman?

The dependence of our survival and our ability to adopt a life plan and live on material things requires that – as Locke intimated[52] – we use things. But how does the sheer appearance of independence in things become a moral concern? If our right to self-determination is secure, should not our final worth imply the self-confidence – at least vis-à-vis whatever does not (claim to) have such a status – to simply reflect upon our distinction from the world of things rather than develop an infinite desire for its conquest? Is it possible that all the talk of self-validation is just an attempt to rationalize some of human history's less appealing features?

The heroic Hegelian effort to derive the private dominion of Blackstonian ownership only from our relationship with things is a way of bypassing Hohfeld's lesson. Its failure is not surprising. As Hohfeld argued, property is irreducibly relational – the interpersonal effects of Blackstonian owners' normative power vis-à-vis others are considerable and, as noted, not easily defensible. For these others – the nonowners – introducing Blackstonian ownership into the state of nature is, potentially, a relational normative threat. Caution may thus be advisable when conceptualizing the state of nature as a rights-vacuum.

4. *Two Lessons*. Repudiating the Hegelian conception of property is not tantamount to disparaging the normative significance of Blackstonian ownership. As Brudner argues, beings with end-status are entitled to a system supportive of their self-determination, of which a crucial component is *some* mastery over things. Justifying Blackstonian ownership, however, cannot sidestep the relational challenge.

Facing up to this challenge will be part of my task in Chapters 3–5, which flesh out property's commitment to self-determination and to the prescriptions it entails: carefully delineated private authority, structural pluralism, and relational justice. The importance of the relational challenge also explains why I dedicate Chapter 7 to the market. Markets, especially labor markets, are probably the most vital legally constructed contexts of human interaction in contemporary property-

Form and Substance

based polities. Fully addressing the morality of property is thus impossible without attending to the legal construction of the market.

Finally, as noted, claiming that property is irreducibly relational does not involve ignoring the nature of the resource at stake. In addition to the functional reasons that Smith emphasizes, the nature of the resource is also significant due to the intrinsic value that people ascribe to the resources they hold. This value is best understood, as I claim in Chapter 3, in terms of our attachment to these resources, which is justified insofar as they reflect our identity.[53] Accordingly, resources are subject to different property configurations. Property law strongly vindicates people's authority over their constitutive resources. By contrast, the more fungible an interest, the less the emphasis that law generally places on its owner's control.[54]

This "personhood" perspective on property raises complicated questions.[55] But the key point here is that this perspective does not marginalize the intersubjective aspect of ownership, thus avoiding the implication that property is the law of things. On the contrary: the reflection-and-attachment phenomenon it relies upon is thoroughly interpersonal. People perceive certain resources as more reflective of their own selves than of others since others – to whom the self's external image is communicated – share with them the same symbolic meaning.

FORM AND SUBSTANCE

1. *A Familiar Dichotomy.* Property, I have argued so far, is intrinsically relational, and property law is best understood as an umbrella of property types rather than as a uniform monistic legal construct. But how are we to understand these types? Should we focus on their form or on their underlying substance, that is, on the property values that these forms serve?

Property law seems to be torn between form and substance. Every student of property remembers – some with joy, others with horror – the system of estates, with its fine distinctions between various present and future interests. Fee simple absolute, fee tail, and life estate are only the beginning of a long repertoire of forms. An intricate taxonomy follows them, including diverse types of defeasible estates, future interests, and concurrent ownerships. This labyrinth of property serves as an apt introduction to the importance and complexity of form in the life of the law and to the rich array of human interaction and organization arrangements that property law constitutes.

But property is also quite obviously about substance. Property is – how can it not be? – about values and normative choices. Homeownership is frequently analyzed as a bulwark of individual freedom and independence. The home, as well as some other holdings, are even regarded as constitutive components of personal identity. Furthermore, property also supplies frameworks for interpersonal arrangements and communities, affects the efficient (or inefficient) allocation of resources, and implicates the distribution of goods and powers in society. Above all – at least from a liberal perspective – property is one of the building blocks in an autonomy-enhancing legal regime.

Is property then a matter of form or of substance? Most of the contemporary property theory takes sides in this purported schism. Many property theorists – ranging from your garden-variety lawyer-economist to members of the "progressive school" of property – follow Bruce Ackerman's "Scientific Policymaker," who downplays the significance of property's form(s) and focuses on its substance.[56] Because property law parcels out rights to use things "amongst a host of competing resource users," the "real question" property faces, in this view, is always "in whose bundle one or another right may best be put" given a certain comprehensive view of the just society.[57]

Other scholars find these approaches "impatient" because, by focusing on ends like social welfare or human flourishing, they fail to appreciate the significance of "the 'gap' between means and ends in property." Bypassing property forms is unfortunate, they insist, because sometimes property's ends are best pursued indirectly.[58] Some property theorists seem to take this insight to its logical conclusion, shifting (or shifting back) the focus of property theory to the architecture of property rather than to the values it vindicates and promotes. This view of property does leave room for values in the landscape of property but implies that reflecting upon these values must follow a foundational inquiry of property's architecture.[59]

2. *Both Substance and Form*. This book resists both positions. Property, I argue, is profoundly about both substance and form in the sense that we cannot understand one without the other. This claim does not simply reiterate the truisms about the limited number of ways in which the various sticks (rights and powers) of property are bundled together, on the one hand, while respecting the various ends that property serves, on the other hand. My claim is that the architecture of property, which is structurally pluralistic, makes a significant – indeed indispensable – contribution to property's normative commitment to self-authorship. The form of property matters and thus requires close attention. Its significance is *not* freestanding, however, and needs to be justified by reference to this *telos*.

The ultimate autonomy-enhancing value of property, I argue, explains the gap at times discernible between its intrinsic and instrumental values – independence, personhood, community, and utility – and the means applied in their pursuit, namely, the *standardized* property types that characterize our law.[60] Moreover, property's *telos* could not have been accomplished had property resisted its structural pluralistic architecture that, in turn, cannot be properly evaluated without reference to property law's liberal *telos*.

To begin with, the forms of property matter because – *pace* Hohfeld – property is not a fully malleable "bundle of sticks," and the possession of any single "stick" by a person is thus not "strikingly independent" of the others.[61] The bundle metaphor does appropriately convey Hohfeld's insight that property has no canonical composition – there is neither an a priori list of entitlements that the owner of a given resource inevitably enjoys nor an exhaustive list of resources that can or should become objects of property.[62] But the bundle metaphor is seriously misleading insofar as it implies a radical disintegration of property,[63] conceiving it as a "laundry list" of substantive rights with limitless permutations. At any given time, property law offers only a limited number of bundles of rights – a *numerus clausus* of types – and the legal system strives to make each type distinctive and coherent.

These types make up an inventory of human interaction frameworks, allowing property law to serve its autonomy-enhancing *telos*. In order to create *effective* frameworks of social interaction and cooperation, property law must, as structural pluralism prescribes, recognize a necessarily limited number of such types while also standardizing their forms. Only in this way can property law consolidate people's expectations so that they can anticipate developments when, for instance, entering marriage or a common-interest community, or when invading other people's rights in a specific form of intellectual property. Thus, as I discuss in Chapter 6, a set of fairly precise rules or informative standards govern each of these property types, enabling people to predict the consequences of future contingencies and plan their lives accordingly.

3. *"Normal Science" and "Paradigm Shifts"*. An autonomy-enhancing property law requires a relatively stable set of standardized property types. A condition for this stability is a measure of respect for the "doctrinalist logic" that guides the daily life of these types' operation. The significance of crafting property forms along these lines, however, does not override the role of property's values. Instead, the forms and values of property simply appear in the legal drama at different times.

The craft of property doctrinalism largely accounts for law's "normal science"[64] – the run-of-the-mill operation of a vibrant system of property law – and thus also for the wide convergence of the ways that property lawyers read the doctrine at any given time and place. At the same time, however, and reflecting the inherent dynamism of property law, the doctrine is amenable to different readings. *Some* legal actors (such as legislators and judges of appellate courts) should thus *occasionally* use new cases and social developments as triggers for the ongoing refinement of the law, that is, as opportunities for revisiting the normative viability of its current understandings.

When conventional understandings of property doctrine are no longer considered obvious, arguments about the doctrine's consequences and their putative injustice break out. At these times (that, metaphorically, could be termed property's "paradigm shifts"), both the existing categories and their underlying animating principles can become subject to debate and reform, possibly leading some property types to fade away, new ones to emerge, and yet others to split or change their character.[65]

At its best, then, property law accommodates stability and growth, shaping and reshaping property types to ensure that a broad spectrum of configurations is available reflecting different ideals of human action and interaction. This ongoing evolution neither undermines the importance of property's forms nor minimizes the caution required when addressing their reconstitution. Yet, property forms are not free-floating logical entities, each with its own inevitable set of incidents. Nor are they merely practices geared at minimizing the information costs entailed by the task of managing scarce resources (although they may well be about this task as well).

A genuinely liberal property law understands property as an umbrella for a set of autonomy-enhancing types. It thus disparages any attempt to discuss property while marginalizing the significance of property's ends. It furthermore allows – at its best even encourages – reform proposals based on a constructive critical investigation of property's immanent promise (albeit all too often unfulfilled) to enhance our autonomy.

The potential for reform attendant on the autonomy-enhancing underpinnings of having multiple property forms is particularly fruitful regarding the (significant) remnants of the estate system. As Chapters 4 and 5 clarify, celebrating property's structural pluralism is not tantamount to sanctioning all the byzantine forms typical of our inherited legal landscape. Quite the opposite: focusing on the autonomy-enhancing role of having a repertoire of forms while refining the scope of the *just* private authority entailed by this liberal *telos* and the requirement of relational justice it imposes, point to potential directions for constructive change. Indeed, as Chapter 6 shows, some episodes in the actual evolution of property law implicitly reflect this notion of reflexive internal critique.

LIBERAL POLITY

1. *Autonomy as the Ultimate Value*. A property theory befitting a liberal polity must be primarily responsive to liberalism's fundamental commitment to people's autonomy. Whatever the other virtues of a

property regime – be it efficiently allocating scarce resources, economizing information costs, decentralizing governance, or promoting civic traits – these *collective* benefits, though significant, cannot be determinative.

In a liberal polity, people have a right to property because, and insofar as, it is conducive to self-determination (or self-authorship), that is, to the right "to have, to revise, and rationally to pursue a conception of the good."[66] The assurance of having "stuff" we may need or want does not capture property's contribution to autonomy, which lies instead in the requirements that property, in both the vertical and horizontal dimensions, places on others: to respect our individual and collective self-determination.

A liberal property law grants owners authority over others regarding given resources, when this authority secures them the possibility of developing their own life plans rather than the plans imposed on them by other persons or by society at large. (The right to exclude is, as noted, a typical *means* for implementing such private authority.[67]) Developing a life plan also implies the ability to revise it, which both explains and justifies the unique (often quasi-immutable) status of the power to alienate and to exit within property systems. This power is the engine of the market, as discussed in Chapter 7.

2. *Autonomy-Based Value Pluralism.* Autonomy is indeed the ultimate value of liberal property. But a liberal property law should not entrench into law only the one most autonomy-enhancing property type. Instead, it must recognize the significance of independence, personhood, and community as intrinsic (even if not ultimate) property values, as well as that of utility as an instrumental one. An autonomy-enhancing property system accommodates all of them within one coherent regime, wherein the right to self-determination is both a side-constraint and the ultimate value that undergirds the significance of all others. These values are crucial to property: they represent the goods people seek to attain by becoming owners or co-owners but can attain if, and only if, property law tailors its rules accordingly (see Chapter 4).

These values – independence, personhood, community, and utility – therefore significantly shape the contents of our property types. Building on varying combinations and different degrees of them, a genuinely liberal property regime develops many autonomy-enhancing property types from which *people* can actually choose.

This pluralistic approach in theorizing about property may appear confusing, if not confused. If *all* values are incommensurable, law is hopelessly indeterminate and alarmingly quietist. But an autonomy-based theory of property is surely *not* pluralistic all the way up, and liberal property does *not* subscribe to foundational value pluralism. The structural pluralism typical of liberal property sharply distinguishes it from foundational pluralistic theories. A liberal property theory is *resolutely committed* to self-determination and fends off any threat to this ultimate value and to its steadfast consequences for property law's justification and design. At the same time, it is also *insistently agnostic* regarding the "dosages" of community and utility that a society chooses to include in its property types.[68]

An autonomy-enhancing system of property should set up a floor of minimally acceptable terms for the property types it instantiates. Property types must not lock people into relationships in ways that undermine their right to rewrite their life stories. On the same grounds, the private authority of each property type must be carefully circumscribed by its putative contribution to owners' autonomy, and all property types must comply with relational justice, meaning respect the self-determination of non-owners. All these, rather than being paternalistic impositions, follow from the idea that autonomy enhancement is property's *telos* and, therefore, the architecture of property cannot include features that, unequivocally, are autonomy-reducing. As long as that floor is respected, a liberal property theory must allow people to select from the choice it offers the property type that works best for their own life plans.

Autonomy thus shapes the macro elements of a liberal property regime – carefully delimited private authority, structural pluralism, and relational justice. Once these three pillars are in place, however, autonomy is and should be far more modest at the level of each property type, allowing each person to determine what is the optimal property type for their own (individual) project.

The flip side of autonomy's modesty is that any given property type is shaped by the balance of its intrinsic and instrumental values – independence, personhood, community, and utility – that creates its unique animating principle (or DNA, as I sometimes call it). These values play a major role in liberal property but are always accommodated only *after* property law faces its autonomy-enhancing *telos*. As discussed in Chapter 3, the normative priority of autonomy plays a uniquely dramatic role in the proper design of property types that enhance people's autonomy only indirectly, notably those dealing with the ownership of the means of production.

3. *Liberal Property and Equality.* The egalitarian connotation of this prescription is typical of liberal property. Besides its commitment (encapsulated in both its first and its third pillars) to eliminate forms of property leading to interpersonal subordination, liberal property also requires, as noted, that everyone be entitled to an autonomy-enhancing property while also acutely aware of property's potentially regressive effects. Thus, as the discussion of these propositions in Chapters 3 and 8 will show, the liberal theory of property perceives the justification of property as a challenge immanent to the ongoing operation of property law.

Finally, because one might suspect that, as with money and utility, the marginal autonomy-enhancement of each additional unit of property is likely to be diminishing, a liberal property law imposes the costs of securing property's legitimacy along these lines on those who are particularly well-off.[69] (Another property-based justification for progressive taxation is that property *necessarily* relies on an economic and cultural infrastructure.[70])

4. *Possible Objection.* Supporters of the dominion conception of property are likely to object. In their view, whereas a liberal polity may well be committed to securing our self-determination and thus our substantive equality, liberalism's conventional understanding of the public–private distinction implies that property law need not, indeed should not, undertake this task. Rather, property law, like private law more generally, should be solely guided by a commitment to individual independence and formal equality.[71] Providing a rich repertoire of property types or imposing affirmative interpersonal obligations is, therefore, none of its business.

This approach leaves matters of self-determination solely to the state background regime of tax and redistribution. It understands private law, and property law more specifically, as the law of dissociated people, whose only duty to one another is to avoid boundary transgressions. As I argue in Chapter 5, such a radical division of labor, which renders our right to self-determination irrelevant to our interpersonal relationships, is misguided because it profoundly undermines the right of self-determination.

Even assuming – a dubious assumption, to be sure – that the state's tax and redistribution mechanisms flawlessly address the vulnerabilities generated by such an unjust property regime, the only consequence is the shift in the dependence of the propertyless from the owners to the state. Furthermore, discarding the responsibility of property law for self-determination sheds the most fundamental liberal commitments from our interpersonal relationships. The significant share of human interdependence in any life plan and conception of the good makes such a legal architecture unsustainable.

Only private law – the law of our interpersonal (horizontal) relationships – can form and sustain the variety of frameworks necessary for our ability to lead our chosen conception of life. And only private law can cast them as interactions between free and equal individuals who respect one another as the persons they actually are.

Given the vulnerability of nonowners to the private authority of owners, liberal egalitarian friends of the dominion conception of property are thus wrong to assume that a supportive background regime, however robust, can adequately face the justificatory challenge created by the introduction of property. But this does not mean that such a background regime is unnecessary; quite the contrary.

Private law – let alone property law – cannot plausibly address property's justificatory challenge on its own, even if it fully adheres to its autonomy-enhancing *telos*. This means that *some* division of labor, which delegates parts of this weighty mission to public law, is not only unobjectionable but rather required if property's legitimacy is to be upheld. In this sense, this book's defense of the liberal conception of property is necessarily qualified.

Liberal property, I will argue, is a necessary component of the landscape in an autonomy-enhancing polity. Though not the only autonomy-enhancing means of liberal law – not even of liberal private law (think contract) – property does have a distinctive and irreducible role. But property's legitimacy cannot be freestanding: property is fully justified only in a genuinely liberal polity, and its legitimacy is necessarily contingent on the performance of a background legal regime that supports the enhancement of autonomy.

3 AUTONOMY AND PRIVATE AUTHORITY

My task in this book is to develop a theory of property premised on a conception of autonomy as self-determination or self-authorship, terms that I use interchangeably. In this account, property empowers self-determining individuals to pursue their conception of the good, and this autonomy-enhancing *telos* legitimizes property and shapes its legal contours. I am *not* claiming that propertyless individuals cannot be self-determining, but rather that property tends to make an important contribution to personal self-authorship.

Understanding property as a potent means for enhancing autonomy departs from some of property's conventional understandings, which are founded on a conception of freedom as personal independence. But recognizing the status of self-determination as property's ultimate value should be natural to liberals, who generally find the thin conception of freedom as independence inadequate.

Basing property theory on self-determination rather than on independence creates space for addressing the role of personhood, community, and utility in the normative infrastructure of property. These values do not function as ultimate, free-standing values of property, unlike their apparent role in some property theories, but neither are they fully specified by the abstract notion of self-determination. Instead, because each of them is either a component of or instrumental to, our life stories, all have a suitable role in an autonomy-enhancing property system as, respectively, intrinsic and instrumental values.

Property's autonomy-enhancing *telos* both explains and justifies its constitution around the idea of carefully delineated *private authority*. Property empowers people by granting them normative powers, which make a critical contribution to their self-authorship. Given that property is profoundly relational, however, these powers necessarily entail vulnerabilities for nonowners. A liberal polity therefore constructs its property law so as to serve the self-determination of owners while constantly attentive to property's possible threat to the autonomy of nonowners.

One critical result of this prescription is that the robustness of owners' authority must be tailored to property's autonomy-enhancing role. This lesson entails radical implications for the ownership of commercial goods, notably the means of production, which serve purely utilitarian purposes. This prescription also implies that (a) property law must be accompanied by a background regime that ensures everyone's ability to become self-authors, and (b) everyone should be entitled to own *some* autonomy-enhancing property.

FROM INDEPENDENCE TO SELF-DETERMINATION

As I noted in Chapter 1 and discuss in greater detail in Chapter 5, the Blackstonian conception of property as "sole and despotic dominion" aptly fits and, indeed, analytically follows from a view of personal independence as property's ultimate justifying value. In this (Kantian) view, independence is not a good to be promoted but a constraint on the conduct of others, a requirement that no person be allowed to tell another what purposes to pursue.[1]

But independence does not exhaust the liberal idea of freedom. A liberal outlook should insist that an individual is free not only in the formal (or negative) sense of not compelled by another's choices but also in the stronger sense of able to make meaningful choices about the course of his or her life. Free individuals, John Rawls writes, act on their capacity "to have, to revise, and rationally to pursue a conception of the good."[2] Individuals can be "free" in the formal sense simply because no one is in a position of control over them, but this conception is too narrow in that it leaves out concerns for the effective realization of their ability to form and pursue a conception of the good.

According to the liberal ideal of freedom, people need a measure of self-determination to lead the full human life they are entitled to. This commitment requires us to respect each person's right to self-authorship and, most definitely, does *not* make this respect contingent on the pursuit or accomplishment of a worthy life plan.[3] Self-actualization is constrained by social and cultural embeddedness. That is the human predicament. But these constraints need not be celebrated, nor need the value of limiting them while expanding our powers of self-authorship be disparaged.[4] Free people are entitled to a degree of self-authorship, to plot their own course through life and exercise some control over their destiny, "fashioning it through successive decisions through their lives."[5]

A self-determining individual should be able to act "according to a plan of life that expresses values formed upon reflection" and to "see in the overall pattern of his or her life the embodiment of such a plan."[6] Starting out with a fully drawn map of the good life may not be possible, and perhaps not even desirable. A conception of self-authorship involving the construction of a preset "narrative arc" for one's life is a form of unfreedom. The antithetical understanding of self-authorship, however, involving free-standing decisions at every fork in the road, is not what follows. Autonomous individuals often choose both long-term and short-term pursuits, and self-determination allows – to some extent even requires – opportunities for people to change and vary their plans.[7]

Indeed, self-authorship lies somewhere in between. Our life story is neither a set of unrelated episodes nor a script fully written in advance. The core notion of an autonomous life, asserting that our accomplishments are the result of our constitutive choices,[8] remains even if we settle for a more modest commitment: we are entitled to act based on our "characteristically piecemeal and incomplete ideas about what makes life better or worse."[9]

Because self-authorship requires the ability to write and rewrite our life story, autonomy puts a high value on people's right to "reinvent themselves." Hence, the significance liberals ascribe to the right to exit, withdraw, refuse further engagement, dissociate, and cut off relationships. Minimally, exit serves a protective function. Leaving is a form of self-defense, and the mere possibility (and thus implicit threat) of exit plays an important disciplinary function. But even without concerns about mistreatment, exit is crucial to autonomy. A self-directed life requires open boundaries that enable geographical, social, familial, professional, and political mobility, which is in turn a prerequisite for the possibility of revision: having second thoughts, looking at things from a different perspective, and starting afresh.[10]

This sketch of autonomy as self-determination implies that autonomy requires appropriate mental abilities[11] as well as a measure of independence. On their own, however, negative rights do not guarantee autonomy,[12] and pursuing our self-determined conception of what gives meaning to life depends on material conditions. As Joseph Raz claimed, "[t]he provision of many collective goods is constitutive of the very possibility of autonomy and it cannot be relegated to a subordinate role, compared to some alleged right against coercion, in the name of autonomy."[13] By the same token, as Raz further explained, personal self-determination requires an adequate range of varied options, allowing effective choice and making autonomy meaningful.[14] This intimate relation between autonomy and pluralism will be the starting point of my analysis of property's structural pluralism in Chapter 4.

At this stage, then, the lesson is that autonomy depends on material conditions and on the availability of a sufficiently heterogeneous inventory of alternatives. This lesson explains why, in a liberal polity, people are entitled to a system of law *supportive* of their ability to shape a life they can view as their own rather than one that merely respects their capacity for uncoerced choice.[15] A liberal law does acknowledge that many (if not most) people often just muddle through life, but remains committed to enabling everyone the *option* of taking some control over the way life unfolds.

PROPERTY AND THE PROMOTION OF AUTONOMY

Some liberals who accept this conclusion may resist the idea of self-determination playing a key role at the core of *property* law as well. Part of their apprehension probably derives from the conventional liberal understanding of the public–private distinction, which I discuss and reject in Chapter 5. But one objection seems to rely on even more primal liberal convictions and should therefore be addressed now.

Alan Brudner argues that placing a good like self-determination at the foundation of property law is problematic. A systemic realization of the right to self-determination, he claims, might require to *fully* submerge the sphere of private sovereignty in our account of the common welfare, implying that individual rights are "variable conclusions of the collective welfare." That cannot be right since nullifying the fundamental equal dignity of persons turns the common good into despotism, a conclusion unacceptable to liberals.[16]

This powerful objection combines two concerns. One derives from the characterization of self-determination as a good – would its promotion by law efface people's (separate) individuality? Another points to the risk of substituting independence with autonomy – would this imply demoting independence to an inferior normative position, perceiving it in strictly instrumental terms? Both these concerns affect the legitimacy of property law in a liberal society. Neither, however, justifies the conclusion that independence should supplant self-determination as property law's ultimate value.[17]

When Brudner raises the specter of the despotism of the common good and the moral necessity of allowing individuals to stand outside their polity, he seems to invoke the famous charge of Rawls against utilitarianism – the dominant consequentialist political theory of our time – as failing to "take seriously the distinction between persons."[18]

Like aggregate welfare, self-determination is a good whose promotion requires both resources and collective action, and a caveat may thus be necessary. For liberals, however, the nature of self-determination as a good cannot suffice for the law to reject it as illegitimate. Unlike libertarians, liberals typically do allow, indeed require, public laws such as taxation to interfere with people's property (and thus their independence) in order to secure the self-determination of others. The reason is that, although it is indeed a good, self-determination is also far different from aggregate welfare.

Self-determination represents a rich conception of freedom. It makes our independence worthwhile – we are all entitled to be free from coercion because this freedom is necessary for each of us to write the story of our (separate though interdependent) lives.

It is on these grounds that liberals such as H. L. A. Hart are unimpressed with Robert Nozick's attempt to "lump together, and ban as equally illegitimate, things so different in their impact on individual life as taking some of a man's income to save others from great suffering and killing him or taking one of his vital organs for the same purpose." With Hart, liberals think that the former alternative does not "ignore the moral importance of the division of humanity into separate individuals and threaten the proper inviolability of persons." With Hart, therefore, they should also recognize the significance of the "unexciting but indispensable chore" of distinguishing "between the gravity of the different restrictions on different specific liberties and their importance for the conduct of a meaningful life."[19]

In other words, acknowledging that independence is subject to autonomy does not lead to the conclusion that an autonomy-based theory of property cannot adequately defend independence.[20] Part of the task of Chapter 5, where I discuss the affirmative obligations entailed by property's relational justice, is to translate Hart's dictum into more specific guidelines. These guidelines derive from the liberal maxim of reciprocal respect for self-determination as such, the nature of legal prescriptions more generally, and rule-of-law concerns. Here is a brief preview:

(a) The duty of reciprocal respect for self-determination cannot constitute an excessive burden because it must neither undermine the autonomy of the involved parties nor create inappropriate interpersonal subordination between them.
(b) Certain practices, such as love or friendship, are rightfully shielded from legal treatment because legal enforcement may destroy their inherent moral value and legal intervention may backfire by displacing internal motivations.
(c) To provide effective guidance to its addressees and constrain the ability of officials to exercise power, law's rules need to be relatively clear, minimizing recourse to individualized knowledge and radically ad hoc judgments.

ULTIMATE, INTRINSIC, AND INSTRUMENTAL VALUES

1. *Independence's Irreducible Value.* Brudner's second concern refers to the relationship between self-determination and independence. The fact that – as I have just claimed – independence is subject to

self-determination, may suggest that the former is but a means to the latter. Wrong.

The value of independence, as hinted above, lies in its contribution to self-determination. Hence, although independence is not an ultimate value, it is not only an instrumental one either. The value of independence is *not* fully captured by "the value of its consequences," or by the value of the consequences it is likely to have, or can be used to produce.[21] If independence is viewed as a means for attaining the autonomy end, our commitment to people's independence is forced into retreat whenever it seems to conflict with the norms that best promote their autonomy.[22] This easy path to the paternalistic revocation of people's independence is intolerable.

This alarming concern is precisely the target of Isaiah Berlin's famous warning regarding the *intrinsic* significance of negative liberty. An instrumental view of independence could end up giving carte blanche to the disregard of people's "actual wishes," claiming they may be driven by "irrational impulse, uncontrolled desires," and the like, "in the name, and on behalf, of their 'real' selves." The resulting coercion and oppression caused by such views led Berlin to insist that "some portion of human existence must remain independent of the sphere of social control" and that "[t]o invade that preserve, however small, would be despotism."[23]

Such worries about abuse do not necessarily preclude thinking about independence in sheer instrumental terms, but the idea that people's actual wishes are mere indicators of what is worthy of respect is objectionable even in the absence of abuse. This objection suggests that an instrumentalist understanding of independence fails to capture its value.[24] Libertarians (and Kantians) may claim that these problems justify thinking about independence as law's (or private law's) *ultimate* value. The choice we face, however, is not a binary one.

2. *Neither Ultimate nor Instrumental.* A value can be "intrinsically valuable," that is, "valuable even apart from [its] instrumental value" or from its contribution "to producing certain consequences" without being also "of ultimate value." Although a value of this type is explained or justified by reference to another, ultimate value, or by its being "a constitutive part" or essential ingredient of that ultimate

value, its contribution to it cannot be encapsulated in instrumental terms.[25]

This notion of an intrinsic, albeit not ultimate, value enables liberalism to embrace a plurality of values without rendering values like friendship or art merely instrumental or collapsing into an unacceptable foundational value pluralism. The lesson for my current pursuit is clear: although independence is not an ultimate value, neither is it merely instrumental – rather, it is an intrinsic value that every self-respecting liberal polity must seriously consider.

This proposition applies throughout the spectrum of property types. It also highlights the indispensable role of the Blackstonian variation within the inventory of property types prescribed by structural pluralism. Finally, the significance of independence to property means that, while the protection of private property from governmental interference need not be absolute, it should, as it is, be legally – or, better still, constitutionally – guaranteed. (I discuss this intricate issue in some detail in Chapter 8.) These are all important implications, but they neither entail nor justify the sole dominion of independence in property's domain, as some property theorists would argue.

Treating independence as an intrinsic though not the ultimate value poses a challenge. We need to make sure that independence does not sidestep the ultimate value (self-determination), of which it is a constitutive component, or transgress other values constitutive of self-determination. Simultaneously, we must beware of demoting independence to the status of merely a means to a superior end. To illustrate the complexity of this task, consider someone for whom healthiness is an essential feature of a good dinner needing to reconcile this conviction with potentially conflicting concerns (such as tastiness).

No magic formula is available for contending with this challenge, which brings us back to Hart's crucial focus on the need for qualitative distinctions between the violations of independence attempted in the name of self-authorship.[26] Brudner appears troubled by precisely this kind of analysis, which he fears may "turn law's rule into politics by other means."[27] With Berlin, I suggest that abandoning "the notion of a final harmony" is less of a concern. This type of judgment is an inescapable feature of the human condition.[28] (Chapter 5 demonstrates the viability of such "Hartian" exercises.[29])

3. *Property's Intrinsic and Instrumental Values.* These remarks on independence do point out that, although the ultimate value of property in a liberal society must be autonomy,[30] autonomy is not the only reason for individuals having property. People have property – they become owners and co-owners – in order to secure property's intrinsic and instrumental values.[31] In addition to independence, property plays an important role in developing our personhood, constructing our communities, and securing the material resources we need in order to achieve our plans and fulfill our goals.

At times, these property values are mutually reinforcing, as is often the case, for example, in the relationship of community and utility: interpersonal capital tends to facilitate trust, which in turn gives rise to economic success, and economic success tends to strengthen trust and mutual responsibility.[32] In other contexts, community and utility push in different directions, with the potential conflict of values increasing even further when we consider independence and personhood as well. Because property's intrinsic and instrumental values are frequently treated as rivals, a pluralistic property theory seems threatened by constant and irresolvable conflicts.

Property law cannot always help people obtain competing goods. But as long as it safeguards people's autonomy and facilitates only those interpersonal interactions that comply with relational justice, a liberal property law need not decide on the proper balance of values and, instead, should support multiple property types affording people options to choose their favorite one.

If property law is to live up to its promise of enhancing autonomy, it must offer people a rich inventory of property types for each sphere of human action and interaction. A genuinely liberal theory of property, then, does *not* imply that independence, personhood, community, and utility are irrelevant to property. Their significance, however, rather than fundamental or free-standing, is both derived from, and thus also circumscribed by, the role of these values in people's autonomous pursuit of their life plans. Yet, given that the autonomy-enhancing role of property follows largely from the freedom to choose between types, and that the key values shaping these types are independence, personhood, community, and utility, these values are nothing short of crucial to property law.

I dwell briefly below on personhood, community, and utility as property values as well as on the role of autonomy as a side constraint to their application.

PERSONHOOD

Discussions of the personhood theory of property often begin with the empirical observation that people perceive some of their holdings as symbolically extending their sense of identity beyond the boundaries of their physical bodies. At times, we express who we are – both to ourselves and to others – through what we have.[33] Margaret Jane Radin emphasized two characteristics of such self-constituting resources: first, people identify their own selves with these resources because they represent their past experiences; second, loss of or damage to this type of resources is experienced as a violation that transcends the financial setback involved.[34]

Perceiving resources as extensions of the self may entail a moral significance that is closely related to property's autonomy-enhancing *telos*. Changing an object, Jeremy Waldron explains, creates a dual relationship between will and object. On the one hand, the person's will has made a difference to the object – there is now something in the object that can only be explained through the workings of this person's will. On the other hand, and more significantly, the object makes a difference to the person, whose willful endeavor at a given point in time can only be explained by reference to the external object of his or her labor. Thus, modifying something in the external world demonstrates a kind of responsibility by registering the product of one's will.

People's will, then, is reflected in the object inasmuch as there is this dual line of effect from the will to the object and back to the will. This reflection is morally significant because, by changing materials, some sort of consistency, permanence, and stability is imposed on the resolutions, plans, and projects of the will. Moral development is thus fostered, with the will becoming more self-disciplined and mature, and abilities and self-conceptions more sustained and developed.[35]

Waldron limits his account to cases of physical changes in an object. But this is too restrictive. The tangible or intangible resources we hold without changing them may also be affected by our wills – and thus express our personalities – in a myriad of ways. These constitutive resources – a subset of our holdings – may be integrated into our lives by being shaped or organized in line with our conception of the self and our private needs, inclinations, and desires, our own life plans. Unlike fungible resources, whose function is merely instrumental, constitutive resources tend to serve as symbols of the unique place we have established for ourselves in our communities and as reflections of our past and present, and, in that way, as external projections of our life stories.[36]

The significance of constitutive resources to our autonomy justifies ensuring their private owners' relatively indisputable authority. This proposition, however, does not collapse into sweeping support for the dominion conception of property. Categorizing property types as constitutive (say homeownership) or fungible (say ownership of financial instruments) implies that only a fraction of the property inventory belongs to the former, privileged category, whereas many typical resources of modern day capitalist regimes are characterless assets without any significance to personhood.[37]

Furthermore, as noted in Chapter 2, the reflection-and-attachment phenomenon is a social process.[38] Our personal investment in external resources is socially constructed, meaning that the taxonomy splitting resources into constitutive and fungible need not be viewed as inevitable. Take the privately owned automobile, which used to be an example of constitutive property.[39] The transition to services like Zipcar and Uber and thereafter to self-driving cars, which is likely to bring about its demise, may well be a reason for celebration rather than despair. Generally, whereas having *some* constitutive property types is substantial for property's autonomy-enhancing *telos*, adhering to the conventional ways of securing a temporal horizon of action is not. Hence, it is appropriate and even desirable to periodically reconsider and, if necessary, revise our constitutive-fungible taxonomy.[40]

COMMUNITY

1. *An Intrinsic Value.* Property is frequently a setting for furthering intrinsically valuable interpersonal relationships. Tasks such as sharing

in the management of a given resource strengthen and enrich the interpersonal capital that grows from cooperation, support, trust, and mutual responsibility.[41] Property types that cater to property's community value understand cooperation not only – at times even not mainly – as a means to economic success but also, or primarily, as a good in and of itself. These property types are one of the ways a group of users turns into a community.

Thus, while all commons property types yield instrumental benefits – economies of scale, specialization and synergy, risk spreading – these benefits are contingent on technological, environmental, social, and cultural circumstances that vary from one setting to the other.[42] Some commons property types, however, offer intrinsic advantages as well that, given the interdependence typical of the human predicament, are germane to any viable understanding of self-authorship. In light of their contribution to self-determination, then, commons property types are necessary features of the landscape in a genuinely liberal property law.[43]

People value interpersonal relationships, forming associations and taking part in collective enterprises not only as a means to some independently specified end: "We human beings are social creatures, and creatures with values. Among the things that we value are our relations with each other."[44] Working together, taking part in a collective enterprise, or participating in a communal activity represent a free-standing value[45] that is constitutive of people's life plans. Much of our self-authorship takes the form of *co*-authorship. The ever-increasing number of projects requiring the daily interactions characteristic of these more social commons property types, tends to produce an intensive, even if partial, fusion. This intensity (and its continuity) stimulates closeness, intimacy, and mutual trust.[46]

Owners in these communities thus partake in a *joint* commitment. They perceive themselves, at least partially, as a "we," a plural subject that is in turn a constitutive feature of each member's identity as an "I."[47] The communal ideal of marriage – of sharing the advantages as well as the difficulties of life – is, of course, a prime example. Sharing life and its projects typically requires spouses to pool their efforts and their rewards, infusing costs and benefits with intersubjective character

Community

so that each spouse operates on behalf of both.[48] In other settings – notably (but by no means only) some religious, ideological, and cultural communities – the commons resource may constitute the center of a way of life that profoundly affects the commoners' self-identity.[49] Social commons property types are thus *loci* in a community whose members "experience group life with a sense of belonging" and consider their community's shared characteristics as "sources of identity" that are "important, even vital, in their lives."[50]

2. *A Liberal Value*. A liberal system of property cannot ignore these truths. Liberalism, properly understood, appreciates the constitutive nature of communities and their significance to the identity of individual people.[51] In turn, a genuine community need not be illiberal. Quite the contrary. Part of what makes our constitutive communities meaningful is that they are realized through voluntary choice, if not *ex ante* then at least *ex post*. Meaningful self-identification and its ensuing significance should be part of the good life for individuals, not a legal duty they must bear regardless of its continuing appeal. In order to guarantee that a given community is good *for* people, law should ensure that individuals participate in social groups only voluntarily.[52]

People, then, are partly constituted by their participation in a community and by their relationship with other members. They cannot be the sole authors of their lives. They should, however, remain the ultimate navigators of their own self-actualization.[53] Committed members of liberal communities, despite their deep identification, do occasionally take a critical perspective of them.[54] They may even decide to exit their communities and abandon that part of their identity.[55]

Barring the legal power to exit, a community's continuity cannot plausibly be taken as an affirmation of its value in its members' life.[56] The phenomenology of a decision to exit a genuine community is interpretive: a member contemplating exit considers to what extent he is defined by his community, and then evaluates himself as that person. It is at this evaluative stage – "is this part of me good, or at least good enough?" – that the individual takes, and indeed should take, center stage.

3. *Liberal Commons.* Achieving the instrumental (economic) as well as the intrinsic (social) goods of commons property types in a liberal environment is a challenging endeavor, mainly because the availability of free exit systemically hinders the success of commons property types. The unilateral right to leave may invite opportunistic behavior and lead people to be distrustful, on their guard, and overly quick to retaliate. Thus, the right to exit that liberal property is committed to, tends to destabilize sharing and trust by thwarting collective action and threatening cooperation, even in long-term relationships.[57]

Law can help to deal with these difficulties. Property types that comply with the prescriptions of the "liberal commons" construct, as Michael Heller and I call it, are actually structured around this challenge. The notion of a liberal commons draws on the insight of Elinor Ostrom that "generalized institutional-choice and conflict-resolution" mechanisms, together with "substantial local autonomy," can enable and sustain commons property regimes.[58] Unlike many of the studies that Ostrom relied on, however, the liberal commons recruits law in order to shore up the liberal right of exit without compromising the commons' success.

Formal law is often inappropriate for establishing the trust, cooperation, and mutual reliance that any successful commons requires for the day-to-day routines of self-governance. Social norms and other modes of social organization and structure, not formal law, govern most daily interactions.[59] Recourse to law on a regular basis would be costly and perceived as unneighborly.[60] But law can nonetheless be helpful and even crucial for the viability of commons property types when it operates in the background of the parties' relationships.

Law can (and often does, as shown in Chapter 4) serve two functions in these property types by providing the infrastructure of the commons institutions and by supplying anti-opportunistic devices that reassure prospective commoners they will not be abused for cooperating. These mechanisms of property governance facilitate interpersonal cooperation, which is a prerequisite for the success of any property type with successive or concurrent interests. They thus characterize a variety of property types, ranging from publicly held corporations, trusts, and landlord–tenant law, through partnerships and common-interest communities, all the way to marriage.

These property types are obviously very different from one another: while some are mostly utilitarian, others are more social and – as I discuss in Chapter 4 – the legal background rules that they provide vary accordingly. But all are aimed at minimizing incentives to abuse the interpersonal trust and cooperation necessary for success. They create a formal "safety net" that reinforces each commoner's trust in others and their willingness to cooperate without focusing on the grave vulnerability that such trust can engender.[61] Thus, well-designed liberal commons property types enable commoners to gain the benefits that flow from mutual trust without taking prohibitive individual risks, facilitating prosperity and cooperation without sacrificing exit.[62]

UTILITY

Welfarist analyses of property abound and there is no need to discuss them in detail here.[63] What is significant for my purposes is to explain why and how they are important to a liberal – meaning autonomy-enhancing – property law.

I begin with the uncontroversial proposition that any humanist polity must respect the welfare of individuals, as well as the importance that people ascribe to securing the means they need to satisfy their preferences and pursue their goals.[64] This proposition, however, is ambiguous. It does not sufficiently distinguish two different ways in which utility can come into play in property law.

1. *Instrumental to Autonomy.* The first way follows directly from the autonomy-enhancing perspective on property. People's welfare should be promoted because it serves as a means for their self-determination, and satisfying their preferences is likewise important since these preferences both reflect and serve their life plans. These propositions imply a significant distinction between, on the one hand, ground projects – the projects that give meaning to one's life and are key chapters in a person's life story – and, on the other hand, sheer preferences.[65] Here welfare is conceptualized as an instrumental good, which is often quite significant but is in principle subordinate to the ultimate good of

self-determination. This means, of course, that the accumulation of capital must not be sanctioned or supported as an end.[66]

This is also why utilitarian considerations can legitimately shape *certain* property types. Enhancing individual autonomy requires that property law offer a rich array of structures for people who are interested in the efficient – and thus beneficial – management of resources. With this autonomy imperative satisfied, the inner life of these property types should be largely devoted to facilitating people's welfare goals. The qualification "largely" is not coincidental: understood in this way, none of these property types should be structured in a way that threatens to efface or excessively limit others' autonomy. I will shortly return to this function of autonomy as a "side constraint" to the application of property's intrinsic and instrumental values.

2. Welfare Foundationalism. There is, however, also another way of thinking about the role of utility in property law that, admittedly, is by far more prevalent in the current use. In this dominant view, the authority of owners and other players in the property drama is perceived as a means for reaching a *collective* goal, namely, *aggregate* welfare. (To be sure, welfarist accounts of property need not be utilitarian: they can aim at maximizing other social welfare functions. But this otherwise significant clarification is immaterial here.)

On its face, this welfare foundationalist view of property may seem similar to the approach I have just embraced, where utility is a critical instrumental value within the liberal conception of property. However, it is dramatically different. It suggests that people's authority over resources has *no* free-standing value and is instead *fully* subservient to aggregate welfare. In turn, if Eric Posner and Glen Weyl are correct, this proposition implies that, because or insofar as private owners' veto power makes efficiency "impossible," ownership should be abolished outright. Our current property system should thus be replaced, as they suggest, with a system in which "[p]eople are not so much owners of property as 'lessees' from society, subject to a special kind of lease that terminates when a higher value user appears, whereupon the lease is automatically transferred to that user."[67]

What matters here is not whether Posner and Weyl are correct.[68] As usual, an economic analysis of property is necessarily contingent since it is highly dependent on specific technological, social, cultural, and environmental variables.[69] But even if they are right, their analysis that – like many other welfarist analyses – reduces everything to preferences, misses at least part of the point of property, which is about owners' autonomy and not only about (individual or collective) welfare.[70]

3. *A Liberal Critique*. The pitfalls of conceptualizing property only in terms of optimizing society's allocation of entitlements or of preference satisfaction are hardly news. They are grounded in John Rawls and Robert Nozick's devastating criticism of welfare foundationalism.

The idea that society should "maximize the net balance of satisfaction over all its members," Rawls famously argued, conflates "all persons into one through the imaginative acts of the impartial spectator," and thus fails to "take seriously the distinction between persons."[71] Moreover, even for one person at a time, preference satisfaction cannot be an ultimate goal.

To see why, recall Nozick's celebrated experience machine. Suppose, Nozick wrote, "there were an experience machine that would give you any experience you desired"; would you plug into it "for life, preprograming your life's experiences"?[72] Nozick's answer – and mine – is negative, and his ultimate reason for it is straightforward. Plugging into the machine "is a kind of suicide" because we humans are concerned not only with our experiences, or with what we do, or even with the sort of person we are. Ultimately, we are concerned with the fact that it is *we* (rather than the machine, or anyone else) who live our lives.[73]

Welfarist foundationalism is definitely correct in refusing to focus *solely* on the act of choosing. The liberal commitment to construct meaningful conditions of choice must not lose sight of potential consequences. But it is equally erroneous to think that only these consequences matter. Individuals are not passive consumers or carriers of well-being, and choice matters because its consequences are part of the chooser's life. Furthermore, the hierarchical character of the plans, projects, and goals that constitute our life stories, as well as their complicated interconnections, defy the simple welfare foundationalist technique of summarizing preferences (weighted by their intensity).[74]

By failing to situate people's welfare and the satisfaction of their preferences in a broader understanding of the self, welfarist foundationalism ends up undermining the very reasons that justify caring about satisfying people's preferences and promoting their welfare in the first place, namely, that these preferences reflect and serve people's life plans, and that people's welfare serves as a means for their self-determination.[75]

4. *Utility and Property.* As my earlier comments clarify, rejecting welfare foundationalism does not mean that there should be no property types whose animating principle is purely utilitarian. Furthermore, nothing in my critique challenges the legitimacy of commandeering property law for collective purposes. The clearest (but certainly not only) case of such "collectivist property types" comes up through the privatization of public services, where property law displaces public forms of governance in order to achieve efficient outcomes.

As noted, insofar as these purely utilitarian property types are concerned, property need not, and often does not, strictly vindicate owners' authority.[76] But even regarding these property types, a liberal polity should resist subsuming autonomy under the aggregate welfare.

To demonstrate this point, consider copyright. The incentives set by copyright law were originally understood in terms of delegating society's interest in fostering culture, research, and development to private individuals and firms.[77] And yet, copyright is by now understood as a potentially constitutive medium of the self, which explains and arguably justifies allocating to authors semi-inalienable rights of "attribution" and "integrity," known as "moral rights."[78] On the other hand, copyright – just as any other property type – must comply with the thin but still noteworthy constraints entailed by property's commitment to relational justice. This commitment, I have argued elsewhere, is a premise of the fair use doctrine, which is the key limit on copyright owners' private authority.[79]

AUTONOMY AS SIDE CONSTRAINT

These last remarks take me back to the role of autonomy as property's ultimate value. The idea of autonomy as a "side constraint" that generally trumps other property values was already implicit in my discussion of community. That discussion was deliberately limited to forms of *liberal* commons,[80] which respect people's right to exit.[81] A liberal property law needs to adopt a similar position regarding welfare. In many cases, promoting the welfarist goals of particular property types does not clash with, and even enhances, the ultimate value of autonomy. When they do clash, however, as Chapter 7 shows in the context of employment, for example,[82] welfarist concerns should generally give way to rules that best promote property's ultimate value of autonomy.

The cautious language of the previous paragraph is not coincidental. The main reason for it is that, in some (many?) cases, the apparent clash between utility or community and autonomy dissolves once we look more closely at the meaning of utility or community for people's autonomy.[83] The vibrancy of certain utility- or community-oriented property types may require curtailing some future choices, a feature that is also typical of many autonomy-enhancing practices and institutions. Indeed, the idea of a plan, let alone a conception of a good life, implies undertaking a future-oriented *commitment*. Thus, insofar as a "Hartian" (complicated, to be sure) analysis of the overall effects of such limitations on people's self-determination shows that they are positive, the incommensurably higher status of autonomy poses no real difficulty.

Other conflicts, however, are real and fundamental and may even require a seemingly impossible trade-off. Although autonomy should take priority in most of these cases, I do recognize that this presumption could be overridden if, and only if, its cost to the utility or community values of property meets a sufficiently high threshold.[84] One category of cases seems clear: in societies afflicted by grave poverty, where even Rawls would no longer insist on the lexical priority of liberty,[85] ensuring food and shelter to everyone may justifiably trump any autonomy-based property claim. There may be further categories of such cases and I cannot hope to fully address these challenges of value incommensurability here. Instead, I flag this concern and note that its impact on liberal property theory seems no more intractable than that on legal theory in general.[86]

THE POWERS OF PROPERTY

Having set these building blocks in place, I can now further refine the ways property serves autonomy. My discussion of property's utility value, as well as the title of this chapter, emphasize that property is not only about provision. Although provision is indeed a significant dimension of it,[87] property is above all about having some *authority* over resources, which is conducive to self-authorship. This authority allows people to employ the (tangible and intangible) external world to ensure their independence and establish their personhood. It can also ease their participation in various kinds of communities and, of course, secure the means for their subsistence so as to provide for their future plans.[88]

Whatever the intrinsic or instrumental property value that is invoked, then, the ultimate value of property is still self-determination and its key feature the authority of an owner. For property to serve these values, owners need to have some authority over others – both other individuals and society as a whole. This means that property, as Chapter 2 corroborated, is thoroughly relational. It also means that, as Morris Cohen famously argued, property law does not merely protect people in their possession. Rather, "the dominion over things" that "the legal order confers on those called owners" empowers them in their interpersonal relations and thus also implies a private "*imperium* over [their] fellow human beings."[89]

Cohen not only emphasized property's relationality[90] but, as this short quote testifies, recognized its connection to property's unique form of empowerment. But whereas Cohen looked at the way the former entails the latter, appreciating the inverse relation is no less significant. Property, as Avihay Dorfman explains, vests authority in owners to determine, in some measure, "the normative standing of others in relation to a resource."[91]

Owners have not only the power to control their resource against nonowners' competing claims but, as Dorfman insists, they also have "the normative power to determine what others may or may not do with it." As Cohen's metaphoric use of *imperium* suggests, this unusual authority implies that property requires nonowners to defer to the owners' authority to prescribe their own normative situation. Property, then, empowers owners by making their intentions a source of demands on others' conduct. A nonowner's respect of the owner's right to property is part of the nonowner's respect of the owner's right to self-determination because, as Dorfman puts it, it implies "a recognition of the owner as reason-providing for that non-owner."[92] To respect people's right to property is to respect their authority to have the last word, that is, to determine theirs and others' normative situation regarding the resource at hand.[93]

Property's empowerment is thus relational through and through, reinforcing Cohen's insistence on the claim that our (power-conferring) system of property is responsible for the vulnerabilities of nonowners. As Cohen argued, my power to control "things [that] are necessary to the life of my neighbor ... confers on me power, limited but real, to make him do what I want."[94] This meaning of "property as power"[95] encapsulates the idea of property's "power as influence," namely, the causal relation between ownership and nonowners' vulnerability that, as I discuss below, challenges property's claim to legitimacy.[96]

Dorfman's account of the *normative* power that property confers on owners highlights another dimension of nonowners' vulnerability (and thus of property's justificatory challenge). Awareness of this dimension is significant because, unlike the influence of property, this power is not contingent.[97] Although property does not always influence nonowners, it invariably subjects them to the owners' Hohfeldian power. Property *necessarily* involves this vulnerability because the law's demand from nonowners to respect the owners' authority is unmediated by any further facts about the world.

As Cohen suggested, the interpersonal implications of the power that owners enjoy vis-à-vis others are not easily defensible because, potentially, property poses a normative threat to others. Although Cohen did not condemn these attributes of private property, he did underscore that "it is necessary to apply to the law of property all those considerations of social ethics and enlightened public policy which ought to be brought to the discussion of any just form of government."[98] In drawing this analogy to the legitimation of government, Cohen may have tried to shed light on the justificatory challenge confronting property, but the parallel does not fully capture its depth.

Dorfman's discussion is again helpful here when he notes that the authority of owners differs from that of public officials. When public officials occupy a position of authority, they purport to represent the state and their demands are therefore justified by reference to legitimate reasons for the state's authority.[99] The authority of owners, by contrast, relies on their subjectivity – their intention, judgment, and point of view – as a free-standing source of legal claims over others. Subjecting nonowners to an authority typified by *such* a profound "accountability deficit" offends the moral equality prevalent between owners and nonowners by virtue of their shared status as private persons.[100]

JUSTIFYING PROPERTY

1. *The Challenge.* Following the recognition of the deep connections between property and power, articulating an adequate justification for property becomes imperative. The authority that property law confers on owners *generates* the vulnerability of nonowners, thereby posing a potential threat to their autonomy. Instantiating a system of property by wielding political power thus faces a significant legitimacy challenge. (Here and throughout the book, I generally follow Allen Buchanan's view of political legitimacy as requiring some benchmark of moral justifiability in exercising "a monopoly, within a jurisdiction, in the making, application, and enforcement of law."[101])

The legitimacy challenge cannot be dismissed by declaring that property is to be founded on a free-standing "authority interest."[102] In and of itself, private authority over others lacks normative significance and, indeed, unless based on a more fundamental interest, it is simply authoritarian, which is precisely why liberal property is *not* private authority *simpliciter*. Liberal property is both grounded in and bound by people's right to self-determination.

Property law can be legitimate and, moreover, it can be just. Its legitimacy, however, cannot be established by focusing solely on its beneficiaries. Property law must be answerable to nonowners, who are the subjects of property's powers. To accomplish this imposing task, a

Justifying Property

liberal theory of property enlists property's contribution (implicit in the previous sections) to people's self-determination – the ultimate normative commitment of any liberal polity.

2. *Power-Conferring Institution.* The difference between the duties that property imposes and the core tort-law duties dealing with our bodily integrity can help to clarify the role of property in facilitating people's ability to develop their own life plans. To assume that people have pre-legal and pre-conventional rights to their bodily integrity seems natural, as does the conclusion that tort law fundamentally affirms the correlative duties against their violation.[103] Property law, by contrast, does not vindicate existing rights. Rather, as just indicated, property is first and foremost *power-conferring*.

Nonowners' duties are certainly relevant to property as well (indeed, they explain the heavy burden of justifying property). But they would be meaningless in the absence of the owners' legal authority, which is the product of property's power-conferring rules. The role of property's duty-imposing rules is to vindicate that authority and to protect the owners' ability to apply the powers enabled by property. These piggy-backing rules would be pointless in a world that does not recognize property as, essentially, a power-conferring institution.

In prescribing the specific content, scope, and implications of the powers conferred by the various property types it promulgates, law actually shapes the interpersonal practices of property rather than merely reflecting them. This was, as may be recalled, the premise of my argument in Chapter 2 – property theory is a *legal* theory.

In the current context, what matters is that, as a power-conferring body of law, property law attaches legal consequences to certain acts in order "to enable people to affect norms and their application in such a way if they desire to do so for this purpose."[104] Property's deference, in other words, is enabling. It enables normative powers regarding tangible and intangible resources, which allow people a measure of control, a say over these resources, in a way *they* deem conducive to *their* own goals.[105]

3. *Temporally Extended Authority over Things.* Property may well deserve its title as "the keystone institution of the liberal social order," precisely because it facilitates people's ability to define and pursue their

projects and commitments with some measure of immunity from intrusions by the state or by other individuals.[106] A liberal property law achieves this goal by offering people, in every sphere of human action and interaction, a rich set of forms of private authority – or property types – from which they can choose what is for them the optimal balance of independence, personhood, community, and utility: property's intrinsic and instrumental values.

For many significant choices, with respect to every property type, property law helps people secure "a temporal horizon of action" that "transforms abstract agents into individuals with concrete identities and abstract choices into individual life plans."[107] Owners' power to bequest further amplifies property's facilitation of people's self-authorship. Self-authorship does not require the unconstrained exercise of this power and is perfectly consistent with the taxation of intergenerational transfers. But *some* power to bequest is important because it enables people to "invest – both financially and emotionally – in a series of projects that define their personal and ethical identity," which "extend beyond their own existence."[108]

Indeed, the temporal extension, which typifies property rights, follows quite closely from property's autonomy-enhancing *telos*. As Charles Beitz explains, because "self-determination consists in the carrying out of higher-order projects," and because each such project "can be seen as composed of a set of plans arranged in a temporal sequence," a successful exercise of self-determination is "an intertemporal achievement." Therefore, "if we allow ourselves the idea of a range of normal life-plans, we can say with some confidence that temporally extended control of things will be indispensable for success in carrying out the vast majority of those plans."[109]

Property is not indispensable for self-determination – a person could, for example, choose a radically ascetic lifestyle, opting to rely on the generosity of others.[110] But it does not seem far-fetched to conclude that, by conferring on individuals the power to employ various property types in the service of their life plans, property does make a crucial contribution to people's ability to realize the right to self-authorship, at least in the world we know and experience.[111] While this contribution depends on the other means that the state offers in support of people's self-determination, property is *not* fully fungible with these other means. The unique autonomy-enhancing function of temporally extending private authority over resources implies that, in a liberal polity, property plays a distinctive and irreducible role.

Property rights, just like people's plans, need not be fully immune from disruption. While machines are supposed to follow operating protocols to the letter, human beings who make plans anticipate some changes. Surprises are, after all, a feature of autonomous life. Constant upheaval, however, is not. Plans may *at times* change and be adapted, and some surprises can be accommodated without undermining self-determination. For plans to be meaningful, however, or even just intelligible, some degree of stability *is* essential.

Hence, a program that radically destabilizes all our holdings, such as that of Posner and Weyl,[112] cannot guide the architecture of a liberal property system. True, liberal property neither does nor should restrict people's ability to limit the significance of their connections with resources to their life story. A person can always decide, for example, not to own her home and be a short-term lessee instead or he can opt for a "tiny house on wheels."[113] Yet, by making autonomy-enhancing property unavailable, Posner and Weyl's program would unduly restrict our options and violate the autonomy-based requirement to expand people's repertoire of choices.

4. *A Formidable Challenge.* The autonomy-enhancing role of property in general, and of a structurally pluralistic property law in particular, are not concerns specific to the better-off. Thus, for example, improving the compliance of property law with structural pluralism implies, as Chapter 4 shows, that it should proactively facilitate home equity insurance and shared equity types. These reforms explicitly address the autonomy (and welfare) concerns of middle- and lower-income households.

And yet, however persuasive, these remarks do not fully address the concerns of nonowners who, as noted, are restricted rather than served by property's empowering function. Justifying property while ignoring the distributive question thus proves impossible: how can a liberal property law guided by a commitment to self-authorship rather than to distributive justice be legitimate, given the burdens it imposes on the "have nots"?[114]

Recall that nonowners' normative liability is the flip side of property's normative powers, whose contribution to owners' autonomy is property's raison d'être. This liability, as I have noted, is amenable to translation into power-as-influence, which in turn tends to generate autonomy-reducing effects. The vulnerabilities of nonowners thus emerge – indeed, become intelligible – only after we decide to endorse the power-conferring institution of property.

5. *A Continuous Challenge.* Vulnerabilities, to be sure, also exist in a state of nature, and some of them may be generated by the possessors of "de facto power." But that power is not equivalent to that of owners after the introduction of property. Because property relations create new and different modes of dependence, Christopher Essert is wrong to claim that, absent property, people's subordination to the power of others would have been aggravated.[115] Even if the degree of domination remains constant, it is still one thing for the state to *allow* significant imbalances in power as influence and quite another for it to *facilitate, authorize, and bring into existence* such dominance by entrenching normative powers into law.[116] The legitimacy of this decision, therefore, depends on the extent to which it can be acceptable to those who will be subject to these powers – a justificatory burden that haunts the liberal case for property.

I use the verb "haunts" deliberately. Property's justificatory challenge is not limited to the moment of its creation and constantly resurfaces. Challenges to justice – be they relational (such as the bigot's attempt to use his property right to deny "undesirables" entry to a mall[117]) or distributive (such as the ways the property regime contributes to the predicament of homeless people[118]) – are inherent in the life of property. They are further exacerbated by certain features of property, notably accession: property leads to more property and thus tends to generate greater inequality.[119]

The law is accordingly required to justify its *consistent* willingness to authorize the power of owners vis-à-vis nonowners who, potentially, attempt to use their stuff. The burden of justification is ongoing and immanent to the life of property in law.

This onerous justificatory challenge could prove insormountable, once we seriously consider the many inequalities of the real world, which this book does not. Grasping the effects of founding property on self-determination, however, may provide at least a preliminary response. They point out, as I claim below, the inherent limitations of property's power in a genuinely liberal property law and, if properly implemented, its rather dramatic distributive connotations.[120]

RISKING PANGLOSSIANISM?

My approach is not risk-free. There is an undeniable and unfortunately not marginal gap between the liberal theory of property and the realities of property in actual liberal systems. This gap may suggest that property is the problem and cannot be part of the solution.

Michael Hardt and Antonio Negri, for example, argue that property, rather than "the foundation of freedom, justice, and development," is bound to be "an obstacle to economic life, the basis of unjust structures of social control, and the prime factor that creates and maintains social hierarchies and inequalities." Property, therefore, must be "transformed into the common," which they understand as "*nonproperty*," namely, "a fundamentally different means of organizing the use and management of wealth," based on "an equal and open structure for access to wealth together with democratic mechanisms of decision-making."[121]

If Hardt and Negri are correct and property is indeed irredeemably evil, a liberal theory of property is at best redundant and at worst an apologetic exercise that might serve to shield oppression and unduly promote intrinsically unjust social practices.[122]

Insofar as their polemical critique attacks the *idea* of liberal property, however, Hardt and Negri are wrong, and the social vision they advance is not very appealing. Celebrating the abolition of property[123] ignores how property can, and should, empower individuals and thus serve their ultimate right to self-determination. Imposing on everyone a "subjectivity" arising from and defined by "social cooperation" cannot "free human conviviality," as they argue,[124] because a happy commons must be one that people *freely* choose. A genuinely liberal property law that proactively expands people's opportunities for individual and collective self-determination while restricting options of interpersonal domination is a far more attractive alternative.

Admittedly, this attractive vision might be illusory in certain settings and its promotion counterproductive. I do not deny that many property systems are normatively corrupt, and some of them even beyond repair, so that attempts to reform them along the lines of the liberal theory of property might actually be distracting.

But these empirical findings, though obviously significant, do not call into question the need for refining the ideal of liberal property. Quite the reverse: to identify a property system as corrupt, we need to know what an ideal one looks like. Understanding property requires us to explore not only its current manifestations but also what it ought to be as well as the standards by which it should be judged.[125] One goal of this book is indeed to bring social scientists and legal academics to examine the performance of existing property systems along *these* lines and not only in terms of their efficiency.

There is yet another reason for refraining from any quick discard of the liberal *idea* of property, notwithstanding its extensive abuse. By neglecting to mine this idea in search of happier practices, critics of property may paradoxically end up confirming its dominion conception, which underlies the manifestations of it that they rightly criticize.[126]

Given the cultural power of the idea of property, losing the battle over its proper interpretation would, by default, needlessly exacerbate our predicament.[127] By contrast, unpacking the liberal *ideal* of property is potentially challenging because it requires, at the very least, a respectable façade of universalism. By setting standards that current practices do not necessarily live up to, the idealized picture can be, and often is, a fruitful basis for social criticism. Even if hypocritical, then, idealism plays a role in any critical engagement.

INHERENT LIMITATIONS OF PROPERTY'S POWER

So consider first the limitations on property's power that, in the liberal conception, are *intrinsic* to property. These limitations are all conditions for property's legitimacy or entailments of its underlying

Inherent Limitations of Property's Power 69

rationale and need not rely on a public requirement from owners to participate in or support the state's responsibilities.

The following analysis takes its cue from an insufficiently recognized lesson of John Locke's discussion of property – that identifying property's fundamental justification is not only crucial in order to legitimate law's support of owners' private authority, but is similarly relevant to properly circumscribe owners' rights. This insight's effect on Locke's system – the so-called spoilage proviso – is quite minimal.[128] But the broader proposition – that property's raison d'être should delimit the scope of owners' authority and prescribe its exact content – is profound and extremely significant.[129]

In a liberal (autonomy-enhancing) property law, the authority of owners is founded on, and justified by, its contribution to self-authorship.[130] This right of self-determination is held to be sufficiently important to merit respect from other individuals and from the state.[131] Therefore, if and to the extent that property's authority contributes to people's self-determination, it is a priori justified.[132] Three conclusions follow from this proposition.

1. *Carefully Delineated Private Authority.* The first is by now familiar. Attuned, as it must be, to property's ongoing justificatory challenge, a genuinely liberal property law must carefully adjust the robustness of owners' authority so that it serves – directly or indirectly – property's autonomy-enhancing role. The implications of this maxim are stark, especially regarding the ownership of means of production[133] and thus the self-determination of workers. This aspect of the liberal theory of property will inform my discussion of the labor market in Chapter 7, but a brief preview may be in place.

Commercial property types, which facilitate the ownership of means of production,[134] may well be valuable because, as noted, resource production indirectly contributes to people's autonomy. Furthermore, even a characterless ownership of shares in your garden-variety for-profit corporation – typified by the principle of separation of ownership and control[135] – is autonomy-enhancing. Share ownership of this type allows individuals to pool resources, limit their liability, and enlist the superior skills, knowledge, and experience of others for managing their money. It thus supports people's welfarist interests and, furthermore, allows them to focus on projects they may view as more intrinsically valuable.[136] Hence, this property type of share ownership is again justified by its *indirect* contribution to people's self-determination.

This means that some measure of private authority over these resources may be important, but it also means that this authority has a strictly instrumental role. Therefore, insofar as these resources are concerned, owners' private authority (including their managerial authority) need not be particularly exacting.[137] The extent of owners' authority over commercial property types – or, for that matter, its duration (think patents) – must not go beyond what its indirect contribution to people's self-determination requires. Moreover, because excessive private authority is autonomy-reducing (for nonowners), *diluting* the authority of owners of these resources may well be necessary, and not only acceptable.[138]

a. *Hobby Lobby*. This conclusion explains, for example, why the (in)famous *Burwell v. Hobby Lobby Store* case[139] distorts liberal property law. Neither a corporation (via its directors) nor its controlling shareholders should be able to expand their private authority by invoking – in the name of the autonomy-based right to religious freedom – exemption from laws of general applicability, especially where such laws protect workers' most fundamental autonomy-based rights.[140]

b. *Authors' Rights*. A similar line of reasoning supports Molly Shaffer Van Houweling's claim that US copyright law would be well-advised to adopt reforms that recognize the interests of authors vis-à-vis the current owners of their past work "to *revive* a work that is no longer being disseminated, *revise* a work that the author thinks can be improved, or *revisit* the substance and/or style of a prior work in a new work." A particularly powerful example comes from some civil law systems, which "allow authors to exploit revised versions of their works even after they have transferred the copyrights to others, subject to an obligation to provide the [current owner] with both indemnification and a right of first refusal for any deal to disseminate the new version."[141]

2. *Antitrust*. Furthermore, and this is the second inherent limitation of property's power, an autonomy-enhancing conception of property

Autonomy and Distribution

implies that antitrust law should not be solely focused on consumer welfare maximization. Rather, it should also appreciate Louis Brandeis' reason for antitrust policy, namely, decentralizing economic power as a means of decentralizing authority.[142] This implies that antitrust law should target all concentrations of private authority, including, for example, concentrations of localized landownership. Similarly, a liberal property law should address the effects of capital accumulation in other contexts, notably the proper regulation of political money.

3. *Relational Justice.* Discussing these broader topics exceeds the scope of this book (I have addressed political money elsewhere[143]). The third inherent limit on owners' authority, however, dealing with relational justice, is squarely within the scope of my current inquiry and is the topic of Chapter 5. In a liberal polity, reciprocal respect for self-determination is the most basic requirement guiding interpersonal interactions.

Owners' authority, then, which a liberal property law sanctions, is to be situated within a broader system of liberal private law. A genuinely liberal private law establishes interaction frameworks conducive to self-determining individuals who respect each other as free and equal agents. Respect for owners' self-determination justifies enlisting law to authorize and coercively enforce the private authority epitomized by property. A reciprocal claim firmly grounds a prescription of relational justice, which is the foundation of owners' obligations and burdens and thus of nonowners' rights and privileges. An autonomy-based conception of property must ensure that owners' rights do not excessively limit (let alone undermine) nonowners' autonomy.

These are paramount features of the liberal conception of property that make it much more likely to be legitimate than its Blackstonian rival. They are indeed *necessary* features of a morally acceptable property regime, but not sufficient without some more direct attention to property's distributive implications.

AUTONOMY AND DISTRIBUTION

Property both empowers and disables, frees and constrains, gives people autonomy and renders them vulnerable. But this does not make property a zero-sum game, in which the only viable question is who gets what regarding any given resource and whether the resulting distribution is just.

While surely important, concerns of just distribution do not exhaust the inquiry of property's legitimacy. A liberal system of property law helps to establish our interpersonal relationships as free and equal individuals committed to respecting each other's right to self-determination. It facilitates thick property types allowing for the many – at times constitutive – interpersonal relationships that are conducive to the ability of all individuals to be, at least to some extent, the authors of their own lives. This promise of liberal property is sufficiently valuable to gain some independent significance behind the veil of ignorance.

And yet, a property system shaped in line with the liberal autonomy-enhancing *telos* cannot ignore distributive justice[144] and must ensure that property's potential empowerment is not limited only to some.

1. *A Just Background Regime.* The first requirement from a liberal legal system that adopts property for the critical purpose of promoting self-determination is to afford everyone the material, social, and intellectual preconditions needed for self-authorship.[145] Property law cannot meet this challenge on its own. Guided by autonomy, property must enlist the mechanisms of tax-and-redistribution law. For property law to deliver its ideal of enhancing people's self-authorship, it must rely on a just background regime that ensures the social and economic conditions (or capabilities) needed to enable people to become and remain self-determining individuals.[146]

Indeed, as Gregory Alexander argues, "[p]ersonal autonomy is possible only in the context of dependence upon communities of other persons who facilitate the development of the capabilities which together are necessary for autonomy as self-governance."[147] In that, Alexander applies to property theory Rawls' claim that our collective responsibility for justice can generate a duty on the part of individuals not only to comply with just institutions but also to support them.[148] As Alexander argues, we are obliged to support "[t]he communities that *enable* our capabilities" so that they "continue to flourish." These vertical duties, as he correctly insists, are "inherent in what it means to

Autonomy and Distribution

own property," because they are entailed by the same normative commitments that underlie property to begin with.[149]

2. *Property for All.* Furthermore, as Dorfman and I have argued, if property is to rely on its contribution to people's autonomy for its legitimacy, it must ensure that this contribution applies to everyone. A genuinely liberal property law, then, cannot be content with public solutions to the problem of inequality. Poverty cannot be fully tackled by allowing nonowners to extend the scope of their free action to resources held by the state (be they public spaces, shelters or, more generally, support for the poor).[150] In the autonomy-enhancing account of property, turning nonowners into private owners by ensuring a *pre*-distribution[151] of ownership for all as the background regime of property law is not merely one possible response to inequality or a possible side effect of such a response. It is *the point*, and thus the core of any acceptable response.[152]

This conclusion draws on Waldron's claim that, unlike justifications of property that rely on a specific causative event (such as Locke's claims of labor or Hegel's claims of occupation), *general* right-based justifications of property that build on its intrinsic importance imply that every human being is entitled to private property.[153] An autonomy-based case for property thus calls for a "radical" distributive program, governed by "a requirement that private property … is something all [persons] must have."[154] State (or private-law based) provision of public access, however broadly defined and applied, may supplement but can never replace private ownership for all.[155] Public access cannot take ownership's place in securing people's self-determination and in structuring interpersonal interactions as relations of freedom and equality.[156]

This proposition may seem utopian, at least when it comes to what for most people is the most important object of ownership – a home. The conclusion that people should have a basic right to housing, however, neither is nor should appear illusory. As Matthew Desmond notes, one of "the most urgent and pressing issues facing America today" is that "fewer and fewer families can afford a roof over their head." Many are evicted because many cities have become exorbitantly expensive to society's poorest families. The fallout of eviction, as

Desmond so powerfully demonstrates, is severe: it "does not simply drop poor families into a dark alley," but "fundamentally redirects their way, casting them onto a different, and much more difficult path" of joblessness, degrading housing (if not homelessness), depression, and illness.[157]

These hardships, Desmond rightly argues, are "shameful and unnecessary" and solutions are within society's collective reach. A universal voucher program for housing such as those successfully implemented in Great Britain or in the Netherlands can be a pragmatic way of implementing the right to housing. It allows families that are eligible because they are below a certain income level, to use the voucher to live wherever they wish so long as the housing is "decent, modest, and fairly priced." Such a program, Desmond predicts, "would change the face of poverty" because families "would find stability and have a sense of ownership over their home and community."[158]

3. *Limits of Property Theory.* I revisit some of these propositions toward the end of the book because the owners' ongoing obligation to contribute to the background institutions necessary for property's legitimacy is crucial to my account of property transitions, as Chapter 8 will show. This obligation becomes particularly acute given the operations of the market, which tend to compound the challenge to property's legitimacy, as Chapter 7 explains.

But the distributive dimensions in the liberal conception of property extend even further and affect health, education, and welfare policy,[159] which I do not discuss. They also demand that we accommodate environmental concerns, given the right to self-authorship and thus to viable ownership of future generations who, without proper attention to intergenerational justice, remain vulnerable to the excesses of current owners.[160]

These omissions, like the exclusion of prevailing systems of taxation and antitrust from the analysis, necessarily leave the question of property's legitimacy open. Indeed, part of my claim in this chapter is that the legitimacy of property depends on the degree the legal system it belongs to complies with the requirement of justly distributing property's potential empowerment.[161]

The rather severe inadequacy of property's distribution in liberal societies today, though seemingly a trite issue, merits mention. An autonomy-enhancing law must commit to set up a background regime that, at the very least, alleviates this predicament. A liberal theory of property, then, can only deal with part of the concerns occupying an autonomy-enhancing polity.

At this stage, I simply assume a legal system that designs its tax policy and its antitrust, health, education, and welfare laws complying with the requirement of justly distributing property's empowering potential. The following chapters will thus shift the focus inward to explore the proper architecture of property law, that is, to study how it can, indeed should, be shaped to serve self-determination in an optimal fashion. Before embarking on this task, however, I need to address one final concern.

CHALLENGE OF NEUTRALITY

Some readers may find that an autonomy-enhancing property theory actually betrays our liberal commitments. According to this argument, my approach violates "the precept of state neutrality,"[162] both in its endorsement of self-determination as property's ultimate value and in privileging a limited, albeit not insignificant, number of property types. This critique combines references to concrete neutrality ("neutrality as a first-order principle of justice") and to neutrality of grounds ("neutrality as a second-order principle of justification").[163]

1. *Concrete Neutrality.* Consider first the challenge of concrete neutrality. The autonomy-based conception of property seems to score quite high on this neutrality test. This is because, practically, property law cannot give equal support to all the possible arrangements that people may want to make. Indeed, it should not even try to do so because having too many options may curtail choice just as much as having too few.[164] Given that law's support makes a difference – very few property types would look as they do and work as well as they do without the active support of law – property law necessarily favors certain types of arrangements over others.

Moreover, law cannot be strictly neutral because choosing a set of legal rules to govern a particular property type lays down one vision of the good in that particular context. Most significantly, an obligation to provide a diverse menu of property types (accompanied by a commitment to broad freedom for further consensual tailoring) is less imposing than its alternative – the one-type-fits-all Blackstonian conception of property.

Finally, can democracy help in securing property's concrete neutrality?[165] Could property law safely rely solely on the choices of our elected representatives as reflected in their legislated products?

Democracy is relevant insofar as it is invoked to highlight that a liberal theory of property grants different polities broad leeway to offer their own menus of property types. As long as they do not coerce one hegemonic vision of property, these menus can vary based on local histories, local needs, local preferences, and local utopian experiments.[166] The liberal theory of property does not imply that this is the *only* legitimate task of democratic property lawmaking. Yet, the crucial role of autonomy in securing property's legitimacy implies, as noted, that autonomy *must* also play a key role in its design.

Democracy alone, then, cannot provide the normative underpinning of liberal property law. Making democracy the foundational value conflates the search for substantive moral truth with that of institutional legitimacy.[167] It also overstates, as Chapter 6 will show, the comparative advantage of legislatures over courts – in terms of competence or legitimacy – in matters of private law.

2. *Neutrality of Grounds.* The remaining challenge may concern the "neutrality of grounds," contesting my endorsement of self-determination as property's ultimate value. The gist of my response to this objection appears earlier in this chapter and I will only restate it here: property is a power-conferring body of law that people can, but need not, invoke or use in pursuing their objectives; therefore, it is hard to think of any intelligible, let alone neutral, alternative to replace self-determination as property's ultimate value.[168]

I am certainly aware of the problems entailed by pseudo-universalist claims that take culturally specific choices and render them

Challenge of Neutrality

as essential. Yet, I resist the innuendo implicit in the neutrality of grounds challenge, claiming that founding property on individual self-determination is a variation of this disguised parochialism.[169]

A measure of suspicion is indeed necessary to counter the tendency to impose contingent preferences as natural or necessary truths. But sociological suspicion should not collapse into skepticism about reason and normativity. I reject the way some critical legal scholars characterize reason itself as a disciplinary technology and normative analysis as arbitrary power.[170] These claims imply a dubious meta-ethical position that ends in relativism, skepticism, or nihilism. By equating normative reasoning with parochial interests and idiosyncratic perspectives, they also undermine any possibility of moral justification, and thus also of moral evaluation and moral criticism.

Humanists can and should be suspicious, but they must resist the trap of helpless relativism that, paradoxically, ends up reaffirming the status quo. The sheer fact that claims of universalism are not always true and are open to potential abuse should not undermine our responsibility or our commitment to work on behalf of what we believe to be universal rights.

The right of every individual to self-determination is the ultimate human right. Therefore, I am unwilling to repudiate autonomy's status as property's ultimate value or, what eventually amounts to the same thing, to embrace a view of autonomy wherein self-determination is merely an option. Arrangements that belittle self-determination must not benefit from law's proactive support, and only a property law that views autonomy as its ultimate value can prevent this unacceptable outcome.

3. *Autonomy Without Perfectionism.* Finally, I wish to clarify the subtle but critical distance between this chapter's account of autonomy and some versions of perfectionist liberalism. Self-determination, I have argued, is property's ultimate value, not a means for securing a rich and satisfying life in terms of human perfection and excellence.[171] As such, autonomy in my account is not implicated in any form of (potentially disrespectful) paternalism: an autonomy-based property law is committed to empowering individuals to form and

pursue *their own* conception of life as long as it does not disparage others'.[172] An autonomy-based property law, therefore, is not vulnerable to neutralist concerns about unequal treatment of different conceptions of the good.[173] Precisely for these reasons, a liberal theory of property subscribes to structural pluralism, to which I now turn.[174]

Structural pluralism requires that law's repertoire of property types for each sphere of human interaction include a sufficient number of partial functional substitutes, offering people alternatives from which *they* can choose. (This proposition implies a vital, even if imprecise, distinction between different *types* and different *rules*: different property types are guided by distinctive animating principles, which implies an appreciable threshold of doctrinal difference.) An autonomy-based structural pluralism also prescribes that one way of securing meaningful choice is to enrich this repertoire with minoritarian or utopian property types.

4 PROPERTY'S STRUCTURAL PLURALISM

VARIETY OF PROPERTY

Imagine a proposal for legal reform aiming to simplify and clarify property law, which recommends the adoption of two simple rules. The first rule prescribes that owners have an *in rem* right to exclude. The second empowers owners (if more than one) contractually to set up their own governance regime. This bill would obviously be radically incomplete, but is that all that is wrong with it? We could think of convenient additions, but is there anything fundamentally necessary still missing for this bill to constitute at least the core of a property regime in a liberal polity?

In this chapter and the following one, I argue that incompleteness does not even begin to capture the shortcomings of this proposal. The deficiencies of this hypothetical bill are far deeper. This bill establishes property as a form of private authority, and thus seemingly complies with property's autonomy-based understanding discussed in Chapter 3 (only seemingly, of course, because it does not properly tailor private authority to its autonomy-enhancing service). But the bill marginalizes, ignores, or possibly even undermines the other constitutive characteristics of property in a liberal polity: its two other pillars. Simply put, this bill is illiberal. One reason for this is that to be genuinely liberal, a property law *must* offer a diverse range of property types.[1]

1. *The Blackstonian Alternative.* My claim opposes property's new (or rather renewed) Blackstonian orthodoxy. The various accounts that belong to this category are different in many significant details, but what matters here is only their common structure – all are critical of the disaggregation of property into a bundle of sticks. By contrast, they

highlight and thus embrace the seemingly underappreciated wisdom of what is perceived as the lay understanding of property as exclusion. They all claim that, although the penumbra of property may include shades and hues, its core is accurately captured by the owner's right to exclude.[2]

Property, in this view, is not "some bundled together aggregate or complex of norms" whose content "mutates from one context to the next." Quite the contrary: it is "a single, coherent right" because its contour is explained and dictated by one interest: the "interest in exclusively using things." Conceptualizing property as a bundle of sticks is thus misleading. Property should instead be understood as "the right to exclusive use," which "correlate[s] with, or can be derived from, the duty of others to exclude themselves from the property." The other sticks within property's bundle are elaborations of what the right to exclude encompasses or entails.[3]

Although property rights do not always confer full-blown Blackstonian dominion, these theorists insist "that exclusion retains its presumptive moral and legal force." They thus conceptualize "efforts to supplement exclusion with various devices governing proper use" as "exceptions." Situating these "refinements" outside property's core does not imply that the interests they serve are insignificant; on the contrary, "these interests' importance enables them to come through the heavy gravitational pull of the exclusionary regime." But property's conceptual structure is nonetheless important because the existence of exceptions should not obscure the basic "core-and-periphery architecture" that typifies property. The "broad presumption" of the law, in this view, is and should be "that owners can dispose of property as they wish."[4]

A genuinely liberal conception of property, I argue, cannot accept this conventional position. Rather than embracing this core-and-periphery architecture, liberals must reject it. Liberals must ground whatever exclusionary rights owners have, as noted, on the right to reciprocal respect for self-determination. They should thus appreciate the many limitations to exclusion that derive from this right and are thus *intrinsic* to property. Chapter 3 addressed some of these limitations; they will be studied further in Chapters 7 and 8 and will be the focus of Chapter 5.

My main claim in this chapter is that "nonconforming" property types should *not* be understood as peripheral "refinements" that are added only if the "heavy gravitational pull" of property's "exclusionary regime" is overcome. Rather, these property types are crucial components of any liberal property regime. Moreover, they are also major components of property law's existing landscape. I begin with this descriptive observation.

2. *Property Heterogeneity.* Property is not, as the bundle metaphor might suggest, a mere laundry list of rights with limitless permutations. Instead, as the *numerus clausus* principle prescribes, property law offers a limited number of standardized forms of property at any given time and place.[5] Understanding property as a formless bundle of sticks open to ad hoc judicial adjustments bears no resemblance to the law of property as lawyers know it or, even more significantly, as citizens experience it in everyday life. On the other hand, neither does the conception of property as a monistic institution revolving around the idea of exclusion.

Some parts of the property drama indeed consist in governing interpersonal relationships of independence along the lines of the Blackstonian paradigm. And yet, the notion that property is fundamentally about exclusion is a great exaggeration.

Property can be understood within the exclusion model only if we set aside large parts of what is conventionally understood to constitute property law. Many property rules that prescribe the rights and obligations of members of local communities, neighbors, co-owners, partners, and family members, cannot be analyzed fairly through terms of exclusion. While exclusion is silent as to the internal life of property, these elaborate property governance doctrines provide structures that facilitate various forms of cooperative, rather than competitive or hierarchical, relationships.

Sharing and cooperation in these doctrines are not the choice of a person who enjoys sole and despotic dominion but constitutive features of the property type, which define the content of that person's property right. An owner's decision to share by inviting someone to enter her premises is qualitatively different from a person's decision to form a co-ownership with others or to join a common-interest community where the majority has wide jurisdiction over a broad subset of management questions. The former expresses an attitude of giving but, at the same time, expresses one's full authority. In the latter, a person expresses what we may call "second-order consent to share" by voluntarily entering into a property type where one shares with others – whether one wants to or not at any given moment – at least some of the authority over the resource.

In shaping the contours of many of these property types, concerns about insiders' governance may be as, or even more, informative than concerns about outsiders' exclusion. As I show elsewhere and mention below, the optimal internal property governance frequently offers a vital clue to the way property law resolves conflicts between owners and third parties.[6]

PROPERTY GOVERNANCE

A thick and rather sophisticated set of property rules deals with the internal life of property. In fact, a significant part of property law is not about vindicating the rights of autonomous excluders cloaked in Blackstonian armors of sole and despotic dominion, but rather about creating governance institutions that manage potential conflicts of interest among individuals who are all stakeholders in one resource or in a given set of resources. These dramas of property law occur, literally, within property; they deal with the internal life of property rather than with its foreign affairs.[7]

1. *First Examples.* Consider, as a starter, the traditional common law doctrine of waste. The law of waste accommodates the property interests of a holder of a present possessory interest, such as a life tenant, and the owner of the corresponding future interest, such as a remainderman. It provides a default governance regime for the relationship between these stakeholders. This regime is required due to the inherent conflict between the parties' property rights. Specifically, while optimal use would maximize the value to both parties, the life tenant has an incentive to overuse the resource during his expected lifetime. "The law of waste forbids the tenant to reduce the value of the property as a whole by considering only his own interest in it."[8]

Waste law applies also in landlord–tenant law because leaseholds are also typified by a temporal division of possession. But modern landlord–tenant law is interested in addressing not only the vulnerability of landlords to the possible opportunism of tenants but rather, and indeed mainly, the mirror image of this concern. Contemporary landlord–tenant law is preoccupied with the ability of landlords to affect the conditions of the premises. While traditional law had recognized a limited number of exceptions to the "no-landlord-duty rule,"[9] many jurisdictions today recognize not only a broad covenant of quiet and beneficial enjoyment but also an implied warranty of habitability.[10]

One may applaud or criticize current landlord–tenant law but no one can hope to provide a reasonable account of it without considering the governance doctrines that play such a crucial role in shaping our contemporary understanding of this property type. (An additional aspect of landlord–tenant law with an equivalent effect on the meaning of leaseholds in modern society is the restriction of landlords' right to select tenants. Like the implied warranty of habitability, this restriction abides by property's commitment to relational justice, which is the topic of the next chapter.)

2. *Trust Law.* The law of waste has largely been superseded in the context of estate planning as well, this time not because of a dramatic change in the way we understand the relationship among stakeholders but rather due to the development of a highly sophisticated mechanism of governance: the trust. As Gregory Alexander explains, trust law includes a "coordinating norm" aimed at accommodating "conflicting investment goals among interest holders whose enjoyment rights are successive." Since this governance regime assigns to trustees considerable management powers over the assets of the trust beneficiaries, trust law also addresses the entailed risks of opportunism by imposing duties of loyalty and care on trustees.[11]

The trust, then, is characterized by its governance regime, which is best understood by exploring how the specific shape of the trustee's managerial authority responds to the need to accommodate the potentially conflicting interests of the settlor, the trustee, and the beneficiaries.[12]

3. *Successive and Concurrent Property Rights.* Governance typifies not only property types whose beneficiaries have successive rights of enjoyment but also property types where the parties' interests are concurrent. These types regulate the relationship inside property among members of local communities, neighbors, co-owners, partners, and family members. While such property types cover a wide range, all are aimed at facilitating the possible economic and social gains of cooperation.

Some of these types, such as a close corporation, are mostly about economic gains, including securing the efficiencies of economies of scale and risk spreading, with social benefits merely a (sometimes pleasant) side effect. Others, such as marriage, are more about the intrinsic good of being part of a plural subject, wherein the raison d'être of the property type refers more to one's identity and interpersonal relationships, while the attendant economic benefits are perceived as helpful by-products rather than the primary motive for cooperation. Either way, the whole point of the elaborate governance structures these doctrines prescribe is to facilitate cooperative, rather than competitive, relationships. It is thus not surprising that the dominion conception of property is particularly inapt for understanding these important property types.[13]

COMMONS PROPERTY[14]

1. *Three Techniques.* Consider the large sections of property law where "partial realignment" of the parties' interests is required before economic and social gains of cooperation can be reaped. The challenge of these property types in a liberal environment is acute given the justified availability of exit, which exacerbates the vulnerability of the parties and thus threatens the very possibility of trust and reciprocity.

To face this challenge, each of these property types contains a governance regime concerning decisions about consumption and investment, about management, and about allocation. These governance regimes are complex and multifaceted. As Michael Heller and I show elsewhere, they include three types of techniques for partially realigning stakeholders' interests: internalizing externalities around individual use and investment decisions, democratizing a set of fundamental management decisions by shifting authority from individual to group control, and de-escalating tensions around entry and exit.[15]

For my current purpose, referring to the core of this regime will suffice: a set of mechanisms for collective decision-making aimed at aligning individual and group goals by aggregating individual preferences or objectives. These conflict-transforming mechanisms range from democratic participatory institutions such as simple majority rule to representative or hierarchical apparatuses such as a condo board in a common-interest community or a board of directors in a close corporation.[16]

2. *Utilitarian versus Social Commons.* The multiplicity of these mechanisms is neither chaotic nor unprincipled. Rather, the particular property configuration that serves as the default for the property type at hand depends on its underlying character. Different property types allow differing emphases for economic success and social cohesion. Property types at the utilitarian end of the spectrum (implicitly) conceptualize their ideal-typical members as "absentee investors." By contrast, at the social end of this property-types spectrum, parties are understood as "active participants." Property law appropriately adjusts the design of the governance regime of any given property type to the location of its typical stakeholders along this utilitarian-social spectrum.

Thus, commons property types where concurrent ownership is predominantly driven by utilitarian reasons are usually highly formal and hierarchical. Management decisions are addressed by *ex ante* rules that establish governing bodies, allocate powers among them, and prescribe procedures for their routine operation.[17] These rules are typically foreground rules: stakeholders and legal players alike expect them to be deployed in the daily life of that property type rather than only at the – inevitably legal – endgame.

By contrast, commons property types that are predominantly social tend to be highly informal and participatory. Parties to neighborly relationships often find formalistic decision-making and resort to law to be the beginning of the end.[18] So, if law is to facilitate such property types, it needs to tread lightly, setting looser and more participatory procedures. In these contexts, governance is understood not only instrumentally but also as a means to intensify the parties' interpersonal relations, which are often intrinsically valuable.

Hence, in such "social property types," republican participatory governance replaces the top-down governance of purely economic types.[19] Typically, the law uses background instead of foreground rules, with a social norm of consensual decision governing the community's daily life while formal majority rule provides a safety net against potential abuse by hold-outs. Similarly, community governance rules also operate indirectly by recruiting third parties to protect community resources, for example, by voiding decisions reached by an insufficient majority or through inappropriate procedures.[20] (This is, of course, a prime example of how property's internal governance, which the dominion conception of property obscures, may dominate property's foreign affairs.)

3. *Common-Interest Communities.* The law of common-interest communities – the fastest growing property type in America and by now a major form of land ownership – provides a rich example of a formal and hierarchical management regime in predominantly utilitarian property types.

A common-interest community has the power to manage its common property and administer its servitude regime in a real estate development or neighborhood.[21] It can raise funds (by way of assessment of fees); manage, acquire, and improve common property; adopt rules governing the use of property, and set procedures to encourage compliance and deter violations.[22]

A common-interest community is managed by an association that, in turn, is governed for most purposes by a representative government: a board elected by its members. The board is entitled "to exercise all powers of the community except those reserved to the members," and members have "the right to vote in elections for the board of directors and on other matters properly presented to [them], to attend and participate in meetings of the members, and to stand for election to the board of directors. Except when the board properly meets in executive session, [members] are [also] entitled to attend meetings of the board of directors and to a reasonable opportunity to present their views to the board."[23]

4. *Participatory Governance.* Compare this formal and hierarchical management structure to the informal and participatory regime applicable in predominantly social property types. One example is the governance of co-ownership in the civil law tradition, where the law prescribes only a basic norm of majority rule accompanied by open-ended rules of disclosure, consultation, and fair hearing.[24] Another example is the rules community property law prescribes for the governance of marital property.[25]

5. *Community Property.* Transactions in the marital estate under community property law require joinder – meaning a joint decision by both spouses – if they involve substantial amounts of money (such as community real estate or a business) or resources that reflect the group identity of the marital community and the personhood of its members (the marital residence and its contents).[26] Joinder is desirable in these contexts to ensure that decisions do indeed aim to improve communal goods – to manage, in other words, the potential conflict between the interest of each individual spouse and the collective good.

This joinder rule is a background rule. It neither prescribes any specific governance procedure nor requires judicial intervention within a functioning marriage. Rather, in most cases where joinder is required, banks and other third parties are recruited to police conflicts of interest. Where such third parties realize that a transaction requires joinder to be binding, they are likely to insist on joinder before entering into the transaction with a single spouse. Thus, while the joinder rule regulates the marital community's foreign affairs, it also – indeed primarily – serves a crucial governance function by indirectly preventing self-serving violations by one spouse in a community.[27]

6. *Profound Pluralism.* These contrasting examples of common-interest communities and marriage are an initial indication of how starkly property law diverges from its monistic dominion conception. In fact, property law sets up a multiplicity of property types, each one covering a specific category of human situations and governed by a distinct set of rules, often expressing different underlying normative commitments. (Differences between property types at times reflect

other considerations as well, and I return to this gap in the next section.)

Doctrines that generally comply with a commitment to independence are thus found alongside doctrines where ownership is a locus of communitarian sharing. The utility value of property tends to figure – albeit quite differently – in both these categories of property types. In others (think patents) it may have an even more prominent role.

The notion of structural pluralism takes this heterogeneity of existing property doctrines seriously. It recognizes the value in understanding property as a category for thinking, given the common denominator of overlapping values and of similar questions in the wide terrain of legal doctrine covered by property. But, along the lines of my discussion in Chapter 2, a structurally pluralistic understanding of property is careful not to confuse a category of thinking with a category of deciding.[28] It thus appreciates that, notwithstanding the attempts to claim otherwise, property's common denominator is not robust enough to illuminate the existing doctrines, or determinative enough to provide significant guidance for their evaluation or development.

Property's pluralism cannot be reduced to the margins by adjusting the application of one core animating principle (say, exclusion) to differing settings. Nor is it confined to exceptional circumstances where "the heavy gravitational pull of the exclusionary regime" is overcome. Rather, property's landscape is profoundly heterogeneous; it is typified by a variety of distinctive property types governed by divergent animating principles.

Proponents of the dominion conception of property claim, as indicated, that rejecting the notion of property as a monistic institution revolving around the core idea of sole despotic dominion *necessarily* leads to an understanding of property as a formless bundle of sticks open to ad hoc judicial adjustments.[29] This binary contrast is both false and misleading. Property need not be confined to a tragic choice between the Hohfeldian Scylla of unprincipled multiplicity and the Blackstonian Charybdis of unacceptable uniformity. There is a principled midway position between these disappointing poles: the autonomy-based conception of property, which is structurally pluralistic.

7. *Autonomy-Based Pluralism*. By grounding property's pluralism on the monistic commitment to autonomy, I depart from some of my prior work, which implies that the value of such pluralism is *free-standing*.[30] Free-standing value pluralism, I have come to realize, cannot plausibly address the urgent and ongoing challenge to property's legitimacy.

In this book, I try to make amends by explaining how a revised version of my earlier position can be founded on the humanistic commitment to self-determination, which *can* secure property's legitimacy. I therefore investigate the implications of this foundation from a two-pronged perspective. First, in terms of the property configurations that cannot be acceptable since they are relationally unjust and thus undermine property's *telos* by infringing the maxim of reciprocal respect for self-determination. Second, in terms of the suitable directions for developing the system for it to be more loyal to this *telos*, hence the prescription to proactively facilitate property's structural pluralism.

MULTIPLICITY AND AUTONOMY

1. *A Rich Mosaic*. Suitably understood, property is neither monistic nor formless. Rather, it is an umbrella for a limited and standardized set of property types that serve as major default frameworks of interpersonal interaction. All these property types mediate the relationship between owners and nonowners regarding a resource, and, in all these types, owners typically have *some* rights to exclude *certain* others. This feature exhausts the DNA of some property types, namely, those that focus on serving the property value of independence, though even there it may be subject to the corresponding demands of relational justice, as Chapter 5 shows. Regarding other types, however, highlighting other intrinsic and instrumental values of property – notably community and utility – the role of exclusion tends to be less prominent. Together, these different property types compose a rich repertoire of alternatives, thus offering people a viable choice in structuring important aspects of their lives.

The particular configuration of entitlements in these diverse property types, as noted, is by no means arbitrary or random and, at least at its best, it is determined by the specific balance of property values (or other possible "local" concerns) characterizing it. The resulting animating principle both constructs and reflects how people are expected to interact when they resort to this property type. Thus, one practical payoff of the structurally pluralistic understanding of property lies in the fact that it resists smuggling normatively disputed claims by way of purportedly conceptual presumptions[31] and situates the normative inquiries regarding property law at the correct level: inside property.

What looks like a random mess from a monistic viewpoint seeking to pigeonhole property law in its entirety under the rule of one animating principle, such as exclusion, emerges as a rich mosaic through a perspective of structural pluralism. This mosaic is valuable: properly interpreted, the profound multiplicity typical of property's landscape can be conducive to people's self-determination. Indeed, for property law to serve people's right to be, to some degree, the authors of their lives, it *must* be structurally pluralistic.

I do not deny that the fee simple absolute – the property type that represents property's core for advocates of the dominion conception of property – facilitates people's independence and, thus, is crucial for liberal societies. But law's support for other property types is equally crucial for autonomy. (I defend this point regarding law's indispensable role, which at this stage is only stipulated, in a few pages.) Precisely on these grounds, a liberal conception of property must resist the attempt to present this singular type as property's essence.

2. *Property Types and Individual Choice*. Recall that the right to self-authorship requires not only appropriate mental abilities and independence but also an adequate range of options. As Joseph Raz explains, for choice to be effective, for autonomy to be meaningful, there must be (other things being equal) "more valuable options than can be chosen, and they must be significantly different" so that choices involve "tradeoffs, which require relinquishing one good for the sake of another." Thus, autonomy emphasizes "the value of a large number of greatly differing pursuits among which individuals are free to choose." While a wide range of valuable sets of social forms is available to

societies pursuing the ideal of autonomy, autonomy "cannot be obtained within societies which support social forms which do not leave enough room for individual choice."[32]

Some decisions may properly be deemed autonomous even in the absence of viable alternatives. A decision not to violate another person's bodily integrity is a prime example. Where only one option is morally acceptable, law's prohibition of the unacceptable options does not undermine people's autonomy and structural pluralism is therefore *not* applicable to the core cases of tort law that are duty-imposing.[33] But property, as I have reiterated, is different. It is a power-conferring institution. Therefore, given the wide variety of acceptable human goods autonomous people should be able to choose from, the liberal state must recognize and actually support a sufficiently diverse set of property types for people to use in organizing their lives.

This commitment to facilitate a plurality of reasonable but conflicting conceptions of the good gives lawgivers some latitude for making choices, where such choices are necessary, among morally acceptable possibilities. It also imposes on them a distinct obligation: to make these choices for people *only* when necessary, thus creating and facilitating a structurally pluralistic legal regime. Liberal property law follows suit by offering a sufficiently diverse range of property types, each incorporating a different value or balance of values.

Each property type should be guided by one robust animating principle that can effectively consolidate expectations and clearly express a coherent normative ideal. This by no means implies that all property rules should be immutable, but rather that each property type should have a distinct character. For property law to serve self-determination, then, it should offer people a rich menu of possible types. Many forms of human interactions are hardly imaginable without such a menu, because just like "language that enables thought[,] without types, our minds would be blank."[34]

The heterogeneity of property types allows law to adjust the form of private authority to specific constraints or needs unique to certain groups or to the resource at issue. Moreover, multiplicity *across* the various spheres of human action and interaction – home, work, commerce, and intimacy – helps property law to respond to the various intrinsic and instrumental values property can facilitate.

3. *Intra-Sphere Multiplicity.* But multiplicity by itself is not enough, because the sheer heterogeneity of property types is not sufficient to bolster people's choices. The availability of numerous property types for commercial activity, for example, does not add options regarding housing. Likewise, freedom is not enhanced if one has a choice, say, between getting married or purchasing a unit in a condominium.

Vital to choice, and thus to autonomy, is the multiplicity of alternatives *within* any given sphere of human action or interaction. A liberal property law must include sufficiently distinct property types within each sphere. Indeed, the diversity of property types is not a sufficient condition for autonomy and the quality of choice is also a concern. Other things being equal, however, availability of choice matters and, in many contexts, a rich repertoire of property types enables people to freely choose their own ends, principles, forms of life, and associations.

Consequently, a genuinely liberal property law provides *intra-sphere multiplicity*, offering more than one option to people who want to become homeowners (e. g., fee simple or a condo), or engage in business (e. g., partnership or corporation), or enter into intimate relationships (e. g., marriage or cohabitation).[35] The diversity of alternative property types enables diverse forms of human interaction and association and thus diverse forms of the good to flourish. Trying to impose a uniform understanding of property on them would undermine the autonomy-enhancing function of property's structural pluralism. Only a sufficiently heterogeneous property law facilitates a sufficiently diverse set of social institutions that are crucial for our autonomy.

4. *Freedom of Contract.* Alongside its rich offering of property types, liberal property recognizes the possibility of contracting around many property rules. (This is currently most highly evident in the traditionally immutable areas of marital property and of servitudes).[36] Generally, parties should be allowed to enter into private agreements that opt out of many incidents of property law's existing forms, tailoring their arrangements to their preferred relationship patterns.

At times, these adjustments are built into the property type: developers can design the homeowners' association's rules that govern common-interest communities. Even when not, however, freedom of contract regarding property types should, overall, abide by the same standards we use for opting out of contract types.[37] Since the good in each of these property types can and often is realized in various ways, law should affirm this plurality. In any event, law should allow citizens in a liberal society to repudiate values recommended by the state and use property types for legitimate arrangements beyond those anticipated by their animating principles.[38] The optionality of property rules is often a precondition for the meaningful realization of the more communitarian values instantiated by certain property types rather than a threat to them, since these values depend on choice and cannot be coerced by law without necessarily destroying them.[39]

NOZICK'S UTOPIA

1. *Why Nozick?* Let me make a brief detour at this stage to recruit an unlikely ally: Robert Nozick. Nozick's *Anarchy, State, and Utopia* is the most renowned libertarian manifesto of recent times.[40] Choosing him as a fellow-traveler is important for two separate reasons.

Nozick's familiar libertarian theory is rightly associated with – indeed, premised upon – the Blackstonian conception of property.[41] I will not repeat here the intense and convincing critique of Nozick's libertarianism.[42] Instead, I use a somewhat neglected argument that Nozick offers on behalf of the minimal state – his argument from utopia – to show why utopians who follow Nozick need to repudiate the dominion conception of property rather than embrace it. The flip side – and no less important – aspect of this reason for my Nozickian detour is that it further clarifies the liberal foundations of property's structural pluralism.

These claims obviously imply that Nozick was wrong to assume that libertarianism can deliver on the promise of his account of utopia. Appreciating the reasons for his error – the deep incoherence between his libertarianism and his utopianism – refines law's irreducible role in securing property's autonomy-enhancing function, which is the second benefit of seeking Nozick as a companion.

2. *Framework of Utopias.* Nozick presents his theory of utopia as an argument that "starts (and stands) independently of" his familiar

claims in support of the night-watchman state, and arguably "converges to their result ... from another direction."[43] For Nozick the utopian, the virtue of the minimal state is that it is not only right but also inspiring.

Nozick's key insight on this front is that utopia must be conceptualized as "a framework for utopias, a place where people are at liberty to join together voluntarily to pursue and attempt to realize their own vision of the good life." In treating us all "with respect by respecting our rights" and in allowing us, "individually or with whom we choose, to choose our life and to realize our ends and our conception of ourselves, insofar as we can, aided by the voluntary cooperation of other individuals possessing the same dignity," this framework for utopias "best realizes the utopian aspirations of untold dreamers and visionaries."[44]

To secure these happy effects, utopia's law must resist the temptation of "planning in detail, in advance, one [utopian] community in which everyone is to live." Instead, it should operate as a "libertarian and laissez-faire" framework, which facilitates "a diverse range of communities," many (maybe most, or even all) of which would be neither libertarian nor laissez-faire, in order to enable "more persons ... to come closer to how they wish to live, than if there is only one kind of community." By facilitating "voluntary utopian experimentation" and "provid[ing] it with the background in which it can flower," this utopian state invites "many persons' particular visions," enabling us "to get the best of all possible worlds."[45]

This ideal of a framework for utopias is compelling. It properly rejects undue collectivism by taking seriously the distinction between persons and insisting that individuals deserve respect for their own autonomy. At the same time, unlike the conception of independence typically associated with libertarian authors, obviously including Nozick, this ideal acknowledges – indeed, builds on – the richer understanding of autonomy as self-determination requiring diverse options.

If Nozick is correct in asserting that only the minimal state with its libertarian credo can bring about this utopia, then the dominion conception of property that this credo is founded on is conducive, and possibly even essential, to autonomy. Nozick, however, is wrong. His exciting vision of utopia defies rather than supports libertarianism.

To see why, we need to: (1) appreciate the robustness of the ideal of a framework for utopias, and (2) realize its profound dependence on law or law-like conventions. While the former step can be read as a friendly extension of Nozick's utopian vision, the latter implies that this vision must rely on the liberal – and not the libertarian-cum-Blackstonian – conception of property.[46]

3. *Layers of Multiplicity.* Nozick envisages a diverse menu of comprehensive lifestyle options, in which "[d]ifferent communities, each with slightly different mix, ... provide a range from which each individual can choose that community which best approximates *his* balance among competing values."[47] But a viable framework for utopias offering a diverse menu of options for interpersonal interaction that people can choose from when pursuing their conception of the good requires more than a variety of all-encompassing communities. Part of modernity's promise, which Nozick undoubtedly espouses, is the option of affiliating with *multiple* groups, enabling people to associate in their various and possibly incongruent or even conflicting capacities.[48]

Moreover, and more substantially for my purposes, self-determining individuals should be able to choose not only from a range of comprehensive options dealing with lifestyles and conceptions of the good but also with more specific decisions confronting them in various spheres of life. These decisions may be less dramatic but they are still significant and, again, disconnected and potentially incompatible components of their life story.

Self-authorship implies not only choosing between life in a "capitalist community" and a *kibbutz*, as Nozick insists,[49] but also choosing whether we want to live in a fee simple absolute or a common-interest community, work as an employee or an independent contractor, do business in a partnership, a close corporation, or a publicly held corporation, and whether to form an intimate bond of marriage or cohabitate.

The liberal commitment to individual self-authorship that makes Nozick's conception of utopia as a framework for utopias so appealing requires, as I have argued in this chapter, a sufficiently diverse set of viable options for all these and many other discrete decisions affecting our interpersonal interactions, in addition to the more comprehensive options that Nozick had emphasized.

LAW'S ROLE

1. *Proactive Facilitation.* So far so good. Nozick the libertarian need not object to any of these observations. But could not all these options, at all these levels, be implemented in the minimal state? Is not the freedom to initiate cooperative arrangements, which Nozick the libertarian relies upon, sufficient for securing the diversity of the menu that Nozick the utopian considers crucial?

Nozick seems to believe that this is indeed the case. Although conceding that his system "does not require" people "to innovate" and that they may "stagnate if they wish," Nozick is not alarmed by this problem as long as his framework provides the "liberty to experimentation of varied sorts."[50] This is of course exactly what property does and should do according to its Blackstonian account. Insofar as property is understood as "sole and despotic dominion," individuals can use their freedom of contract to tailor their interpersonal arrangements so that they best serve their own utilitarian, communitarian, or other purposes.[51] So can the imaginary bill that this chapter started with support Nozick's vision of a framework for utopias, which is indeed the proper ideal for a liberal polity?

No, it cannot. The state's obligation to foster diversity and multiplicity cannot be properly met through a hands-off or passive approach on the part of the law. Why? Because such an attitude "would undermine the chances of survival of many cherished aspects of our culture."[52] A commitment to personal autonomy, as shown below, requires that a liberal state, through its laws, work actively to "enable individuals to pursue valid conceptions of the good" by providing them a multiplicity of options.[53]

My brief discussion of waste law[54] provides a simple example of law's indispensable role. Waste law is needed because, in the relationship between life tenants and remaindermen, contractual freedom is insufficient. Had they been required to negotiate their relationship through contract, the situation would have been one of bilateral monopoly and transaction costs might have been too high, even if we set aside the possibility that the remaindermen might be children (born or even unborn).[55]

Similar impediments to contract (transaction costs in the broad sense of the term) pervade many other property types. Understanding the various governance forms in property's more cooperative types as merely convenient substitutes for what parties would do absent such doctrines thus fails to appreciate the role that law plays in these property types. In certain contexts and for some parties, social norms and other extra-legal reasons for action, or the possibility of *ex ante* explicit contracting, may be enough. But in many others, a hands-off policy and a hospitable attitude toward freedom of contract can hardly suffice to overcome the endemic difficulties of asymmetric information and collective action.

At least in a liberal environment, where exit is always legally available, participants in cooperative interpersonal relationships are particularly vulnerable to one another. Property law's active empowerment in providing institutional arrangements, including reliable guarantees against opportunistic behavior, is therefore likely to be essential to the viability of these challenging, though still promising, types of interpersonal relationships.[56]

These straightforward examples generalize. Many property types that participate in a Nozickian menu of options cannot be realistically actualized without the active support of viable legal institutions (or law-like social conventions). To see why this is the case, we need to consider the insights of both lawyer-economists and critical scholars.

2. Material and Cultural Effects. Economic analysis of private law investigates its incentive effects and forcefully demonstrates, as noted, how many of our existing practices rely on legal devices serving to overcome numerous types of transaction costs – information costs (symmetric and asymmetric), bilateral monopolies, cognitive biases, and heightened risks of opportunistic behavior, which generate participants' endemic vulnerabilities in most cooperative interpersonal interactions.[57]

Merely enforcing the parties' expressed intentions would not be sufficient to overcome the inherent risks of such endeavors. If many (if not most) of them are to be viable alternatives, law must provide the background reassurances that help to ensure the trust so crucial for success. Even where parties are guided by their own social norms, law often plays an essential role in providing them background safeguards, a safety net for a rainy day that can help to establish trust in their routine, happier interactions.[58]

But law's effects are not only material. Because property law (like private law more generally) tends to quietly blend into the backdrop of our lives, its categories play a crucial role in structuring our daily interactions.[59] Thus, alongside these material effects, many of our conventions – including many social practices we take for granted – become available to us only due to cultural conventions that are often legally constructed.[60] This is especially true in modern times.

Hence, were these notions not legally coined, people would not only have to consider the transaction costs of constructing these arrangements from scratch but would also face "obstacles of the imagination" merely coming up with the options in the first place. Indeed, the property types that law establishes play a vital cultural role. Like other social conventions, they serve a crucial function in consolidating people's expectations and in expressing normative ideals regarding the core categories of interpersonal relationships they participate in constructing.

On its face, a pluralistic repertoire of legally entrenched types might dilute imagination vis-à-vis its monistic alternative. But even if, or to the extent that, structural pluralism may indeed entail such a "crowding out" effect, this effect seems to be overwhelmingly offset by the greater range of options provided by property types. These options would cease to exist, or become available only in rather circumscribed settings – or only to those who can afford such costly tailoring – were it not for the support of the law.[61]

Both the material and the cultural functions of property imply that freedom of contract, though significant, cannot possibly replace active legal facilitation. Lack of legal support is often tantamount to undermining – maybe even obliterating – many cooperative types of interpersonal relationships and thus people's ability to seek their own conception of the good.

This gap between the Blackstonian conception of property and Nozick's utopian vision admittedly relies on people's fallibility, notably their cognitive failures and the way they tend to prefer their self-interest to the interests of others. But these imperfections cannot be dismissed as contingent features that need not bother Nozick the utopian. While their import may vary from one empirical context to another, these human features are sufficiently ingrained to render irrelevant if not self-defeating any purportedly utopian theory that ignores them.[62]

3. *Laws for Utopia.* The state's obligation to enhance autonomy by fostering diversity and multiplicity, which is the impetus to Nozick's conception of utopia, cannot be properly fulfilled through the passive legal attitude represented in the conventional account of property espoused by Nozick.

In some contexts (notably in the commercial sphere) powerful economic forces catalyze the demand for options, so the task of property law can and should be mostly reactive. But in other spheres of interpersonal interaction – think work, intimacy, or home – where collective action problems or other (say, cognitive or distributive) difficulties inhibit the development of new property types, the lack of market demand cannot delimit the state's obligation.

The liberal commitment to self-authorship, therefore, requires the state, through its laws, to enable individuals to pursue their own conceptions of the good by *proactively* providing a multiplicity of options for interpersonal interaction. The genuinely liberal state cannot circumvent the prescription of structural pluralism demanding that, for each major category of human action and interaction, law should include a sufficiently diverse repertoire of property (and contract) types, each governed by a distinct animating principle, meaning a different value or balance of values.

Endorsing Nozick's framework for utopias as the proper vision for the liberal state means discarding the libertarian credo of the minimal state and the dominion conception of property it is founded on. Nothing short of the sturdy legal edifice of structural pluralism – namely, a sufficiently varied inventory of property (and contract) types for each sphere of social life – will do if private law is to be guided by this autonomy-enhancing utopian promise.

One lesson of this chapter is that autonomy as self-authorship may be threatened not only by having too much law. The absence of law, the failure of property law to proactively support a sufficiently diverse range of types within a given sphere of interpersonal activity, may undermine autonomy just as much.[63]

True utopians should not be deterred from this seemingly surprising conclusion of "laws for utopia." To be sure, law – including laws for utopia – always implicates power, defined as "the capacity to influence people's actions and interests."[64] And yet, in line with its utopian underpinnings, property's structural pluralism tends to *curb* law's coercive effects vis-à-vis its monistic counterparts.

Admittedly, at pathological moments of breakups followed by litigation, the coercive power over the litigants that a pluralistic legal regime assigns decision makers may be no different from that allocated by a monistic system. But it is no greater either. In any event, the drama at the endgame of interpersonal relationships and legal institutions should not obscure the significance of the *ex ante* choices available to people entering and shaping these relationships. From this perspective, a structurally pluralistic property law opens up options for choices instead of channeling everyone to the singular possibility privileged by law. When property law complies with the prescriptions of structural pluralism, individuals can navigate their own course, bypassing certain legal prescriptions and avoiding their implications as well as the power of those who have issued them.[65]

BLACKSTONIAN OWNERSHIP

The significance of multiplicity for self-authorship, I have argued thus far, refutes the proposition that exclusion should be the essence of liberal property, and offers instead the prescription of intra-sphere multiplicity. But what are the implications of this proposition for the status of Blackstonian property? What are its more specific guidelines regarding the proper evolution of property law? And how does it affect our understanding of the *numerus clausus* principle? The remainder of this chapter focuses on these takeaways.

An autonomy-based understanding of property should not privilege the fee simple absolute by treating its characteristics as fundamental features of property as a whole while suppressing other property types as mere variations on a common theme, or marginalizing them as peripheral exceptions to a solid core. Blackstonian ownership, therefore, should not be conceptualized as the "core" or the "default" of our understanding of property.[66]

Objecting to these excesses, however, does not mean dismissing the role of Blackstonian ownership altogether. Quite the contrary: its inclusion in the repertoire of property law adds a *crucial* option, which contributes to self-authorship. Blackstonian ownership is singular among property types in its zealous protection of our independence. By shielding individuals from the claims of others and from the power of public authority, this particular property type guarantees a relatively untouchable private sphere that is a prerequisite to personal development and autonomy.[67]

As I argued in Chapter 3, independence is not our ultimate value, but it is not merely instrumentally valuable either. As a constitutive component of self-authorship, independence is intrinsically valuable.[68] The intrinsic value of independence explains the unique place of Blackstonian ownership in a liberal property system. It implies that the eradication or marginalization of the fee simple absolute (and of any equivalent property type) could entail an excessive restriction of liberty (and privacy) because it would erase the alternative of private sovereignty and thus eliminate the option of retreat into one's own safe haven. The intrinsic value of independence prescribes that a liberal polity *must* offer individual natural persons the realm of solitude that such strong ownership represents.[69]

Two conclusions follow from the unique role of Blackstonian ownership. The first is that, although indeed singular in its indispensability, Blackstonian ownership should not aspire to exclusivity or hegemony. Indeed, it functions best as part of a liberal repertoire of property types conducive to self-authorship.

A second, related conclusion touches on the legitimate scope of Blackstonian ownership. Since the role of the fee simple absolute is to ensure individuals private sovereignty over resources necessary for their independence, it should cover *only* the type of resources and the scope of sovereignty needed to secure that purpose. Beyond such property-for-safe-haven rights – think about property law's privilege of homeownership, for example[70] – other (notably utilitarian) property rights are not as intimately connected to their owners' independence.[71]

Thus, as I have repeatedly argued, the authority of owners of these property rights – notably owners of means of production – need not, and often should not, be overly demanding and overly expansive. In these cases, and especially where the claim of nonowners to access the resource at hand is important for *their* own self-authorship, owners' dominion should be carefully circumscribed and should furthermore be subject, as it often is, to other people's right to entry or to inclusion. Chapters 5 and 7 revisit and expand this important lesson.

DEVELOPING AN ADEQUATE RANGE OF TYPES

1. *Partial Functional Substitutes.* A liberal conception of property celebrates the existing multiplicity of property law. To support autonomy, the doctrinal subdivision of property should follow, as to some extent it does, the "property types" construct. A property type is autonomy-enhancing when it is guided by one robust animating principle that can effectively consolidate expectations. This means that property types are narrow and that relatively many are offered. Thus, a property type should be split if it addresses values that diverge too widely.[72]

Moreover, property types should function as *partial functional substitutes* for each other within any given sphere of human action and interaction. They need to be adequate substitutes because choice is not enhanced with alternatives that are orthogonal to each other; on the other hand, their substitutability should not be too complete because types that are too similar do not offer meaningful choice.

Commercial property types are a good illustration, offering a wide repertoire of types that includes partnership (notably LLCs and LLPs) and various types of corporate forms (from closely held corporations to public corporations).[73] Each of these property types is characterized by its own governance structure and set of solutions to the typical

Developing an Adequate Range of Types

difficulties (notably agency costs) that would probably have inhibited such business activities but for their legal facilitation.[74]

The shifting relations among lawyers in firms offer a vivid example. As one article notes, "For those lawyers who entered the legal profession 20 to 30 years ago, becoming a partner at a major law firm was like entering a marriage."[75] Now, many of these firms have reorganized as limited liability partnerships to maximize revenue, facilitate entry and exit of lateral partners, and shield individuals from liability. The choice of property type can go the other way too. In many cases, lawyers are leaving corporation-like law firms for marriage-like partnerships. As one lawyer said, describing such a move, "The biggest cultural aspect of our firm is that it is based on the old-fashioned partnership. We're partners first and business colleagues second."[76]

2. *N and Δ*. But what constitutes a normatively adequate range of existing property types within a given sphere? This question raises two interrelated concerns. As Ori Aronson puts it: (1) "what is the 'pluralistically optimal' *amount* of alternatives a state is required to (strive to) provide," and (2) "what is the 'optimal' degree of *variance* the state should seek to maintain among the given alternatives."[77]

Addressing these questions – which Aronson terms "the N question" and "the Δ question" – across the various spheres (home, commerce, work, and intimacy) wherein property plays a chief role, involves complex judgments. It requires us "to take account of our knowledge of how people choose and how choice mechanisms can be tweaked ... through strategic design of the supply side."[78] A full-blown account of structural pluralism also requires us to identify with some precision the dimensions whereon property types may vary – such as the duration of the property right, the owner's degree of control and scope of authority, and the main features of their internal governance structure – an inquiry that, in turn, may be resource-specific. Such a research agenda is beyond the scope of this book.

Some preliminary answers are nonetheless available, and at least insofar as the noncommercial contexts of property are concerned, probably sufficient. (In the commercial sphere, by contrast, market forces seem to have taken care, as noted, of property's structural pluralism.) Liberal law's obligation of intra-sphere multiplicity indicates that, for people's choice to be meaningful, N should not be too small. Conversely, if N becomes too big, choice can be curtailed for cognitive, behavioral, structural, and political economy reasons.[79] Similar issues arise for the Δ question – too small (and maybe also too much) variation among types means individuals have insufficient choice among the various (balances of) values that property can facilitate.

An autonomy-enhancing property theory implies that property's multiplicity should probably be *expanded* to include a manifold repertoire of sufficiently distinct types in all relevant spheres of life, including home, work, and intimacy. Thus, while the marginal value of adding another distinct type is at some point likely to be nominal in terms of autonomy, pluralism implies that law's supply of these multiple property types is not to be guided solely by demand. Demand for certain types generally justifies their legal facilitation, but the absence of significant demand should not foreclose adoption of these types when they add valuable options – meaning differing property types complying with the prescriptions of relational justice – that significantly broaden people's choices.

So long as the boundaries between the multiple property types are open and nonabusive navigation of these options is a matter of individual choice, the liberal commitment to autonomy does not require the hegemony of the Blackstonian conception of property otherwise known as the fee simple absolute. Nor does this commitment undermine the value of other, more communitarian or utilitarian property types. On the contrary, the availability of several different but equally valuable and attainable interpersonal frameworks makes autonomy more meaningful by facilitating people's ability to choose and revise their forms of interaction with other individuals regarding various types of resources.

3. *Internal Critique and Reform.* I do not claim that existing property law perfectly complies with this happy liberal picture, and it would be quite surprising if it did. Liberal property's structural pluralism is not a description of property law but an interpretation of one of its characteristic features and, as such, a platform for its internal critique and constructive reform.

Developing an Adequate Range of Types 105

Legal reform is surely in place when a property system's compliance with the prescriptions of structural pluralism is only nominal such as, for example, if the nondominant types it offers are inherently problematic (if they are internally oppressive, or tend to generate grave inefficiencies, or do not protect from risks of opportunism or of an internal deadlock). Further reform is needed given the failure of contemporary property law to offer sufficient property types, which the next section addresses.

Moreover, the autonomy-enhancing rationale of property's structural pluralism suggests that reform is also called for because not all existing property forms – certainly not some of the estate system's remnants still in place – function as a liberal property theory requires.[80] Indeed, it is not by chance that many of these bizarre remnants, such as the three different forms of reversionary future interests (reversion, the possibility of reverter, and right of entry), were not mentioned in this chapter. Fortunately, the American Law Institute has previously recommended reducing the number of forms,[81] and the Restatement (Fourth) of Property may adopt this recommendation to streamline the estates system.

And yet, I hope that the existing property types discussed in this chapter, and obviously the multiplicity typical of property law, demonstrate that these pitfalls are to be viewed as blemishes in a system that, charitably, can be interpreted as structurally pluralistic and thus autonomy-enhancing. This reconstruction does suggest that some urgent reforms are needed, which is indeed partly the purpose of such an exercise. These reforms, however, need not be understood as revolutionary but simply as attempts to urge property law to live up to its (implicit) autonomy-enhancing promise.

I do not deny that run-of-the-mill property *cases* are not concerned with these matters and are largely governed by specific doctrinal configurations in the existing repertoire of property types. This is not merely a reminder of an empirical truism. It is also a necessary feature of a structurally pluralistic property regime that, in order to function, let alone to serve its autonomy-enhancing role, must consolidate people's expectations so that they can anticipate developments when interacting with any given property type. Thus, a set of fairly precise and relatively stable rules governs each of these property types, enabling people to predict the consequences of future contingencies and to plan and structure their lives accordingly.

The ongoing process of reshaping property types is, indeed, often rule-based and usually addressed with an appropriate degree of caution (see Chapter 6). And yet, the possibility of repackaging highlighted by Hohfeld implies that the existing types, as well as their underlying animating principles, are always *potentially* subject to debate and reform.[82] As I argued in Chapter 2, by accommodating form and substance, property can accommodate stability and growth.[83] This dynamic feature of liberal property assures that understanding property as encapsulating ideals of interpersonal interaction is, as Chapter 6 demonstrates, a source of critical engagement and constructive reform.

MISSING TYPES

1. *When and What to Add.* Ensuring sufficient diversity of valuable property types is a core feature, benefit, and indeed obligation, of a property law regime committed to individual autonomy. A liberal property law must include sufficiently distinct property types for the diverse social settings and economic functions wherein law facilitates interpersonal interactions. Only such a rich repertoire can enable people freely to choose their own ends, principles, forms of life, and associations.

At times, though, more choice may actually be autonomy-reducing and intra-sphere multiplicity should then be curtailed. Excessive multiplicity might obstruct choice – a "paradox" that cognitive psychologists have documented – and in certain contexts trigger boundary disputes arising from *ex post* opportunistic maneuvering. Multiplicity is also autonomy-reducing where the market structure generates a race to the bottom that may systematically undermine the autonomy of weak parties (think of, say, markets for unskilled workers at times of non-negligible unemployment). Finally, certain property types may be particularly vulnerable to the risk of interest group rent-seeking.[84]

Missing Types 107

These cognitive, behavioral, structural, and political economy reasons delimit the circumstances in which law should proactively enrich our repertoire of property types. They should always be considered but, often, they either do not apply or their effect is only marginal. An autonomy-enhancing law should then support establishing emerging types, even if the demand for new types is low.

Legal systems can hardly be expected to routinely invent new property types. Carrying out the state's obligation to enhance choice in such a top-down fashion is not necessarily desirable given the comparative disadvantage of state institutions vis-à-vis private individuals and firms in coming up with appropriate innovations. Hence, at least in typical cases, carriers of the property law need not (maybe even should not) engage in innovative design.[85] Rather, they should proactively look for innovations, such as those based on minority views and utopian theories that have some traction but would fail if left to people's own devices.

Formally instantiating a new property type may not always make a difference. To perform its autonomy-enhancing work a new property type needs to be sufficiently prominent socially, a demand that (especially regarding new minoritarian property types) could entail a significant entry barrier. To ensure that structural pluralism does not remain the law in the books, liberal property law should address this impediment. While it cannot, without violating liberal neutrality, grant these types long-term special protection or subsidies, it can, and in the suitable cases should, treat these property types on a par with infant industries and offer such support on a *transitory* basis.

2. *Homeownership*. Take homeownership as an example illustrating where property law offers some choice and where it can offer more. Property law already offers a relatively rich menu of homeownership models. In addition to traditional forms such as the fee simple, leasehold, and commons property, we now have an increasing array of shared-interest residential developments, including condominiums and cooperatives. Nozick's mention of the *kibbutz* may, however, imply that even on this front the menu may be incomplete.[86]

But what about the route *to* homeownership? There are at least two promising directions for innovative private law types that are currently advanced in response to *public* concerns. Interest in the first type – home equity insurance – has been reinvigorated by the subprime mortgage crisis and is probably more pertinent to middle-income families. The second – shared equity homeownership – comes up in discussions of affordable housing for lower-income households. The public macro-concerns are important, but these proposals are valuable even without them given their contribution to property's autonomy-enhancing *telos*.

The first type – home equity insurance – demonstrates the implications of structural pluralism to *contract* law, when complying with the obligation of the liberal state can generate the benefits of providing "off-the-rack" contractual arrangements for new insurance and financial products. These products allow homeowners to share or offload the risk of their home decreasing in value due to changes in the state of the neighborhood or in the overall housing market.[87] Helping middle-income households separate house-as-home from house-as-investment along these lines is an effective tool for complying with the prescription of intra-sphere multiplicity.[88]

Unfortunately, for lower-income households that cannot afford to buy in the first place, this tool does not offer a viable alternative to renting. Therefore, for people of modest means, the commitment to autonomy requires *property* law to facilitate models of shared equity homeownership. These models – notably community land trusts, limited equity cooperatives, and deed-restricted homes – link "low- and moderate-income people with affordable owner-occupied housing" by combining three features: "(1) they lower the initial cost of purchasing a home; (2) they limit the gain a homebuyer can receive on resale, thus generating a relatively affordable price for a subsequent buyer; and (3) they frequently provide stewardship to maintain community values and help homeowners retain and maintain their homes."[89]

For these models of tenure to thrive, they may have to overcome the occasional monitoring problem[90] and, typically, need to rely on some public (or public-spirited) sponsorship.[91] Friends of liberal property, who appreciate how its autonomy-enhancing *telos* at times requires a supportive background regime that ensures conditions for self-determination,[92] should not be deterred by these challenges.[93] Indeed, they should welcome initiatives that "may produce near-term financial benefits for those who would otherwise be unable to buy a home," and "help individuals purchase homes in neighborhoods with higher home values and education levels than they would have been able to otherwise."[94]

3. *Work and Intimacy.* Examples of reforms that would expand the repertoire of property types, thus fitting property law more successfully to its autonomy-enhancing *telos*, are also found in other major spheres of life. Consider briefly one example from the sphere of work and one from that of the family.

A worker cooperative is a jointly owned and democratically controlled enterprise; an entity with a class of worker-members "whose patronage consists of labor contributed to" the corporation, and who must always maintain a controlling interest in the business.[95] Although worker cooperatives have existed for over a century,[96] Massachusetts was the first state to enact, only in 1982, a law specifically supporting worker cooperatives as a corporate form.[97] Since then, eleven more states have passed worker cooperative acts[98] that helped solidify this property type in the public consciousness, providing a framework to promote the survival and growth of worker-cooperatives.[99] For example, California's recent Worker Cooperative Act makes it easier for worker-owned businesses to raise capital and scale up hiring.[100]

California also provides an example of structural pluralism in the sphere of intimacy. California and eight other states differ from the majority of states, where title theory governs property questions during an intact marriage while equitable principles govern the allocation of entitlements upon divorce. California's default regime for marital property is community property, whose basic principle is that spouses are equal owners of all property acquired during the marriage due to either's effort, regardless of how the property is nominally titled. This principle is translated into a tripartite governance regime: while major decisions are governed by a rule of joint management,[101] others are subject to the exclusive management authority of one of the spouses, or to a residual rule of equal management whereby either one can make decisions.

I have discussed this regime in some detail elsewhere, pointing to it as the concretization of an animating principle that conceptualizes marriage as a liberal egalitarian community.[102] What matters for my purpose here is a seemingly marginal aspect of this system that far upgrades it beyond the equitable division regime that governs marital property elsewhere. In states like California, spouses can transfer ("transmute") specific assets of their holdings to "regular" forms of concurrent ownership, such as joint tenancy or tenancy in common (and vice versa).[103] By contrast, equitable division states (such as New York) do not have the community property type in their repertoire. This asymmetry implies that "community property plus transmuting" states comply (at least to an extent) with the prescription of intra-sphere multiplicity, while "strictly equitable division" ones do not. This deficiency is only partially ameliorated in roughly half of the equitable division states, which recognize the tenancy by the entirety form.[104]

Much more remains to be said regarding the spheres of work, to which I return in Chapter 7, and of intimacy. In sharp contrast with the substantial inventory of types characteristic of the commercial sphere, law needs to proactively enlarge the repertoire offered in these two spheres. I have addressed this challenge in a book I coauthored with Michael Heller that focuses on celebrating structural pluralism in *contract*,[105] and I hope that the brief discussion here suffices to demonstrate its reformist potential. The co-participation of property and contract in the core liberal challenge of offering a structurally pluralistic legal infrastructure for our interpersonal relationships is to be expected, given the continuity of property and contract noted in Chapter 2.[106]

NUMERUS CLAUSUS

1. *Between Standardization and* Numerus Clausus. Besides a rich variety of state-sponsored frameworks, an autonomy-based private law must offer, wherever feasible, a residual category allowing autonomous individuals to "invent" their own private forms of interaction.[107] Although imperfectly, contract law generally complies with this prescription.[108] By contrast, property law's *numerus clausus* principle, at least in its prevailing understanding, fails to offer a salient and vibrant residual category of private arrangements.

Property's autonomy-enhancing *telos* fully justifies the *numerus clausus* as a principle of standardization. Law's list of property types is commendable because it facilitates stable categories of state-supported property types by standardizing their incidents. For law to consolidate people's expectations in compliance with the prescriptions of both structural pluralism (as noted above) and the rule of law (to be discussed in Chapter 6), it must recognize a necessarily limited number of categories of relationships and resources.

The conventional understanding of the *numerus clausus* principle, however, goes further. It stands for the proposition that "property rights exist [only] in a fixed number of forms,"[109] so that private arrangements can enjoy the status of property only if they are pigeon-holed into the *delimited* menu of state-recognized property forms. But even the most sophisticated attempts to justify this dimension of the *numerus clausus* principle are not fully persuasive.

2. *Unconvincing Accounts.* Thus, although ostensibly it seems to be a needed anti-fragmentation device to address anticommons difficulties,[110] there are "much more direct and cost-effective methods of preventing excess fragmentation of property rights." In any event, "the size of parcels or the number of co-owners" generates fragmentation problems much more pressing than those caused by unlimited property forms.[111]

Another prominent justification for the *numerus clausus* principle treats it as a means for reducing the communication costs of third parties, who need to determine the attributes of property rights in order to avoid violating them or to acquire them from present owners.[112] But because the pertinent concern of such third parties is to verify the ownership of rights, it can often be satisfied through less onerous means, namely, via legal mechanisms – recordation or (better) registration – that provide effective notice.[113]

Verification costs do not exhaust the information costs of novelties. The way information is structured affects the costs of processing it,[114] and how far the costs of novelties can be cured by notice is an empirical question. But while these information costs should not be dismissed too lightly, an autonomy-enhancing property law should strive to ensure that they do not frustrate people's ability to opt out of state-favored forms.[115]

Therefore, though law's traditional facilitation of standardized property types along structural pluralistic lines is laudable, a liberal property regime should reconsider the hostility of *numerus clausus* toward tailor-made property rights. This deficiency is addressed to a limited extent by the trust, which allows the settlor to "engage in many types of complicated carving up of interests."[116] But trust law does not fully redress this deficiency, notably due to the beneficiary's dependence on the trustee.[117]

Liberal property law is, of course, perfectly justified in proscribing idiosyncratic arrangements insofar as they entail negative external effects, both social (e. g., segregation) and economic (e. g., fragmentation), or as they impinge on individual rights (either those of the parties themselves or of third parties). But these concerns are addressed, as they should be, even respecting state-sponsored property types.[118] They can, and should, similarly limit the ability of people to tailor their property arrangements in accordance with the way they prefer to shape their interpersonal relationships, but they do not establish an a priori obstacle to such private orderings.

3. *Residual Category.* People may legitimately want to accommodate their property arrangements to their particular needs and circumstances. In a liberal society, citizens should be free to reject many of law's messages and at least some of the values recommended by the state, and a liberal property law must facilitate this option. People should thus be able to create their own idiosyncratic frameworks of interpersonal interactions and not merely idiosyncratically adjust state-sponsored frameworks. This does not mean that property law must adopt a *numerus apertus* (open list) principle, allowing "bizarre rights" to be registered or recorded on par with law's standardized types and thus require every third party to further inquiries.[119] Instead, it means that, like contract law, property law should also include *one* residual category for private arrangements in addition to the state-sponsored property types.[120]

Designing such a category and making it sufficiently salient and vibrant is not a trivial task; however, there are two apparent guidelines: (1) The significance to people's autonomy of opening up this option justifies investing some technological effort in developing effective means of providing notice to third parties as to the content of such an arrangement (technological advances suggest that, in our era, this task should not be overly burdensome). (2) Both the risks of possible misunderstandings due to its idiosyncrasy or ambiguity, and the costs of administering such a residual property type, should be allocated to the parties of such an arrangement rather than to these third parties. This reform can rely on the successful experience of Spanish law, whose registration system roughly corresponds to the lines of this and the previous paragraphs.[121]

★ ★ ★

In sum, a liberal property law must honor law's commitment to self-authorship by offering a repertoire of property types for interpersonal relationships sufficiently distinct from one another, so as to provide meaningful choices in all spheres of social action and interaction.

A liberal property law must also ensure that all these property types comply with the maxim of reciprocal respect for self-determination. As I argue next, this prescription of relational justice requires that people treat each other as free and equal persons, respecting each other not only as mere bearers of a generic human capacity for choice but as the persons they actually are.

5 PROPERTY'S RELATIONAL JUSTICE

Liberal property, I argued in Chapter 3, relies on its contribution to owners' self-determination, which others are obligated to respect. The justification of authorizing owners' private authority and its coercive enforcement by the state is premised on people's interpersonal obligation of reciprocal respect for self-determination, making property's legitimacy contingent on its compliance with this fundamentally liberal understanding of just relationships. Reciprocal respect for self-determination is thus not only a potential external constraint on the liberal conception of property but inherent in its raison d'être.

This notion of relational justice, which Avihay Dorfman and I have developed in recent years,[1] is not limited to a negative duty of non-interference that is the correlative of others' right to independence. Respect for others' self-determination is hollow without *some* attention to their predicament. Equally, relational respect for self-determination cannot be content with a formal conception of equality that abstracts away the particular features distinguishing one person from another. While interpersonal independence does not depend on the distinctive features of others, respecting their self-determination necessarily requires that we respect them as they actually are.

This chapter argues that a liberal property law is indeed committed to reciprocal respect for self-determination (rather than independence) and thus also for substantive (rather than merely formal) equality. This claim sharply contrasts not only with the dominion conception of property but also with the conventional approach to the private–public distinction, which views private law as that part of our law that is resistant to demanding interpersonal claims. Per this view, even if the commitment to people's self-determination and thus to their substantive equality has some bearing on the law, it should not affect private law, meaning that individuals are not required to treat others with care or concern when utilizing their private property. As long as they do not harm anyone, they are entitled to a strictly self-interested attitude.

I begin this chapter with an analysis of the conceptual, normative, and descriptive failings of this conventional approach toward the private–public distinction, significant not only for their own sake but also because they help to refine the alternative view at the focus of this chapter.

KANTIAN PROPERTY

The notion of a sharp division of labor between the state's responsibility for providing a fair starting point for all and the responsibility of individuals for pursuing their ends using their fair share seems commonplace, and is held by Kantians, Hegelians, and many liberal egalitarians.[2] Ernest Weinrib and Arthur Ripstein's elaborations of Kant's theory of private law, and specifically of property, offer its most sophisticated articulation. Property in this Kantian view – which I present here as *the* Kantian view even though some scholars offer competing understandings of Kant[3] – is a stronghold of interpersonal independence. Working in a different tradition, Philip Pettit's neorepublican view of property is strikingly similar to the Kantian account, and thus subject to much of the critique that follows.[4]

Kantians do not subscribe to the libertarian ideal of the nightwatchman state. Indeed, the reverse. Beside its role as the guarantor of people's property rights vis-à-vis one another, the Kantian state functions as the authority responsible for levying taxes "in order to fulfill a public duty to support the poor."[5] Strong property rights and a viable welfare state cluster together as a matter of conceptual necessity.

1. *From Independence to Property.* The starting point of this analysis is Kant's conception of the right to personal independence: each person is entitled not to be subordinated to the desires, choices, circumstances, or needs of any other particular person. Autonomy "can be compromised by natural or self-inflicted factors no less than by the deeds of others," while independence "can only be compromised by

the deeds of others." Independence is exhausted by the requirement that no one can tell anyone else what purposes to pursue. "It is a constraint on the conduct of others, imposed by the fact that each person is entitled to be his or her own master." Independence entails only a negative duty that "is not compromised if others decline to accommodate you."[6]

This understanding of the right to independence implies that rights, even when related to issues beyond the physical self, *must* be absolute. If people are to be allowed, as they should be, "to exercise their freedom by controlling external objects of choice," these objects must be under their sole discretion so that all others are bound by the power of the proprietor's will.[7] Property "comprises the external means" one uses "in setting and pursuing purposes," so that "if someone interferes with your property, they thereby interfere with your purposiveness." Therefore, the right to property must "limit the conduct of others in relation to particular things."[8] Indeed, although one's property is not "an extension of [one's] body," one's property rights "are broadly parallel to [one's] rights with respect to [one's] body ... because the form of [that right] – the way in which it constrains the conduct of others – is the same."[9]

2. *Property and Poverty.* But allowing "one person coercively to restrict another's freedom through unilateral acts that establish proprietary rights to exclude" is problematic, because it allows the proprietor "to subordinate others to his or her purposes," and is thus "inconsistent with innate equality of all." This is a profound difficulty since it threatens to undermine the very independence that prompted the introduction of property rights. A full-scale regime of such rights of private property confines people's "rightful possibilities ... to what might be left over from others' efforts at accumulation." This may make their ability to satisfy their basic needs or even their survival "dependent on the goodwill or sufferance of others," or force them to subordinate themselves, "making [themselves] into a means for [these owners'] ends."[10]

The introduction of property rights thus creates a conceptual tension since these rights, which are required for independence, are also what threatens it. The Kantian theory of property suggests two ways of

Kantian Property

breaking this impasse. Both acknowledge that "a purely unilateral act of acquisition can only restrict the choice of all other persons against the background of an omnilateral authorization." Both ways, then, rely on the legitimating authority reflecting the transition from a lawless state, where individuals can take from others at will, to "the civil condition of law-governed society" capable of protecting each person's independence.[11]

First, Kantians argue that "ownership is legitimate when one person's acquisition is related to acquisitions by others through a general system of acquisition." The operative term here is "general," because the system ties each acquisition "to the availability of acquisition to others," signifying a "reciprocity among all potential acquirers," and thus "conformity to the innate right of everyone." The point "is not merely that everyone can be an acquirer, but that all the acquisitions taken systemically are the ground for the legitimacy of any particular acquisition." Only the state system of acquisition "renders any particular acquisition binding on everyone else," because it allows each acquirer to state that "I can acquire *because* you (and everyone else) can acquire."[12]

Kantians seem to acknowledge, however, that the sheer *opportunity* to acquire cannot plausibly be tantamount to a recognition of the system's legitimacy or otherwise legitimate its effects on nonowners. Hence, their second – and ultimately main – response: "The only way that property rights can be made [legitimately] enforceable is if the system that makes them so contains a provision for protecting against private dependence."[13]

The danger that some people will be "reduced to a means for others" given their "possible inaccessibility [to] the means of sustenance" is eliminated, in this view, by the state's "assumption of the duty to support the poor." This duty is a "*collective* duty imposed on the people" and is aimed at resolving the "*systemic* difficulty that property poses" so that "no one's subsistence is dependent on the actions of others." Thus, although the poor are only "beneficiaries of a duty" and not holders of a right,[14] the state's operation of this duty reestablishes people's nondependence on others for their survival.[15]

3. *The Social Contract.* This "civil condition is formed through a social contract ... that unites the will of all." This social contract

"is not a historical event" but "an idea of reason in terms of which the legitimacy of the state can be conceived." This "notional union of all wills" is crucial: it transforms unilateral acquisitions of unowned things "to an omnilateral act, to which everyone as possible owners of property implicitly consents and whose rights-creating significance everyone acknowledges."[16]

No valid social contract can be formed if some people "are completely beholden to the choice of another," as is the case when there is no public duty to support the poor. The legitimacy of private property does require the state, through the legislature, to take upon itself the duty to support the poor, but does not depend on the details of this tax legislation. The result of the legislation is legitimate as long as "everyone acts in his or her official capacity," so that the legislation "is not an instance of one person unilaterally choosing for another" but reflects "the public purpose of creating and sustaining a rightful condition." If so, then the "details of [such] legislation" are "accidental from the standpoint of right," even if the result is not "one that is most advantageous to you, or even to everyone."[17]

MISSION IMPOSSIBLE

There is nothing objectionable in the notion that public law should ensure a background regime that can help make property legitimate. Part of my claim in Chapter 3 actually was that, to address the legitimacy challenge that property law cannot plausibly face on its own, a liberal regime *must* resort to mechanisms such as the law of tax and redistribution. But the Kantian position is different. In this view, public law does not supplement the efforts of property law but undertakes the task in its entirety.[18] Is this *radical* division of labor feasible, when our *entire* responsibility for other people is delegated to the state? And if it is, is it normatively appealing? The answer to both these questions is no.[19]

1. *Two Ambiguities.* A radical division of institutional and moral labor between private and public law is not viable, even in a closed economy.[20] One way of tracing the difficulties facing this idea can begin with two ambiguities in the Kantian account of property.

One concerns the threat that strong property rights pose to propertyless people. On the one hand, Kantians seem to recognize that ownership is a source of economic, and therefore social, political, and cultural rights and powers, whose correlative are other people's duties and liabilities. Property's threat to nonowners is thus potential dependence and applies, for example, to the numerous cases of propertyless workers who only rent living spaces or even live on the employer's land without renting.

On the other hand, the justified complaint of the propertyless in these Kantian accounts seems much more limited and concerns only the satisfaction of basic needs or the accessibility of means of sustenance. This minimalism is troublesome because, as discussed in Chapter 3, not only do property rights threaten the survival of nonowners but property relations also introduce new and different modes of dependence. Even if everyone's basic needs are secured, the private authority that property creates entails interpersonal inequalities that generate dependence and even subordination. Independence can hardly be secured without addressing these inequalities.

The other ambiguity relates to the remedy that can address the threat of property and thus legitimate its introduction. The Kantian insistence that the unilateralism of proprietors' conduct can only be validated by omnilateral authorization implies a high threshold of legitimacy, seemingly requiring that all affected parties can reasonably be assumed to have consented to the resulting regime. It is thus puzzling that, for Kantians, this requirement hardly entails any implications – as long as the form of tax-and-redistribution legislation is in place, its details are a matter of politics rather than of right.

If omnilateral authorization is not to be reduced to an ideological device of legitimation, the broad (even if hypothetical) consent it stands for must at least be plausible.[21] Survival and the satisfaction of basic needs, then, cannot be our only concern and procedural adequacy cannot exhaust the justificatory burden at stake. Given the threat of dependence posed by property rights, Kantians can justify the renunciation of all interpersonal obligations (beyond duties of noninterference) only if they can plausibly demonstrate that the public law of tax and redistribution is likely to remedy the injustices entailed by private law, at least in terms of interpersonal dependence if not in terms of distribution. This burden of persuasion is insurmountable for three reasons.

2. *Justice and Politics.* The first reason is straightforward. The realities of interest group politics in the promulgation of tax legislation in liberal democracies make egalitarian tax regimes, such as one based on Rawls' difference principle, a matter of political theory and not of empirical reality.[22]

This unfortunate result is inherent in the idea of democracy. Democratic legislatures are expected to reflect the grammar of democratic politics, which is a hybrid of preferences and reasons.[23] Thus, there is a critical difference between justice and democracy: while "justice conceptually *can* count preferences as relevant reasons," democracy "*must* always take (some) account of people's preferences."[24] As long as these preferences diverge from what justice demands, their translation into legislative pronouncements will likely fall short of what a just scheme of tax and redistribution requires.[25]

3. *Cultural Effects.* The Kantian account of property may exacerbate this disparity between distributive ideals and real-life redistribution through public law, given the role that our understanding of property in defining mutual legitimate claims and expectations plays in our daily interactions. I address these cultural effects of property (and their limitations) elsewhere.[26] My claim here is more limited. I assume that people view owners' responsibilities and what they perceive to be their legitimate interests as somehow influenced by the conception of ownership applied by our private law. If so, the self-regarding attitude generated by the dominion conception of property supported by Kantians, may undermine the hope of endorsing policies targeting the requirements of distributive justice when we come to shape our public law. In Rawlsian terms, this means that a private law regime grounded in relational independence might threaten the *stability* of a just public order by failing to attract the support of the people subject to its basic structure.

I am not disputing – indeed, I fully recognize – that people can and often do apply disparate, and at times even opposite, standards in different normative spheres. Yet, our stance in one sphere may sometimes affect our stance in another and, in such cases, we should take these consequences into account. The possibility that a private law regime permitting *extreme* indifference to the predicament of others might dilute the responsiveness to claims from distributive justice is a case in point.

People who are *never* required to pay attention to the fate of others in many of their interactions affected by private law are likely to doubt or belittle the legitimacy of others' claims to a *significant* portion of their resources when asked to pay taxes. Of course, exact correspondence between the normative underpinnings of private law and of the public law on tax and redistribution is neither possible, required, nor even desirable. But *complete* divergence in this context is probably impossible as well. While acknowledging the benefits of public law beneficence, private law should beware of fostering attitudes that might hinder a just public order.[27]

4. *Dependence on The Welfare State.* Finally, even if a sufficiently redistributive tax scheme somehow emerged, it would probably fail to erase the distortions of an independence-based private law system in terms of unjustified interpersonal dependence. Even if government largesse is recognized as an entitlement, dependence does not fade and, instead, shifts from the context of private law to that of the individual's relationship with the state via the welfare bureaucracy.[28]

The Kantian response to this concern is that "dependence involves a relationship with someone who, without breaching a duty, can withhold a benefit necessary for one's survival," and that because the state is under a duty to support the poor and "has no motivation to withhold support," the receipt of state support "does not make the needy subservient to the will of others."[29] This response, tellingly articulated without mentioning the bureaucrats who run the welfare system, is premised on a surprising analogy to the parent–child relationship[30] and is clearly far removed from everything we know about the workings of modern welfare states.[31]

Kantians may reply that the expected noncompliance of state officials is irrelevant to an *ideal* theory of law that, by definition, is aspirational. The noncompliance of officials, even if endemic, can be set aside insofar as it relates to the truth of the "ought" judgment, and thus normative assessment, pertaining to these officials. But the issue at hand refers to the "ought" judgment about *other* agents: citizens. The unfeasibility of officials' compliance with the utopian vision of state bureaucracies is surely part of the morally relevant background circumstances, even regarding an aspirational theory of private citizens.[32]

The notion of a welfare state without dependence is indeed detached from real life and from almost any imaginable welfare system run by real people. Yet, its difficulties notwithstanding, a welfare state is clearly superior to a society where charity is poverty's sole remedy.[33] A welfare state, as noted in Chapter 3, is a necessary element in a legal regime seeking to make property legitimate but is still not a panacea. By pushing the *entire* burden of social responsibility and distributive justice to the welfare state, Kantians (and other division-of-labor liberals) do not avoid the problem of dependence.[34]

MISSION UNDESIRABLE

Even if the Kantian strict division of labor between private and public law could somehow be viable, it would be highly undesirable and could not possibly legitimize the Blackstonian conception of property. This was my argument in my coauthored work with Dorfman, on which much of this chapter relies.

1. *Pitfalls of a Strict Division of Labor.* The core idea of division-of-labor liberals, aptly captured in Kantian property theory, is that the liberal commitment to individual self-determination – and thus to substantive equality – is purely vertical. Both John Rawls and Ronald Dworkin, for example, understand these values as the sovereign's virtues – the defining features of the polity's responsibility that do not, indeed should not, affect our horizontal relationships. Assuming that the state complies with its vertical obligations, all that free individuals are required to do is respect each other's independence and formal equality. In other words, as long as we avoid crossing interpersonal borders, we bear no responsibility for each other's autonomy and need not be concerned with claims for substantive equality.[35]

In this conventional understanding, private individuals may be enlisted only to support just basic institutions, a duty making their responsibility purely accessory and conditional.[36] This construction, then, implies a clear indictment of any form of primary and independent interpersonal responsibility.

The exclusion of any concern for the predicament of others from our conception of private law is deeply troublesome, and particularly objectionable with respect to our understanding of property. Support for a strict division of labor exacerbates the alarming implications of property's spectacular private authority highlighted in Chapter 3, aggravating the concomitant vulnerability (if not subordination) of nonowners.

The dominion conception of private property places at the core of private law dissociated persons whose only (direct[37]) duty to one another is to avoid transgressing boundaries. By supporting only horizontal obligations of noninterference and denying any duties of interpersonal accommodation, this understanding leaves intact, and thereby *authorizes*, the interpersonal vulnerability that constitutes the main threat to the legitimacy of property. Thus, even assuming that, contrary to my conclusion in the previous section, public law measures flawlessly address the vulnerabilities resulting from such an unjust property regime, a strict-division-of-labor regime would certainly fail to comply with the ideal of respecting one another as substantively free and equal human beings.

The canonical liberal commitments to individual self-determination (and not merely independence) and thus to substantive (and not merely formal) equality should not be cast out from our interpersonal relationships. Discarding liberalism's most important commitments from the realm of private law is troubling due to two facts of the human condition: interdependence and personal differences.

The deep interdependence of our practical affairs is evident in all our interactions, ranging from fairly trivial transactions to the most crucial relationships in our lives such as those related to family, friends, work, and other significant positions we come to occupy in society. These interactions can be voluntary or involuntary – we invite others and are invited by them to join projects, be it because social interaction is critical to the project or because enlisting others makes it possible or practical. Our projects may also affect the legitimate interests of other people, including some not directly involved in the joint project.

These forms of interaction affect our lives generally, and certainly our success. The dominion conception of property, as Chapter 4 showed, renounces the responsibility of private law for the facilitation of these interactions, compromising the significance of our interpersonal relationships to our conceptions of the good life.

Moreover, and specifically meaningful for this chapter, the significance of our standing in relation to others also implies that interactions developing under conditions of interdependence should be assessed as just or unjust. In this context, the dominion conception again proves disappointing, especially given the existence of personal differences, namely, given that we all constitute our own distinctive personhoods in light of our own peculiar circumstances.

2. *Private Responsibility for Justice.* The dominion conception of property replaces a concern for what relating to one another as free and equal agents means to *real* people with a concern for what this means to equal abstract beings. In assigning responsibility for addressing our personal differences solely to public law, this conception implicitly rejects any claims that private individuals may place on one another as a matter of relational justice.

This outright rejection of relational justice reflects – and indeed perpetuates – an undervalued perception of what interpersonal relationships mean for our conceptions of the good life. This failure is troublesome even in societies where just public-law arrangements ensure all citizens adequate opportunities to realize their full freedom in their private lives.[38] Relational justice, in other words, is not reducible to distributive justice – it deals with a demand of justice that is free-standing.

In a world of perfect, or even significant, interpersonal detachment, this worry could perhaps be set aside. But interdependence implies that our horizontal interactions are too significant to our autonomy and social equality to be so easily supplanted by vertical arrangements, however just they might be.

Consider the private owner of a boutique café who decides not to let customers enter the premises adducing some morally arbitrary grounds, such as their sexual orientation. Suppose, more particularly, that this café is the only one to practice discrimination against gay people in Manhattan (or, say, San Francisco) so that, in its liberal surroundings, there are easy substitutes and no discernible external effects (material or cultural) to the owner's bigotry. In this hypothetical, there is nothing that public law justice can or should do: it is a simple private law case in which one private person (who *really* values his or her independence) disrespects the self-determination of another person on the basis of the latter's sexual identity.[39]

This case vividly illustrates the indispensable dimension of private responsibility for justice, one that the foreground justice advocated by division-of-labor liberal egalitarians denies on grounds of formal equal independence. Even a widespread egalitarian ethos among private persons and a public commitment to provide for background justice, as this case shows, could not rehabilitate a property law that authorizes private owners to discriminate against others re decisions of exclusion.[40]

3. *Property's Legitimacy and Relational Justice.* Without a doubt, the justice of property law is partially dependent on background distributive justice, as noted in Chapter 3. This dependence notwithstanding, property law is still charged with the justice-based task of determining terms of interactions carefully attentive to the (substantive) freedom and equality of *both* parties.

Thus, a system of property that facilitates, authorizes, and (given property's irreducible legal foundations) even constitutes interpersonal interactions while impervious to *any* demand of relational justice, can hardly be acceptable to free and equal individuals. Ascribing any form of consent to nonowners, to whom the argument for this system's legitimacy is owed above all, is not merely hypothetical but counterfactual.[41] Hence, the Blackstonian conception of property at the core of the radical division of labor presumed between private law and public law cannot possibly meet property's justificatory challenge, especially given the accountability deficit constitutive of the unique private authority typical of property.[42]

To be acceptable, property law must repudiate the dominion conception of property while recognizing interdependence and personal differences. The liberal commitments to individual self-determination and to substantive equality are just as crucial to our horizontal relationships as they are to our vertical ones, although their implications in these different dimensions are not the same.

RELATIONAL JUSTICE

Law's recognition of owners' authority, then, cannot be justified by reference to their aloofness. Their property rights are not merely constraints on the permissible means of others, nor merely limits (analogous to certain physical limitations) on what is available to nonowners. The value of property hangs on the respect from others – both other individuals and the polity as a whole – that ownership implies for the owner's right to self-determination (see Chapter 3). Owners' authority is to be founded on a requirement of *reciprocal* respect and recognition among self-determining persons.

In this view, property is part of a certain vision of being *with others* in the world. A genuinely liberal private law vindicates our claims of relational justice – the dimension of justice that focuses on the terms of our interactions as private individuals rather than as citizens or as subjects of state institutions. It casts our horizontal, interpersonal relationships as interactions between free and equal individuals, respecting one another as the persons they actually are.

For people – owners and nonowners alike – to treat each other as equals, the terms of their interactions must be premised on reciprocal respect for self-determination and not merely independence. Given personal differences and the significance of our interdependence to our self-determination, these terms must be predicated on the conception of the person as a substantively, rather than formally, free and equal agent.

Private law should thus strive to ensure a reasonably fair *relational* starting point from which parties can realize their respective freedoms. As long as the parties' relevant personal qualities are not intrinsically inimical to the ideal of relational equality, then, private law – especially property law – cannot ignore them. It merits note that this maxim of relational justice can go beyond what may be required by the prescription to carefully delineate owners' private authority set in Chapter 3.

The commitment to relations of respectful recognition with others, which grounds relational justice's prescription of interpersonal accommodation, also constrains the conceptions of the good and other personal choices that may legitimately require accommodation. Some personal choices, policies, and conceptions of the good will, by definition, deny specific others the very standing that would enable them to relate to the deniers as equals – the animating ambition of the murderer, the racist, and the bigot, for example, is to repudiate their victims' equal standing.

Besides this principled limitation, however, private law must take account of the parties as they actually are, accounting for their constitutive characteristics and circumstances as well as the choices pertaining to their "ground projects" (the projects that give meaning to one's life as opposed to one's brute preferences[43]). Given that these individual features are crucial to people's self-determination, they are highly relevant to private law. An autonomy-enhancing conception of property thus requires precisely the kind of accommodative structure that the dominion conception of property precludes.

By contrast, overemphasizing personal differences is not a precondition of interpersonal respect. A world that renders a specific type of accommodation redundant – through a technological improvement or by reshuffling a social practice – would often represent an improvement over a world that does require such an accommodation. But as long as personal differences systematically impact many of our social practices – and it would be hard to imagine a world where they do not – interpersonal respect does entail some measure of interpersonal accommodation.

At times, relational justice requires *active* accommodation as in many workplace instances.[44] In other cases, such as those dealing with nondiscrimination considered below, relational justice implies *not* considering certain characteristics when making decisions. Be that as it may, when it applies to owners, relational justice ensures that law does not confer property rights that authorize violations of reciprocal respect for self-determination.

To reiterate: the prescription of relational justice runs directly from owners to nonowners. While its specific implications may depend on the state's background regime and its compliance with the demands of distributive justice, it is not reducible to distributive justice. Relational justice does not substitute our Rawlsian duty to support just institutions, which remains intact. It does not target inequality in the overall distribution of resources (or opportunities) in society. Relational justice focuses on the acceptable terms of interpersonal interactions and establishes the demands of justice among private persons. Owners are required to comply with relational justice in their private capacity instead of as citizens of a particular state or as agents enlisted by the state to act on its behalf.[45]

RELATIONALLY JUST PRIVATE AUTHORITY

1. *The Challenge*. But is not this injunction of relational justice bound to undermine the unique private authority of property? This private authority, as I argued in Chapter 3, is justified due to its crucial contribution to securing (vertical and horizontal) respect for people's self-determination. Critics of relational justice may worry that it would completely destroy property's private authority since it implies that "everyone has a standing duty to see to it that particular other persons with whom they are interacting lead autonomous and successful lives."[46] Alternatively, if the commitment to relational justice is ineliminable, does this not imply that the private authority granted to certain owners in property law is actually unjustifiable?

These questions highlight a deep tension intrinsic to an autonomy-based account of property and, therefore, pose a substantial challenge that cannot be dismissed.[47] Yet, following the guidance of H. L. A. Hart's dictum on the "unexciting but indispensable chore" of making qualitative judgments in any credible autonomy-talk,[48] my effort is to show that, although the tension between private authority and relational justice cannot be dissolved, it can be contained, and that its circumscription is principled rather than ad hoc.

Relationally Just Private Authority

2. *Three Limitations.* To see why, consider the three limitations on the application of relational justice, derived from the liberal maxim of reciprocal respect for self-determination, from the nature of legal prescriptions more generally, and from rule of law concerns.

a. *Inherent Limits.* Some limitations on the scope of relational justice derive from this very ideal. The duty of accommodation is not an all-encompassing requirement to accommodate each and every person in every single area of their practical affairs. What the duty typically establishes are fair terms of interaction in and around one sphere of action, applying to a particular context or event and regarding one person (or class of persons) at a time. Furthermore, and most importantly, the burden to perform an interpersonal duty of accommodation grounded in relational justice cannot be excessive because it must neither undermine the autonomy of the parties involved nor create interpersonal subordination between them.[49]

b. *Nature of Law.* Other limits emerge from the nature of legal prescriptions. Some relationships (such as love or friendship) are rightfully shielded from any legal treatment, either because legal enforcement might destroy their inherent moral value or because legal intervention might backfire by crowding out internal motivations. Relational justice does not require anyone to be anyone's friend.[50]

c. *Rule of Law.* Finally, there are limits to the legal application of relational justice originating in the rule of law maxim (discussed in Chapter 6) requiring that effective guidance be provided to law's addressees, thus also constraining officials' ability to exercise power. This maxim, which is deeply ingrained in any autonomy-based legal regime, helps to defuse the potentially intrusive and demanding aspects of accommodation. This effect is attained by setting out clear categories and doctrines for individuals to adequately discharge their duties on the one hand and, on the other, allowing them to exercise their rights of accommodation.

These rule of law techniques – drawing, for example, a firm distinction between law's treatment of private homes and the rules applicable to other forms of land ownership – create an intersubjective frame of reasoning capable of guiding participants' deliberation and behavior by minimizing recourse to individualized knowledge and radically ad hoc judgments. At times, rule of law concerns – and other institutional considerations – also explain why at least some of the burden of translating the prescriptions of relational justice into law is performed by legislators and regulators, and not (or not only) by judges.[51]

These three limitations imply that relational justice should not, and if properly implemented does not, threaten the possibility of an autonomy-enhancing property law. Equally, appreciating the autonomy-enhancing role of private authority need not – indeed should not – ignore or marginalize the demands of relational justice. As I claim in the remainder of this chapter, a legal system guided by property's autonomy-enhancing *telos* can and should shape the scope and the distribution of owners' authority in a way that properly responds to these demands.

3. *Structural Pluralism.* It is convenient to start this inquiry by considering the implications of property's structural pluralism on property's ability to comply with the prescriptions of relational justice. Structural pluralism implies, as indicated in Chapter 4, that different property types can, and should, take differing forms. Thus, while some property types justifiably confer on owners a robust autonomy-enhancing authority – the right to a basic home or home-like space is again an obvious example, at least in the conventional understanding[52] – other property types may delimit this authority.

Even these non-Blackstonian property types typically involve *some* authority over nonowners since the indispensability of *some* owner authority derives from the irreducible property–autonomy nexus. But insofar as *these* property types are concerned, the authority of owners need not, and often should not, be particularly exacting.

Regarding these property types, and especially where nonowners' access to the resource at hand counts for their own self-determination, owners' dominion should be qualified, as it often is, including by ensuring entry rights to other (and other categories of) people. Concerning most property types (especially commercial ones), Felix Cohen rightly pointed out that private property is often subject to limitations and obligations, and "the real problems we have to deal with are problems of degree, problems too infinitely intricate for simple panacea solutions."[53]

Limits on nonowners' deference to owners' authority are quite prevalent in property law. I have no pretense to cover all these doctrines in this chapter and focus instead on three examples that are best understood as instances of relational justice. Other manifestations include, for example, the right to access beaches, the right to roam, the implied warranty of habitability, and copyright's fair use doctrine.[54] My first two examples – the law of public accommodations and the law of fair housing – limit the right of individual or group property owners to exclude by, respectively, insisting that some nonowners do not physically enter their land and refusing to sell or lease it to them. The third example deals with affirmative burdens that owners assume as part of their responsibility to accommodate nonowners' self-determination.

PUBLIC ACCOMMODATIONS

1. *Veteran Property Type.* Public accommodations law is one of the most persistent doctrines of land law in the Anglo-American tradition. At its core is the instance of the common innkeeper, whose premises "have been subjected from time immemorial to special rules" prescribing a duty "to receive and provide lodging in his inn for *all* comers who are travelers."[55] In the United States, as Joseph Singer's meticulous research reveals, the scope of this common law doctrine has been the subject of some curious historical developments.

Before the Civil War, such a broad duty to serve the public probably applied to "all businesses open to the public." But later, "when the right to access was explicitly extended for the first time to African-Americans," this duty was deliberately cut back so that only innkeepers and common carriers were obligated, while other public places were entitled "to exclude patrons on the basis of race."[56]

The current state of the law, as Singer further elucidates, is also somewhat puzzling. In some jurisdictions, the applicable statutory materials do not cover the entire array of either public accommodations or invidious discrimination. Some statutes do not explicitly prohibit race discrimination in retail stores, while others do not cover gender discrimination, and only one state has openly announced a common law doctrine whereby "all places open to the public have an obligation to serve people who enter their establishments unless they have a good reason not to do so." Nevertheless, Singer's suggestion that the normative DNA of public accommodations law implies that "businesses open to the public [do] have a duty to serve the public without unjust discrimination"[57] is persuasive.

2. *Relational Justice.* Such a general right to entry is a straightforward entailment of property's relational justice, though obviously this right is subject to the owner's authority to prescribe reasonable rules of conduct appropriate to the purpose of the premises at hand.[58] Nonowners' right to enter public accommodations is firmly grounded not only in a public law prescription of antidiscrimination, but also in the very normative commitments that underlie the"public accommodations" property type.

Public accommodations law applies to privately owned places that are deliberately open to the public. This feature surely affects the possible infiltration of public law norms into the regulation of such private properties.[59] But it is also – more in keeping with my current purposes – relevant to the appropriate construction of the property type at hand. It implies the right to entry, given its significant implications for the autonomy of potential entrants and the attenuated consequences of its recognition for the autonomy of public accommodations' owners.

An unqualified right to exclude from public accommodations would have detrimental effects on other people's self-determination. In contemporary society, the ability to physically enter such places is a precondition for accessing many social and economic opportunities crucial for personal development.[60] Moreover, and in some sense more fundamentally, an owner who prevents people from entering a restaurant, hotel, theater, or shopping mall because of who they are deeply disrespects, and indeed undermines, their self-determination.[61] Therefore, liberal property law, committed as it is to relational justice, cannot authorize such exclusion.

An unqualified right to exclude would undoubtedly have strengthened the independence of public accommodations' owners, but is hardly justified given the nature of the resource at hand. The personhood value of property easily explains the difference between ownership of a hotel or a retail store and ownership of a home. Our home is one of our quintessential constitutive resources. Its direct contribution to self-determination implies that it should be a priori shielded from regulation.[62] By contrast, commercial businesses are typically held purely instrumentally by their owners, which are frequently corporations. Insofar as these public accommodations are concerned, the personhood value of property seems indifferent to a legal prescription of nonowners' right to entry.

3. *Hard Cases?* Some "mom and pop stores" that reflect their owners' prejudices, and some similar and potentially much larger businesses of owners who refuse to subscribe to the conventional understanding of the commercial sphere in instrumental terms, appear to be more difficult. These cases seem to generate "a standoff from the perspective of personhood."[63] At least where the owner's refusal to engage relies on sincere objections grounded in his or her own (say religious) conception of the good, both parties seem to raise strong claims of self-determination. Three features of property's commitment to relational justice nonetheless explain why limiting owners' right to exclude is justified even in this type of cases.

The first feature is the rule of law considerations that circumscribe, as noted, the reach of property's demands to relational justice. Indeed, one reason antidiscrimination laws include a list of *categories* is that this method allows both owners and others to ascertain and assess precisely what accommodation requires. Historically, these antidiscrimination laws can be described as the state commandeering private individuals into the service of correcting past societal failures. The enumeration technique of contemporary antidiscrimination law, however, can and should be understood as law's means to a *more* inclusive commitment to the demands of relational justice. For this reason, and in appropriate cases, both legislatures and judges should be able to add new categories to it. (I discuss the role of judges in the development of property law in Chapter 6.)

Even more notably, in line with my general observations regarding the inherent limitations of introducing the prescriptions of relational justice into law, consider how legal duties of inclusion interact with human agency. Rules of accommodation purport to furnish duty holders mandatory reasons for action. As Dorfman explains, a critical distance exists between the normative grounds of a given reason and the motivation for conforming with its demands. This gap between reason and motivation, which is particularly important within the domain of legality in a liberal society,[64] delimits the ambition of property law to give owners a reason to act in ways respectful of others. A liberal law only compels owners (and other persons, of course) to act in conformity with this demand rather than because of it.[65]

Finally, and most crucially, recall that relational justice constrains the class of choices and conceptions of the good that can legitimately require interpersonal respect only to those that recognize others' equal status. When facing the challenge of reconciling the autonomy-enhancing role of private authority with the autonomy-based injunction of relational justice, therefore, a liberal property system can easily dismiss the personhood claims of a public accommodation owner if they reflect prejudices that deny others' equal standing.

4. *Objection.* Dorfman, who coauthored much of this chapter, criticizes this account and outlines an alternative approach. His critique is premised on a sharp divide between bigotry and authentic religious persuasion that, in his view, disrupts the justifications just mentioned. His account relies on a distinction between cases where property rules are formative of the human interaction and those where they are merely incidental. Where property rules are constitutive and law "opens up a category of human interaction in and around resources that could not have been formed prior to it," private discrimination is categorically prohibited because a liberal state must not *empower* interpersonal relationships of subjection. By contrast, where property law "merely supervenes on preexisting social ties," a liberal law should accommodate "religiously-grounded refusals to interact with others" even if, by *allowing* owners to rely on their property rights, it *facilitates* such a refusal.[66]

I resist both prongs of this argument. First, I find the formation/facilitation distinction unsatisfactory. I am less troubled by borderline

Fair Housing

cases, which Dorfman acknowledges, than by the distinction itself. According to this distinction, as long as the type of interaction at issue "*can* arise" independently of the owner's status as such, his reliance on his ownership is deemed incidental.[67] This approach not only sets an unacceptably low threshold that tends to naturalize social frameworks often legally constructed but is also objectionable given property's justificatory challenge.

A liberal law, as Chapter 3 indicated, must not instantiate a property regime that sanctions violations of reciprocal respect for self-determination. I fail to see why the fact that relationships of subjection *could* have occurred based on the parties' preexisting social ties legitimizes a law that "only" facilitates or aggravates such subjection. Even if property law's normative powers are not strictly required for such subjection to develop, their (ab)use in this way cannot legitimately be authorized. A liberal law must not add power to acts of relational injustice.

Nor do I see a difference between the uneducated bigot and the misguided but sincere religious believer. As Dorfman himself argues,[68] a liberal law should focus on action and reasons for action rather than on the actors' motivations. Property law must not facilitate relational injustices even (or is it especially?) when they are based on an authentic denial of others' equal right to self-determination.[69]

Finally, Dorfman uses the example of freedom of speech as evidence that "legal authorization need not implicate the law or the state in endorsing or approving the authorized behavior."[70] But the analogy of property to freedom of speech is dubious. Recall that, unlike free speech, property is essentially a power-conferring legal institution, as shown in Chapters 2 and 3. Property, therefore, cannot be justified as our innate rights are, and law's involvement in property law is qualitatively different from its involvement in the doctrines of duty-imposing institutions. Law's constitutive role in property law implies that it cannot abdicate its responsibility for any of its consequences.

FAIR HOUSING

1. *Refusals to Sell or Lease.* Public accommodations law, I have just argued, reflects more than a good public policy and follows the

interpersonal injunctions of a liberal law encapsulated in the notion of relational justice. The law responds to the two mundane truisms that motivate the commitment to relational justice: people's interdependence and their personal differences. It is one thing for the state to respect its constituents as free and equal individuals and quite another to live in a society that expects individuals to comply with the ideal of just relationships between free and equal agents. Similar convictions underlie modern fair housing laws.

In contemporary society, a residential dwelling is the paradigm of a person's safe haven. The home is a bastion of individual independence, shielding us from the demands of others and from the power of public authorities, while providing us with an almost sacrosanct private sphere that is a prerequisite for our personal development and autonomy. Concomitantly, decisions about inclusion (and thus also exclusion) regarding residential dwellings are taken to express friendship or intimacy, whose value resists legal regulation. Thus, while it may be unethical for an owner to refuse to let another into her home on grounds of religious objection, property law defends the owner's right to do so and conceptualizes such behavior as the inevitable result of our residential practices.

But ownership of a residential dwelling includes other normative powers that do not affect the owners' privacy, intimacy, or friendships and, therefore, do not exclude law's commitment to relational justice. Suppose that A is interested in selling or leasing his dwelling but refuses to accept B as a buyer (or lessee) only because of B's religious persuasion. Or suppose that B wishes to purchase A's unit in a common-interest development but the board withholds its consent to the sale on racial grounds.

Because buying or leasing a dwelling implies the fact of our interdependence, they expose certain classes of people to discrimination by some homeowners and landlords. The law justifiably interferes by insisting that these interactions be consistent with the demands of relational justice. Deciding on one's residence is often a major act of self-authorship that also plays an important role in other significant aspects of people's life, such as their work or their children's education. The requirement that the parties treat each other as substantively free and equal individuals does not undermine the point of these residential practices.

Fair Housing

2. *Convoluted Explanations.* Advocates of the dominion conception of property have some difficulty in fully capturing the indisputable objection to these discriminatory practices. They can show that, even if property law is founded on a thin commitment to independence and formal equality, there may be circumstances that justify stripping owners of their entitlement to exclude potential buyers. This is the case when not enough housing opportunities are available to non-owners. Allowing owners to make their selling or renting decisions based on discriminatory considerations would then make nonowners "fully subject" to these owners' choices.[71] Since private owners and landlords neither exhaust nor control the supply of residential dwellings, however, discriminatory practices on the part of owners and landlords do not, in principle, *necessarily* entail a state of dependence on the part of nonowners.[72]

Alternatively, proponents of the dominion conception of property suggest that duties of accommodation and antidiscrimination in the commercial sphere are justified because commercial sellers should be understood as *quasi*-state actors.[73] This view may be plausible if narrowly applied to commercial actors providing essential services and forming local monopolies, such as the early modern common carrier[74] or today's utility companies and dominant actors of the platform economy. It fails, however, when extended to all other commercial actors. Neither the corner café owner discussed earlier nor a local real estate developer is in any important sense a state actor or public servant, not even a *quasi* one.[75]

Many critics of the public–private distinction and scholars indifferent to it (e. g., lawyer-economists) reach surprisingly similar, and unsurprisingly disappointing, conclusions. These scholars are bound to treat the identity of the agent responsible for eliminating discrimination in selling or renting residential dwellings solely as an issue of institutional design. For them, what matters is that, at the retail level, members of groups that are discriminated against enjoy fair equality of opportunity in buying or renting the dwellings they prefer, and at the wholesale level, that residential dwellings be sufficiently integrative.[76]

3. *Relational Justice.* For relational justice, by contrast, the prohibition against obvious discrimination by private owners is not contingent on how the state carries out its responsibility for eliminating all forms of

injustice in the context of residential dwellings. Refusing to consider would-be buyers on discriminatory grounds fails to respect them on their own terms and does not treat them as free and equal individuals.

Relationally just terms of interaction between persons engaging in the context of buying or renting residential dwellings mandate that owners and landlords set aside certain considerations, such as their racist preferences, when making selling or renting decisions. Relational justice requires that would-be buyers should not bear the consequences of adverse assumptions that owners make about them based on personal qualities they actually possess (or are even perceived[77] as possessing).[78]

Regardless of whether the state supplies sufficient housing options while sustaining integrative residential communities, property law must not leave intact – and thereby authorize – social relationships that violate the equal standing and the autonomy of the person subject to discrimination. The imperative to establish relationally just terms of interaction among persons buying or renting residential dwellings cannot be sidestepped. Fair housing legislation implements this prescription by prohibiting discrimination in the sale or lease of residential dwellings based on such considerations as race, gender, language, nationality, religion, disability, familial status, and sexual orientation.[79]

The scope and contents of the accommodation duties incumbent on owners in connection with the selling or leasing of residential dwellings are partially set by reference to contextual considerations.[80] Thus, when the leasing entails cohousing (of landlord and tenant), the internal logic of the practice of residential dwelling exempts owners from accommodative duties. The Fair Housing Act's exceptions for single families and small owner-occupied multiple-unit dwellings seem to rely on this rationale but, arguably, overextend it.[81]

The irreducible relational injustice of discriminatory selling and leasing practices highlights the difficulty that plagues the famous case of *Shelley v. Kraemer*.[82] By deciding that judicial enforcement of racially restrictive covenants is unconstitutional because it implicates courts in endorsing racial discrimination, the Supreme Court seems to suggest that racial covenants are not void, meaning they can be enforced privately.[83]

Racial covenants, however, do not only violate the Fourteenth Amendment's Equal Protection Clause, which expresses the vertical dimension of substantive equality – the dimension that captures the relationship between the state (acting through the courts) and the persons excluded by such covenants. They are also an obvious violation of liberal property's relational justice. Therefore, even the most strictly law-abiding citizen, who follows the law without *any* consideration of potential sanctions for noncompliance,[84] need not – indeed must not – grant any weight to a racially restrictive covenant.

Private owners should refrain from resorting to considerations such as racist preferences not only in order to support the state's effort to comply with its duty toward potential victims of discrimination. The commitment of liberal property to relational justice offers a free-standing distinctive justification for this demand, which neither fulfills nor supplants the state's obligation to curb discrimination in the housing market. Racially restrictive covenants, therefore, should be deemed void per se, irrespective of whether their enforcement is pursued through the courts.

Understanding the free-standing grounds of this relational justice prescription is particularly important when the collective goal of social integration is making strides. Thus, reports show a decline in residential segregation, which would significantly destabilize some aspects of the fair housing regime that rely on its integration rationale.[85] Even if these reports are confirmed, however, appreciating the significance of the other, relational, rationale of a fair housing regime vindicates its continuous importance.[86]

OWNERS' RESPONSIBILITIES

1. *Uncontroversial Responsibilities.* Finally, consider my third example of property's relational justice – owners' responsibilities. Reference to the special responsibility often entailed by property is not a particularly surprising claim. Even arguing that responsibility accompanies land ownership is not really controversial, at least since Tony

Honoré's classic description of the incidents of ownership.[87] In some cases, this responsibility imposes constraints on landowners as to what they can do with their property, especially regarding uses that threaten or hinder the quality of life of others (e.g., their neighbors).[88] In other cases, at the focus of Chapter 8, landowners bear an uncompensated disproportionate share of the burden entailed by public actions designed to enhance communal well-being.[89]

Both types of owners' responsibility play a role when assessing the gap between the portrayal of ownership as "sole and despotic" and its actual legal manifestations, though neither necessarily challenges the subtler, Kantian view of property. Negative duties or constraints are trite in the Kantian system of rights. Acting "in a way that is characteristically damaging" is an obvious wrong, so the nuisance duty to refrain from "interfering with another's ordinary use and enjoyment of his or her land" is easily justifiable.[90] Likewise, contributing to the background regime of the state (and also, arguably, the local community) does not necessarily offend the Kantian architecture of interpersonal independence and, as shown, is indeed one of its constitutive components.

2. The Misfeasance–Nonfeasance Distinction. Yet, there is one subset of owners' responsibilities that Kantian property must reject and the autonomy-based conception of property happily embraces. Reciprocal respect for independence implies that the distinction between misfeasance and nonfeasance is the signature of private law, its organizing normative idea that, therefore, should be strictly observed.[91] A sharp misfeasance–nonfeasance distinction vindicates the maxim "a person acts at her own peril," suggesting that nonowners bear the entire risk of making mistakes with respect to others' property.[92] As long as owners have not caused this risk, they bear no affirmative responsibility for minimizing it.

The misfeasance–nonfeasance distinction is indeed relevant to any liberal legal system – and thus to our private law, and more specifically our property law – but only up to a point. Unlike its Kantian interpretation, this distinction does not require that we should discard *every* responsibility to affirmatively serve people's self-determination. Private law, like law generally, is cautious about affirmative interpersonal

Owners' Responsibilities

duties to aid others, in part because they may excessively interfere with people's autonomy[93] (and also because imposing a rescue obligation may dilute the ethical value of altruism while, pragmatically, drawing lines between easy and hard cases may be difficult[94]). Placing limits through a negative duty on a person's course of action is typically less intrusive on that person's autonomy than dictating – through an affirmative duty – what that course of action should be.

This understanding of the intuitive bite of the misfeasance–nonfeasance distinction does *not* imply that people should not bear duties to aid others. Rather, it implies that, whether in specific situations or in general and all else being equal, when deciding on people's moral and legal responsibility to aid others, considerations of autonomy can be more weighty. This constraint means that affirmative interpersonal duties must address the self-determination of both parties to an interaction. Again, the actual workings of property law manifest the type of "Hartian" qualitative judgments needed to accommodate private authority and relational justice.[95]

3. *Property and Easy Rescue.* Thus, property law singles out categories of cases where the responsibility placed on duty-bearers infringes on their independence but does *not* gravely jeopardize their self-determination. It discards a regime of *caveat emptor*, which limits the responsibility of vendors and landlords to the negative duties enshrined in the traditional doctrines of misrepresentation and concealment, instantiating instead an affirmative duty to disclose.[96] Property law likewise rejects the view that owners bear no responsibility for guiding nonowners in the fulfillment of their tort duty (such as the duty against committing trespass to land or chattels).[97] The reverse is true: doctrines of consent, mistake, and proprietary estoppel, as well as burdens arising from registration or recordation law, encapsulate affirmative duties and burdens incumbent on owners to give clear and reasonable notice to nonowners in order to reduce some accidental mistakes.[98]

These and other – think, for example, adverse possession or innocent accession doctrines[99] – carefully limited burdens are justified. They all derive from the owners' obligation to accommodate nonowners' self-determination and do not unduly impinge on owners' independence. Rather than merely adhering to the thin conception of freedom as independence and thus strictly limiting property's role to vindicating each individual's right to noninterference, property law duly honors the right to self-determination of all parties to an interaction. And while independence can be fully vindicated with strict duties of noninterference, relational justice – grounded in our right to self-determination – may require some affirmative duties to aid others.

UNJUST PROPERTY TYPES

1. *Reconsidering Property Types.* Largely, property law complies with the obligation of reciprocal interpersonal respect for self-determination. Yet, proper recognition of this obligation requires a critical inquiry into doctrines and rules that do not. Gaps between current law and the demands of relational justice are not surprising. Not only are they a usual feature of interpretive legal theories seeking to flesh out the *implicit* normative underpinnings of legal doctrines but they also reflect that the obligation of interpersonal accommodation is rarely, if ever, the only value at stake.

The strong interdependence underlying this obligation is typically manifest in social practices composed of events, actions, and attitudes understood to exemplify, embody, or constitute a substantive good or goods. Because each such practice is supposed to be rationally conducive to the pursuit of its underlying good, it is typically informative regarding the contents of the interaction terms in the particular context.

In the easy cases that fully conform to relational justice, practices simply fine-tune the abstract injunction of relational justice. In the more challenging ones, the particular practice does not comply with the demands of relational justice, and we must then consider the existence and ultimate strength of countervailing values.

Where the legal infrastructure of a particular social practice is relationally unjust, property's architects need to decide whether the values underlying that practice defy relational justice. If they do, the practice can be abolished, reinstated despite this flaw, or, if possible, reformed by making it congruent with relational justice.

Some relationally unjust practices seem beyond rehabilitation, their repressive nature leaving no moral choice but to discard them altogether. Slavery is an obvious example of a practice indisputably undeserving of charitable transformation. But in small-scale instances of flatly illiberal social practices, the option of transformation is quite attractive, when the successful reconciliation of a social practice with the demands of relational justice can dispel a conflict of values.

2. Marital Property. Consider the history of the marital community ideal as a locus of sharing and trust. Marriage law, including marital property law, has a long, persistent, and shameful tradition of abusing this ideal to shield subordinating patriarchal structures. "When we look seriously at the distribution between husbands and wives of such critical social goods as work (paid and unpaid), power, prestige, self-esteem, opportunities for self-development, and both physical and economic security, we find socially constructed inequalities between them, right down the list."[100]

People may of course engage in many joint endeavors where equality is not necessary, as is true of many business enterprises. But conceiving marriage in these terms, with one spouse having a recognized controlling interest in the property that partially constitutes the marriage and, correspondingly, in marital decisions, would be perverse because marriage is an enterprise far more pervasive than any other. Disparity in the control of marital property moves beyond mere inequality (which an individual may voluntarily choose as a means to other ends) to subordination (which systematically denies the substance of any ends that individual may have chosen).

Some scholars have proposed a radical solution – giving up marriage altogether.[101] There are valid pragmatic reasons for resisting this option. Due to its thorough and long-term nature, marriage is one of the few relationships that can produce the communal goods of interpersonal trust, caring, and commitment. Attempts to erase marriage, therefore, are likely to be futile: people will continue to partner even in the absence of legal marriage, but will do so without the protections against subordination that law can provide.[102]

The option of transforming rather than eradicating marriage also raises a matter of principle by questioning the purported conflict between nonsubordination – an obvious component of the relational justice maxim – and the communal goods of marriage. An oppressive marriage is not only unjust, depriving the subordinated spouse of a voice and a viable option of exit and thus posing a threat to self-determination, but actually precludes the realization of intimacy, caring, commitment, emotional attachment, and self-identification.

Because "[o]ne committed and loving partner cannot unequivocally rejoice in his life with his partner if he knows that the other finds the relationship oppressive in some way,"[103] a nonegalitarian marriage deprives *both* spouses of the unique collective goods of marriage. Reforming marriage law so that it complies with the obligations of relational justice would thus also further its compliance with its communitarian DNA.

This reconstruction process requires that the marital community be bound by a commitment to nonsubordination, while adjusting doctrines governing marriage to this construction of it as an egalitarian liberal community. I have attempted to pursue this complex task elsewhere.[104] In the current context, I will only point to it as a vivid illustration of a (relatively) happy reconciliation between a nonconforming social practice and the demands of relational justice.

Marital property law also highlights the contribution of a legal regime to unacceptable governance practices of domination and oppression. No decent property law, and certainly not one grounded in liberal property's commitment to self-determination, should ever allow itself to be used as a means for proactively advancing patriarchal arrangements. Nor are other commons property arrangements, including the prevalent property type of common interest community, immune to the risk of internal oppression.[105] The relational justice pillar of liberal property implies that the legitimacy of law's support for any of these commons arrangements must depend on a minimal bill of rights for their members.[106]

3. *Between Private and Public.* Marital property law is also an instance of another challenge confronting a liberal private law – facing up to the responsibilities of the liberal state to secure distributive justice (or, for that matter, democratic citizenship and aggregate welfare).

Unjust Property Types 145

A genuinely liberal property law must abide by the maxims of private authority and of relational justice while remaining sensitive to these public concerns. As usual, no easy formula is at hand for coping with this task.

Consider the question of whether marital property law should address the issue of gender discrimination. Ostensibly, gender inequality is a public concern external to marital community and thus meriting address only in a collectivist understanding of property. Yet, gender inequality is not a problem merely for women individually but also for the institution of marriage since serious disparities between the post-divorce financial status of men and women[107] give men greater bargaining power within the marriage, raising the specter of subordination.[108]

If both spouses entered and left marriage equally able to earn an income in the market, the rule of equal property division prevalent in both community property and equitable division regimes would be perfectly consistent with egalitarian marriage. But although equal division sends a message of equal entitlement and partially neutralizes one spouse's greater market power vis-à-vis the resources of the marital community, it falls short of adequately addressing this challenge.[109] This predicament, which mainly affects heterosexual couples, suggests that the remedial response of a marital property law compliant with relational justice can, inevitably, only be imprecise – mitigating the devastating consequences of gender inequality for marriage without imposing the entire burden of it on the spouses.

The recent practice of rehabilitative alimony fulfills this role.[110] Rehabilitative alimony does not require a former spouse to equalize an ex-spouse's financial situation for the remainder of their lives. Such an arrangement would impose a prohibitive exit tax, undermining not only the autonomy of the spouses but also the community as a whole, constituted as it is (and should be) of voluntary attachments.

Rehabilitative alimony, then, expressly aims at self-sufficiency. Its purpose is merely to cover the education or training of spouses with the smaller income so as to enable them to support themselves better after the divorce.[111] These awards are inherently time-limited, restricting their impact on exit. Admittedly, rehabilitative alimony does place some of the burdens of gender discrimination on the alimony-paying spouses, but this is hardly unfair because they too benefit from the arrangement. To the extent that they desire the unique goods arising from communal marriage, they benefit from lessening the threat that gender inequality poses to genuine community. A limited alimony obligation enables them to participate in and benefit from a good marriage without unduly compromising their autonomy.[112]

4. *Hard Cases.* I do not deny that there are *really* difficult cases of genuine conflict between the demands of relational justice and the animating good of an – otherwise just – particular social practice. These hard cases involve *liberal* practices typified by a *principled* insensitivity to interpersonal accommodation.

One example relates to the reach of relational justice's injunction of nondiscrimination to social practices adopted as part of the infrastructure sustaining meaningful (say, religious or cultural) communities. Communities of this type require some demarcation from the broader society and, possibly, also a measure of practical and symbolic exclusion beyond the boundaries of the home. The duty imposed by fair housing laws to accommodate protected classes of people whose personal characteristics are the outcome of chance cannot be qualified by these specific communal concerns. Yet, intricate questions may arise regarding characteristics subject to personal choice, such as religion or familial status. These issues raise difficult normative questions leading to hard cases that can be properly determined only by reference to an overall theory of justice rather than to relational justice alone.

★ ★ ★

My topics in this and the previous chapters – carefully delineated private authority, structural pluralism, and relational justice – are the three pillars of property in a liberal polity. But my mission in this book is not yet accomplished.

A theory of property, as I argued in Chapter 2, is necessarily a *legal* theory and must therefore focus on the work of society's coercive normative institutions. Much of the analysis thus far took account of law's power and its normativity. It is now time to pay attention to the legal institutions that develop and apply property law, to study the institutional setting(s) where property's structural pluralism and its relational justice, as well as the intrinsic and instrumental values of property and its ultimate commitment to self-determination, can or should be pursued. This institutional embeddedness of property also implies that a theory of property should examine whether these tasks can be accomplished without violating the rule of law.

Finally, in a liberal democracy, property and property law are likely to be dynamic. Alienability is a hallmark of property in liberal polities, while a significant subset of the regulatory measures enacted by democratic (typically local) governments change the entitlements of property owners. These dynamic aspects of it require students of property to account for the justice of the market and to question the proper regime for addressing legal transitions.

6 MAKING PROPERTY LAW

Making property law means more than identifying a legitimate and substantively appealing conception of property. It also requires answering three further (and somewhat related) questions. First, what are the appropriate institution(s) for creating, interpreting, and developing property law (the institutional question)? Second, to what extent can a legal system that embraces the liberal conception of property also comply with the rule of law? Third, what are the limits (if any) of the authority of property law's architects?

A comprehensive institutional analysis of property exceeds the scope of this chapter and may necessitate access to social scientific tools that I lack. It requires attention to the relative strengths and weaknesses of varied institutions in applying and evaluating different kinds of considerations as well as to the putative bases of their respective legitimacy. In performing this task, one should consider the particular institutional setup of diverse jurisdictions (by subnational unit or across countries) as well as potentially helpful overlaps and crossovers, and explore the impact that interest groups and sociocultural associations may have on different institutions. One should furthermore be mindful of the implications entailed by the institutional characteristics of the enforcers of property rights for the question at stake.

My goals in what follows are more limited: to demonstrate the relevance of my substantive theory of property to these inquiries and to draw some preliminary conclusions regarding the liberal theory of property developed in the previous chapters.

With respect to the first question, I argue that, subject to a few exceptions dealing with general limitations of judge-made law, an autonomy-based account of property allows judges to play an important and legitimate role in the development of property law. With regard to the second question, I contend that a structurally pluralistic property regime whose development is guided by an autonomy-enhancing *telos* is unlikely to violate the rule of law. Finally, insofar as the third question is concerned, I claim that a liberal theory of property may justify treating property as a human right. This status, I further contend, implies that the very core, minimal requirements of property's relational justice should serve as a premise for criticizing domestic rules and as the foundation of aggrieved parties' standing vis-à-vis those who wronged them.

PROPERTY'S CORE AND THE INSTITUTIONAL QUESTION

Thomas Merrill and Henry Smith's discussion of the *numerus clausus* principle is the most important account for drawing the connection between the core of property and the institutional question, that is, who or what should make property law.[1] Merrill and Smith argue that the *numerus clausus* captures a deep feature of property. As a principle of "judicial conservatism regarding innovation in the system of property rights," it implies that property is by essence less amenable to judge-made law than the rest of private law. Appreciating this principle's rationale may well require judges, in their view, to altogether avoid the business of affecting – creating, modifying, or abolishing – property rights, leaving this task entirely to legislatures.

To see why, recall Merrill and Smith's claim mentioned in Chapter 4, stating that the regulation of property as a fixed menu of options aims at reducing the communication costs of third parties who need to determine the attributes of these rights (both to avoid violating them and to acquire them from present owners). This account finds the distinctive features of property in its effects on "classes of individuals who fall outside the zone of privity."

Merrill and Smith argue that legislation holds significant comparative advantages over adjudication in communicating information to third parties. In particular, two characteristics of adjudication render it an "inhospitable forum" for creating or modifying property rights, and thus justify channeling parties interested in such changes to the legislature.[2]

First, whereas common law rules need to be extracted from a complex body of case law, legislated rules "are set forth in a canonical text which is easy to identify and usually terse," making them clearer and thus cheaper to grasp. Second, whereas decisional rules evolve incrementally and resolve questions regarding such issues as their scope and precise effects as they arise in the adjudicated cases, legislation tends to deal comprehensively and with lesser frequency with the multiple questions evoked by any innovation. This, again, economizes the gathering of needed information.

Merrill and Smith argue that these comparative advantages of legislation over adjudication are significant enough to override the public choice problems of "the legislative process emphasized by supporters of common-law courts," which they find to be less significant "in the context of reforming property regimes [than] elsewhere."

Clarity and comprehensiveness are indeed important features of legislation and they affect the system's communication costs. However, as indicated, the standardization of property captured by the *numerus clausus* principle cannot be justified by the concern of communication costs.[3] Accordingly, communication costs cannot justify a sharp preference for legislative rule-making in property matters.

That said, Merrill and Smith's more fundamental insight, that property's standardization generates an important lesson to the institutional question, is nonetheless crucial. Standardization is a critical characteristic of property, and it is indeed informative to investigate the institutional question against this particular feature of property law.

Property's standardization does play an indispensable role in creating and sustaining important default frameworks of interpersonal interaction with respect to resources that consolidate people's expectations. Liberal property's commitment to such structural pluralism explains and justifies *numerus clausus* as a principle of *legal* conservatism and, as I noted in Chapter 4, structural pluralism requires some degree of legal stability. But this foundation of property's standardization implies that *numerus clausus* is not a blueprint for a priori judicial abstinence: it does not make the required conservatism of the judiciary conceptually or qualitatively different from that of the legislature.

An inquiry into the proper division of labor between the legislature and the judiciary concerning property rule-making requires, instead, a comparison of their expected *performances* in accomplishing the task incumbent on liberal property – developing a repertoire of just interpersonal interaction frameworks. It further requires examining the *democratic legitimacy* of their doing so. The following analysis of these questions is admittedly partial since it is not informed by any empirical (and thus necessarily contingent) data on either institution.[4] But even the idealized pictures of lawmaking I refer to are nonetheless informative because they serve as benchmarks, which affect the pertinent actors' understanding of their role as well as the expectations of their professional groups and the public at large.[5]

PERFORMANCE

1. *Stability versus Stagnation.* Property's structural pluralism and, even more fundamentally, its core function as a tool of autonomy-enhancing planning, account for the typical stability and conservatism of property. Property lawyers should surely be cautious not to engage in a "blind imitation of the past" by upholding doctrines whose "grounds have vanished."[6] However, structural pluralism's reliance on stability implies that they should appreciate the added value of adherence to tradition in property matters, even beyond the more general value of following legal tradition.

The restraint imposed by the virtues of stable expectations and effective transmission of the various animating principles underlying our property types is important but by no means unique to judges. Rather, to the extent that the character of property justifies an attitude of forbearance and temperateness, this approach should guide judges and legislators alike.

Restraint is not synonymous with stagnation. Expectations can be stable even if rules are not frozen in time, as long as the rules are not revisited too frequently.[7] The proper frequency must also be affected by the pace of other developments, for instance in technology, pertinent to the property type at hand. Equally, and to avoid the risk of romanticizing the law, we must not be overly deferential to its existing doctrine. Both the normative principles underlying existing property types and law's means for their instantiation should therefore be challenged and, occasionally, properly reexamined.

2. *The Growth of (Property) Law.* Property law has indeed evolved throughout its history. New property types have emerged (consider equitable servitudes, common-interest communities, and various types of intellectual property), old types have been marginalized and at times vanished (such as the fee tail[8]), and many others have been modified. In some cases, the reform of a given property type has been relatively radical (as was the case with leaseholds[9] and marital property[10]). Sometimes, more moderate options seemed in order, such as restating the doctrine pertaining to a property type in a way that brings its rules closer to its underlying commitments (one example here is the *Restatement of Servitudes*[11]).

Both legislatures and courts were involved in these developments. If property's narrative is about developing stable frameworks of just interpersonal relationships regarding resources, as it should be in a liberal polity, it is hard to justify excluding judges from lawmaking. The reason is that, in the liberal conception of property, the creation and modification of property types often is, or at least should be, triggered by challenges bearing on the desirability of the normative underpinnings of property types, their responsiveness to their social context, or their effectiveness in promoting their contextually examined normative goals.

3. *Legislation and Common Law.* Challenging property law to live up to our property types' animating principles, or to shape these or new types in a way that promotes other worthy goals, can definitely come from the legislature. But why discount the possibility or the desirability that such challenges might come about via the adjudicatory process? In fact, at least given the virtues of what Karl Llewellyn, an astute student of the common law tradition, described as its "Grand Style" – the "functioning harmonization of vision with tradition, of continuity with growth, of machinery with purpose, of measure with need," mediating between "the seeming commands of the authorities and the felt demands of justice"[12] – adjudication is a perfectly appropriate forum for developing property law.

Llewellyn was wary of romanticizing law's carriers but also careful not to fall into the trap of cynicism. He acknowledged that "distortion to wrong ends [and] abuse for profit or favor" are part of the life of the law. But he also understood that these are always deemed to be disruptions, which are "desperately bad." And against them, there is "in every 'legal' structure ... [an implicit] recognition of duty to make good." This demand of justification is not just "an ethical demand upon the system (though it is [also] that)." Rather, it is "an element conceived to be always and strongly present in urge," one that cannot be "negated by the most cynical egocentric who ever ran" the legal system.[13]

Thus, inherent dynamism runs alongside the case law system's "demand for moderate consistency, for reasonable regularity, for ongoing conscientious effort at integration." This dynamism, triggered in moments of property law's "paradigm shifts,"[14] represents a perennial quest "for better and best law" – a relentless "re-examination and reworking of the heritage." Judges have a "duty to justice and adjustment," which means the "on-going production and improvement of rules."[15]

In the common law tradition, judges face this duty in a distinctive institutional setting, typified by the procedural characteristics of the adversary process and by the professional norms that bind judicial opinions, notably the requirement of a universalizable justification. These characteristics encourage judges to develop what Felix Cohen terms "a many-perspective view of the world" that "can relieve us of the endless anarchy of one-eyed vision," a "synoptic vision" that is "a distinguishing mark of liberal civilization."[16]

Moreover, because adjudication is always situated in a specific human context, judges have constant and (relatively) close access to human situations. This feature of adjudication is the flip side of the legislative comprehensiveness emphasized by Merrill and Smith. This contextuality of judicial encounters with abstract principles of justice, Herman Oliphant observed, serves as an "alert sense of actuality" that "checks our reveries in theory." It provides judges with "the illumination which only immediacy affords and the judiciousness which reality alone can induce," and it encourages them to shape law "close and contemporary" to the human problems with which they deal.[17]

To clarify: as Llewellyn explained, the claim is *not* that "the equities or sense of the particular case or the particular parties" is determinative.[18] Rather, the idea is that judges develop the law while "testing it against life-wisdom," benefitting from "the sense and reason of some significantly seen *type* of life-situation."[19] Therefore, if the development of property law indeed is (as I claim it should be) an ongoing dialogue about our property types, aimed at their reconstruction along the lines of the autonomy-enhancing trio of carefully delineated private authority, structural pluralism, and relational justice, this unique feature of adjudication must count as a significant comparative advantage.[20]

4. *Limits of Adjudication.* None of this implies that there are no functional difficulties with judicial property lawmaking or that there are no limitations to its proper domain. But these problems are not unique to property or particularly acute in property matters, nor do they apply across the board of property law. Without attempting to be exhaustive, it seems safe to mention three significant categories of cases limited to particular subsets of property doctrines in which judicial caution is warranted. They are premised on three familiar and general limitations of judicial competence:

a. At least in its conventional rendition, adjudication does not involve the creation of complex and elaborate regulatory schemes that may at times be required in order to create or to modify a property type. Legislation is required, for example, for the creation of a formal registration of property rights,[21] as well as for the establishment of administrative agencies, such as the Office of Fair Housing and Equal Opportunity, which may be needed for ensuring the sustained compliance of a property type with the requirements of relational justice.[22]

b. Contexts requiring specialized knowledge and expertise, such as innovative technologies or complex market ramifications, may call for judicial deference to governmental agencies equipped with such technical expertise.[23] Similarly, in certain contexts, the task of prescribing the governance regime of a property type or the specific obligations that ownership entails requires complicated, and at times not fully principled, determinations of both line-drawing and detail. This is why some of these rules are products of adjudication while others were enacted by legislatures and regulatory agencies often after the common law has set a vague standard, which legislators and regulators are better suited to implement.[24]

c. Finally, some modifications, such as the annulment of an existing property type, generate widespread excessive redistribution so that their retroactive application, as the common law usually applies, is inappropriate.[25] Certain cases are obviously exceptions, as when people's reliance on the preexisting system was illegitimate given that system's violation of property's own justificatory premise: slave-owners' reliance was indeed unworthy of legal protection.[26] In other cases, however, the fact that legislatures can and typically do apply their norms prospectively and, moreover, can provide explicit or implicit compensation or set up other ameliorating means for the transition period, such as grandfather clauses,[27] may count as a significant reason for judicial caution.

LEGITIMACY

1. *Comparative and Contextual Analysis.* When judged from the viewpoint of comparative performance, then, property seems quite amenable to judicial development, subject to its general conservative tilt and to the three local qualifications just mentioned. But this functional analysis can only provide a partial defense for judicial engagement in the shaping of our property types. A full defense requires a parallel analysis of the liberal ideas of political legitimation.[28]

I obviously do not challenge the legitimacy of legislatures taking part in the development of property law. They should refine and enrich our repertoire of default frameworks for interpersonal relations because, at least in a democracy, these elected institutions are, or are generally presumed to be, "well suited to represent the multiple interests involved in ... property law, and to reach compromises when necessary."[29] (I deliberately qualify this statement, anticipating the last sections of this chapter.) This simple proposition requires significant judicial deference in contexts of newly enacted legislation,[30] and legitimizes legislative responses to judicial activism in other contexts.

As with expected performance, however, the legitimacy of judicial activism in property must be addressed in comparative terms and without assuming that the legislature's authority necessarily implies the exclusion of the judiciary. Unless this dichotomy is simply stipulated, this question of legitimacy must be carefully and contextually examined.[31]

Thus, one need not reject the significance of public deliberation in the pursuit of the common good highlighted by the supporters of deliberative democracy[32] in order to appreciate that such deliberation is both impossible and undesirable across the broad range of public decisions,[33] especially since, even if we are content with the deliberations of elected representatives, their intensity and quality are not uniform across the board.

To determine the proper domain of judicial creation and modification of property types, if any, we need to examine the potential bases for the democratic legitimacy of judicial rule-making in property matters. Though I could not possibly hope to provide an adequate account of democratic legitimacy here, the following remarks should suffice to support the claim that the legitimate scope for judicial rule-making in property is in fact rather broad.[34]

2. *Coauthorship.* Consider first the notion that state power can be legitimate only if it is a product coauthored by the citizens. As noted, the ideal of coauthoring property law must not be axiomatically attached only to the legislative process.[35] Rather, a commitment to citizens' coauthorship requires a comparative account of meaningful participation and deliberation in legislation and in adjudication. This account can either look at the participation of the citizens directly or via elected representatives, or focus on the participation of the subset of citizens who are most likely to be affected by the property law development at hand.

In general, participation and deliberation will more likely be found in legislation than in adjudication because lawmaking is legislation's only task, whereas in adjudication it emerges as part of the resolution of discrete disputes.[36] But the broad or representative participation that

Legitimacy 157

might significantly foster collective coauthorship does not seem typical in legislation on property matters.

Thus, some property doctrines, such as the law of co-ownership or of common-interest communities, may seem too mundane a subject for real democratic deliberation.[37] By contrast, where the creation or modification of property types provides significant opportunities for rent seeking, as in the repeated extensions of the term and scope of copyright, the legislative process tends to be dominated by interest groups promoting narrow distributive goals,[38] and thus cannot meaningfully count as collective coauthorship.

It is more realistic to expect participation by the parties directly affected by the proposed development of property law. But insofar as this participation is concerned, adjudication fares quite well and in some contexts better than legislation. The adjudicatory adversarial process fares well because, as noted, it invites disagreements on questions of facts, opinion, and law. It thereby creates a forum where the judges' normative and empirical horizons are constantly challenged by the participating parties' conflicting perspectives, which present a microcosm of the social dilemma at hand.[39]

Moreover, as Neil Komesar shows regarding tort law, at times adjudication seems to provide a qualitatively better forum for the participation of affected parties. One instance are cases where there is a sharp "distinction between *ex ante* and *ex post* stakes," so that the low ex ante probability of harm may obscure an important perspective rendered vivid in the ex post litigation triggered by the unfortunate realization of such harm.[40] Certain important developments of property types such as marital property, cohabitation, and leaseholds by the judiciary may also fit well into this category.

3. *Accountability.* But legitimacy should perhaps require only decision makers' accountability rather than citizens' participation. Accountability is a more modest standard: it does not require active participation or deliberation but merely insists that decision makers be responsive to citizens' values and preferences.

As with participation, the accountability requirement may in the abstract appear as a trump card favoring elected legislators over unelected judges, given that reelection is a rather potent incentive for responsiveness. But my previous observations regarding skewed participation in property matters detrimentally affect legislators' responsiveness as well. If a property matter is either politically marginal or dominated by interest groups, the legislators' expected responsiveness is likely to be rather limited. Moreover, why simply dismiss the possibility that judges can be responsive?

As Llewellyn insisted, in their opinions, judges need to "account to the public, to the general law-consumer" on a regular basis and in detail; they must persuade not only their brethren but also the legal community, including losing counsel, "that outcome, underpinning, and workmanship are worthy" and that their judgment was formed "in terms of the Whole, *seen whole*."[41] While real-life adjudication surely falls short of these ideals, having these standards in place is nonetheless significant because it affects judges' utility function and thus informs judicial behavior, as even the tough-minded portrayals of judges as maximizers of their utility function admit.[42]

4. *Easy Cases*. Finally, recall that liberal property is structurally pluralistic and that it allows a broad realm of freedom of contract.[43] This means that, while certain developments of liberal property law generate additional obligations on people,[44] others do not. The previous paragraphs aimed to address the legitimacy challenge posed by the former category but should not obscure the latter group of cases. In these cases – where the development of property law generates additional frameworks of interpersonal interaction that enrich the repertoire of available options open to tailor-made adjustments, or where it weakens third-party obligations vis-à-vis the status quo, and where freedom of contract implies that people can avoid law's prescriptions – judicial activism in property seems particularly innocuous.[45]

BOTH LEGISLATURES AND COURTS

The creation of new property types and the modification of existing ones are major events in the development of our social frameworks of interpersonal interaction. They shape and reshape our social order, adjusting it to new circumstances, challenges, and opportunities.

In a democracy, legislatures have an important role to play in such developments. In certain contexts – as where a property innovation requires a regulatory structure, depends on specialized knowledge available elsewhere, or involves excessive widespread redistribution – judges should generally avoid taking part in this drama. They should likewise be significantly deferential regarding newly enacted property legislation.

But these qualifications of judicial authority are not unique to property, and other than them (or parallel ones I may have failed to mention), there seem to be no good reasons, either from expected performance or from legitimacy, for a heightened degree of judicial passivity in property matters. Judges must respect property's stability, but so must legislators. Still, when appropriate, both legislators and judges should utilize their distinct comparative advantages in order to create new property types and to modify existing ones so as to enrich and refine our repertoire of default frameworks of just interpersonal relations.[46]

PROPERTY AND THE RULE OF LAW

Property law, I have argued thus far, is composed of a heterogeneous set of property types. By facilitating a diverse inventory of property types, property law participates in the liberal state's obligation to empower people to make choices among viable alternatives, and thus be the authors of their own lives. One implication of this aspirational nature of liberal property is that the various property types are subject to ongoing normative reevaluation and possible, if properly cautious, reconfiguration. They are thereby forced to adhere to their autonomy-enhancing promise as frameworks of just interpersonal interactions. This is a happy account of property. But does it comply with the rule of law despite its multiplicity and dynamism?

Henry Smith argues that it does not; indeed, that it cannot. A structurally pluralistic conception of property, he claims, can hardly be distinguished from the bundle understanding of property and both irreparably undermine stability.[47]

Smith contends that stability is not "yet another detachable feature or lever to be dialled up or down" or "a factor to be balanced whenever we are deciding on the supposedly separable sticks in the bundle." Rather, stability is "a feature that can only be evaluated as an aspect of the system." And while it may be important for the system to serve "values like community, autonomy, efficiency, personhood, labor, and distributive justice," we must reject the idea "that doctrines are part of an issue-by-issue balancing of [these values]."[48] Whereas Smith has focused his critique on my account of structural pluralism, similar criticism has been launched against my claim that relational justice plays a critical role in property (and private law more generally).[49]

For Smith, the only alternative to the dominion understanding of property is "to invoke a plethora of general principles to be balanced as specific situations present themselves." And given that "ad hocery itself is not a feature that can easily be dialled down," he concludes that nothing separates my account of property from the understanding of property as "an ad hoc, unstructured bundle."[50]

Smith argues that the objection of legal realists like me to defining exclusion as property's baseline is misguided because it downplays and may undermine the important function of concepts as "mental shortcuts," which are relatively indifferent to context and can thus reduce information costs and uphold the overall architecture of property. Rejecting the dominion conception of property, he therefore suggests, might substitute rigidity with "near-chaos." Only the presumption of exclusion, Smith concludes, can assure that we keep the bundles "lumpy" and "opaque" and avoid "hard-to-predict ripple effects through the entire system."[51]

This critique must be taken seriously. The conception of property as a formless bundle of sticks open to ad hoc judicial adjustments does not, as I repeatedly noted, accurately represent property law. Furthermore, and more significantly for this chapter, if an autonomy-based conception of property necessarily collapses into such unstable nominalism, it also undermines the two key aspects of the rule of law: the requirement that the law be capable of guiding its subjects' behavior, and the prescription that law may not confer on officials the right to exercise unconstrained power.[52]

Bundles should, as Smith argues, remain "lumpy," and ad hoc "issue-by-issue balancing" should indeed be avoided. But these justified prescriptions do not undermine (or challenge) the liberal conception of property, which neither requires nor should imply adopting the dubious nominalist approach to adjudication that indeed undermines law's guidance. Quite the contrary: because property types are supposed to consolidate expectations and express ideal types of interpersonal relationships, an autonomy-based property regime supports, even requires, that our (properly narrow) property types be relatively stable and internally coherent.

This means that each such property type is governed by fairly precise rules alongside informative standards founded on the animating principles of these types, enabling people to predict the consequences of future contingencies and to plan their lives accordingly. The plurality of property values makes the molding of property types' animating principles a challenging endeavor for both legislators and judges. But as I claim in what follows, we have no grounds for doubting that the normative contextual inquiry that typifies most common law developments defies the rule of law.

To clarify: I do not claim that no property law system would score better than an autonomy-based one in terms of guidance or constraint, but simply that a liberal property regime seems to score quite highly on both fronts. Thus, if one supports a threshold conception of the rule of law, this regime would probably pass it. Even barring such a threshold – meaning a view in which the rule of law and substantive virtues must always be balanced – the following analysis implies that adding the concerns of the rule of law is unlikely to lead to abandoning the autonomy-based regime, at least when compared with alternative (i.e., monistic) approaches to property law.[53]

GUIDANCE

Smith's critique can be recast in terms of the understanding of the rule of law (associated mostly with Joseph Raz) as the requirement that law provide people effective guidance.[54] While seemingly thin, the guidance conception of the rule of law, which is often divided into lists of formal requirements,[55] is intimately connected with people's self-authorship. By requiring that government actions be "bound by rules fixed and announced beforehand," the rule of law enables people "to foresee with fair certainty how the authority will use its coercive power in given circumstances, and to plan [their] affairs on the basis of this knowledge."[56]

Indeed, "the rule of law respects the capacity of the individuals who are subject to the law to choose and pursue pathways through life by weighing up reasons and by anticipating how the law is liable to impinge upon their potential decisions through grasping the content of legal rules."[57] Only a relatively stable and predictable law can serve as a "safe basis for individual planning," which is a prerequisite to people's ability to form definite expectations and future goals. Law's participation in securing stable "frameworks for one's life and action" increases predictability in one's environment, and thus facilitates people's "ability to choose styles and forms of life, to fix long-term goals and effectively direct one's life towards them."[58] When legal decisions are "anchored in stable general legal doctrines, made for publicly available reasons, [and] applied faithfully," people "feel at home within the framework of the law, and ... have the confidence and self-reliance to plan their life."[59]

This guidance conception is often associated with the idea that the rule of law is the law of rules,[60] namely, that law's prescriptions must be concrete and sufficiently clear and determinate to be followed "without first resolving the very normative questions [they] are designed to settle" or "considering whether the local outcome of the rule conforms to the values [they are] supposed to advance."[61] By contrast, open-ended standards that allow judges to consult law's underlying commitments in each case jeopardize this virtue of "the rule of rules."[62]

On its face, the normative dynamism of an autonomy-enhancing property law, which invites judges to participate in property lawmaking, threatens the rule of law as guidance. As Frederick Schauer argues in his critique of the common law tradition, if normative commitments can always upset existing doctrinal propositions or require that they be discarded or modified, the doctrine is incapable of constraining its application and can no longer serve as behavioral guideline.[63]

But Schauer is mistaken. To explain his and Smith's error, I need to unpack some of my early propositions in Chapter 2 as per the way liberal property accommodates stability (in its times of "normal science") and growth (in "paradigm shifts" moments).[64] An example of property's growth can demonstrate why, properly interpreted, the liberal conception of property conforms to the rule of law prescription of guidance. This liberal conception also fits property's preference for rule-based decision-making insofar as this preference is indeed justified (which, as will be shown, it not always is).

THE BIRTH OF COMMON-INTEREST COMMUNITIES

Neponsit Property Owners' Ass'n v. Emigrant Industrial Savings Bank[65] is the first major decision on the enforceability of the assessment covenant, whose validity at that time (1938) was in doubt.[66] This makes *Neponsit* a significant milestone in one of the most important developments of American land law in the last century: the emergence of common-interest communities, a property type that is now a major form of land ownership. *Neponsit* is the landmark decision that enlisted servitudes law into facilitating the governance of this property type.

As the New York Court of Appeals noted, *Neponsit* had unquestionably intended that the covenant assessment should run with the land. The difficulties posed by this case were elsewhere, in the "age-old essentials of a real covenant" set by "ancient rules and precedents." These rules state that "a covenant will run with the land and will be enforceable against a subsequent purchaser" if two conditions are met. First, if the covenant "is one 'touching' or 'concerning' the land with which it runs," and, second, if "there is 'privity of estate' between the promisee or party claiming the benefit of the covenant and the right to enforce it and the promisor or party who rests under the burden of the covenant."[67]

Does "an affirmative covenant to pay money for use in connection with, but not upon, the land which it is said is subject to the burden of the covenant" touch or concern the land? The "touch and concern" test developed in old English cases is, says the court, "too vague to be of much assistance." The court acknowledged that some prior cases imply that only negative covenants "which compel the covenanter to submit to some *restriction on the use* of his property, touch or concern the land" and, therefore, affirmative covenants do not run with the land. It also noted, however, that notwithstanding this seemingly bright line distinction, there are cases that enforce promises to pay money "as covenants running with the land, against subsequent holders of the land who took with notice of the covenant."[68]

A confusing state of the doctrinal landscape along these lines is indeed typical for times when conventional understandings of property doctrine, which govern property's normal science, become increasingly challenged. As my discussion in Chapter 2 implies, such pressures tend to upset the implicit sense of obviousness insiders share as per "on-the-wall" interpretations of the doctrine and invite readings of the doctrine in ways that have hitherto been "off-the-wall."[69]

Acknowledging the emerging difficulties of classifying the increasing number of exceptions and of formulating "a rigid test or definition which will be entirely satisfactory," the *Neponsit* court moves on to state "a reasonable method of approach" to such cases, namely, "a covenant which runs with the land must affect the legal relations – the advantages and the burdens – of the parties to the covenant as owners of particular parcels of land."[70]

Applying this test to the question at hand allows the court to conclude with a rather bright line rule regarding the specific issue of assessment covenants. While the payments at hand serve "public purposes" upon land other than the land conveyed to a grantee's predecessors in title, through that conveyance grantees obtain "not only title to particular lots, but an easement or right of common enjoyment with other property owners in roads, beaches, public parks or spaces and improvements in the same tract." For these property owners to fully enjoy them in common, these improvements "must be maintained." This happy outcome can be achieved only if the burden of paying this cost is "inseparably attached to the land which enjoys the benefit."[71]

The court had to pass yet another hurdle: no definition of "privity of estate" in connection with covenants that run with the land covered the relationship between a property owners' association and a subsequent purchaser. The *Neponsit* court alluded to the rather tortuous privity doctrine but refused to have its analysis defeated by the doctrine's technical details. "Only blind adherence to an ancient formula devised to meet entirely different conditions could constrain the court to hold that a corporation formed as a medium for the enjoyment of common rights of property owners" lacks standing "to enforce the covenant upon which such common rights depend." Thus, the court held that a corporate plaintiff like *Neponsit*, which "has been formed as a convenient instrument by which the property owners may advance their common interests," should be able to enforce the covenants at hand.[72]

Neponsit set bright line rules on the standing of property owners' associations and the validity of the assessment covenant. It also articulated the principle animating the doctrine of covenants, thereby serving as the springboard for the development of common-interest communities, which is the fastest growing property type in America. On both fronts, *Neponsit* demonstrates the happy cohabitation of liberal property and the guidance conception of the rule of law.

STRUCTURAL PLURALISM AND RULES

Consider first *Neponsit's* bright line rules establishing the validity of assessment covenants and the standing of homeowners' associations,[73] which were (almost literally) necessary preconditions for the subsequent flowering of common-interest communities. This simple observation attests that property's structural pluralism can, and indeed should, distance itself from the dubious nominalist approach of case-by-case adjudication.

Property's structural pluralism – or, for that matter, its relational justice – neither requires nor implies focusing on the equities of the particular case or parties. Nor should it imply rule-sensitive particularism, the approach that allows judges to depart from rules whenever the outcome of a case so requires, while accounting for both substantive values and the preservation of the rule's integrity.[74]

Property's structural pluralism does not suggest substituting clear rules with open-ended discretionary decision-making. Instead, it stands for the proposition that reasoning about property rules should involve reasoning about the property type at hand and not about property writ large. Given that the number of property types is limited and the role of the property values that inform their animating principles is confined to law's more deliberative moments – most dramatically the moments of property's "paradigm shifts" – we need not assume that property's structural pluralism cannot be rule-based.[75]

Furthermore, to perform their autonomy-enhancing function in consolidating expectations and expressing ideals of interpersonal relationships, our property types *must* be relatively stable and predictable. This means that property's structural pluralism is not only capable of setting bright line rules but in fact, if properly executed, is inclined to do so.

Indeed, the property values of independence, personhood, community, and utility, as well as property's fundamental commitments to (carefully delineated) private authority and relational justice, neither are nor should be invoked as reasons for outcomes of specific property cases but rather as reasons for property rules or (informative) standards.

Respecting property's stability implies that the moments of property's growth should not be too frequent, and that the potential detrimental implications of destabilizing property law should always be considered. In between paradigm shifts, "on the wall" or routine interpretations of the doctrine are properly taken for granted. But certain legal actors (legislatures *and* judges) should, in these more reflective moments, take these values – the normative infrastructure of our property types and of property law as a whole – as integral to their legal analysis. These moments of "jurisprudence of ends" invite a critical examination of the continued validity and desirability not only of a property type's constitutive rules, but also of its animating principle and, at times, of the menu of property types as a whole.[76]

INFORMATIVE STANDARDS

Besides prescribing rules regarding the validity of assessment covenants and the standing of homeowners' associations, *Neponsit* transformed the doctrinal analysis of covenants more generally. *Neponsit* criticized the technical nuances of the doctrines of touch and concern and of privity. Admittedly, it did not overrule their complex requirements. Nevertheless, it paved the way for their substitution with more substantive elements that focus on the role of covenants in landowners' endeavors to pre-regulate their relationships in their capacity[77] as members of a common-interest community. This reconstruction recruits the law of covenants to the mission of facilitating landowners' common enjoyment of certain improvements and advancing their common interests.[78] Both the critical and the reconstructive sides of this part of *Neponsit* are relevant for my purposes.

In criticizing the confusion of covenant law's preexisting doctrinal rules, the *Neponsit* court reminds us that, at times, a complex set of rules may not serve as an adequate guide for action. Regulating a wide range of conduct is complicated, and an attempt to do so with bright line rules at times generates technical nonintuitive complexity. Such complexity, in turn, could undermine the guidance value of rules, especially where its subtleties are detached from any reasonable understanding of the animating principle that can plausibly govern the pertinent area of the law.[79] In such circumstances (and *Neponsit*'s reconstructive side comes into play here), commitment to the rule of law implies allowing, or even preferring that the conventional understanding of a legal doctrine be formed around a somewhat vague but nonetheless informative standard.[80]

The reason for this preference is that a guidance-friendly standard enables its addressees (or their lawyers) to figure out its intended content and thus to predict future effects and possible applications. They can then monitor or modify their behavior accordingly.[81] Standards that refine the animating principle governing a specific doctrine along these lines – informative standards, as I call them – are therefore generally unobjectionable, and often welcome. By contrast, open-ended references to justice, fairness, good faith, or reasonableness, as these are interpreted by the presiding law applier given the specific circumstances of the case at hand, fail to ensure predictability. They should therefore generally be objected to as an invitation to ad hoc discretion, which affronts the rule of law,[82] or else interpreted as a source of more specific rules and informative standards.[83]

Neponsit's focus on the role of covenants in facilitating landowners' ability to enjoy the potential benefits of common-interest communities is a good example of an informative standard. By refining the animating principle of an emerging property type and making it sufficiently stable (meaning it is not revisited so frequently as to make law incapable of guiding behavior), such an informative standard can facilitate the gradual creation of more bright line rules that implement its prescriptions. Furthermore, entrenching such an informative standard may culminate in the doctrine's conventional understanding – its "on-the-wall" interpretations – which helps legal subjects (or, typically, their lawyers) to anticipate the content of this property type and its realm of application.[84]

Hence, where bright line rules cannot adequately serve as a guide for action, structural pluralism is likely to be *more* predictable than its monistic counterpart due to its use of multiple and relatively small categories. These categories – or property types – are sufficiently distinct from one another and internally coherent, meaning each one is generally guided by one animating principle: one property value or specific balance of values. Such animating principles are robust enough to function as informative standards, which can credibly guide people's expectations.

This comforting conclusion is particularly valid when compared to the alternative presented by property monism, involving recourse to the principles underlying property law as a whole that, given its deep heterogeneity, are inevitably thin and thus hardly informative.[85] (Think about the profound indeterminacy of the proposition that, "generally," property implies the owner's sole and despotic dominion but, at times, this dominion is "properly" curtailed due to "regulatory" or "public policy" countervailing concerns.[86])

CONSTRAINT

In line with the actual legacy of American legal realism (as opposed to some of its extreme voices),[87] the potential dynamics of a liberal property law and its commitments to structural pluralism and relational justice do not undermine law's stability. The predictability of

Constraint

property law (like that of law more generally) follows from the social practice of law[88] – namely, the conventional understanding of the doctrine, not the blackletter law as such – and is served rather than impeded by property's structural pluralism.

This conclusion, however happy it is in terms of guidance, may still seem alarming in terms of another understanding of the rule of law. The conception of the rule of law discussed so far has focused on the subjects of law and their guidance, whereas the conception of the rule of law as constraint, to which I now turn, focuses on the government.[89]

Consider the notion that the rule of law is the flip side of the rule of man. As Albert Venn Dicey maintained, a literal interpretation of this maxim is "absurd" because political institutions "are made what they are by human voluntary agency." A more substantive understanding of this contrast, however, implying that the rule of law stands for "the absence of arbitrary power on the part of the government," is meaningful.[90]

Unrestrained power is objectionable, both because of its potentially devastating burdens and because it renders us mere objects, dominated by the power-wielder.[91] The rule of law addresses these grave concerns by imposing "effective inhibitions upon power and the defense of the citizen from power's all-intrusive claims."[92]

As Jeremy Waldron explains, the rule of law as a constraint stands for an aspirational idea, wherein law must be guided by "justice and the common good that transcend the self-interest of the powerful." Its main mission, therefore, is "to correct abuses of power"[93] and to "take the edge off human political power, making it less objectionable, less dangerous, more benign and more respectful."[94]

Accordingly, the rule of law requires "a particular mode of the exercise of political power: governance through law." It thus maintains that "people in positions of authority should exercise their power within a constraining framework of public norms, rather than on the basis of their own preferences, their own ideology, or their own individual sense of right and wrong."[95]

In a sense, insofar as liberal property follows the guidance aspect of the rule of law, it also addresses the concerns of unconstrained judicial power, because the requirement to identify and articulate a general norm imparts *some* element of impersonality.[96] But if there are no further constraints on judges' discretion when they rethink the constitutive rules and informative standards of a property type, the rule of law would still be in jeopardy.[97] Unbridled judicial discretion invites subjective or self-serving "normative" preferences.[98] It therefore poses "the specter of the usurpation of power by an unaccountable elite," misrepresenting political decisions "as if they were matters of law," and thus making "the rule of law ideal ... a fraud."[99]

This is, of course, a concern that informs many critiques of judge-made law and thus of the common law tradition.[100] As such, it requires a sophisticated articulation of the idea of law and the distinctive features that set it apart from politics, notwithstanding the profound indeterminacy of pure doctrinalism. I have analyzed this at length elsewhere[101] and hinted at it earlier in this chapter when discussing the legitimacy of judge-made property law and will not return to it here. Instead, I will again use an example from the law of common-interest communities to demonstrate the constraints that an autonomy-based conception of property imposes on (good faith) judges in their infrequent deliberations about property's paradigm shifts.

REVISITING *SHELLEY* V. *KRAEMER*

In *Shelley v. Kraemer*, the Supreme Court held that judicial enforcement of racially restrictive covenants is an exercise of state action that violates the Fourteenth Amendment.[102] *Shelley* and the legislation that followed it embedded the antidiscrimination norm in the DNA of the law governing sale or rental of residential dwellings. It is hard to think of a liberal property regime that can doubt the validity of this prescription.

Recall, however, that the decision in *Shelley* did not refer to any property reasoning (a feature I criticized in Chapter 5[103]). In fact, as Carol Rose argued, *Shelley*'s reasoning also poses "a 'state action' enigma" because both prior and later decisions show that the bare potential for judicial enforcement of private arrangements does not transform them into state action.[104]

Rose's solution to this puzzle seems to me unsatisfactory.[105] But her more general claim that *Shelley* presents "some of the best instincts of property law" is precise.[106] *Shelley*'s invocation of a right to fair housing need not be understood as an external limitation or qualification of the owner's exclusionary prerogative but as an internal entailment of the right to property in common-interest communities.

At least partly, this was also seemingly the premise in *Noble v. Alley*, *Shelley*'s Canadian twin, when it invalidated racially restrictive covenants because they referred to the identity of users/owners rather than to any actual use of the pertinent land.[107] Not only is this reasoning from within property, but it also (implicitly) relies on the DNA of the property type of covenants as a means to facilitate landowners' ability to commonly enjoy the benefits of private land use controls. Understanding covenants in these terms makes reference to the *identity* of ostensibly users/owners suspicious.

From the perspective of liberal property, *Noble* is an easy case, which is overdetermined by property's most fundamental features. *Noble* is a straightforward application of liberal property's relational justice, as the discussion of fair housing in Chapter 5 demonstrates. *Noble*'s conclusion also coheres with the animating principle of common-interest communities, which *Neponsit* refined. Its holding is grounded in the very reasons and the very property values that justify law's support of this property type.

Thus, thinking about common-interest communities as a property type aiming to foster the community value of property and conceptualizing covenants along the lines of the animating principle identified in *Neponsit*, vindicates *Noble*'s property-based reasoning. This perspective sanctions exclusionary practices of residential communities only in limited circumstances. It implies that, in general,[108] limits on entry are authorized if, but only if, they are necessary to exclude "bad cooperators," who are likely to jeopardize the success of the commons property.[109] This means that courts need to supervise the criteria for admission to such communities and how they are actually implemented. One implication of this prescription is that rejections of applicants for admission must be reasoned, and the reasons should be sufficiently detailed so that both their factual and evaluative components can be properly scrutinized.[110]

Indeed, when the analysis of a property type (such as a common-interest community) is informed by its animating principle that, in turn, is examined by reference to property's ultimate commitment to self-determination and thus to its prescription of relational justice, it is not wholly open-ended. Here, as elsewhere, the requirement to explicitly apply "Hartian" judgment, which needs to be normatively and contextually justified, is a real constraint.[111] I do not deny that there may be hard cases where such an inquiry might lead to a standoff. Hard cases, however, can scarcely threaten our ability to use reason as the arbiter for prescribing property rules or refining the animating principle of a property type. Hard cases do not, in other words, undermine property law's determinacy or its integrity.[112]

Quite the reverse: an autonomy-based theory of property, guided as it is by the commitments to carefully delineated private authority, structural pluralism, and relational justice, generates reasonably specific property-based criteria for evaluating the law and guiding its development. The plurality of intrinsic and instrumental values involved in molding the animating principles of our property types does make this a challenging enterprise.[113] But as long as a normative contextual inquiry eliminates both unjust and arbitrary results, any remaining concern on this front is surely ameliorated by property's structural pluralism.

Moreover, as discussed in Chapter 4,[114] a structurally pluralistic property regime constrains the power of lawmakers – who, as fallible human beings, make mistakes and may prefer their self-interest to the public good – because it opens up options. By providing a rich repertoire of property types for each sphere of action and interaction, a liberal property regime allows individuals to navigate their course so that they can bypass certain legal prescriptions. This built-in mechanism, which dilutes the coercive power of property law where it complies with structural pluralism, again implies that it is in fact *more* compatible than its monistic counterpart with the rule of law as constraint.

LIBERAL PROPERTY AND THE RULE OF LAW

The compatibility of an autonomy-based property regime with the rule of law is thus ingrained in its foundational features. Its commitment to stability and predictability, given its dual mission of stabilizing expectations and expressing the principles animating our property types, together with its even more fundamental commitment to employ multiple and relatively small categories sufficiently distinct from one another and internally coherent, facilitate people's self-determination.

The commitment to stability and predictability is crucial from a rule-of-law perspective because it requires property law to employ bright-line rules whenever possible or, otherwise, resort to informative standards. The commitment to small categories is even more critical. Only small categories can plausibly rely on animating principles that are sufficiently determinate to function as informative standards, and the multiplicity of property types dilutes the power wielded by the carriers of property law, be they judges or legislatures.

Indeed, the contrast with the large heterogeneous categories advocated by friends of the dominion conception of property invites the question of whether their monism can plausibly comply with either the guidance or the constraint injunctions of the rule of law.

THE HUMAN RIGHT TO PROPERTY

1. *Universalist Foundation.* Both domestic legislatures and domestic courts (and in appropriate cases also domestic administrative agencies) thus participate, as they should, in the development of property law. In a liberal polity, however, their power is subject to some limitations. The last assignment of this chapter is to study these limitations and point out some of their repercussions (a task continued in Chapter 8). To do so, I return to the first page of this book, which mentions property's status as a human right.

To be valid and viable, property certainly requires institutional constitution, elaboration, implementation, and enforcement. But as I noted at the start[115] and hope to have established in the previous chapters, an autonomy-based system of property is not contingent in the Benthamite sense. The conventions that sustain liberal property are ones that any humanist polity *must* develop.[116]

Recall that the normative foundation of property, the ultimate premise of its legitimacy, rests on its prominent role in enabling people's self-determination and sustaining their interpersonal relations as free and equal persons. Therefore, property is not fully dependent on the state for its legitimate existence, despite the state's comparative advantages in promulgating property's conventions.[117]

2. *Neither Pre-Political nor Apolitical.* Although a human right property need not be addressed as pre-political or apolitical. In fact, liberal property emphatically rejects both these familiar but problematic positions. It does not view property as part of the natural law, which sets the baseline of the social contract and, therefore, the bounds of its legitimate demands.[118] Nor does it perceive property, as do the Kantian and Hegelian views discussed in Chapters 2 and 5, as part of an apolitical private law, pertaining to "morally self-sufficient" persons regarded "as ends outside of human association" who are thus indifferent to "common ends and member obligations even in a civil condition."[119]

Indeed, as a power-conferring convention, property can neither be pre-political nor apolitical. The human right to property cannot be about respect for autonomy's prescriptions only with regard to the legitimate *limits* of the social contract, some of its familiar treatments notwithstanding.[120] The duties of nonowners and of the polity as a whole to respect property are thus qualitatively different from the (natural?) duty incumbent on us to refrain from interfering with the external freedom of others.

Furthermore, the three pillars of liberal property – carefully delineated private authority, structural pluralism, and relational justice – all follow from the requirement that both specific others and the polity as a whole respect each person's right of self-determination. As such, these pillars do not precede our social contract but inform how it should *actively* design our horizontal and vertical interactions.[121]

3. *Not Necessarily Statist.* Political does not mean contingent or fully state-based, however. Property is not a convention *simpliciter*; it does not serve only as a solution to a recurring coordination problem, although it certainly plays this role as well. As a human right, property – or, rather, liberal property – is crucial for people's self-authorship, suggesting that it differs from other standard conventions. By enacting or developing[122] the conventions that liberal property relies on, society

empowers people "to become full agents," engaging in relationships of mutual recognition and respect. Given liberal property's potential contribution to people's autonomy, a polity committed to respect for people's dignity or normative agency – that is, to human rights – is obliged to have (or establish) such a convention.[123]

This proposition generally justifies the constitutional – or constitution-like – protection of property that characterizes liberal states (see Chapter 8), though still leaving room for legitimate variations. The state is, quite understandably, an obvious locus for promulgating the conventions that constitute law's repertoire of property types given its comparative advantages – in terms of both legitimacy and competence – in performing the necessary tasks of elaborating, implementing, and enforcing people's property rights. Even in our era of increasing transnational interconnectivity, the state is still "the most comprehensive legally-based social organization of the day."[124]

These advantages, however, do not turn property into a fundamentally state-based construct. Unlike the dominion conception of property, at least in its Kantian version,[125] the autonomy-based account of property is, at its core, non-statist.

The reasons for insisting on this characterization are only partly contingent. Contingently, confining our attention to property within specific borders is increasingly unsatisfying given the receding impact of social (as well as economic and cultural) interstate boundaries and the current globalization trends. The growing presence – in terms of quantity, intensity, and quality – of transnational interpersonal interactions justifies thinking about property (as well as about contracts and torts) as substantive concerns of transnational law.

Herein lies the conceptual and non-contingent reason for the non-statist significance of the human right to property: this right transcends the state because its normative weight is largely irrelevant to our relationship with or through the state. Property's horizontal dimension governs our interactions with others in their capacity as private individuals rather than as co-citizens.

Admittedly, even in this context, property's effective instantiation may depend on the state (given the reliance of property's legitimacy on a background regime that actively ensures distributive justice). Yet, since these interpersonal relationships are not mediated through the state and their significance is not a function of their consequences for society as a whole, property rights are not, need not, and indeed should not be tied to specific national systems.

This conclusion suggests that transnational interactions involving property rights should be subject to at least some minimal prerequisites of relational justice. This proposition, in turn, implies that the scholarly debate re the (statist or cosmopolitan) scope of distributive justice obscures the free-standing dimension of *relational* justice, which is relevant across borders even if, for the sake of the argument, our distributive obligations are statist.[126] This dimension turns neither on our role as co-participants in global institutions nor on our involvement in unjust structures.[127]

An era typified by extensive transnational interpersonal interdependence requires the recognition of some core mandatory norms of *interpersonal* human rights. This is obviously a broad claim that I have tried to defend elsewhere.[128] For my current purpose, it suffices to demonstrate its possible implications insofar as the human right to property is concerned.

THE GLOBAL LAND RUSH

Consider the recent predicament affecting members of numerous rural communities, especially in developing countries, whose reliance on access to land is threatened by transfers of land they do not hold formal title to. As one report documents, in many of these large-scale land acquisitions – the so-called land rush (or green rush) – "those who are selling or leasing land are not the ones who are actually using it," a situation often generating displacements.[129]

The formal legal regime in the transnational markets where these transfers take place allows potential buyers to accept as a given, and indeed rely on, property rights as prescribed by the host country. The reason is that the conflicts-of-law rule pertinent to land points to the *lex situs*, stipulating that title will be determined according to the law in the jurisdiction where the property is situated.[130] There is an exception to this rule, dealing with grave infringements of human rights that the courts of other countries would refuse to sanction. But the rare cases

The Global Land Rush 177

that invoked this exception dealt with deprivations of hitherto recognized property rights, such as a Nazi statute that purported to strip fleeing German Jews of their rights by annulling their German citizenship.[131]

Perceiving property as a human right highlights the inadequacy of the conventional analysis when applied to transnational encounters and their necessary reform. This reform has two aspects: substantive and structural. Substantively, it entails a different understanding of the concept of "grave infringements" of the human right to property; structurally, it implies that the obligation to respect this right is not only vertical, but also horizontal.[132]

I begin with the structural aspect, which is particularly important in the land rush context often typified by unrepresentative, indeed unaccountable, governments.[133] Because the significance of the human right to property is not limited to people's relationships in their capacity as citizens, the demand to respect the property claims of members of these rural communities is not directed merely to their governments or to courts of other jurisdictions. The legality of the vertical interactions between the buyer and the state and between the state and the displaced person cannot render redundant the horizontal dimension of interaction between the buyer and the displaced person.

The human right to property commands the unmediated respect of all the participants in the transnational practice of property. Insofar as the global land rush involves violations of this human right, "buyers" are participants in, and not merely implicated beneficiaries of, these infringements. The buyer who fails to respect the entitlement of the displaced person to control the purchased land violates an interpersonal human right and thus commits a transnational private wrong.

But how could these land transactions constitute violations of the right in question? They may not count as rights violations as long as private international law defers to domestic property rules, save for cases of outrageous expropriations mentioned above. This regime, however, is inadequate because it fails to respect the horizontal dimension of the human right to property and because this right is attacked not only in cases showing excessive deprivation of recognized property rights.

Thus, the human right to property in its liberal conception is also undermined if a state's property system fails to recognize people's claims in ways flatly inconsistent with property's normative foundations. This dimension is obscured by the conventional understanding of the human right to property.

By contrast, the liberal conception of property, founded on self-determination, implies that this human right can also be violated by omission, namely, by a failure to recognize such a right even where such recognition is mandated. In some cases, then, such as the rural communities affected by the land rush, although land users may lack formal title, their claims to private authority over the land are sufficiently backed by the most foundational property values. These claims must therefore be recognized and secured before any other measure of economic development is adopted.[134] Failure to do so should be deemed an arbitrary deprivation of the human right to property. Although this implication of the liberal conception of property is yet to be recognized, the emerging international soft law on these issues does fortunately provide some support for it.[135]

★ ★ ★

The outer boundaries of the legitimate authority exerted by any domestic lawmaking body regarding property necessarily rely on our understanding of property as a human right. Insofar as the transnational context is concerned, this inquiry is clearly in its early stages and the last few pages should accordingly be read more as an invitation to a dialogue than as its conclusion.[136] Research on this very same question in the constitutional context is, by contrast, already rich and sophisticated, deserving the more elaborate discussion and more definitive conclusions that Chapter 8 is devoted to. Before I address the perennial question of property in transition, however, I need to study the implications of property's embeddedness in the market.

7 JUST MARKETS

Property and markets are not fully intertwined. Although one cannot think about the idea of a market without thinking about property – property, after all, is one of the market's foundational building blocks – it is possible to think about property without thinking about markets. Still, *liberal* property and markets are so deeply connected that a liberal theory of property cannot ignore the market. A liberal theory of property must explain how property can remain loyal to its liberal commitments in the context of large-scale economies heavily reliant on the operation of markets.

This challenge is particularly acute regarding market relationships where what is sold is labor rather than goods. Property is a – if not *the* – major source of many autonomy-reducing features of existing labor markets.[1] In the workplace, the power of owners threatens the autonomy of nonowners because "[c]laims for worker voice are seen as antithetical to" the management's "power to govern," purportedly "conferred by the employer's ownership of the means of production."[2] In the established view of the employment contract, this power to govern entails a hierarchical structure of subordination that "requires obedience on the part of the employee to the employer's lawful instructions."[3]

The significance of work to people's life therefore implies that property's legitimacy, or at least desirability, depends on refashioning labor markets so that the employers' ownership of the means of production does not undermine the workers' self-determination. The convoluted relationship between property and labor suggests that one cannot address the justice of property without attending to the operation of the labor market.

In this chapter, I aim to sketch the liberal vision of a just market, specifically, a just labor market.[4] This task appears possible in light of one of the main lessons of Chapter 3, stating that, in an autonomy-based property law, the private authority of owners of means of production – and thus the scope of legitimate managerial power – should be carefully delimited.[5] This lesson can also be derived from analogous implications of the liberal theory of contract law that I have developed elsewhere.[6]

My discussion of labor markets does not explore all the implications of an autonomy-based reconstruction of the relationships between workers and their employers, who own the means of production.[7] Nevertheless, it does show that the prevailing "worker-protective legal framework for employment relations" need not be defended only by principles exogenous to liberal property and liberal contract.[8] Many of these rules, rather than external constraints, are principled entailments of a proper understanding of the liberal ideas of property and contract, and thus of the market. The current legal framework has many shortcomings, some of them quite blatant, and these liberal conceptions do not quickly yield blueprints for overcoming them, but I still hope to demonstrate that taking these conceptions as foundational does hold promise.

This attempt requires to define what a market is and to refine the relationship between property and markets. Only then can I show that liberal property can retain its essential characteristics in a large-scale, market-based economy if, but only if, it complies with the requirements of just liberal markets. Meeting these (rather exacting) requirements is important not only for its own sake but also because focusing on labor markets helps to refine our understanding of liberal property itself. Although both goods and services can be traded in the market, an autonomy-based conception of the market should – and indeed can – ensure that the commodification of human labor does not blur the line between selling one's property and employing oneself in the service of another person.[9]

WHAT IS A MARKET?

1. *Pre-theoretical Definition.* Markets are complex social institutions heavily dependent on, if not strictly constituted by, a thick legal

infrastructure. In the various forms they assume, markets play a key role in domestic and transnational interactions. The contemporary omnipresence of markets may account for their tendency to attract both enthusiastic advocates and zealous critics. Indeed, much of the literature on the morality of the market mirrors the conflicting attitudes reflected in Albert Hirschman's famous dichotomy of the *doux-commerce* and self-destruction theses, either celebrating or denouncing the market.[10] I have no pretense to summarize or evaluate this voluminous literature here, let alone the multifaceted reality it analyzes.

My current objective is more modest. Refining understanding of the relationship between property and the market and then clarifying how (or under what conditions) markets can serve rather than hinder the autonomy-based commitments of liberal property theory, needs at least a rough account of what a market is. This seemingly simple question, however, turns out to be quite tricky.

Some accounts of the market are built around a model of an ideal market, a strategy that often makes sense. Given their assumption that markets aim to maximize efficiency, it is reasonable for economists to (explicitly or implicitly) treat the perfectly competitive market, typified by perfect information, full rationality, and no transaction costs, as the ideal market.[11] By contrast, an account highlighting the moral virtues that markets tend to inculcate would opt for a picture of the ideal market as revolving around the institutionalization of civilized exchange among strangers.[12]

Given my task in this chapter, I cannot follow this strategy and, instead, need to resort to a broader and less judgmental (meaning pretheoretical) account, articulating the common properties of the heterogeneous trading activities we typically call markets. Therefore, I begin with John O'Neill's definition of markets as "social and institutional arrangements through which goods [or services] are regularly produced for, distributed by and subject to contractual forms of exchange in which money and property rights over goods [or entitlements regarding services] are transferred between agents."[13]

2. *Markets and Law.* As this definition clarifies, markets are robust infrastructures that enable systemic, repeatable acts of exchange. For markets to function, property rights and modes of their legitimate

transfer need to be defined and respected, and contracts honored and enforced. For markets to go beyond barter exchanges, they also need to rely on a common, accepted, liquid currency, namely, money (widely understood as any generic means of exchange).

Property, contracts, and money play key roles in the constitution of contemporary markets. Without implying that markets cannot exist without law – law-like social conventions can, and have, facilitated markets[14] – this simple observation does mean that, where law exists, its prescriptions provide at least some of the foundations of the market.[15] Indeed, appreciating the heavy reliance of markets on law (especially at present) denotes that, as property theory is a species of legal theory (as I claim in Chapter 2), so is a theory of the market. It also explains why the claim that, absent market failures, law should refrain from intervening in the market is conceptually confused.[16]

3. *Voluntary Exchange.* O'Neill's definition emphasizes that markets institutionalize specific types of transactions. Market transactions are voluntary undertakings and they are "two-way transfers, leaving no doubts about reciprocity or future payments (unlike one-way transfers such as gifts, which may or may not carry an implicit duty to reciprocate)."[17]

Both of these features point to core characteristics of the market. The voluntariness of market transactions indicates that "[m]arkets call up our power as individual decision makers who can veto as well as sign on to exchanges, and they give scope to the exercise of these powers."[18] The distinction between a market and a gift exchange suggests that, while the latter "aims to realize a shared good in the relationship itself," the former – exchange through market transaction – focuses on realizing "distinct goods for each party."[19]

4. *Markets' Heterogeneity.* Markets' focus on voluntary exchanges will occupy much of the following discussion.[20] At this stage, the exclusion of gift exchanges from the definition of markets deserves closer examination. Some scholars, including O'Neill, learn from this exclusion that "market relations are essentially impersonal."[21] Elizabeth Anderson's influential account of the "norms structuring market relations" goes even further. These norms, Anderson claims, "embody the economic ideal of freedom: they are impersonal, egoistic,

exclusive, want-regarding, and oriented to 'exit' rather than 'voice'."[22] Some markets are indeed characterized by several of these traits, but my definition of the market does not view any of them as part of the market's essence.

The role that Anderson's definition plays in her account resembles that of an ideally efficient or virtuous market in the accounts I started with. Because she highlights the dangers of market imperialism, Anderson focuses on market interactions as different as possible from other types of interactions. For my purposes, however, her definition is again unduly restrictive. As William Jackson notes, beside markets of impersonal trading "such that sellers and buyers compete anonymously and aim only to obtain the best available price," often "traders take part in relational exchange": they "develop personal relationships going beyond their impersonal roles" and thus "no longer respond to price alone." Therefore, there is no reason to assign anonymous trading a privileged status in "a 'marketness' scale."[23]

Indeed, markets are complex phenomena with many manifestations. They involve different types of goods and services and can be structured around different property and contract types. This heterogeneity justifies a cautious attitude toward definitions of the market and also counsels some suspicion of overly broad normative judgments of them, be they celebratory or critical. Indeed, to anticipate what will follow in this chapter, it suggests that Lisa Herzog might be correct when she claims that current instantiations of the market are not inevitable and markets can in fact be "more supportive of individual autonomy and personal growth."[24]

PROPERTY AND MARKETS

Let me turn to my second preliminary inquiry, touching on the connection between property and markets. The previous section spelled out the role that property – and thus property law – plays (alongside contract and money) in the constitution of any market. Now, I need to look at the reverse side of this relationship and explain why the current entanglement of property and markets is not wholly fortuitous. The simple reason is that liberal property tends to be alienable, and thus also divisible. There are valid reasons for limiting alienability as well as divisibility, but in a liberal property system, inalienablility is the exception, not the rule.

James Penner holds it need not be so.[25] Whereas the right to give is conceptually inherent in ownership, he argues, the right to sell is not because "gratuitous sharing and giving" are "entailed by the right of exclusive use [since] when we give something to someone, we treat the use of the donee *as our own use*." Selling is different, he claims, because "in general I could not care less what a contractual transferee does with the property he receives from me in an exchange, since his use does not implicate any of my interests."[26]

Penner's view of alienability relies on his specific genre of exclusion theory, in which "the right to property is a right to exclude others from things which is grounded by the interest we have in the use of things."[27] My reference to it here is not meant to reiterate my critique of exclusion theory (or to question Penner's sharp dichotomy between gift and exchange[28]). For my purposes, what matters in Penner's provocative view, stating that property and contract create "completely different realm[s] of human interaction,"[29] is that it is such an outlier.

Indeed, Tony Honoré's inclusion of the power to alienate, specifically the power to sell (and mortgage) as a typical – even canonical – incident of "the 'liberal' concept of 'full' individual ownership,"[30] is quite consensual.[31] "The ability to transfer" is, in this conventional wisdom, one of property's "most important attributes."[32] As such, it is mentioned as almost a matter of course in the statutory references to the rights of owners – be it of chattels, patents, copyright, trademarks, publicity rights, and goodwill – as well as in rights to oil, gas, minerals, water, and timber.[33]

Admittedly, some property rights can neither be sold nor given away,[34] and others can be given away, but not sold.[35] Liberal systems do not necessarily attach unlimited power to alienate to property rights, and I return to some of these limitations toward the end of this chapter, but these are widely understood as exceptions to the rule.[36] In liberal polities, the shift from being an owner to being a transferor is obvious. It is no coincidence that the "emergence of the modern system of private property" is "often described as a steady march toward free alienability, with the fetters of feudalism removed slowly over the centuries."[37]

Alienability typifies ownership in our time, when property systems are dynamic. For liberal property, founded on a commitment to self-authorship, this dynamism is not contingent.[38] For property to live up to its promise of empowerment, it cannot be static. The right to self-authorship requires a right to discard one story and begin another. Without alienation, "persons would be trapped in and determined by their property."[39]

Although property and contract are distinct legal categories, the connection between their liberal conceptions is particularly strong, as noted in Chapter 2. Both liberal property and liberal contract are founded on an autonomy-enhancing *telos*, and both serve as frameworks for a respectful interaction conducive to self-determination.

Property, then, is not only a constitutive building block of the market deeply affected by its operation. What follows from the autonomy-enhancing *telos* common to liberal property and liberal contract is that a liberal property law is also likely to opt for market arrangements, as per O'Neill's definition discussed earlier.

Markets are potentially conducive to people's self-determination because alienating resources and entitlements enables geographic, social, familial, professional, and political mobility, which is often a prerequisite for meaningful autonomy. Markets are also central to self-authorship because they facilitate people's ability to legitimately enlist one another in the pursuit of private goals and purposes, both material and social, thus enhancing their ability to be the authors of their own lives.

AUTONOMY-BASED MARKETS?

In the next section, I will attempt to show how markets, when properly configured and calibrated, can contribute to our freedom along these two lines. Before proceeding, however, I need to differentiate between the autonomy-based view and two other approaches more frequently associated with markets. Critics like Herzog indeed aspire to reconfigure the market precisely because of the current predominance of these competing conceptions. Furthermore, I need to clarify that even an autonomy-based market is insufficient to support autonomy and may, moreover, entail some autonomy-reducing consequences. Just like property, then, for markets to be legitimate, they require a supportive background regime.

1. *Markets for Welfare.* One of the two conceptions of the market I will *not* be defending is most frequently tied to welfarist commitments. The *telos* of the market, in this view, is to maximize utility. Eric Posner and Glen Weyl, for example, argue that the market economy is the only game in town because "the market is the appropriate [social design] to achieve the greatest good for the greatest number." Its systemic superiority in allocating resources efficiently lies not only in Frederick Hayek's celebrated account of the market's ability to "obtain information about people's tastes and productivity ... and supply it to those who needed to know it, without the involvement of a government planning board." An even more fundamental comparative advantage of the market, as Ludwig von Mises argued, is that it "miraculously cuts through" the otherwise "computational nightmare" confronting any system seeking to achieve allocative efficiency. As Posner and Weyl explain, the market is "programmed" to allocate resources efficiently by elegantly harnessing and combining the "distributed human computational capacity." In this sense, the market is similar to "a giant computer composed of these smaller but still very powerful computers."[40]

Markets certainly serve goals such as efficiently allocating resources and entitlements (as well as rewarding desert, inculcating virtues, and spreading power). But a liberal polity, committed as it must be to individual autonomy as its ultimate value, cannot accept welfare maximization as the market's normative *foundation*. As I argued in Chapter 3, though typically endorsing utility as an instrumental value, a genuinely liberal law of the market renounces welfare foundationalism.[41]

In fact, it is not clear whether welfarism is fully committed to the idea of the market. If exchange and competition are wholly subservient to an ultimate *welfarist* goal of optimizing allocative efficiency, it is possible to envision (as Posner and Weyl do) the replacement of markets with a more efficient mode of economic organization.

Autonomy-Based Markets?

Indeed, once people's preferences can be deducted from data about their behavior or their physical and psychological attributes, their choices may no longer be necessary. By the time the total capacity of digital computers surpasses that of human minds (c. 2050), the market's welfarist function of harnessing the power of individual human minds could (and from a welfarist perspective probably should) be replaced by machines. Digital computers will be able to learn "the statistical patterns in human behavior [and] use this information to distribute goods (and jobs) as well as, or possibly better than, people can choose goods (and jobs) themselves."[42]

Analyzing the human (or is it post-human?) predicament under the rule of "big data" is unnecessary for my purposes. The key issue here is: if the preferences revealed through people's operations in the market are merely tools for implementing the market's program of allocating entitlements so as to achieve the greatest good for the greatest number, the market may well become unnecessary.

As such, welfarism's contingent support for the market is not necessarily disappointing. The deeper problem is that it ends up undermining the very reasons that justify caring about satisfying people's preferences and promoting their welfare in the first place, that is, the role of these preferences in people's life plans and the way social welfare can serve their self-determination.[43]

A liberal theory of the market celebrates the potential contribution of efficient markets to self-determination – its help in fulfilling people's preferences and expanding the resources available for their various goals – without losing sight of welfare's subservience to autonomy. Welfare foundationalism is objectionable because it ends up throwing out the baby with the bathwater: people are not data points of preferences or joint carriers of the aggregate social welfare. They are agents with projects entitled to govern their own lives.[44] The market cannot plausibly be justified by welfare foundationalism.

2. Markets for Negative Liberty. The second prevalent conception of the market does not devalue human freedom so bluntly. According to this understanding, markets should be founded on *negative* liberty. Most freedom-based advocates of markets indeed refer to it as freedom *from* the interference of others, whether individuals or the state, possibly explaining the frequent association between libertarianism and "free market" advocacy.

Many have criticized the claim or, more often, the implicit presupposition that markets can be free in *this* way by accentuating how markets depend upon the power of law.[45] My observations regarding the legal foundations of the market[46] follow a somewhat refined version of this critique, and I will not attempt to rehabilitate the libertarian, or "neoliberal," understanding of the market.[47]

Indeed, the account of a liberal market outlined in this chapter is diametrically opposed to the one acclaimed by libertarians. Understanding contract and property as empowering devices places self-determination, not negative liberty, at the market's moral core. The possibility of an autonomy-based conception of the market explains why Herzog rightly insists that, although there is "so much that is wrong with today's markets," we should not give up hope of improving this flawed reality since markets can become "something different from what they are today."[48]

Nothing in my following claims concerning the market's role in enabling mobility and expanding options should thus be read as suggesting that market formations will *always* facilitate, enable, or even secure people's self-determination, or that markets – even in their best possible form – are sufficient for the task. Indeed, my claims in Chapter 3 regarding the preconditions for the legitimacy of the legal instantiation of property[49] apply to markets as well.

3. *Autonomy as the Market's Telos.* If markets are to serve self-authorship, the expanded choice afforded by the market must rely on and be guided – and at times be limited – by its autonomy-enhancing *telos*. This chapter is largely dedicated to unpacking this prescription by exploring the proper architecture of the genuinely liberal market – studying how it can, and should, be shaped so as to optimally serve self-determination.

Understanding the market as a means for self-determination also implies that markets cannot function well as a stand-alone autonomy-enhancing device. A liberal polity enlisting markets in the service of self-determination should thus be committed to the creation of a background regime that secures the social and economic conditions (or capabilities) enabling individuals to be self-determining. This prescription, which I have already discussed with respect to property, is particularly urgent due to some (unfortunately inherent) harsh consequences of the market's operations, beyond the externalities generated by specific market interactions.

Consider, for example, changes in supply or demand triggered by technological transformations, which may leave very few options to workers possessing skills that have become obsolete. More generally, consider the market's dependence not only on people's preferences but also on their ability to pay, as well as the role that both luck and misfortune play in its operations. Markets, then, often generate consequences diverging from their autonomy-enhancing end goal.[50]

These consequences can be quite significant, portending the introduction of new patterns of hierarchical relations antithetical to the market's own (autonomy-enhancing) ideal. Therefore, they must be treated as unfortunate (even if inherent) pathological effects of the market.[51] Because these effects often cannot be properly addressed within the law of the market, they need to be remedied by the background regime, which thus becomes essential to the market's legitimacy or, at least, to its normative desirability.

TWO ROLES

Keeping these caveats in mind, it is now time to point out how, in two main ways, markets are potentially conducive to people's autonomy. First, they allow individuals the mobility that is a prerequisite for self-determination, and second, they expand the options available to individuals to function as the authors of their own lives. In these two roles, markets contribute *directly* to self-authorship and, as noted, efficient markets may also make an *indirect* contribution by virtue of their welfarist implications.

1. *Mobility*. Markets enable mobility through the alienation of resources and entitlements. The possibility of liquidating one's holdings enables exit, thus making people's right to withdraw from or refuse further engagement with others meaningful. Exit serves a protective function because leaving is a form of self-defense, and the mere

possibility of exit plays a disciplinary function. But even if possible mistreatment is not a concern, exit is essential to autonomy because it enables the substantial market mobility crucial to a self-directed life.[52]

This mobility of the market is famously contrasted with social relationships of servility. As Adam Smith (as well as John Stuart Mill and Karl Marx) argued, markets substitute fixed status and command with flexible relations based on interest, persuasion, and consent. They thereby undermine hierarchies where loyalty is taken for granted and need not be enlisted and accounted for. The market can thus liberate individuals from predetermined roles and social positions, releasing them from excessive dependence on the authority of others.[53]

Some critics of the choices that markets open up present them as a postmodern identity game, where people playfully slip off commitments to other persons and projects and move on to others just as easily as they change clothes with shifting fashions. They note that a constantly changeable individual whose life is a "series of unrelated episodes" is "not an autonomous individual, but rather one who lacks any sense of self and whose life lacks any narrative form." Since the market thereby undermines the conditions necessary for the settled dispositions and commitments that define what it is to have a self, so the argument goes, it actually ends up endangering autonomy.[54]

Although some (extreme) forms of consumerism may deserve this critique, the *idea* of the market does not. To begin with, recall that markets are not uniformly responsive only to price and that market governance does not necessarily imply impersonality. This critique, then, confuses a given market form, typical of some one-shot exchanges and of norms governing consumer goods, with the essence of the market.[55] But many market transactions, usually (but by no means only) in labor markets, are relational. They rely on strong interpersonal commitments and a good dosage of voice, leading to the creation of thin and at times even thick communities.[56] These contractual communities preserve exit, as they should, but its phenomenology is very different from the postmodern caricature of the market and premised on an occasionally critical view of the relationship and its continuous value in the parties' lives.[57]

Moreover, although anonymous one-shot trading is the hallmark of many market formations, even they need not threaten autonomy.

Insofar as these calculative market types characterize interactions that are strictly utilitarian, they often contribute to autonomy, though at times indirectly. Thus, for example,[58] a purely instrumental conception of consumer contracts allows people to make quick and *secure* consumption decisions, freeing them up to engage in more valuable projects.[59] More generally, trading that does not rely on prior social bonds is important even outside the consumer context because, as noted, it opens up opportunities for self-determination that might otherwise be unavailable. One recent example is the "access economy," allowing people to replace long-term possession with casual use.[60]

2. *Expanded Choice.* Markets are not only about exit and mobility but just as much about entry and commitments. The moral significance of contract, the centerpiece of the market, is precisely that "it allows persons to create obligation where there was none before," thereby giving free individuals "a facility for extending their reach by enlisting the reliable collaboration of other free persons."[61] Contract is conducive to self-determination because it enables people to recruit others to advance their own material and social goals, purposes, and projects. Contract expands the range of meaningful choices people can make to shape their own lives. It enhances our ability to be the authors of our lives by expanding our repertoire of secure interpersonal engagements beyond the (by definition limited) realm of gift-based interactions.

The market extends these autonomy-enhancing functions by further broadening the scope of choices between differing projects and ways of life. Markets create a structure that respects and facilitates divergent ends. Individuals can unbundle their resources according to their own priorities and "gain from the skill and knowledge of others [they] need not even know and whose aims could be wholly different from [their] own."[62] Because "[i]n a market system there is no preordained pattern of value to which individuals must conform," markets multiply the alternatives people can choose from and facilitate experimentation. They "allow people to make their own judgments about what they want to buy or sell, how hard they want to work, how much they want to save, what they value and how they value it, and what they wish to consume."[63]

At its best, the market functions as an enabling device for self-authorship. It enables individuals to act upon their own goals, values, objectives, and life plans without subordination to other individuals or to collective decision-making procedures.[64]

3. *Careful Design.* Markets are powerful institutions that significantly impact individuals, affect relationships, and shape societies. They can both support and threaten our autonomy. Markets are problematic when they undermine relational or distributive justice, or improperly treat utility as an intrinsic rather than instrumental value (thus commodifying people or their interpersonal relationships). Many market configurations do involve such pitfalls but the *idea* of the market as an arena for alienating entitlements in competitive terms need not entail these implications, at least not in full.

It should by now be clear that the doctrines prescribing the specific content, scope, and implications of the powers conferred by the various property and contract types promulgated by law shape – and not merely reflect – the market's interpersonal practices. To "fix the bugs" of the market in its current form, then, we must reconfigure the ideal that the market should represent and redesign it accordingly.[65]

The various goals that justify the complex legal arrangements sustaining markets should thus be subject to critical scrutiny. Promoting social welfare, rewarding desert, inculcating virtues, and spreading power, are all worthy objectives that deserve their prominent status in this crucial exercise. But at least for a liberal polity, facilitating self-authorship must be *the* fundamental goal.

Markets *can* play a vital autonomy-enhancing role in enabling mobility and expanding options. Appreciating the significance of these functions and their emancipatory potential implies that liberal polities should strive to organize markets – to shape the law of the market – in line with the market's autonomy-enhancing *telos*.

Law can help in configuring markets suited to enhance people's autonomy. Antitrust laws, which prevent concentrations of private power that reintroduce excessive dependence and vulnerability, are necessary features of an autonomy-based law of the market. But they are not sufficient. Two further characteristics of a liberal market will be hardly surprising to this book's readers. Markets with autonomy-enhancement as their primary goal should proactively ensure meaningful choices in every major sphere of human action and interaction, and must thus be structurally pluralistic. Structuring markets so as to serve autonomy also requires universal participation (or opportunity to participate) and, more broadly, compliance with the prescription of reciprocal respect for self-determination, meaning that interactions in and around the market must be governed by the maxim of relational justice.

In what follows, I do not reiterate my discussions of structural pluralism and relational justice but show instead how these two prescriptions go beyond property law and apply – or should apply – throughout the law of the market, and specifically in the labor markets at the focus of this chapter.

STRUCTURAL PLURALISM

A state committed to the use of market mechanisms to enhance autonomy is obliged to offer a sufficiently broad range of property and contract types in all spheres for the market to perform its function.

Law's carriers need not engage in innovative design but, as usual, look for and proactively support innovative types that can broaden people's choices, such as those based on minority views and utopian theories. Facilitating intra-sphere multiplicity also involves providing options for "partial exit" from the market itself: offering property and contract types supporting business models based more on sharing and collaboration and less on competition and profit maximization.[66]

This obligation of intra-sphere multiplicity, as noted in Chapter 4, has the greatest hold in less commercial spheres, especially in the housing and labor markets. Chapter 4 addressed some reform proposals in the housing sphere and here I discuss some suggestions in the labor markets, all subject to the minimal requirements of relational justice, which I discuss shortly. They are also tentative since, as noted, where multiplicity is more likely to undermine rather than, as usual, expand the autonomy of weak parties, it should *not* be applied.[67] This exception is particularly relevant in markets for unskilled workers at times of nonnegligible unemployment potentially leading to monopsony, when multiplicity may generate a race to the bottom that would systematically curtail autonomy.[68]

1. *Dependent Contractors.* The traditional structure of employment contracts offers a binary choice between employee and independent contractor status. Emerging forms, however, such as workers who provide their own equipment and control their own hours but are still subject to others' authority (as in Uber), call for additional categories. These new varieties, found most notably in the platform economy, require law to adapt the means for securing relational justice (consider, e.g., occupational health and safety, antidiscrimination, or fair pay and working time regulations).[69] With such – far from trivial – adjustments in place, these additional forms may open up new opportunities, most notably in emerging economies.[70]

2. *Job-Sharing.* Other options diverge even further from the existing employment landscape. Job-sharing – not to be confused with work-sharing[71] – has emerged as a particularly attractive form of flexible work arrangements.[72] It allows employers to hire new parents, older workers not yet ready for retirement, and others who want less work in their work/life balance. Job-sharing can thus be understood as a form of divisibility, which opens up opportunities for alienability and is thus autonomy-enhancing.

Job-sharing first became popular in the United States in the legal profession, when attorneys sought to work shorter hours but were restricted by workload demands and personnel budgets.[73] Then it spread to large companies, half of which now offer some type of job-sharing arrangement, usually informally negotiated.[74] The federal government has also encouraged the creation of public sector workplaces with job-sharing opportunities.[75]

The current versions of job-sharing, however, do not exhaust the potential of this contract type. Law can be instrumental in expanding its availability outside the federal government and beyond the lawyer and large firm contexts. Eliminating legal obstacles to the growth of job-sharing arrangements is a first, necessary step.[76] Other countries, such as Italy, have gone even further, proactively facilitating job-sharing by defining it as a distinct contract type.[77] This last step renders job-sharing more culturally salient and makes it more economically viable by stabilizing contractual defaults regarding responsibility, attribution, decision-making mechanisms, time division, sharing space and equipment, and availability on off days.

3. *At Will/For Choice*. An autonomy-based approach to the labor market would also revisit the current regime in all American states (except, oddly, for Montana), where employment-at-will is the default version for employees not on a fixed term contract.[78] Structural pluralism suggests that, instead of choosing between the "at will" and the "for cause" regimes as defaults, states would be advised to enact two parallel employment types. Employers would need to opt for one of them, making sure of notifying prospective employees of their choice. This regime would provide workers with a clear indication of this fundamental characteristic of the employment relationships each firm offers.[79]

This reform is particularly timely since about 85% of nonunion employees can be fired at-will, but empirical studies show that most employees incorrectly believe their employment can be terminated only "for cause."[80] The question of whether this structural pluralistic employment regime is preferable to a mandatory "for cause" one (assuming this was a viable option) is more complicated. An at-will employment doctrine deepens the structural inequality of power between employers and employees, and its acceptability then depends on the presence of mandatory countermeasures strong enough to still secure relational justice.[81]

RELATIONAL JUSTICE

1. *Inclusion and Nondiscrimination*. If markets are understood as means for self-determination, they need to be inclusive. The reason is (maybe surprisingly) straightforward. Conceptualizing the right of self-authorship as the ultimate value of both property and contract means that the law's facilitation of the market needs to be justified by reference to its role in providing people with choices. Given that self-authorship is a general, right-based justification, this proposition

implies that every human being is entitled to such choices and that a sufficiently diverse set of options must be available to all. Recognizing the horizontal effect of the right to respect for one's self-determination adds a crucial interpersonal dimension to this injunction: the maxim of relational justice. Even in the most restrictive interpretation, this injunction proscribes discriminatory limits on participation in market practices.[82]

Antidiscrimination rules do feature in contemporary doctrines governing the market, notably in relation to the employment and housing spheres. Yet, they are typically justified by reference to equal opportunity and social integration commitments or as means for improving the efficient functioning of markets. The rationales of equal opportunity and integration perceive nondiscrimination as an external imposition on the market's operation, a price exacted in the name of exogenous, worthy public causes. In all three rationales, antidiscrimination rules are contingent on the availability of other state-driven means for securing equal opportunity and social integration or improving the operation of the market. When these public ends are, or can be, secured otherwise, antidiscrimination rules may not be needed and thus, in some views, may even become unjustified, if not illegitimate.

By contrast, in an autonomy-based understanding of the market's building blocks (property and contract), antidiscrimination rules – including rules that instantiate *fair* equality of opportunity in the workplace – are not external constraints on the market limiting its putative commitment to efficiency or to negative liberty. Instead, insofar as these rules ensure inclusion, they are necessary for *perfecting* the market's realization of its most fundamental *telos*, its raison d'être. If the law of the market is to empower its subjects' self-determination so as to be justified by reference to people's right to self-authorship, it *must* be inclusive.

Legal reforms that extend autonomy and open up markets by alleviating discriminatory barriers are thus best understood as devices entailed by the idea of the market. They are means of urging the law of the market to live up to the market's implicit ideals, the very ideals that Adam Smith celebrated. An autonomy-based law of the market must ensure that its rules serve the self-determination of *all* its subjects and cannot authorize private parties to decide whether they can discriminate against their fellow humans.[83]

2. *The Specter of Domination.* Inclusion and nondiscrimination do not exhaust the relational-justice-based obligations of market participants. If markets are to serve people's self-determination and not only their independence, the law of the market cannot rely, as it does in its conventional portrayal, on a formal conception of equality seeking to abstract away the particular features distinguishing one person from another and must ensure, at least to an extent, their equal standing regarding their interactions.

This view of relational equality is substantive and not merely formal. In a significant subset of the laws of the market – dealing notably with business contracts between firms – formal equality is the all-things-considered best proxy for a state of affairs where the participants' relationship is roughly one of substantive equality. When relationships are not usually substantively equal, however, an autonomy-enhancing law can no longer legitimately use this proxy.

The law governing the employment market is an apt illustration. Liberal law needs to ensure that employers' authority is not distorted "into a relation of domination,"[84] returning the relationship to the very pattern the market is supposed to supplant.[85] This concern obviously turns graver when law's background regime, purported to guarantee workers the preconditions for autonomous life, becomes too meager as is the case in many contemporary societies.[86]

3. *Labor Law.* The commitment to relational justice is thus the essence of labor law, which promotes and supports the workers' collective bargaining.[87] As the introductory section to the Wagner Act explicitly states, the purpose of allowing labor unions is to address "[t]he inequality of bargaining power between employees who do not possess full freedom of association or actual liberty of contract and employers who are organized in the corporate or other forms of ownership association."[88]

As Claus Offe explains, the power relationship between capital and labor is structural: capital is unitary whereas labor is fragmented. The capital of each firm is "always united from the beginning" because its constituent parts are "entirely unrecognizable and indistinguishable."

Labor, by contrast, is "both indivisible and 'non-liquid'," which means that "each individual worker controls only one unit of [labor] power and, moreover, has to sell this under competitive conditions with other workers who, in turn, have to do the same."[89]

By giving workers the chance to bargain collectively and to place themselves on a more equal footing with employers, labor law attempts to solve this structural inequality,[90] and thus to redeem the legitimacy of employment contracts *qua* (liberal) contracts, that is, as means of empowering people's self-determination.[91]

Some may fear that unionization per se may not suffice to meet the concerns of relational justice in employment markets and that, to distinguish contract from subjugation, individualized contracting should effectively be abolished.[92] But this concern is exaggerated. Current labor law may fail to equalize the bargaining power of employers and employees. But the ability of individual employees, unionized or not, to bargain in the shadow of labor law can, if properly reconfigured,[93] make a real difference.[94] So long as unionization remains (or becomes) a viable and serious option, nonunion employee contracts may shield under the protective shadow of labor law.[95]

4. *Workers' Inalienable Rights.* Labor law, therefore, can help reinstate relational justice in the labor market. But more is needed. Just employment relationships require more than curbing employers' power. Workers' self-determination must be secured, in turn implying that "the basic paradigm of an employment relationship as one in which an employee labors under the control of an employer" must, to some extent, be eroded.[96]

Some features of contemporary employment law already comply with this prescription by specifying an inalienable infrastructure of just relationships dealing with topics like workplace safety, minimum wage, and nondiscriminatory treatment.[97] Relational justice may well justify further reinforcement of workers' autonomy by spelling out a workplace bill of rights protecting them against managers' arbitrary and unaccountable authority, particularly – but by no means only[98] – insofar as they purport to regulate workers' lives off-hours.[99] One example comes from the Grand Chamber of the European Court of

Human Rights, which ruled that an employee's legally protected right to privacy was violated when his employer monitored personal messages he had sent from a company account.[100]

5. *Owners-Employers' Limited Private Authority.* Finally, and most basically from the standpoint of liberal property, the prescription of its first pillar, which carefully circumscribes the private authority of means of production owners, implies that owners-employers' private authority must not include normative powers potentially infringing any of these workers' rights.

Consider the scope of the owners-employers' right to exclude. A liberal theory of property must endorse the famous *State v. Shack* holding, stating it is "unthinkable" that an owner-employer "can assert a right to isolate" migrant farmworkers employed and housed in his property. A farmer-employer's private authority does not entitle him to deny the worker's privacy or the opportunity to receive in his living quarters visitors (including aid workers) of his own choice.[101]

A similar line of analysis explains why the Supreme Court's *Lechmere* decision[102] is unfortunate not only from the perspective of labor law,[103] but also from that of liberal property. Ownership of factories, farms, and other types of both tangible and intangible property that serve as means of production *must not* include a right to exclude labor organizers and activists, insofar as such an exclusion might jeopardize the workers' right to unionize that, as noted, is entailed by the liberal commitment to relational justice.[104]

Nor does ownership of the means of production, as Joseph Singer correctly argued, need to imply that owners' decision to close a plant leaves workers remediless.[105] I cannot consider here the specific rights – from notice and information to supervised negotiation and first refusal – that may ameliorate the possible devastating effects of plant closures and similar dramatic decisions on the autonomy and welfare of workers, without unduly burdening owners. But in a liberal system of property, where the private authority of owners of means of production is carefully delineated and workers' claims to relational justice are properly acknowledged, these rights cannot be easily dismissed.[106]

Indeed, these and other doctrines that courts use (or can use or develop) can narrow the permitted gap between the required commitment of relational justice to substantive equality and the pragmatic use of formal equality as an imperfect proxy. They help to realize the ideal of the market as underwriting horizontal relationships based on free interaction, substantive equality and thus, most fundamentally, reciprocal respect for self-determination.[107] Markets that diverge too much from the prescription of relational justice are not only "noxious markets [that] undermine the conditions that people need if they are to relate as equals."[108] More fundamentally, their structuring of interpersonal relationships also subverts the very ideal of interactions between equals underlying the market's liberal *telos*, and indeed, its ultimate legitimacy.

★ ★ ★

Thus far, I have demonstrated that the pillars of liberal property also play (or should play) a significant role in the constitution of autonomy-enhancing markets. In what follows, I add two additional autonomy-based prescriptions that liberal markets must follow.

The first prescription echoes the commitment to exit characteristic of liberal property:[109] autonomy-based markets should set limits on the power to alienate whenever it erodes our ability to rewrite our life story and start anew. The second sharpens the distinction between welfare-based and autonomy-based conceptions of the market. Since utility should be understood as instrumental to the markets' ultimate value, which is autonomy, the law of the market must avoid the commodification of people and interpersonal relationships. In some subsets of the settings it governs, then, it should resort to techniques of incomplete commodification ensuring that, while entitlements are exchanged, interactions retain a personal aspect.

CHANGING PLANS

1. *The Future Self.* Self-determination requires that people should have the right to write the story of their lives. As Michael Bratman

Changing Plans

explains, humans are planning agents, which implies "*diachronic rationality constraints*" and, in turn, means that "prior intentions provide a rational default for present deliberation."[110] A liberal law of the market follows suit. It offers the normative power to make contractual commitments and properly assumes that, insofar as these commitments are indeed part of the current self's plan, the future self is presumed to adhere to them.

But self-determination also requires that people should have the right to *rewrite* the story of their lives. New "ordinary desires and preferences" may not suffice. Nonetheless, planning agency implies only "defeasible constancy: constancy in the absence of supposed conclusive reason for an alternative." In other words, the intertemporal constancy required by planning agency must be "sensitive to the fact that sometimes an agent supposes there are conclusive reasons for change."[111]

Thus, because changing plans is not necessarily a pathology, not all limits on alienability are prima facie troubling. Indeed, the autonomy-based foundation of alienability noted early on in this chapter implies that law's suspicion toward restraint of alienation is not only a response to the reasons of imperfect information, strategic barriers, cognitive failures, or externalities.[112] These familiar rationales are not insignificant but are contingent and, at least theoretically, responsive to technologies or legal techniques that could overcome hindering rationality deficiencies or other pertinent market failures. A genuinely liberal law of the market offers a different understanding of people's decisions to change their plans, one that respects their right to reinvent themselves.

If the ultimate commitment of the law of the market is to autonomy, people's ability to enlist one another in the pursuit of private goals and purposes must not overwhelm their right to exit relationships. The right to exit, as noted, is a pillar of the autonomy-based case for the market because self-authorship requires the ability to write and rewrite our life stories. This lesson is not only vital for property but equally decisive for the other building block of the market – contract.

A liberal contract law, beyond enabling us to make credible commitments, should always be alert to its potentially detrimental implications for the autonomy of the parties' future selves. Safeguarding our ability to start afresh by limiting the range, and at times the types, of enforceable commitments we can undertake is thus imperative. The same law that confers on people the normative power to commit themselves through contracts in the name of enhancing their self-determination, then, cannot ignore the impact of these contracts on their future selves.[113]

This tension is inherent in contract's very essence – *any* act of self-authorship constrains the future self – requiring contract law to carefully define the scope of the obligations it enforces and circumscribe their implications. Though seemingly obvious, this statement encapsulates a crucially difficult challenge confronting an autonomy-enhancing contract law: to identify categories of excessive limitations on the exit of contractual parties – that is, on promisors' freedom to change their mind – that undermine a party's autonomy to the point of making these limitations unenforceable.[114]

2. *Limits of the Power to Commit*. No formula is available for resolving this difficulty. But acknowledging the ability to revise and even discard one's plans as an entailment of the normative underpinnings of contract at least provides a strong, principled justification for several doctrines that might otherwise seem puzzling. Before considering the potentially negative external effects of placing limits on exit, then, their implications on the future self require attention. This more fundamental inquiry is not redundant even barring any plausible concern re imperfect rationality.

People's right to change course helps explain the *unilateral* right to terminate long-term contracts that, at least regarding contract types such as agency contracts, is semi-inalienable.[115] (This rule neither does nor need imply that employment contracts must be at-will since its autonomy-based foundation is not easily applicable to employers who own the means of production.)

Similarly, the right to rewrite our plans justifies some restrictions on the enforceability of employee non-compete agreements,[116] which have become endemic in recent years,[117] as well as on the advance sale of future wages.[118] Finally, the value ascribed to the ability to change plans may also help justify rules ensuring that contractual commitments are not overly dogmatic, such as the doctrines governing excuse and the blanket refusal to specifically enforce contracts to render personal service.[119]

Consider specific performance in slightly greater detail. Being able to change plans provides a firm foundation to the common law position, where specific performance is unavailable whenever damages are "adequate to protect the expectation interest of the injured party."[120] Other things being equal (for the promisee), contract in the common law tradition rightly opts for not compelling the promisor to act in accordance with the contractual script, allowing her to choose between doing so and covering the promisee's expectation.

Civil law jurisdictions reject this position and make specific performance widely available, but they do make an exception regarding service providers. On that front, no difference prevails between common law and civil law: both steadfastly resist granting specific performance compelling a person to work.[121] This deep-rooted and widespread rule is not an imposition on the logic of contract,[122] but the implementation of contract's *internal* logic of self-empowerment, which proscribes these excessive impositions on the self-determination of the future self.

INCOMPLETE COMMODIFICATION

1. *Utility Surplus as a Means.* Founding markets on self-determination requires that market transactions be voluntary undertakings and that a sufficiently diverse set of contractual options be available. Moreover, as I have argued earlier, the utility surplus – the material benefits these transactions generate – is to be viewed as an *instrument*, a means to the superior end of promoting the parties' autonomy.

Satisfying the parties' preferences is a significant concern in this view of the market because (but only to the extent that) it is conducive to self-determination. Utilitarian considerations – even when pertaining only to the contracting parties – should thus generally be subservient to the market's ultimate value of autonomy and, therefore, preferences that undermine self-determination should generally be overridden.[123] The law of the market cannot legitimately further transactions where enhancing the parties' welfare threatens their self-determination.

My discussion of the future self captures a subset of these cases but does not exhaust this category. In some types of contract, even beyond the obvious example of slavery, the instrumentalization of people could go as far as effacing their humanity by preempting their self-determination.[124] This risk of allowing the means (utility) to overwhelm the end (self-determination) is particularly acute in the context of employment.

Although Marx's account of the proletariat's plight may not be an accurate description of postindustrialized labor markets generally, there are still employment settings that dehumanize workers. Sweatshops typified by "deplorable working conditions that include low pay and long working days, unhealthy and unsafe conditions and a regime entailing elements of force and degradation," are extreme cases.[125] Workers, however, are treated as disposable commodities in many other contexts, currently described as "unacceptable forms of work."[126]

In some hard cases, such employment conditions may be legitimate as, for example, when one generation voluntarily undertakes derogatory obligations to secure the prerequisites of autonomy to its successor. As a rule, however, an autonomy-enhancing market cannot sanction transactions that involve such commodification.[127]

Addressing this crucial aspect of the labor market is obviously an enormous task that, like a full discussion of other features of an autonomy-enhancing market, exceeds the scope of this chapter.[128] Automation may afford partial relief to dehumanized work but raises vexing new difficulties of its own.[129] Yet, there is room for three general observations.

2. *Intrinsic Limitations and the Normalization Concern.* My first observation is by now familiar: although the perspective advanced in these pages does not deal with all the moral qualms evoked by some contemporary labor markets, it generates a uniquely powerful critique. Some labor markets undermine the very ideal of the market as autonomy-enhancing and are thus condemnable *qua* markets. Examples are markets involving repetitive or otherwise unfulfilling, fungible work that, together with a hierarchical structure at the workplace and the number of hours spent at work, cannot be reasonably understood as a means to, let alone as components of, the workers'

self-determination.[130] Proponents of the market who celebrate its contribution to people's self-authorship cannot but object to these practices and work to eradicate or transform them.

Setting a fixed floor of minimum labor standards seems easy when targeting arrangements that overwhelm people's sense of self, as in the sweatshops context. It may prove harder in other contexts, however, such as that of working hours, because these standards may be subject to Jürgen Habermas' powerful critique of their normalizing effects. By prescribing a floor of legitimate agreements, law forces employees "to conform their behavior to a 'normal' work relation," so that its "presumptive beneficiaries" end up *paying* for its attempt to secure their self-determination "with dependence on normalizing intrusions" that limit their ability to "autonomously pursue a private life plan."[131]

This is a particularly troubling charge, relevant also to some of the rules discussed above in the context of relational justice. Any *uniform* judgment touching on minimum requirements in the respectful treatment of others is bound to embrace the *majoritarian* view on that matter. Allowing easy opt-out from these rules would typically exacerbate these concerns, given the systemic inequality in the bargaining power of the parties, while a mandatory rule that anticipates minoritarian life plans would hardly count as an improvement. These responses only highlight Habermas' challenge of normalization, which is particularly devastating for an autonomy-based view of the market.[132]

This is truly a dilemma without easy solution. One response to Habermas' challenge could be to prescribe *multiple* floors, in line with liberal law's commitment to structural pluralism. Recall that the troubling normalization effect is the inevitable outcome of employing a *uniform* floor. A liberal law conscious of contract's power-conferring essence, then, should strive to offer a choice of diversified minimal-arrangements packages, attempting to include among them floors that anticipate minoritarian forms of life.

I do not claim that this strategy is flawless.[133] Even when choice is offered, not all can choose the formula that best secures their autonomy; *standardized* floors may not fit some people. Offering a plurality of floors for employees to choose from, however, does make a real difference that is not only quantitative but also qualitative. If law's spectrum of floors is indeed sufficiently diverse and if it includes minoritarian alternatives, law leaves its "presumptive beneficiaries" with some real choice and also avoids the risk, or rather the irony, of mainstreaming people's life plans in the name of respecting their self-determination.

3. *Incomplete Commodification.* My second observation on how labor markets can avoid threatening the agency of workers is that the context of these markets seems particularly inviting to what Margaret Jane Radin calls the "incomplete commodification" strategy. In this strategy, money changes hands but the interactions nonetheless retain a personal aspect. As Radin notes, the complete decommodification of work is now not possible and may well be undesirable. But the labor market can be regulated to prevent workers' degradation to the status of completely monetizable and tangible objects of exchange. The labor market can take into account workers' personal contribution and recognize, even foster, the noncommodified significance of their work and of their relations with other people in the workplace.[134]

4. *Voice.* My third and final observation is that this regulation should help improve the workers' voicelessness. This observation builds on the idea that the market need not imply impersonality and thus need not always preclude voice.[135]

In many market contexts, as noted, the hegemony of exit over voice and the interaction's impersonal nature need not hinder their function in the service of self-determination. But the specific subset of labor markets addressed now, traditionally epitomized by "grinding assembly-line jobs that hardly anyone could treat as humane work,"[136] and, more recently, by precarious forms of work that inhibit workers' "ability to establish and maintain stable families and households" and are typified by "unsafe and unhealthy conditions,"[137] is different. In these settings, workers' voicelessness is particularly troubling because it implies that they no longer have any control over a large part of their day.[138]

Rehabilitating these labor markets requires bringing them back to the universe of, at least potentially, autonomy-enhancing markets. This purpose, in turn, necessitates ameliorating these workers' subordinate position,[139] either by facilitating their union representation or through other means for granting them a say in workplace decisions to ensure recognition of their non-fungible status.[140]

MARKETS AND LABOR

Liberal property, I have argued early on in this chapter, is typically alienable, which makes property and markets more than only contingently intertwined. When we shift from markets for goods to markets for services, part of the challenge is to preserve the autonomy-enhancing functions of alienability without turning it into *alienation*. Lisa Herzog's account of the two visions of the self in the market, associated with the views of Adam Smith and of Hegel, powerfully captures this dilemma.

Labor markets are empowering. While most people do not have "the independence that comes from landownership," almost everyone "has, or can acquire, human capital." This is why labor markets are potentially transformative: they allow everyone to "participate, on an equal legal footing," that is, "to choose freely whom to work for … rather than depending on one single employer, as had been the case in feudalism." By "getting trained, collecting experience and developing expertise," people can acquire marketable skills and improve their condition; they can thus, at least partly, write the story of their own lives.

For labor markets to perform this transformative function, people must be able to "make wise use" of their human capital. (This is the charitable understanding of the term "human capital," which is otherwise quite offensive.) Thus, just as with respect to other forms of capital (read: property), each person should be able to stand apart from his or her human capital, "serenely choosing the usage that leads to the highest return." People "must not see their professional activity as 'constitutive' for their identity" and as an essential part of themselves. For workers to put their human capital to a different use without losing their identity, they must regard their ability to work as something they can sell in the market to the highest bidder. Their human capital can then be understood as "something they *have*, not something they *are*."[141]

There are, of course, numerous difficulties with this picture, which is quite different from the way most actual labor markets function or can function. What matters here is that it *fully* instrumentalizes work, in effect requiring people to treat their choice of vocation on a par with, say, their mundane choices as consumers, which are properly understood as sheer preferences. But work is different.

At least since the decline of feudalism, work has figured prominently in people's adult lives *not only* as a means to an end. Although surely that as well, work is also a ground project.[142] Unlike brute preferences we may or may not satisfy, people's ground projects – for many, work is the quintessential one – are chapters of their life story; these are some of the projects that give meaning to one's life.[143] Instrumentalizing work may indeed empower people in autonomy-enhancing ways: the religious connotations of vocation and the accompanying idea that, after choosing a profession, one's "professional identity is in a deep sense part of who one is"[144] may well be overly cumbersome. Exit and the ability to start afresh are important for self-authorship on this front as well. And yet, a *full* instrumentalization of work might rob people of some of the most obvious possibilities of making their life stories meaningful.

By focusing on labor markets, I have tried to demonstrate in this chapter how an autonomy-based conception of the market can meet this challenge. The conceptual and normative difficulties in the idea of selling one's labor are real, but a view of the market that puts self-determination rather than either aggregate welfare or individual independence at its core is best situated to properly address these challenges. It can, moreover, offer the general parameters of the road that thus far has not been not taken but can, and should, guide liberal architects of the law as they narrate its next episodes.

An autonomy-based law is happy to enlist the market to enable people's mobility and enrich their repertoire of choices, but is also acutely attentive to the distinction between brute preferences and ground projects. It thus guards against excessive commodification of people's work, proscribes unwarranted impositions on their future self, and ensures that their interactions do not fall below an acceptable threshold of relational justice. It also carefully refrains from

Markets and Labor

marginalizing the broader picture, where the justice of the market is partially dependent on a background regime that guarantees the conditions of individual self-determination. Rather than striving for exclusivity, a truly liberal conception of the market is confidently attuned to its distinct autonomy-enhancing tasks: enabling mobility and expanding choice, while acknowledging the indispensable role of other social institutions in enabling these vital functions.

★ ★ ★

My mission in this book is almost done, but one major feature of liberal property is still missing. Property rights change over time and these transitions profoundly challenge liberal property. How should a legal system premised on the notion that property is neither a natural right nor a sheer creature of positive law respond? Under what circumstances should owners be entitled to compensation for losses they incur from these transitions, and why? Every student of property law grapples with these difficult questions and the confusing case law that they triggered. The liberal conception of property offers a distinctive answer, which Chapter 8 develops and defends.

8 PROPERTY TRANSITIONS
(with Michael Heller)

PROPERTY AND TIME

Time plays a key role in this book. The last two chapters discussed two reasons why time matters to the life of property: over time, owners effect voluntary changes to property in order to carry out their life plans and the state imposes involuntary changes (from the individual owner's perspective) in response to changing circumstances, shifting needs and wants, and revised public goals. For the state to function – and to remain justified on liberal principles – the government must have this ability to adjust ownership. However, state-initiated transitions to ownership – implemented through governments' police and takings powers – are potentially devastating to the owners' ability to be the authors of their own lives.

This chapter focuses on these property transitions. Although many of them are triggered by pragmatic reasons, they raise profound questions for any theory of property, especially a liberal one. Property transitions simultaneously constitute a core requirement for the legitimacy of liberal property and a continuous existential threat and, therefore, the risks and costs they necessarily entail call for a principled treatment.

VULNERABILITY AND STABILITY ACROSS TIME

1. *Two propositions.* A liberal theory of transitions builds on two propositions involving liberal property across the dimension of time. The first addresses the legitimacy challenge that property always

Vulnerability and Stability across Time 211

faces – this proposition concerns itself primarily with the self-determination of nonowners. The second involves the critical dimension of time in the core liberal justification for the private authority of owners. I have already explored these propositions in Chapter 3 and will briefly expand on them here to make their connection to justified property transitions more transparent.

The first proposition arises from the vulnerability of nonowners, who necessarily suffer whenever property law recognizes any private authority by owners over scarce resources. Because nonowners are continuously vulnerable, the challenge to property's legitimacy is, in turn, continuous as well. That is, property must be legitimated not only at the (real or imagined) moment of its creation, but throughout its life. The law must *continuously* ensure both that the justified background conditions that make property legitimate persist, and that the scope of the private authority that owners exert over nonowners continues to conform to its justificatory foundations over time.

The second proposition concerns the role that property plays in the enhancement of owners' autonomy. Property can serve autonomy, I claimed, partly because the private authority it confers is stable. This stability is what intimately connects property to the idea of a plan, which in turn plays a key role in the notion of self-determination. On these grounds, I argued, for example, that the architecture of a liberal property system cannot plausibly follow a program that constantly destabilizes all our holdings. Constant instability is inconsistent with any reasonable conception of a plan.

In Chapter 3, I discussed these two propositions – the temporal dimension of property's legitimacy challenge (addressing nonowners' vulnerability) and the temporal dimension of its liberal justification (securing autonomy-enhancing stability) – separately, each on its own terms. But they are actually profoundly connected, and awareness of how they can be reconciled proves key to the basic liberal approach to property transitions. To see why, consider first how property's legitimacy challenge can accommodate stability, and then how property's autonomy-enhancing function does not require freezing ownership rules.[1]

  2. Interrelation of Change and Stability. I begin with the requirement that property be legitimate not just at its creation but continually, through the life of the institution. Even if a property regime is perfectly justified at inception, then, it must be periodically reexamined to ensure that it still complies with property's demanding justificatory challenge. But property's legitimacy challenge does not require these reexaminations and the possible reforms they may entail to be particularly frequent. The discussion on the evolution of property law in Chapter 6 implicitly assumes this sensible refinement: property law has built-in resources for intermittent reappraisals, not for constant upheaval.

Conversely, property's stability requirement, which is crucial for supporting our ability to plan, demands resistance to *constant* change but not to *any* change. Property's liberal *telos* does imply rejection of a radical destabilization of holdings that would utterly frustrate property's autonomy-enhancing function. Yet, the stability property requires does not imply stagnation. We can advance our life plans even when there is some change. Our plans, big and small, tend to be evolving and often adaptive.[2]

THE TRANSITION INTUITION

To anchor the intuition that some but not all property transitions are legitimate – and indeed required in a liberal property regime – an analogy to the old common law rules regarding ownership of shoreline land when the waters rise or recede may be helpful.

1. *Accretion and Avulsion.* Under these rules, which date back to Roman law, an owner's land remains at the shoreline boundary so long as changes happen slowly and imperceptibly. The owner's land grows as soil is deposited and shrinks as the land erodes. That is "accretion." Slow additions or subtractions from ownership similarly fall within this accretive principle, ensuring both property's stability and its legitimacy.

But when a sudden change occurs, called an "avulsion," the original boundary remains unchanged.[3] The owner does not get the new chunk of land attached to the old, nor does the owner lose land that has suddenly sunk underwater. Again, this accords with a basic intuition

The Transition Intuition

about property: changes that are too big or too sudden undermine the owners' ability to plan and, therefore, the state should not have the ability to impose them on owners without compensation (with one important caveat that I address later in this chapter).

Any change – big or small, sudden or gradual – alters to some extent the status quo, of land specifically and of ownership more generally. But (as noted in Chapter 6) this does *not* make all changes the same. The law of accretion and avulsion recognizes differences, as does the law of property transitions more generally. Expectations about property are not stable only if frozen across time.[4] Moderate incremental changes are not necessarily offensive to self-determination because they do not disrupt the ability of owners to plan.[5] Plans often accommodate external changes, and anticipating moderate gradual changes does not make the idea of planning futile.

These observations suggest a principled bifurcation of the universe of property transitions. In brief, owners' private authority over scarce resources does not imply immunity from moderate state-imposed gradual changes. All transitions detrimentally affect some owner's property rights, but only a subset of them collide with the liberal idea of property, which must incorporate some amenability to change if property is to remain legitimate.[6] The same fundamental normative propositions that justify the liberal conception of property in the first instance also guide the differing legal treatment that we should accord property transitions.

The proper demands of our right to self-determination require a high degree of stability in property rights, and those same proper demands also impose on owners the obligation to accept a certain measure of change. These changes, without compensation, should be understood as part of the accretions that a reasonable individual in a liberal polity must accept to ensure the continued legitimacy of his or her property. They can thus be seamlessly accommodated in a system of liberal property.

By contrast, sudden and dramatic changes *are* disruptive of property's contribution to self-authorship. Regulations that intrude too far too fast on our individual autonomy are the avulsions of regulatory change. Therefore, a liberal property system conceptualizes *this* type of change as a taking, which must be compensated.

2. *The Liberal Property Pact.* In a nutshell, this is the idea of "the liberal property pact."[7] Later, I will also defend it as an elaboration of another lesson of Chapter 3, namely, that property owners have a responsibility to support the continuous justice of their system of property.[8]

My main tasks in this chapter are conceptual and normative: to refine the idea of a property pact and its jurisprudential necessity, and to defend the normative appeal of the *liberal* pact in particular. Our property pact, properly understood, is not a "historical compact" but rather a core feature of *any* legal regime. The pact is responsible for regulating the distribution of the risks and costs of legal transitions. A *liberal* property pact determines this distribution so that owners incur the risks and costs of legal accretions but not of legal avulsions.

Like other features of liberal property discussed in these pages, the liberal pact fixes the broad strictures of a justifiable system of property without attempting to fully substitute local, and thus necessarily contextual, determinations. But, again as usual, these theoretical reflections entail some helpful doctrinal payoffs: (1) They point to two unacceptable versions of the pact from the standpoint of liberal principles, which may seem like straw men but have been surprisingly dominant in American takings jurisprudence. (2) They refine the pact's liberal boundaries, that is, they delimit the rare cases of legal accretions that should trigger compensation and legal avulsions that must not. (3) They offer guidance for how to resolve or dissolve some (in)famous puzzles of existing takings doctrine.

LUCAS'S COMPACT

Michael Heller – the coauthor of this chapter – and I are not the first to invoke the idea of a property pact. Justice Scalia introduced an early version in his well-known discussion in *Lucas v. S.C. Coastal Council.*[9] Much of Justice Scalia's account is indefensible: he refers to a nonexistent "historical compact" and he interprets the pact in a way that offends liberal notions of property. But metaphors are important, so Justice Scalia's contribution must be acknowledged, even while its deficits are pruned away.

Justice Scalia wrote, the idea "that title is somehow held subject to the 'implied limitation' that the State may subsequently eliminate all economically valuable use ... is inconsistent with the historical compact recorded in the Takings Clause that has become part of our constitutional culture." Therefore, he added, where "the State seeks to sustain [such] regulation ... it may resist compensation only if the logically antecedent inquiry into the nature of the owner's estate shows that the proscribed use interests were not part of his title to begin with."[10]

What are these implied limitations of landowners' title? The conventional interpretation of *Lucas* – aptly supported by some of Justice Scalia's language – points to the preexisting State common law of property and nuisance. It is "unexceptional," Justice Scalia writes, to recognize the power of the State to prohibit expressly what "was *always* unlawful," and thus merely "duplicate the result that could have been achieved in the courts." But, he wrote, South Carolina's Beachfront Management Act was unlikely to fall into this narrow category, because "[i]t seems unlikely that common-law principles would have prevented the erection of any habitable or productive improvements on petitioner's land."[11]

This strategy for interpreting the property pact is indefensible, as Justice Blackmun detailed in dissent.[12] To redeem Justice Scalia's positive contribution, we must cut away three problematic features of his attempt to set a baseline for takings law: (1) His reliance on nuisance as the baseline. (2) His distinction between adjudication and legislation. (3) His description of the pact as historical.

1. *Nuisance as Baseline.* First, Justice Scalia's use of nuisance law as the baseline for limitations on ownership is curious because it follows his own harsh deconstruction of the "nuisance exception."[13] Landowners' title, according to this exception, never includes the authority to harm and, therefore, even changes in nuisance law that dramatically diminish the value of property cannot trigger compensation. But by refusing to allow construction on a vulnerable beachfront lot, the state denied Lucas a use that was indeed arguably harmful. Thus, the prohibition should have been plausibly subject to the "noxious use" per se exception, even within the terms of Justice Scalia's understanding.

Justice Scalia, however, contested the ability of this rule to "serve as a touchstone to distinguish regulatory 'takings' – which require compensation – from regulatory deprivations that do not require compensation." He argued that "the distinction between regulation that 'prevents harmful use' and that which 'confers benefits' is difficult, if not impossible, to discern on an objective, value-free basis." This distinction, he added, "is often in the eye of the beholder" such that it is possible "to describe in *either* fashion" the same set of "ecological, economic, and esthetic concerns" depending "primarily upon one's evaluation of the worth of competing uses of real estate."[14]

Unfortunately, Justice Scalia's demolition of the nuisance rule did not offer a constructive way to determine which side of the harm/benefit line Lucas's lot fell on.

2. *Adjudication versus Legislation.* Similarly, Justice Scalia's repeated references to common law suggest that the baseline of property must be strictly limited to adjudicative, as opposed to legislative, rules. But this assertion is certainly misguided. As Justice Blackmun insisted, "There is nothing magical in the reasoning of judges long dead. They determined a harm in the same way as state judges and legislatures do today."[15]

Indeed, a few years later, in *Stop the Beach,* Justice Scalia overruled himself on precisely this point. In the latter case, he wrote that the identity of the "particular state actor is irrelevant" for takings purposes.[16] In his argument supporting the creation of a judicial takings doctrine, he asserted, "it is no more essential that judges be free to overrule prior cases that establish property entitlements than that state legislatures be free to revise pre-existing statutes that confer property entitlements, or agency-heads pre-existing regulations that do so."[17]

So, the judge/legislator line offers no more help in evaluating Lucas's claim than does Justice Scalia's reconstructed nuisance rule.

3. *Historical Compact.* Finally, it is hard to substantiate the "compact" Justice Scalia invokes if it is understood – as he presents it – in historical terms, that is, as one that reflects the long-term *factual* "understandings of our citizens regarding the content of, and the State's power over, the 'bundle of rights' that they acquire when they obtain title to property."[18]

Justice Blackmun's summary of the long history of courts upholding "bans on particular uses without paying compensation, notwithstanding the economic impact, under the rationale that no one can obtain a vested right to injure or endanger the public"[19] is irrefutable. Indeed, this rejoinder is devastating to Justice Scalia's approach, if the property pact were properly conceptualized in empirical terms.[20]

So, *Lucas* is a deeply problematic opinion, as Justice Scalia himself noticed in *Stop the Beach*. But we all lose an important insight if we simply reject Justice Scalia's invocation of the necessity of a pact underlying property transitions. Some such pact must exist if we are to escape the "positivist trap," that is, if property means something different from just the momentary constellation of state regulations.

Indeed, the pact is a central, existing feature of all liberal property systems. And the pact can easily be rehabilitated and take pride of place if it is properly conceptualized as the legal construct prescribing and delimiting the state's Hohfeldian power over our property rights.

To be useful in analyzing property transitions, especially for a theory that is not overly parochial, the property pact must be understood in *jurisprudential* terms, rather than as a *historical* fact. The property pact is a heuristic devise, analogous to the social contract. But the property pact deals with a specific aspect of our social contract. To refine its jurisdiction and specific contribution to law, it should thus be jurisprudentially situated.

RULE OF CHANGE

A property pact prescribes the foundational limits of the state's authority to revise our property rights. A pact thus informs our expectations regarding the stability of existing property law. More precisely, it informs our ability to develop *protected* (or *reasonable*) expectations regarding our property. When our expectations are protected – in compliance with the property pact – that means individuals should not be required to incur a significant concentrated burden when the state modifies them.

1. *When Are Expectations Justified?* The idea of property's protected expectations is not an easy one. Law never protects expectations – or

even reliance – per se. Rather, it protects expectations (or reliance) if and only if they are justified, and the question of whether they are justified is, at least partially, a function of the applicable law.[21] As Friedrich Hayek noted, "[t]he protection against disappointment of expectations which the law can give in an ever changing society will always be only the protection of some expectations but not of all," so that the task of a just law "can ... only be to tell people which expectations they can count on and which not."[22]

This uncontroversial proposition applies not only to claims with regard to *first-order* expectations that may ultimately end up not being legally grounded. Arguments based on the mere fact of actors' reliance on existing law – which assume *second-order* expectations per law's stability – are also hopelessly question-begging. For example, the sheer fact of reliance on previous judicial pronouncements cannot plausibly vindicate the binding power of precedent. Without some independent legal recognition of precedent as a source of law, reliance on judges' utterances is neither called for nor worthy of legal protection.[23]

Nor can a credible understanding of a property pact rest on sheer empirical observation of citizens' expectations. A zoning regulation that revises a landowner's existing rights, for example, may be predictable, but nonetheless considered a taking if it oversteps the scope of acceptable non-compensable changes of the applicable property pact. Likewise, an unpredictable change cannot be said to have taken an established property right if it either clarifies the law or changes property entitlements in compliance with the operative property pact.[24] If the legal system's property pact prescribes that no transition relief will be provided for certain types of doctrinal changes, then "one cannot reasonably expect relief to be forthcoming."[25]

2. *Second-Order Rules*. This analogy between the precedential power of courts' rulings and the role of a property pact in shaping owners' *protected* expectations is not coincidental. Just like the norms that prescribe the status of rulings (of certain courts) as a source of law, the types and degree of protected reliance on existing law are also a function of what H. L. A. Hart called law's secondary rules or – more specifically – one of the legal system's rules of change. Hart famously discussed three types of secondary rules (rules about rules): rules of

Rule of Change

recognition, rules of change, and rules of adjudication. Rules of recognition and rules of adjudication specify, respectively, "the ways in which the primary rules may be conclusively ascertained ... and the fact of their violation conclusively determined."[26]

My focus here is on the system's *rules of change*. Rules of change prescribe how the primary rules of conduct may be introduced, eliminated, or varied.[27] The familiar rules of change deal with the procedure whereby utterances of legislatures or judges can affect the state of the law. (The rule of *stare decisis* belongs to this category.) They imply that changes in the system's primary rules are effective only if executed by the proper officials who followed certain stated procedures.

The property pact addresses a different aspect of the same mission: it allocates the risks and costs of transitions in our property rules. Unlike the mission of the other rules of change, this mission necessarily relies on some view of fair distribution. A property pact prescribes that for a revision (that complies with the institutional and procedural rules of change) to take effect, the costs of transition must be fairly distributed.[28] It must be designed, as Justice Black noted in *Armstrong v. United States*, "to bar Government from forcing some people alone to bear public burdens which, in all fairness and justice, should be borne by the public as a whole."[29]

3. *Property Pact as a Rule of Change.* Understanding the property pact as a Hartian rule of change suggests that the property pact is an *essential* ingredient in *any* property regime, constitutive of the (secondary) rules of the game regarding property. In this light, Justice Scalia's own preferred version of the property pact is unacceptable, as shown below. But his pact metaphor – which stresses the *inevitability* of having a second-order norm for allocating the burdens of property's transitions – is nonetheless valuable.

This inevitability means that the transparency of the property pact is significant. As with other rules of change, it is vital that lawyers – along with owners and other citizens – know (or at least can know) what it says. Take again the practice of respecting precedent. There are many ways of implementing it, all acceptable, but it is critical for courts not to treat the choice of how to extract the *ratio decidendi* on a case-by-case basis. Similarly with the property pact: different polities can make their choices and, as noted, there are even many versions of liberal property pacts. (Recall that a liberal theory of property leaves ample space for contextual concerns that are likely to vary across jurisdictions.) But whatever version they choose should be relatively stable and transparent, something the current regulatory takings law is not.

A transparent property pact has one notable feature: it addresses the circularity critique of the frequent reference to "legitimate" or "justified" or "reasonable" expectations or reliance (or, for that matter, of "vested" rights).[30] In other words, refining the notion of a property pact, which requires prescribing its specific contours, is important to stabilize, and indeed render legible, citizens' *justified* expectations regarding the state's legitimate power over their property.

Finally, Justice Scalia's use of the pact metaphor is on target to the extent he rightly conceptualizes the rule of change for property transitions in *civic* terms. The most familiar rules of change, as noted, deal with institutional and procedural aspects of legal transitions, but these aspects do not exhaust the drama of transitions.

The aspect we focus on here is rightly referred to in civic terms because it addresses the proper distribution of transitions' risks and costs, that is, it speaks to our responsibilities as co-citizens. As the rule of change that delimits the state's power over our property, the property pact prescribes some of our civic responsibilities in our capacity as owners.

TWO UNACCEPTABLE PACTS

Identifying the concept of a property pact as part of the Hartian set of rules of change is an important step, but a preliminary one. Appreciating the necessity for the *existence* of the property pact says nothing about its appropriate *content*. There are many plausible versions of the property pact.

Three stylized possibilities will be presented in the following pages, all claiming some textual support in American takings jurisprudence. I begin by explaining why the two extreme positions – of no civic responsibility and no governmental constraints – are unacceptable.

Focusing on their flaws is important, both because of their relative prominence in the takings debate and because they help clarify the distinctive *liberal* property pact.

1. *The Libertarian Pact.* Justice Scalia's judgment in *Lucas* adequately conveys one possible property pact. For the state to win its case on remand, Justice Scalia emphasized, "South Carolina must do more than proffer the legislature's declaration that the uses Lucas desires are inconsistent with the public interest," or assert "that they violate a common-law maxim such as *sic utere tuo ut alienum non laedas.*"[31]

Rather, as the state "would be required to do if [South Carolina] sought to restrain Lucas in a common-law action for public nuisance," they could impose the entire cost of transition on Lucas only if their justification was premised on "background principles of nuisance and property law that prohibit the uses he now intends in the circumstances in which the property is presently found."[32]

This version of the property pact, read at face value,[33] would seem to require transition relief for *every* change (as opposed to mere clarification) of *every* rule or incident pertinent to property. It prescribes that *all* the costs (and all the risks) of such transitions are incurred by the public and none by landowners. In other words, while this putative pact does not object to legal changes that affect the value of specific holdings, it bars any incidental reconfiguration of the distribution of generic wealth, excepting, perhaps, a *de minimis* one.

This means, for example, that every time the impact of a public project on the landowner is disproportionate to the burden (if any) carried by other beneficiaries of that use, compensation would be required. Such a rule dictates that owners must not sustain burdens that are disproportionately heavy in comparison to those sustained by other beneficiaries of the public action.

I call this version of the pact "the libertarian pact," and it is the one mostly associated in American Supreme Court jurisprudence with Richard Epstein's blueprint for takings law.[34] Because property transitions typically burden some citizens more than others, virtually every regulation of property is a compensable taking if the libertarian pact dominates judicial decision-making. Stability trumps the continuous justification of property in this version.

2. *The Progressive Pact.* Justice Stevens's dissenting opinion in *Lucas* presents a sharply contradictory approach. "Arresting the development of the common law," he claims, is "profoundly unwise," because "[t]he human condition is one of constant learning and evolution – both moral and practical."[35] That "new learning" – for example, our new "appreciation of the significance of endangered species," of "the importance of wetlands," or "the vulnerability of coastal lands" – is properly implemented by legislators, who thus "must often revise the definition of property and the rights of property owners."[36] Therefore, "[t]he rule that should govern a decision in a case of this kind should focus on the future, not the past," and it should reflect "our evolving understandings of property rights."[37]

This version of the property pact is reminiscent of Justice Brandeis's dissent in *Penn Coal. v. Mahon*, where he founds his objection to the birth of regulatory takings law on a particularly attenuated interpretation of the "reciprocity of advantage" test that obtains by the sheer "advantage of living ... in a civilized community."[38]

Call this "the progressive pact." Some progressive authors advocate, in this spirit, a regime that sanctions, indeed expects, significant civic sacrifices extending to all economically beneficial uses of one's land. These authors perceive most government injuries to private property as ordinary examples of the background risks and opportunities assumed by property owners.[39] Thus, they read in the takings clause "a strong presumption" that, in a democracy, "normally" the fact that regulations "take property without just compensation" does not render them illegitimate.[40]

This view implies a broad no-compensation rule, with a few pockets of exceptional categories. An injury to individual property that benefits the public, even while disproportionately burdening a specific individual with the weight of public interest, is legitimate in this view as long as it can be justified by "general, public, and ethically permissible policies."[41] This progressive pact aims to ensure the continuous legitimacy of property, but sacrifices the stability owners require to implement their life plans.

Whereas libertarians tend to conceive every regulation of property as a compensable taking, progressives tend to conceptualize any regulation as implied by the owners' background expectations, meaning that no new regulation should trigger compensation. In a liberal theory of property, both these positions must be rejected.

LIMITS TO THE LIBERTARIAN PACT

The libertarian position is unacceptable because, if property has no internal resources for adjustment, nothing can ensure that a property regime will be continuously justified. There are two reasons for this proposition, one intrinsic to the idea of autonomy-enhancing property and the other derived from the background regime necessary for property to be legitimate.

The intrinsic reason was introduced at the beginning of this chapter. Owners have a justified claim to stability but not to stagnation and, therefore, not to immunity from change of any kind. Moreover, because property's justification depends on its ability to continuously ensure a background regime that guarantees everyone the material, social, and intellectual preconditions of self-authorship, a stagnant property system cannot plausibly be legitimate.

1. *Insights from Economic Analysis.* The robust economic analysis of takings law helps in refining this proposition. This literature is mostly interested in the welfarist implications of various possible rules, which is inappropriate here, but the insights of these economic accounts on the incentive effects for owners can still be illuminating for my purposes.[42]

For example, they point out in what circumstances compensation should be paid to prevent risk-averse landowners from underinvesting in their property. Compensation is likewise often warranted to create a budgetary effect that forces governments to internalize the costs of their planning decisions (assuming public officials are responsive to budgetary shifts). Both considerations – dealing with the incentives of landowners and potential landowners and of public officials, respectively – are relevant to members of marginal groups with little political clout, and to private owners who are not professional investors and may have purchased a small parcel of land with their life savings. In these cases, economic analysis may suggest compensation for regulatory change.

In other types of cases, however, full compensation should *not* be granted, if the law aims at providing private landowners and public officials with proper (read, for now, efficient) incentives. For example, when land is owned as part of a diversified investment portfolio, full compensation may lead to inefficient overinvestment, while the possibility of uncompensated regulatory change is likely to lead to an efficient adjustment of the landowner's investment decisions commensurate with the risk that the land will be put to public use.

Similarly, landowners who are members of powerful and organized groups (and only such landowners) can use nonlegal means to force public officials to weigh their grievances properly.

Thus, economic analysis suggests that compensation practices vary depending on the identity of the affected owners. An indiscriminate regime of full compensation, just like its opposite rule of no compensation, might distort the officials' incentives. Both rules systematically encourage officials to impose the burden on the nonorganized public or on marginal groups even when the best planning choice would be to place the burden on landowners that belong to the more powerful or organized groups.

Both sides of this analysis are instructive. The intensified vulnerability of homeowners to uncompensated transitions will inform my critique of the progressive pact. What is crucial here, though, is the flip side of the coin, combining these economic insights with the lessons of the preceding autonomy-based analysis.

2. *Implications for the Libertarian Pact.* Full compensation for any derogation of the value of commercial holdings, as just shown, may not be needed to produce efficient investment decisions. Nor is it always necessary or justified from an autonomy standpoint: private authority over *such* resources (in the commercial context) need not – and in many cases should not – be overly demanding, as I have recurrently argued. Fewer changes are avulsive when owners can diversify their holdings and are able to bring effective political pressure to bear on governmental decision-makers.

The other half of the economic account, dealing with the disciplining effects of compensation regimes on the public authority, is likewise important. The economic analysis warns against the potentially inefficient and regressive effects of a regime that recasts every regulation as a compensable taking. Such a regime frustrates the necessary flexibility of property, which is required to ensure that it is continuously responsive to the concerns of nonowners.

Moreover, endorsing a property pact that prescribes transition relief for every change of every legal rule denotes we have no civic duties respecting transitions. Such excessive protection defies the Rawlsian maxim of individuals' duty to support just institutions, a duty that even Nozick eventually endorsed.[43] In the context of property, as shown in Chapter 3, this duty translates into the duty of owners, inherent in the meaning of ownership, to support the continued justice and viability of their system of property.[44] Since Justice Scalia's favored property pact of "no civic responsibility" contravenes this duty, it must be rejected if property is to be justified in liberal terms.

LIMITS TO THE PROGRESSIVE PACT

The progressive pact is diametrically opposed to its libertarian counterpart. It implies that, no matter how sharp or rapid a change, if the state says you no longer have property, then by and large nothing was taken and no compensation is due. Under such a pact, which sanctions – indeed expects – significant civic sacrifices, the landowner almost always loses takings claims. But this pact is no more acceptable than the libertarian pact, again for two reasons mirroring the pitfalls of the libertarian pact.

1. *Are All Changes Accretions?* A property pact almost without any governmental constraints implies that property can always be dramatically altered. All changes are accretions and none are avulsions. At least vis-à-vis our public authorities, then, property no longer plausibly serves its own autonomy-enhancing *telos*.

The progressive pact would not undermine property's contribution to people's self-determination in a world that complied with a utopian vision of state bureaucracies, but that is not our world. Therefore, as explained in Chapter 5,[45] a credible theory of property must be responsive to the autonomy-reducing effects of such an open-ended government authority to adjust people's property rights.

Property transitions endanger all property holders, rich and poor. Moreover, both central and local governments may be corrupt despite attempts to structure them in the spirit of civic virtue. In our nonideal world, corruption of public-spiritedness can take various forms, and some of its more troubling manifestations are not necessarily crude infirmities of the administrative process but more systemic and subtle problems, such as strong interest groups capturing public authority.

2. Implications of Interest Group Power. Property owners who belong to strong and organized groups will typically defend themselves even in the absence of legal protection. As the economic analysis pointed out, in the absence of such protection, the weaker the property owner, the greater the danger of injury from government action. Those endangered include dispersed individuals as well as individuals belonging to marginal groups lacking political power.[46]

A property pact that might encourage "those citizens with disproportionate influence and power in the political process, including large corporations and development firms" to victimize the weak,[47] cannot be justified. No property system can be acceptable if it allows the autonomy-reducing effects of transitions to systemically concentrate on "the least politically powerful" members of society.[48]

3. Rejecting Individual Sacrifice. These observations also inform the second reason for rejecting the progressive property pact. In a just property system, owners have, as noted, a civic duty to support law's autonomy-enhancing background regime. The unhappy trajectory of victimization just noted implies that Justice Stevens' favored property pact might end up as a platform of sacrifice, one that contravenes, rather than manifests, a credible claim of Rawlsian civic responsibility.

Sacrifice for one's community has a long and not very happy history. The greater good, on behalf of which calls for sacrifice are made, tends to efface individuals. As Jean Hampton clarified, selflessness is not a virtue we should celebrate. While human "saints" are often revered by those whom they beneficially serve, the subordination of their individual selves (and of their own needs) to moral deliberation may well be morally blameworthy. Indirectly, self-sacrificers may be harming the very people they care for by teaching "the permissibility of their own exploitation by submitting to, and even supporting, their subservient role."[49] No wonder, then, that in eminent domain cases, law insists on compensation and does not perceive the sacrifice of landowners as an appropriate manifestation of the property pact.[50]

THE LIBERAL PACT

The two extreme formulations of the property pact, respectively standing for no civic responsibility and no government constraints, are both unacceptable. But existing takings law is not the all-or-nothing affair implied by the libertarian and progressive pacts either.

As with the waterfront land this chapter started with, so it is with property generally; the Supreme Court itself often suggests that the right answer on compensation is "sometimes." The state can neither ask for the complete self-sacrifice progressives might allow nor be limited to the libertarian's no-contribution position.

The Court does compensate sometimes, but gets there by jumping between libertarian and progressive poles based on momentary majorities. This arbitrary oscillation does not make for satisfying or stable jurisprudence. We can do better, and the liberal property pact points the way.

1. *Ad Hocery is not the Solution.* Daniel Farber, who is sympathetic to "the court's reluctance to embrace" either a "libertarian assault on the modern state or complete deference to regulators," defends the resulting ad hockery (known as the *Penn Central* test[51]) as the inevitable consequence of an effort to "square the circle." He writes, "We no longer believe that the shape of property law and the rights of property owners stem from natural law." But "if property is created by state law, and state law includes the power to modify property rights, then how can a change in state law be a violation of property rights?"[52]

Farber correctly identifies the challenge, but he is wrong to suggest that refusing to choose between two extreme positions inevitably implies that we must settle with the "muddled" predicament of existing takings doctrine.[53]

Ad hockery is offensive both to the rule of law and to property's own liberal commitment to secure owners' ability to plan. Therefore, an ad hoc transition regime is objectionable. It is also unnecessary: Farber's skepticism notwithstanding, there *is* a principled position in between these two objectionable alternatives.[54]

2. *The Liberal Pact in Practice.* Recall that, as Chapter 6 claimed, property's status as a human right need not rely on any dubious preconventional understanding. Property is a convention, but every polity that respects people's ultimate right to self-determination must adopt a property system that follows property's autonomy-enhancing *telos*. Furthermore, as shown throughout this book, this liberal *telos* is not only the source of property's justification but also the most fundamental design principle for property's primary rules.

Property's autonomy-enhancing *telos* similarly can, indeed should, shape the system's secondary rules. The liberal pact introduced at the start of this chapter is the principled rule of change befitting a polity that recognizes property for its contribution to people's autonomy and is properly committed to ensuring its ongoing legitimacy.[55]

The liberal pact responds to property's autonomy-enhancing *telos*, which commands a polity to entrench property's stability. At the same time, it also allows for sufficient dynamism so as to ensure that the private authority of owners is not improperly augmented and that they comply with the property-based civic duty of keeping the property system both just and viable. Not surprisingly, commitment to liberal property already infuses the Court's jurisprudence.

3. *Justice Kennedy's Innovation.* Perhaps surprisingly, the best statements of the liberal property pact come from Justice Kennedy, whose takings jurisprudence has been underappreciated. Perhaps his insights have been slighted because his reasoning was so fragmentary and partial. Indeed, Justice Kennedy never made much progress in defining a coherent jurisprudence that tracks the liberal understanding of property. But he did point in the right direction through his lonely attempts to resist the two extreme positions criticized above.

Justice Kennedy's concurrence in *Lucas* can serve as a starting point. He maintains that, to assess an owner's loss, reference must be made to "reasonable, investment-backed expectations." He acknowledges the difficulties of this test when he worries about an "inherent tendency towards circularity," but insists it "is not circular in its entirety" because "[t]he expectations protected by the Constitution are based on objective rules and customs that can be understood as reasonable by all parties involved."[56]

But what are these "rules and customs"? Herein lies Justice Kennedy's most important contribution. "The Takings Clause," he writes, "does not require a static body of state property law," and "reasonable expectations must be understood in light of the whole of our legal tradition."[57] This is the insight that animates the liberal property pact.

It is instructive to pause and indeed reflect on the tradition – the common law tradition – and what it implies for the idea of citizens' reasonable expectations. The common law unapologetically applies new rules even to pending cases.[58] This rule of change was often justified by proclaiming that judges merely find the law. But as even traditionalist (friendly) students of the common law acknowledge, at least in some cases judges do not merely make such declarations.[59]

4. *Judging and Property Accretion.* More precisely, as Karl Llewellyn noted, "judges in fact do both at once." Common law adjudication is creative in the sense of "the sharp or loose phrasing of the solving rule" and its "limitation or extension and ... direction." But this creativity is considerably constrained by the "given materials which come to [the judges] not only with content but with organization, which not only limit but guide, which strain and 'feel' in one direction rather than another and with one intensity rather than another." Thus, the typical story of the common law (at its best) is one of "on-going renovation of doctrine, but touch with the past is too close ... the need for the clean line is too great, for the renovation to smell of revolution or, indeed, of campaigning reform." This is why judicial decisions are "*found* and recognized, as well as *made*."[60]

Llewellyn's description of this process implies that, when judges act, they generally aim to constrain themselves to legal accretions rather than legal avulsions. He observes that cases are decided with "a desire to move in accordance with the material as well as within it[,] ... to reveal the latent rather than to impose new form, much less to obtrude an outside will." Llewellyn is *not* talking about following precedents but about an attempt to bring the solution to the new case into harmony with "the essence and spirit of existing law." The instant outcome and rule must "fit the flavor of the whole"; it must "think with the feel of the body of our law" and "go with the grain rather than across or against it"; it should conscientiously seek "integration" rather than rupture.[61]

Benjamin Cardozo's account of this incremental dynamism captures its normative foundation. Cardozo describes this canonical feature of the common law tradition as an "endless process of testing and retesting" that aims at removing mistakes and eccentricities and preserving "whatever is pure and sound and fine."[62] Law is legitimate, in this view, if and only if it is typified as a quest for justification.[63] Law's dynamism, as long as properly cautious and not too frequent, is the anchor of this quest "for better and best law" and, therefore, of our judges' "duty to justice and adjustment," thus implying a relentless "re-examination and reworking of the heritage" and an "on-going production and improvement of rules."[64]

This account of "the whole of our legal tradition" implies that its rule of change perceives gradual changes as legal accretions that an individual in a liberal polity must accept. To be sure, even gradual changes that emerge out of ongoing efforts to normatively readjust and improve the law impose *some* concentrated risks and costs. But a citizen, who plays a dual role "both as one of society's subjects and as one in whose name its authority is exercised,"[65] is duty-bound to incur these costs.

So long as the evolutionary drama of law does not include sudden and dramatic changes – namely, legal avulsions – a party who has been adversely impacted by the transition should not be afforded any relief. The common law is justifiably unapologetic regarding its rule of change because incurring the costs of legal accretions is a civic responsibility; an entailment, if you will, of our Rawlsian duty to support just institutions.

At the same time, by circumscribing our civic duty in this way, this rule of change also implies that our expectations of protection from legal avulsions are "reasonable." It guards us from significant abrupt changes because, as coauthors of our laws, we are deemed to incur only the risks and costs of legal accretions.

5. *Stop the Beach*. Against this understanding of legal tradition, Justice Kennedy's pronouncement in *Stop the Beach*, a case that

fittingly but entirely coincidentally turns on the Florida law of accretion and avulsion, is particularly apt. "Incremental modification under state common law," he writes, does not take property, "as owners may reasonably expect or anticipate courts to make certain changes in property law."[66] That, in rough form, is the liberal property pact.

The rule of change in the common law tradition implies that citizens share the risks and the costs of (judicial) transitions *because* these changes all take the form of legal accretions.[67] (In the rare exceptions of legal avulsions in property matters, common law courts should apply the change only prospectively.[68])

The liberal property pact echoes this rule of change in a context that includes other types of legal transitions as well, not just judicially created ones. Some of the changes in property rights effectuated by legislatures and agencies are incremental, while others are abrupt; some impose only moderate concentrated costs, and others quite significant ones. Moderate incremental changes that affect our holdings are part of our "background" risks and opportunities, just like those covered by the black letter law of Florida regarding accretions. The avulsions of regulatory change are not incremental; they are – as they should be – compensable takings.

BOUNDARIES TO THE LIBERAL PACT

The liberal pact implies that there are limits to the concentrated burden that any individual owner should bear, although we are all duty-bound to continuously support the state's responsibility to ensure that its property system is both just and viable.

There are many legitimate versions of the liberal property pact. Polities may adopt preferred formulations that set different boundaries between legal accretions and avulsions. A liberal pact, I have argued thus far, is guided by the happy convergence of the temporal horizons of liberal property's stability and dynamism requirements. Thus, neither the fact that the pedigree of an owner's title is impeccable nor that it was perfectly just at inception means that it should be immune from change. Owners should expect legal accretions and incur their burden because they are not only society's subjects but also the coauthors of property law and its beneficiaries.

A liberal property pact presupposes that the owner is part of the benefitted community – a co-citizen of the pertinent state or member of the relevant locality, which is why the owner is indeed justifiably expected to incur the burden of such legal accretions. Another presupposition of the liberal pact is that the owner's private authority, which the legal transition at hand detrimentally affects, was initially justified. This is why the liberal pact insists that *only* legal accretions, and not legal avulsions, can go uncompensated. Things are, or at least should be, very different when either of these presuppositions does not apply.

1. *Noncitizens and the Pact.* First, the power of a polity to detrimentally affect property rights must be limited to the rights of its own members (or else of people who voluntarily put their property under its jurisdiction by, for example, purchasing real estate within its borders). Others cannot be legitimately expected to support that polity's tasks even if they are perfectly legitimate.

This first boundary is powerfully expressed by the contemporary international law of occupation. In sharp contrast to prior law, which equated occupation with conquest, the Hague Regulations of 1899, explains Eyal Benvenisti, delimit "the occupant's exercise of authority" based on the same "principles of self-determination, democracy, and human rights" that inform the contemporary understanding of legitimate national sovereignty. The occupant must "protect the life and property of the inhabitants"; and its "authority to manage public property and modify existing legislation" is strictly limited "under the constraints of necessity and the immediate goals of the occupation."[69]

This is the first principled boundary of the liberal property pact: it is limited in scope to owners legitimately subject to the state power derogating from our property rights.

2. *Non-Compensable Avulsions.* The second boundary delineates the types of property rights eligible for protection in a liberal property pact. The protection against legal avulsions provided in a liberal property pact must not serve as a sanctuary allowing legitimation of property rights that were unjust to begin with. Employing it for *that* purpose

would be an abuse of its very foundations, as a rule of change that guarantees property's ongoing justifiability.

The second boundary points to a few categories of easy cases and then to somewhat harder ones. The easy cases involve private authority that could not plausibly be justified by reference to people's ultimate right to self-determination and thus could not plausibly belong to a liberal system of property in the first place. The *liberal* property pact protects from legal avulsions only owners of at least prima facie justified property.

Echoing the idea embedded in "the whole of our legal tradition" that law must always attempt to improve its justifiability,[70] the liberal pact ought to beware from fostering within the citizenry a complacent attitude toward the legitimacy of existing property law. Rather the opposite: especially given the intrinsic normative difficulty of any claim to private authority, the liberal property pact unapologetically destabilizes holdings of morally tainted entitlements.[71]

By denying coverage to such legal avulsions, the pact may instead cultivate an attitude of cautious – maybe even suspicious – acceptance of the moral propriety of positive law, while anticipating, indeed, expecting its moral improvement.[72]

a. *Slavery.* Slavery is the most conspicuous case in this category. Slavery "was supported by the United States' legal system for a long period of time." Article I, section 9 of the Constitution was understood "to limit Congress' power to regulate slavery," and the Fugitive Slave Act provided that slave owners "may pursue and reclaim" fugitive slaves, imposed sanctions on those who aided escaped slaves, and prescribed legal obligations to aid in the capture of escaped slaves. Thus, although never without opposition, slavery was "more than simply a social and economic institution. It was also an established legal institution."[73]

It is therefore (disgracefully) clear that "when the Nation came to understand that slavery was morally wrong and mandated the emancipation of all slaves, it, in effect, redefined 'property.'"[74] Emancipation eliminated a property type and, at least from a doctrinal perspective, this property transition was abrupt.[75] It was a legal avulsion, and thus prima facie compensable. Yet, Morris Cohen was clearly correct to claim that "the state [is not] ethically bound to pay [the former owners] the fair market value of their slaves."[76]

Slavery's law exemplifies the most powerful incidence of unjust property law because making human being slaves is the ultimate case of denying their self-determination. The liberal property pact's protection against legal avulsions, therefore, cannot imply that slave owners have *any* reasonable protected expectation from a system founded on unjust private authority. Emancipation was an avulsion that cannot plausibly be deemed a compensable taking.[77]

Lesser, but still unjustified, foundations to owners' title lead to the same conclusion, as the South African constitutional property clause exemplifies. It prescribes that the "amount of the compensation" for expropriation must be "just and equitable, reflecting an equitable balance between the public interest and the interests of those affected," emphasizing that "the public interest includes the nation's commitment to land reform, and to reforms to bring about equitable access to all South Africa's natural resources." Furthermore, among the factors to be considered in determining what just and equitable compensation is, the clause mentions both "the history of the acquisition and use of the property" and "the extent of direct state investment and subsidy in the acquisition and beneficial capital improvement of the property."[78]

b. *Fair Housing Act*. Likewise, the US Supreme Court has unhesitatingly validated, without compensation, legal avulsions that removed incidents of existing property rights when those incidents violated basic norms of relational justice. Thus, public accommodations laws, as Chapter 5 argued, prevent owners from applying their right to exclude so as to contravene property's intrinsic, autonomy-based justificatory foundations.

Therefore, the Fair Housing Act did not violate the Fifth Amendment, though it was an avulsion. The Court held that, even if any member of the class regulated by the Act suffered "an economic loss" not shared by others, that loss is "of no consequence."[79]

c. *Community Property*. Similarly, a liberal pact must not build up any expectations as to the stability of a patently illiberal property governance regime.

The traditional governance doctrine of community property law belongs to this dishonorable category. It "gave a husband, as 'head and master' of property jointly owned with his wife, the unilateral right to dispose of such property without his spouse's consent." Striking down this gender-based discrimination, held the Court, justifiably invalidates the mortgage a husband gave on the home he jointly owned with his wife without her knowledge or consent, even though it was given prior to the state legislature's revision of this illegitimate governance regime.[80]

Indeed, as Cohen noted, "history is full of examples of valuable property privileges abolished without any compensation." Regarding legislative abrogation of property rights that could not be initially justified on liberal grounds – Cohen mentioned the right of nobles under feudalism "to hunt over other people's land" – it would indeed "be absurd to claim that such legislation is unjust."[81] Not all avulsions are takings.

3. *Harder cases.* There are also harder cases, for which it may not be enough to consult the autonomy-based premises of the liberal property pact. For example, where the relevant owners are commercial actors, the sophisticated economic analysis of legal transitions can, and indeed should, be consulted to refine the pact's proper boundaries. This literature identifies cases indicating that people's investment decisions are more efficient if they are encouraged to anticipate legal transitions and adjust their behavior accordingly.[82] Because the private authority of such owners is only indirectly conducive to their autonomy, a liberal property pact should adopt the pertinent economic insights.

Consider a deregulation scheme that causes incumbents significant losses in a market previously isolated from competition. As a matter of positive law, in many cases incumbents are not awarded any compensation for these losses, even if – maybe especially if – their monopoly power and rents were initially sanctioned by law.[83] The new avulsive law, in other words, is generally valid even with no compensation, notwithstanding the fact that it imposes on such incumbents the (often significant) cost of collective improvement.

This result is justified because, usually, there are no good reasons for respecting reliance on the continuation of a practice of charging prices that contain monopoly elements. Such super-competitive pricing, even if legal, should not be deemed an entitlement subject to regulatory protection.[84] Only when the previous regulation was meant to induce investment is it justified for the law to protect the investment, and then only to the extent necessary to achieve that purpose.[85] But if, for whatever reason, the incumbent cannot point to any (or any remaining) losses from stranded investments induced by the prior regulation – losses it now sustains as a result of competitive entry – then it would be inappropriate to compensate the incumbent.[86]

A similar analysis may justify Justice Stevens's suggestion (in his dissent in *Lucas*) that where a state "decide[s] to prohibit the manufacture of asbestos, cigarettes, or concealable firearms, for example," it need not "pay for the adverse economic consequences of its decision."[87] A potentially significant financial setback in cases of such legal avulsions may be desirable because it may cause the relevant actors (particularly commercial actors) to internalize the bad effects of such practices, that is, to insure or self-insure against the possibility of such legal transitions. Commercial actors who engage in legal, but harmful, activities must not be immunized against responsibility for the external effects of their practices.[88]

RECONSTRUCTING TAKINGS LAW

I conclude this chapter with its final doctrinal payoff, outlining how the liberal property pact can help to clarify and potentially improve on America's convoluted takings jurisprudence.

The pedigree of the liberal property pact, as Justice Kennedy implied, is well rooted in the common law tradition and method. It also, even more importantly, reflects a deep commitment to (liberal) property's autonomy-enhancing *telos* and to a balanced and principled conception of civic responsibility. Rendering the liberal property pact transparent would further its legitimacy, facilitate its compliance with the guidance and constraint requirements of the rule of law, and help rationalize puzzling – many say incoherent[89] – takings doctrines.

The liberal property pact, to be sure, does not provide a precise solvent of hard cases. But it does cabin disagreement and allows principled steps forward in takings jurisprudence. I work out in detail the various doctrinal queries elsewhere.[90] For the purposes of this chapter, it is enough to outline some takeaways.

Reconstructing Takings Law

1. Judicial Takings. Consider first the most recent puzzle of this tortuous body of law. Most takings jurisprudence deals with regulatory or legislative initiatives that harm landowners. In *Stop the Beach*, however, a plurality held that the same doctrines may also apply in cases where "a court declares that what was once an established right of private property no longer exists." The crux of the plurality's reasoning for adding this category of judicial takings was that "[t]he Takings Clause bars *the State* from taking private property without paying for it, no matter which branch is the instrument of the taking."[91]

Commentators have debated the question of whether there is a reason to treat judges differently from legislators and regulators.[92] Yet, as noted, once the liberal pact is properly situated as the pertinent rule of change of property law, much of this debate becomes superfluous.[93] The plurality in *Stop the Beach* is correct when insisting that the identity of the state actor does not in principle affect the takings analysis. But the convergence between the liberal pact and the traditional common law rule of change that still largely captures the judiciary's *modus operandi*, explains why a doctrine of judicial takings is simply unnecessary in the vast majority of cases.[94]

So long as judges develop the law in line with their traditional rule of change of "all accretions and no avulsion," the liberal pact prescribes that a party who has been adversely impacted by the transition should not be afforded any relief.

Judicial takings doctrine is fine in theory and an empty set in practice.

2. Eminent Domain versus Regulation. The liberal property pact provides a structurally analogous explanation for an otherwise perplexing schism between eminent domain and regulatory takings doctrines. Full compensation is *always* forthcoming in eminent domain cases, but regulatory takings doctrine finds only a (small) subset of cases that require full compensation.

Most, if not all, applications of the power of eminent domain law trigger significant and nonincremental losses on private owners, that is, they constitute legal avulsions. Hence, so long as eminent domain law does not recognize the option of partial compensation, the liberal pact would be "forced" to opt for a uniform full compensation rule.[95]

This explanation implies, however, that the so-called per se rule of "permanent physical occupation" that the Court announced in *Loretto v. Teleprompter Manhattan CATV*[96] cannot be justified. The problem with this rule is not only, as the dissent highlighted, that the "distinction between a permanent occupation [that is deemed a taking] and a [mere] physical invasion [that is not]" is plagued with difficulties.[97] The difficulty is more fundamental: a permanent occupation of a marginal and not particularly significant part of an owner's land (as was the case in *Loretto*) is not *necessarily* a legal avulsion and, consequently, should not necessarily trigger compensation.[98]

3. *Revisiting Penn Central.* The liberal pact also offers answers to some of the confusing questions of the *Penn Central* balancing tests, which cover most of the cases requiring courts to decide when a regulation of land crosses over into a regulatory taking requiring compensation.

A liberal property pact, as indicated, makes the *Penn Central* test of "investment-based expectations" meaningful. The pact reformulates the test in terms of a normative inquiry regarding the proper scope of civic responsibility and directs its interpreters to focus on the pace of the relevant property transition. This principled investigation is the antithesis of ad hockery.

4. *Reciprocity of Advantage.* Similar considerations must guide the liberal pact's understanding of the "reciprocity of advantage" test. The reciprocity of advantage concept has been part of regulatory takings from its very early days,[99] but courts still oscillate between two diametrically opposed understandings of its content.

Some interpret it narrowly, requiring that the restricted parcel receive a reciprocal benefit embedded within the specific public project, activity, or regulation. Others follow Justice Brandeis[100] and read reciprocity of advantage in a much broader sense, requiring only that the injured landowner be a member of the benefited community. In this broad reading, the landowner need only share in the general welfare-enhancement generated by the public action or by other beneficial public actions, even if this benefit is outweighed by the burden now sustained.[101] These opposing extreme interpretations spring, of course, from the libertarian and progressive pacts discussed (and rejected) earlier.

There is, however, an intermediate interpretation of the reciprocity of advantage test. This conception of reciprocity absolves the public authority from paying compensation if, and only if, the disproportionate burden of the public action in question is not overly extreme and is offset, or is likely in all probability to be offset, by benefits of similar magnitude to the landowner's current injury that he or she gains from other – past, present, or future – public actions (which harm neighboring properties).[102] Elsewhere, I discuss some manifestations of this interpretation in the existing case law, including *Penn Central* itself.[103] The concern here is only its fit to the liberal property pact.

This conception of long-term reciprocity does not require that the burden be offset by present benefits from the same transaction. Other public actions that supply roughly equivalent advantages may also be taken into consideration. In rejecting the libertarian position of strict short-term accounting, long-term reciprocity refuses to reduce citizenship and membership to monetizable exchanges, recognizing instead owners' responsibility toward their fellow community members.

At the same time, however, this conception of reciprocity rejects the progressive position. It does not find the mere fact of the landowner's membership in the community to be of enough advantage to offset any concentrated loss an owner may suffer. It requires probable, and not only theoretical, long-term reciprocity, and insists – as per the liberal pact's instructions – that a property transition can be deemed a legal accretion only if the current concentrated burden is not too extreme. Overly severe transient imbalances are deemed legal avulsions, and treated as compensable takings.

5. *Diminution of Value.* The liberal property pact also informs understanding of the "diminution in value" test. It strongly supports the demise of the so-called conceptual severance strategy, in which – consistent with the libertarian pact – a given parcel is divided (horizontally, vertically, or functionally) so as to diminish the denominator and thus amplify the severity of the owner's concentrated loss.[104]

Instead, to provide a credible assessment of whether such a loss is still within the proper scope of civic responsibility sanctioned by a liberal property regime, the diminution in value test must apply the "parcel as a whole" standard, as the Court indeed ruled in *Murr v. Wisconsin*.[105] Moreover, the liberal pact also sheds light on how to properly set the *numerator* for this calculus. It implies, again in line with the *Murr* holding, that, to determine "the amount of value retained by the owner despite a regulation," the analysis should not only include the regulated lot but also take account of increases in the value of the owners' other related lots.[106]

These constraints relate back to the initial justifications that animate the property pact. Here, the concern is to ensure that owners have sufficient stability to carry out their life plans. Looking at the "parcel as a whole" most directly approaches this liberal requirement.

6. *The Public Interest.* The final *Penn Central* test, dealing with the significance of the public interest, can also be accommodated in the liberal pact, but the weight it currently carries cannot.

Contemporary takings doctrine suggests that this test significantly affects the *Penn Central* inquiry. Current law includes a capacious list of "legitimate regulations" categories, whose impositions "do not constitute unconstitutional takings of property … *regardless of their impact on owners*" and subject only to "a narrow set of exceptions." In these types of cases, "if the regulation serves a legitimate public purpose," even "very large economic impacts can be imposed without compensation." In the current context, it is enough to mention one such category: "regulations that promote the *general welfare*," such as zoning laws, which "are valid without compensation, even if only a few owners are affected, as long as [they were not] unfairly single[d] out."[107]

Zoning laws and similar general welfare laws are certainly important, and their inclusion within the state police power evokes no qualms. But, as with the "public use" requirement of eminent domain law, their public significance should only go to this point of validity or legitimacy.[108] Indeed, even a particularly compelling public interest in the use of a property does not generally imply that the owner should incur the burden of what is otherwise a legal avulsion. Barring extreme contingencies, such a burden could be spread over the entire citizenry or over the project's beneficiaries through taxation and other measures, from which compensation could be paid.

The sheer significance of the public interest can hardly justify requiring owners to expect to incur the cost of the avulsions of regulatory change.

7. *The Nuisance Test.* This critique of the impact of the public interest on the *Penn Central* balancing doctrine also implies that the nuisance *per se* rule should be revisited.

The intuitive power of this doctrine is understandable and indeed justified. Recall that there are good reasons to situate harmful practices – even if legal – outside the boundary of the liberal pact's protection against legal avulsions. Injurious industries should expect the law to force them to internalize their external harms and, therefore, must not be shielded against property transitions even if they take the form of a legal avulsion.[109] Some types of legal transitions that define a previously unobjectionable use as a "nuisance" squarely fall into this framework. But not all do, and regarding *those* types of newly defined "nuisances," the liberal pact's protection from legal avulsions may well be necessary.

Consider the *Hadacheck* case. The city of Los Angeles "came to the nuisance" of Hadacheck's brickyard and then, through its newly enacted zoning ordinance, made his operations unlawful. It was undisputed that Hadacheck had invested in that particular piece of land precisely because it was distant from the city. It was also undisputed that the ordinance almost wiped out his investment, diminishing its value from $800,000 to $60,000.

And yet, Hadacheck's claim that without compensation the ordinance was tantamount to an unlawful taking, was rejected. The Court conceded that this use of the police power "may, indeed, seem harsh in its exercise, [and] usually is on some individual," but quickly added that "the imperative necessity for its existence precludes any limitation upon it when not exerted arbitrarily." The fact that the reduction in the value of Hadacheck's land was very significant (92.5%) was of no moment to the Court. "There must be progress," it proclaimed, "and if, in its march, private interests are in the way, they must yield to the good of the community."[110]

This is an unnecessarily harsh outcome, and one inconsistent with the liberal property pact. The difference between causing a harm that thereafter becomes actionable and engaging in an activity that turns harmful only when others become one's neighbors is clear to anyone except to the supporters of Justice Scalia's overly skeptical (Coasean) propositions about nuisance.[111] The law, to be sure, justifiably requires landowners "to contemplate and expect the possibility that the adjoining land may be settled, sold or otherwise transferred and that a condition originally harmless may result in an actionable nuisance when there is later development." Coming to a nuisance is thus properly not an absolute defense to a nuisance claim. But it is still, and justifiably so, "a factor to be considered in determining whether the nuisance is actionable."[112] When coming to the nuisance implies a legal avulsion, even the civic responsibility expected from a wealthy owner like Hadacheck respecting a commercial property must be circumscribed.[113] Huge losses, such as the diminution in the value of Hadacheck's land, can hardly comply with the liberal pact.

★ ★ ★

American takings law deserves detailed treatment. Its main tests are mentioned here only to illustrate the potential of the liberal pact to guide this labyrinthine body of law toward a principled and normatively attractive reconstruction. The sketch of this reconstruction also shows that, notwithstanding the rhetorical power of the libertarian and the progressive pacts in the case law, neither version of the pact can plausibly fit the doctrine as it exists or as it should be.

The distinction between legal accretions and avulsions, which the liberal pact captures, is indeed crucial to a proper treatment of legal transitions in a liberal polity. This distinction relies on property's autonomy-enhancing foundations: property's empowering potential and the gravity and persistence of its justificatory challenge. These foundations also clarify the boundaries of the liberal pact's application, namely, why occupiers cannot invoke it to legitimize property transitions and why beneficiaries of a clearly unjust property regime cannot use it as a shield.

9 AFTERWORD

Property leaves very few people indifferent – it usually has either friends or foes. Friends of property tend to celebrate property's many contributions to our collective, notably economic, goals. They also highlight property's role as a bulwark of personal independence. Property's foes are not very impressed. They insist that, for the vast majority of people, property actually generates and perpetuates inequality and dependence. Some critics resist reconstructive efforts and see these grave defects as perpetual, concluding that property needs to be uprooted rather than reformed.

When we look at the world around us, there is much to be said in favor of the more critical approach to property. Rising inequality, especially in wealthy countries, becomes the most pressing problem of our time, and the valorization of property seems to be a, if not the, culprit. Critics are also correct to be troubled by property's self-confident status in liberal thought.

Property's justificatory challenge, as shown, is much heavier and much more pressing than its friends take it to be. It is heavier both because property generates new vulnerabilities and because these vulnerabilities cannot be eliminated solely through an ameliorating background regime. It is also more pressing because it continuously resurfaces: the need for justification haunts property throughout its life in law, not only at its inception. This momentous justificatory challenge, I have argued, cannot be adequately met either by an independence-based account of property or by one that founds property only on its benefits to the collectivity.

Yet, the conclusion that property must be declared the enemy does not summarily follow. Property need not be understood as either a bulwark of independence or in collectivistic terms. When presupposing this binary structure, property's foes may end up entrenching these indefensible conceptions, thus misrepresenting some of property's current pathologies as its inevitable implications. But whether or not property's adamant foes find themselves in this particularly unhappy position, they miss out on property's great humanistic promise. Properly understood and carefully designed, property law can make a critical contribution to everyone's self-determination.

In this book, I have attempted to avoid these unfortunate consequences without falling into the quietism that threatens overfriendly accounts of property. Rather than delving more deeply into property's many real-life pitfalls and joining forces with those who call for its demise, I have tried to persuade you that an autonomy-enhancing theory *can* – if (but only if) properly configured – justify property. Much of my attention was thus devoted to fleshing out the three principles this theory prescribes – carefully delineated private authority, structural pluralism, and relational justice – and to illustrate the many more specific prescriptions of these three pillars of liberal property.

The result should be read as an exercise in radical reconstruction, one that is unapologetic about its charitable interpretation of the idea of property, while openly acknowledging its many – and at times significant – departures from property's existing manifestations.

Liberal property offers a worthy humanistic ideal. A legal system that embraces this ideal provides a diverse set of stable frameworks of private authority that are conducive, indeed indispensable, to people's ability to set up – on their own or with the cooperation of others – long-term plans. Property law can be legitimate – moreover, it can be just – if the private authority of each property type is properly circumscribed, if they all comply with relational justice, and if law's background regime both assures that everyone can have the authority typical of full private ownership and secures to us all the material, social, and intellectual preconditions of self-authorship.

Liberal property builds on important features that typify current property law. I have even claimed that its descriptive fit surpasses that of both its efficiency and its independence rivals. Thus, the idea of private authority typifies *all* property systems, and while technological developments that affect its welfarist impact tinker with its manifestations, they do not challenge its persistence.

Afterword

But property law does *not* match the dominion picture of independence theories. Law persistently offers a deeply heterogeneous inventory of relatively stable – and thus rule-of-law friendly – property types, each with its own animating principle, which offers a distinctive balance of property's intrinsic and instrumental values (independence, personhood, community, and utility). Following a structurally pluralistic architecture, property law typically pays close attention to the design of these property types' inside affairs and thus to their governance regimes.

Finally, many of the derogations from the sole and despotic dominion imagery, which is commonplace in both the efficiency and independence schools of property, seem to respond to the pressure of justification that drives much of liberal property's architecture. These dominion-qualifiers lend themselves to the maxim that owners' private authority must carefully follow its service to autonomy, and must not include powers that undermine others' right to self-determination in defiance of relational justice. Likewise, the regime governing property transitions – notwithstanding its doctrinal confusions – roughly responds to the liberal property pact, which reflects the intricate temporal dimensions of both property's autonomy-enhancing *telos* and its insistent requirement of ongoing justification.

This positive prong of this book's thesis – the claim that current property law offers a promising starting point – does not, however, imply that current law should be congratulated, let alone celebrated. I do not contend that the happy picture of liberal property approximates the law in the books – let alone the law in action – as we find it here and now, and I have no intention to belittle the gap between ideal and reality. Quite the contrary.

A radical reconstruction leverages on our commitment to property's most exalted ideals as a response to this threatening gap, and aims to pressure the architects of property law to bring it closer to its most defensible normative underpinnings. Property's autonomy-enhancing *telos* is inspiring, and the genuinely liberal property law that follows from it can confidently rely for its legitimacy on people's foundational obligation of reciprocal respect for self-determination. True friends of property should therefore follow suit and resolutely adopt whatever reforms are needed in order to bring it about.

I obviously do not know if this will happen, but I think that the effort would pay off. In the worst-case scenario, we would come out with reasons for discarding the system we have. Rather than simply assuming that a corrupt property regime is doomed, we may, for example, determine that it is beyond repair if (but only if) we conclude that the likelihood of meaningful reforms taking place is negligible and that the alternative is more acceptable. In such an extreme predicament, this would be the only responsible conclusion. But why presuppose that our predicament is so extreme? Before reaching such a conclusion of despair, a liberal theory of property offers a set of constructive reforms that property's foes should at least consider. These reforms are all guided by liberal property's autonomy-enhancing *telos*. Some aim at proactively expanding people's opportunities for both individual and collective self-determination, others at carefully restricting their opportunities for interpersonal domination and relational injustice.

Thus, liberal property requires that property's heterogeneity, which is already prominent in the commercial sphere, should also typify the other spheres where private authority over resources is conducive to self-determination: housing, work, and intimacy. It requires law to properly guarantee intra-sphere multiplicity of property types by adding property types that function as partial substitutes for each other in these spheres. It further instructs lawmakers to resort to minoritarian and utopian types in this endeavor and to add a residual type for privately designed arrangements.

No less significant than these prescriptions are liberal property's reform guidelines regarding the way some property types should be amended so as to eliminate – or at least ameliorate – their autonomy-reducing effects. Some of these guidelines follow property's relational justice, implying that all remaining oppressive governance regimes and discriminatory legally-authorized practices should be uprooted. Another guideline involves the reinterpretation of the human right to property as one that is operative horizontally (and beyond national borders) and not only vertically, and is undermined not only by failing to protect property rights but also by failing to recognize such rights. Finally, taking property's autonomy-enhancing *telos* seriously calls for a significant reorientation in the legal construction of markets, especially labor markets. Because owners' private authority must be tailored to its service to people's autonomy, the authority of owners of means of production must be diluted, which implies that managerial authority must be shrunk and workers' rights – both individual and collective – properly vindicated.

This has been a long journey. This book should not be read as a conclusive statement on property but as an invitation to social scientists, reformers, and theorists alike. I hope that social scientists will use its conceptualization of liberal property to develop tools for empirically assessing the performance of diverse property systems against property's great humanistic promise of self-determination. In turn, I invite reformers who appreciate this promise to introduce the vital – and necessarily local and contingent – culturally specific considerations and pragmatic concerns that must be integrated into and properly refine liberal property's prescriptions if they are to become actual blueprints. Finally, I encourage other theorists, who are intrigued, but not fully (or not at all) persuaded, to refine, add, or challenge the liberal theory of property I have offered in these pages.

For better or worse, property has been with us throughout the ages and is not going anywhere. It is our joint responsibility – as social scientists, reformers, and theorists – to evaluate its effects and try to do our best to make it better.

NOTES

Chapter 1

1 The most notable Lockean pitfalls are the tortuous path from the no-spoilage proviso to an endorsement of a full-blown money economy, the dubious (implicit) claim that nonowners have no right to complain about appropriations so long as enough and as good means of subsistence remain, even if they suffer nonmaterial harms, and the feeble contention that, by mixing one's physical labor with an object that originally belongs to everyone in common, one is able to obliterate others' rights to that object and establish absolute ownership of it. For a survey of some of the pertinent literature, see GREGORY S. ALEXANDER & HANOCH DAGAN, PROPERTIES OF PROPERTY 9–12 (2012). The best treatments of Locke's theory of property are JEREMY WALDRON, THE RIGHT TO PRIVATE PROPERTY 137–252 (1988) and GOPAL SREENIVASAN, THE LIMITS OF LOCKEAN RIGHT IN PROPERTY (1995). Founding property on labor is particularly problematic in contemporary society, where "labor and economic production are increasingly socialized," and individuals "are immersed in the common, cooperative circuits of production and reproduction." MICHAEL HARDT & ANTONIO NEGRI, ASSEMBLY: HERETICAL THOUGHT 91, 94 (2017).
2 *See* G.A. Res. 217 (III) A, Universal Declaration of Human Rights, art. 17 (Dec. 10, 1948) (announcing that "[e]veryone has a right to own property," and that "[n]o one shall be arbitrarily deprived of his [or her] property"). To be sure, the right to property is not included in all the international instruments that form the canon of human rights law. See, e.g., *Property, Right to, International Protection*, MAX PLANCK ENCYCLOPEDIA OF PUBLIC INTERNATIONAL LAW, http://opil.ouplaw.com/view/10.1093/law:epil/9780199231690/law-9780199231690-e864?rskey=K1Flqx&result=10&prd=EPIL (last updated July 2009).
3 For an attempt to introduce these liberal tenets into contract theory, see HANOCH DAGAN & MICHAEL A. HELLER, THE CHOICE THEORY OF CONTRACT (2017).
4 *Cf.* T.M. SCANLON, WHY DOES INEQUALITY MATTER? 108–09, 113 (2017).

5 The demanding requirement of "effective realization" is more often attached to political rights. Yet, it must also apply to property because property is not only a means for enhancing people's autonomy but also a source of vulnerability for others, and thus a possible setback to autonomy.

6 My formulation here is deliberately cautious, recognizing the possibility of self-authorship without planning as, for example, in a commitment to adopt a specific attitude regarding a set of future contingencies (say, I decide I will be a good family man).

7 This book does not probe the separate, though related, question of delineating the proper domains of the market and the state (and, therefore, does not engage with the privatization debates). Its only – quite minimal – presupposition on these matters is that the state is important because of its role in supplying the background regime required by liberal property and because self-determination relies not only on people's capacity as individuals, but also on their capacity as co-citizens. Citizenship, in other words, is both instrumentally and intrinsically valuable, and a liberal theory of property accordingly assumes a liberal state that secures distributive justice, democratic citizenship, and sufficient overall welfare.

8 *See* Joseph William Singer, *Democratic Property*, in RESEARCH HANDBOOK ON PRIVATE LAW THEORIES (Hanoch Dagan & Benjamin Zipursky eds., forthcoming).

9 RESTATEMENT (FIRST) OF PROPERTY intro., §§ 1–5 (1936).

10 2 William Blackstone, COMMENTARIES ON THE LAWS OF ENGLAND *2 (Univ. of Chi. ed. 1979) (1765–69).

11 *See* Jeremy Waldron, *Property Law*, in A COMPANION TO PHILOSOPHY OF LAW AND LEGAL THEORY 6 (Dennis Patterson ed., 1999).

12 *See* Carol M. Rose, *Canons of Property Talk, or, Blackstone's Anxieties*, 108 YALE L.J. 601 (1998); David B. Schorr, *How Blackstone Became a Blackstonian*, 10 THEORETICAL INQ. L. 103 (2009).

13 *See* Carol M. Rose, *Property as Storytelling: Perspectives from Game Theory, Narrative Theory, Feminist Theory*, in PROPERTY AND PERSUASION: CHAPTERS ON THE HISTORY, THEORY, AND RHETORIC OF OWNERSHIP 25 (1994).

14 Thomas W. Merrill & Henry E. Smith, *The Morality of Property*, 48 WM. & MARY L. REV. 1849, 1850 (2007). *See also, e.g.,* Thomas W. Merrill, *Property and the Right to Exclude*, 77 NEB. L. REV. 730, 730 (1998); J.W. HARRIS, PROPERTY AND JUSTICE 29–30, 34, 65–66 (1996); J.E. PENNER, THE IDEA OF PROPERTY IN LAW 103 (1997).

15 ARTHUR RIPSTEIN, FORCE AND FREEDOM: KANT'S LEGAL AND POLITICAL PHILOSOPHY 91 (2009).

16 ERNEST J. WEINRIB, CORRECTIVE JUSTICE 275 (2012).

Chapter 2

1 JEREMY BENTHAM, THE THEORY OF LEGISLATION 113 (R. Hildreth trans., 2nd ed. 1914).

2 As the text implies, this claim is conceptual and normative, not historical. Therefore, it applies even to legal systems – the common law would be the obvious suspect – wherein rights were consolidated only *after* the articulation of duties as well as to the remedies for their breach.

3 Any attempt to justify property's power-conferring rules while ignoring its autonomy-enhancing implications necessarily relies on the dominion conception of property and thus begs the question. *Cf.* Hanoch Dagan & Michael Heller, *Autonomy for Contract, Refined*, 38 L. & PHIL. (2020); PRINCE SAPRAI, CONTRACT LAW WITHOUT FOUNDATIONS 8 (2019).

4 *See* Hanoch Dagan & Roy Kreitner, *The Character of Legal Theory*, 96 CORNELL L. REV. 671 (2011).

5 For legal insiders, I hope that my previous work, where I delved into the details of many of the doctrines I cover in these pages, assures the credibility of my account.

6 *Cf.* H. L. A. HART & A. M. HONORÉ, CAUSATION IN THE LAW (1959).

7 *Cf.* Christopher McCrudden, *Legal Research and the Social Sciences*, 122 L.Q. REV. 632, 648 (2006).

8 Thomas Merrill and Henry Smith explain that the "architectural approach to property" distinguishes "what property does from how it does it," and emphasizes "the latter, however intertwined these aspects may be." They clarify that they do not claim that "the many purposes property serves ... can be reduced to a single metric (such as utility)." But then they add that they "do think that the kind of quasi-utilitarianism of law and economics can serve as a provisional lingua franca," and insist that "one cannot understand property except in terms of function and how that function is served." *See* Thomas W. Merrill & Henry E. Smith, *The Architecture of Property*, in RESEARCH HANDBOOK ON PRIVATE LAW THEORIES *2, 4, 20 (Hanoch Dagan & Benjamin Zipursky eds., forthcoming). *See also, e.g.,* Henry E. Smith, *Systems Theory: Emergent Private Law*, in THE OXFORD HANDBOOK OF NEW PRIVATE LAW (Andrew Gold et al. eds., forthcoming).

9 The distinction between the two impacts of autonomy on property law – as a condition of its legitimacy and as a criterion for evaluating its justness – implies that autonomy plays both a pre-political and a political role.

10 On the distinction between invention, discovery, and interpretation, see MICHAEL WALZER, INTERPRETATION AND SOCIAL CRITICISM 1–32 (1987).

11 Another way to formulate this is to say that falsifiability may not be the right concern for interpretive theories, and rival interpretations are examined by their relative ability to persuasively and coherently identify and account for the core features of the object of their investigation.

12 *See* Hanoch Dagan & Avihay Dorfman, *Against Private Law Escapism: Comment on Arthur Ripstein*, Private Wrongs, 14 JERUSALEM REV. LEGAL STUD. 37, 39–45 (2017).

13 *See infra* Chapter 3 text accompanying notes 123–126.
14 I return to this issue in Chapter 3 to address the concern of Panglossianism it invokes.
15 As the text implies, the liberal conception of property understands exclusion as a means to property's private authority.
16 *See, e.g., respectively,* Thomas W. Merrill & Henry H. Smith, *The Property/Contract Interface*, 101 COLUM. L. REV. 773 (2001); Arthur Ripstein, *Private Authority and the Role of Rights: A Reply*, 14 JERUSALEM REV. LEGAL STUD. 64, 82–83 (2017).
17 There are, of course, differences between law's protection of property rights and its protection of contractual rights: notably, unlike the former, the latter is typically dependent on the defendant's interference with improper motive or improper means. *See* DAN B. DOBBS ET AL., HORNBOOK ON TORTS 1096 (2nd ed., 2016).
18 *Cf.* Dagan & Heller, *supra* note 3.
19 I do not deny that, in a sense, the idea of private authority conceptually precedes structural pluralism and relational justice. As I argue in this chapter and below, both structural pluralism and relational justice are entailed in the commitment to self-determination that justifies constituting property around the notion of private authority. Precisely on these grounds, however, I also insist on the claim that structural pluralism and relational justice are both essential features of the *liberal* idea of property: the legitimacy of instantiating the idea of private authority depends on these requirements.
20 In other words, a *pure* conceptual analysis of property lacking *any* normative ambition is innocuous. Thus, for example, a modest interpretation of the Blackstonian conception of property can be unobjectionable. For this to be the case, its sole claim could be that, because exclusion is *often* a means of securing property's autonomy-enhancing *telos*, property *typically* involves *some* exclusion. This reformulation of the Blackstonian view ensures that, in the terms adopted below, property is a category of thinking rather than a category of deciding. It also emphasizes that the right to exclude, which often does help to secure property's private authority, is a means to an end and should thus be calibrated with an eye to that end. Clarifying this instrumental role of exclusion also precludes the claims entailed by the robust Blackstonian understanding, namely, that structural pluralism is a possible add-on to property's core and that relational justice is likewise a regulatory override exogenous to property.
21 This qualification refers to possible cases of strategic exit from (or entry to) property types.
22 Put differently: outside the realm where only one moral option is available – and is thus governed by duty-imposing legal doctrines – autonomy *implies* choice. Having only one or very few options in these other realms makes one experience life as subject to legislation rather than as self-legislating. *See infra* Chapter 4 text accompanying notes 32–34.

23 *See* Hanoch Dagan, *Doctrinal Categories, Legal Realism, and the Rule of Law*, 164 U. PA. L. REV. 1889, 1910, 1915–16 (2015).
24 *See* Hanoch Dagan, *Fiduciary Law and Pluralism, in* OXFORD HANDBOOK OF FIDUCIARY LAW 833 (Evan Criddle et al. eds., 2019).
25 As the text implies, categories of thinking are useful for learning because they typically share at least some essence. This essence – here the notion of private authority – helps refine the questions but does not determine the answers.
26 *See* Avihay Dorfman, *The Society of Property*, 62 U. TORONTO L. J. 563 (2012).
27 *See* Merrill & Smith, *supra* note 16, at 785–86. Indeed, even regarding what some see as property's signature – its third party effects – its differences with contract are more quantitative than qualitative, and both are best analyzed by reference to the same normative apparatus. *See, respectively,* Ben McFarlane & Andreas Televantos, *Third Party Effects in Private Law: Form and Function*, 1 OXFORD STUD. PRIVATE L. THEORY (2020); HANOCH DAGAN, PROPERTY: VALUES AND INSTITUTIONS 17–26 (2011)
28 *See* HANOCH DAGAN & MICHAEL A. HELLER, THE CHOICE THEORY OF CONTRACT (2017); Hanoch Dagan & Michael Heller, *Freedom, Choice, and Contract*, 20 THEORETICAL INQ. L. 595 (2019); Dagan & Heller, *supra* note 3.
29 The shift from enforcing barters to enforcing contracts is, in this sense, parallel to the shift from protecting possession to vindicating ownership.
30 *See* Hanoch Dagan, *Two Visions of Contract*, 119 MICH. L. REV. (forthcoming).
31 RESTATEMENT (FIRST) OF PROPERTY ch. 1, Introductory Note (1936).
32 *See* Wesley Newcomb Hohfeld, *Fundamental Legal Conceptions As Applied in Judicial Reasoning*, 26 YALE L.J. 710, 720 (1917) ("A right in rem is not a right 'against a thing'").
33 *Id.*, at 721.
34 *See* ARTHUR RIPSTEIN, FORCE AND FREEDOM: KANT'S LEGAL AND POLITICAL PHILOSOPHY 93 (2009); Ernest J. Weinrib, *Ownership, Use, and Exclusivity: The Kantian Approach*, 31 RATIO JURIS 123 (2018).
35 Henry E. Smith, *Property as the Law of Things*, 125 HARV. L. REV. 1691, 1693–94 (2012).
36 Henry E. Smith, *The Thing about Exclusion*, 3 BRIGHAM-KANNER PROP. RTS. CONF. J. 95, 117, 96 (2014).
37 *See* Kenneth J. Vandevelde, *The New Property of the Nineteenth Century: The Development of the Modern Concept of Property*, 29 BUFF. L. REV. 325, 366–67 (1980). This position is still prevalent in civil law countries such as Germany. *See* Yun-chien Chang & Henry E. Smith, *An Economic Analysis of Civil Versus Common Law Property*, 88 NOTRE DAME L. REV. 1, 40–41 (2012).
38 *See* Henry E. Smith, *Intellectual Property as Property: Delineating Entitlements in Information*, 116 YALE L. J. 1742 (2007). For a view in which property only deals with tangible things, see Simon Douglas & Ben McFarlane,

Defining Property Rights, *in* Philosophical Foundations of Property Law 219 (James Penner & Henry E. Smith eds. 2013).
39 Smith, *supra* note 36, at 122.
40 *Id.*, at 96.
41 *Id.*, at 113.
42 For more on the functional front, see Lee Anne Fennell, *Lumpy Property*, 160 U. Penn. L. Rev. 1955 (2012).
43 *Cf.* Katrina M. Wyman, *Property as Intangible Property*, 1 Oxford Stud. Private L. Theory (2020). *See also* Lee Anne Fennell, *Property as the Law of Complements*, *in* Research Handbook on Private Law Theories *2, 12 (Hanoch Dagan & Benjamin Zipursky eds., forthcoming) (arguing that "A welfarist approach to the field requires continually identifying anew those packages of resources that are most valuable in combination, and crafting property law to match," which means that "the most important attribute for a modern property system to possess" is "reconfigurability").
44 A discussion of the regime that should govern the resources of the public domain is beyond the scope of this book. The best treatments of this matter are Carol Rose, *The Comedy of the Commons: Custom, Commerce, and Inherently Public Property*, 53 U. Chi. L. Rev. 711 (1986); Christopher Essert, The Nature and Value of Public Space (unpublished manuscript).
45 Smith, *supra* note 36, at 118, 96 (my emphasis).
46 Henry E. Smith, *The Economics of Property Law*, *in* 2 The Oxford Handbook of Law and Economics 148, 153 (2017).
47 *See* Mark A. Lemley, *Ex Ante Versus Ex Post Justifications for Intellectual Property*, 71 U. Chi. L. Rev. 129, 143 (2004); Oren Bracha, *Give Us Back Our Tragedy: Nonrivalry in Intellectual Property Law and Policy*, 19 Theoretical Inq. L. 633 (2018).
48 Merrill and Smith are likely to resist this conclusion. For them "[t]he most basic architectural – and, in that sense, foundational – principle is that property is about things." While they agree that "property is concerned with the rights and obligations of persons," they insist that "the critical qualification is that property concerns the rights and obligations of persons *with respect to things*," and that "[t]he presence of a thing is what distinguishes property from other types of interests of importance to persons." Merrill & Smith, *supra* note 8, at *6–7. But how does the latter (definitely correct) proposition support the former one on the primacy of the thing, especially given their own (again correct) proposition that "[t]he law plays a variable role in determining what constitutes a thing eligible for treatment as property"? *Id.*, at *6.
49 Alan Brudner with Jennifer M. Nadler, The Unity of the Common Law 96, 106, 116–17, 132 (2013).
50 *Id.*, at 114–15, 118.

51 Brudner clarifies that a Hegelian account of property does not treat "insatiable acquisitiveness as natural to rational agents" and, instead, "relativizes it to an immature phase of human development where dignity is equated with the person's mastering the non-human world." While such an account "faces up to the egocentrism at its base," it "then shows how acquisitiveness is moderated as the dignity in owning becomes integrated into the life sufficient for dignity – a life that includes limitations on property for the sake of self-determination, family life, corporate life, and citizenship." Alan Brudner, *In Defense of Embedded Atomism: A Reply to Critics*, 1 CRIT. ANAL. L. 343, 346 (2014). Chapter 5 criticizes at some length the Kantian strategy of making responsibility for our self-determination wholly external to property. My critique of that position applies to the Hegelian account of property as well.

52 *See* JOHN LOCKE, TWO TREATISES OF GOVERNMENT 303 (Peter Laslett ed., 1960) (1690).

53 *See infra* Chapter 3 text accompanying notes 33–36.

54 *See generally* HANOCH DAGAN, UNJUST ENRICHMENT: A STUDY OF PRIVATE LAW AND PUBLIC VALUES 40–49, 63–108 (1997).

55 Think, for example, of retirement funds, which are fungible but nonetheless intimately related to our self-authorship and even to our (future) personhood. For similar complexities, see Bruce G. Carruthers, *The Meanings of Money: A Sociological Perspective*, 11 THEORETICAL INQ. L. 51 (2010).

56 *See, respectively*, Thomas W. Merrill & Henry E. Smith, *What Happened to Property in Law and Economics?*, 111 YALE L.J. 357 (2001); Gregory S. Alexander et al., *A Statement of Progressive Property*, 94 CORNELL L. REV. 743 (2009).

57 BRUCE A. ACKERMAN, PRIVATE PROPERTY AND THE CONSTITUTION 26–27 (1977).

58 *See* Henry E. Smith, *Mind the Gap: The Indirect Relation between Ends and Means in American Property Law*, 94 CORNELL L. REV. 959, 959, 962–63, 989 (2009).

59 *See* Smith, *supra* note 35. *Cf.* Larissa Katz, *Property's Sovereignty*, 18 THEORETICAL INQ. L. 299 (2017).

60 My account in this respect resembles those of both Kantians and Hegelians, who also argue for a conceptual connection between property's form and its substance. Our respective accounts of what this form is and of the substantive value(s) it vindicates are of course very different.

61 Hohfeld, *supra* note 32, at 747. This text epitomizes the by now almost canonical association of Hohfeld with the conception of property as a bundle of sticks. For an interesting claim to the contrary, see Andrew Halpin, *The Value of Hohfeldian Neutrality when Theorising about Legal Rights*, in NEW ESSAYS ON THE NATURE OF RIGHTS 1 (2017).

62 *See* Hohfeld, *supra* note 32, at 720, 733–34, 746–47.

63 *See* Thomas C. Grey, *The Disintegration of Property*, in PROPERTY 69 (J. Roland Pennock & John W. Chapman eds., 1980).
64 The reference here to "normal science" and later to "paradigm shifts" evokes, of course, Thomas Kuhn's distinction. *See* THOMAS S. KUHN, THE STRUCTURE OF SCIENTIFIC REVOLUTIONS (1962).
65 *Cf.* Hanoch Dagan & Roy Kreitner, *The New Legal Realism and The Realist View of Law*, 43 L. & SOC. INQ. 526, 548–49 (2018).
66 JOHN RAWLS, JUSTICE AS FAIRNESS: A RESTATEMENT 19 (2001).
67 *See* Lee Anne Fennell, *Property Beyond Exclusion*, 61 WM. & MARY L. REV. 521, 572 (2019) (concluding that exclusion is "just one possible technology of doing property work," which for Fennell is "pairing inputs and outcomes.") *Cf.* Merrill & Smith, *supra* note 8, at *9. ("The exclusion right is a means to end, which is the allocation of the right to control assets to particular persons.")
68 *See* Dagan & Heller, *supra* note 3.
69 As the text implies, once we focus on property's autonomy-enhancing work, we should figure out how to think about its just distribution. Maximizing the number of people who are autonomous authors of their own lives may be one attractive option, but implementing this option, or any other, requires a more holistic view of potentially autonomy-enhancing means (such as health care or education). This inquiry goes beyond what a theory of property can – or should – answer.
70 *See* MICHAEL OTSUKA, LIBERTARIANISM WITHOUT INEQUALITY 11–40 (2003); Reuven S. Avi-Yonah, *Why Tax The Rich? Efficiency, Equity, and Progressive Taxation*, 111 YALE L. J. 1391, 1404 (2002); Tom Malleson & Igor Shoikhedbrod, On the Very Idea of Private Property: Towards a Socialist Retrieval (unpublished manuscript).
71 *See supra* text accompanying notes 15–16.

Chapter 3

1 ARTHUR RIPSTEIN, FORCE AND FREEDOM: KANT'S LEGAL AND POLITICAL PHILOSOPHY 14, 34, 45 (2009).
2 JOHN RAWLS, JUSTICE AS FAIRNESS: A RESTATEMENT 19 (2001). While Rawls's second moral power – the capacity to abide by fair terms of cooperation provided others are also willing to do so – could have supported some of the arguments of this book, I deliberately invoke only the first power, which only defines rational autonomy and thus falls short of Rawls's conception of liberal autonomy. My aim is not to offer a Rawlsian theory of property, but rather to develop an argument that builds on premises of liberal thought as uncontroversial as possible and thus, necessarily, rather thin.
3 *Cf.* Ian Carter, *Respect and the Basis of Equality*, 121 ETHICS 538, 559 (2011).

4 *See, e.g.,* Yochai Benkler, *Siren Songs and Amish Children: Autonomy, Information, And Law*, 76 N.Y.U.L. REV. 23, 34, 39–40 (2001).
5 JOSEPH RAZ, THE MORALITY OF FREEDOM 369 (1986).
6 ALAN BRUDNER WITH JENNIFER M. NADLER, THE UNITY OF THE COMMON LAW 135 (2013).
7 *See* RAZ, *supra* note 5, at 384. *Cf.* Michael E. Bratman, *Time, Rationality, and Self-Governance*, 22 PHIL. ISSUES 73, 82 (2012).
8 As Joseph Raz explains, by embracing goals and commitments, "one progressively gives shape to one's life, determines what would count as a successful life." RAZ, *supra* note 5, at 387.
9 JAMES GRIFFIN, ON HUMAN RIGHTS 149, 151 (2008).
10 *See* ALBERT O. HIRSCHMAN, EXIT, VOICE, AND LOYALTY 21–29 (1970); Leslie Green, *Rights of Exit*, 4 LEGAL THEORY 165, 171, 176 (1998); Michael Walzer, *The Communitarian Critique of Liberalism*, 18 POL. THEORY 6, 11–12, 15–16, 21 (1990).
11 As Raz notes, "If a person is to be maker or author of his own life then he must have the mental abilities to form intentions of a sufficiently complex kind, and plan their execution. These include minimum rationality, the ability to comprehend the means required to realize his goals, the mental faculties necessary to plan actions, etc." RAZ, *supra* note 5, at 372–73.
12 H.L.A. Hart, *Between Utility and Rights*, 79 COLUM. L. REV. 828, 836 (1979).
13 RAZ, *supra* note 5, at 207.
14 *Id.*, at 372, 398.
15 *See* BRUDNER, *supra* note 6, at 254–55.
16 *Id.*, at 110–11, 151, 154, 158, 255, 262, 354, 356.
17 Brudner argues that independence and self-determination can be accommodated as the two equal cornerstones of liberal life. But as I explain elsewhere, his heroic effort cannot work. *See* Hanoch Dagan, *Liberalism and the Private Law of Property*, 1 CRIT. ANAL. L. 268 (2014).
18 JOHN RAWLS, A THEORY OF JUSTICE 27 (1971).
19 Hart, *supra* note 12, at 834–35.
20 *Contra* Arthur Ripstein, *The Contracting Theory of Choices*, 38 LAW & PHIL. (2020).
21 *See* RAZ, *supra* note 5, at 177.
22 *Cf.* WILL KYMLICKA, CONTEMPORARY POLITICAL PHILOSOPHY 123–24 (1990).
23 Isaiah Berlin, *Two Concepts of Liberty*, *in* FOUR ESSAYS ON LIBERTY 118, 126, 132–33 (1969). *Cf.* FRIEDRICH. A. HAYEK, THE CONSTITUTION OF LIBERTY 16–17 (1960).
24 *Cf.* David Enoch, *Hypothetical Consent and the Value(s) of Autonomy*, 128 ETHICS 6, 30–35 (2017).

25 RAZ, *supra* note 5, at 177–78. As the text implies, I interpret Raz's category of intrinsic value in line with what Christine Korsgaard would call extrinsic non-instrumental value; that is, a value that derives its value from some other source but is nonetheless valued for its own sake. *See* Christine M. Korsgaard, *Two Distinctions of Goodness*, 92 PHIL. REV. 169, 170 (1983).

26 *See supra* text accompanying note 19.

27 BRUDNER, *supra* note 6, at 40.

28 BERLIN, *supra* note 23, at 168–69, 200.

29 Kantians obviously argue that the *idea* of independence rules out these kinds of qualitative judgments, and in the Kantian conceptual apparatus it indeed does. But Hart's point – or at least the way I understand it – is that this binary conceptualization distorts the way the value of independence functions in our practical reasoning.

30 This does not mean that autonomy cannot *also* be instrumental for other values. For example, for friendship to be valuable, it needs to be autonomously chosen.

31 Readers may ask why these are *property* values rather than merely values that property owners endorse. The query, in other words, is what is the role of *law* with respect to *these* values? Or why is it not enough for law to enhance our autonomy by establishing and sustaining the power-conferring institution of "generic" (Blackstonian?) property? This is a pertinent question, and I address it in some detail in Chapter 4.

32 *See* Philip Pettit, *The Cunning of Trust*, 24 PHIL. & PUB. AFF. 202, 209–10 (1995).

33 *See, e.g.,* HELGA DITTMAR, THE SOCIAL PSYCHOLOGY OF MATERIAL POSSESSIONS: TO HAVE IS TO BE (1992).

34 *See* Margaret J. Radin, *Property and Personhood*, 34 STAN. L. REV. 957, 959, 977 (1982); Margaret J. Radin, *Residential Rent Control*, 15 PHIL. & PUB. AFF. 350, 362–63 (1986). *See also* Russell W. Belk, *The Ineluctable Mysteries of Possessions*, in TO HAVE POSSESSIONS: A HANDBOOK ON OWNERSHIP AND PROPERTY 17, 35–37 (F. W. Rudmin ed., 1991).

35 *See* JEREMY WALDRON, THE RIGHT TO PRIVATE PROPERTY 353, 364–65, 369–70, 372–73, 378, 385 (1988). *See also* Peter G. Stillman, *Property, Freedom, and Individuality in Hegel's and Marx's Political Thought*, in PROPERTY: NOMOS XXII 130, 135 (J. Roland Pennock & John W. Chapman eds., 1980).

36 *See* Dudley Knowles, *Hegel on Property and Personality*, 33 PHIL. Q. 45, 52, 56–57 (1983); C. Edwin Baker, *Property and Its Relation to Constitutionally Protected Liberty*, 134 U. PA. L. REV. 741, 746–47 (1986). *Cf.* STEPHEN R. MUNZER, A THEORY OF PROPERTY § 4.3 (1990).

37 *See* MARGARET JANE RADIN, REINTERPRETING PROPERTY 12 (1993). *Cf.* Daniel Markovits & Alan Schwartz, Rights and Remedies in Private Law (unpublished manuscript).

38 *See supra* Chapter 2 text following note 55.
39 *See* Belk, *supra* note 34, at 21–22, 25, 27–35.
40 *See* Hanoch Dagan, *Why Markets? Welfare, Autonomy, and the Just Society*, 117 MICH. L. REV. 1289, 1305 (2019).
41 *See* Gregory S. Alexander, *Dilemmas of Group Autonomy: Residential Associations and Community*, 75 CORNELL L. REV. 26, 41–42 (1989); Robert C. Ellickson, *Property in Land*, 102 YALE L.J. 1315, 1345, 1395 (1993); Robert McC. Netting, *What Alpine Peasants Have in Common: Observations on Communal Tenure in a Swiss Village*, 4 HUM. ECOLOGY 135, 143 n.13 (1976).
42 Hanoch Dagan & Michael A. Heller, *The Liberal Commons*, 110 YALE L.J. 549, 561–63 (2001). In certain contexts, the instrumental benefits of the commons have become more salient with the decline of the welfare state. *See* Eva Vriens & Tine de Moor, *Mutuals on the Move: Exclusion Processes in the Welfare State and the Rediscovery of Mutualism*, 8(1) SOCIAL INCLUSION 225 (2020).
43 *But see* Ugo Mattei, The State, the Market and Some Preliminary Questions About the Commons, http://ideas.iuctorino.it/RePEc/iuc-rpaper/1-11_Mattei.pdf ("The commons are radically incompatible with the idea of individual autonomy as developed in the rights-based capitalistic tradition.").
44 Samuel Scheffler, *Relationships and Responsibilities*, 26 PHIL. & PUB. AFF. 189, 200 (1997).
45 *Cf.* JON ELSTER, THE CEMENT OF SOCIETY: A STUDY OF SOCIAL ORDER 187 (1989); Henry Hansmann, *When Does Worker Ownership Work? ESOPs, Law Firms, Codetermination, and Economic Democracy*, 99 YALE L.J. 1749, 1769–70 (1990).
46 *See* MARGARET GILBERT, LIVING TOGETHER: RATIONALITY, SOCIALITY, AND OBLIGATION 222–23 (1996). *Cf.* Shyamkrishna Balganesh, *Unplanned Coauthorship*, 100 VA. L. REV. 1683 (2014).
47 *See* GILBERT, *supra* note 46, at 2, 8. *Cf.* Étienne Balibar, *Philosophies of the Transindividual: Spinoza, Marx, Freud*, 2(1) AUSTRALASIAN PHIL. REV. 5 (2018) (Translated by Mark G. E. Kelly). The text below implicitly explains my reservations about transindividualism. It also implies that, while both libertarians and some of their harshest critics equate individualism with atomism, liberals should – as many do – reject the atomistic conception of the individual, appreciating the constitutive role of communities and the profound effects of culture on self-identity.
48 *See* HANOCH DAGAN, PROPERTY: VALUES AND INSTITUTIONS 201 (2011).
49 *See, e.g.*, ANDREW GRAY, INDIGENOUS RIGHTS AND DEVELOPMENT: SELF-DETERMINATION IN AN AMAZONIAN COMMUNITY 109–11 (1997); Angela R. Riley, *Recovering Collectivity: Group Rights to Intellectual Property in Indigenous Communities*, 18 CARDOZO ARTS & ENT. L.J. 175, 194 (2000). In these cases, "the community is [partly] identified by the resource managed in common, while the resource is in turn [partly] identified by the

community that manages it." Maria Rossaria Marella, *The Commons as a Legal Concept*, 28 L. & CRIT. 61, 66 (2017).

50 *See* GREGORY S. ALEXANDER, PROPERTY AND HUMAN FLOURISHING 81–82 (2017).

51 *See, e.g.*, JOSEPH RAZ, ETHICS IN THE PUBLIC DOMAIN: ESSAYS IN THE MORALITY OF LAW AND POLITICS 155–74 (1994); Chaim Gans, *The Liberal Foundations of Cultural Nationalism*, 30 CAN. J. PHIL. 441 (2000); Avishai Margalit & Moshe Halbertal, *Liberalism and the Right to Culture*, 61 SOC. RES. 491 (1994).

52 In other words, although Charles Taylor is right to highlight the way in which "irreducibly social goods" rely on "a common understanding that we have formed a unit, a 'we' who understands together," he is wrong to claim that this "we" is "by definition analytically undecomposable." Charles Taylor, *Irreducibly Social Goods*, in PHILOSOPHICAL ARGUMENTS 127, 139 (1995).

53 *Cf.* RAINER FORST, THE RIGHT TO JUSTIFICATION: ELEMENTS OF A CONSTRUCTIVIST THEORY OF JUSTICE 131 (Jeffrey Flynn trans., 2011); RUTGER CLAASSEN, CAPABILITIES IN A JUST SOCIETY: A THEORY OF NAVIGATIONAL AGENCY 47–48, 62–63 (2018).

54 As accountable agents, then, people must preserve the "standpoint of sheer negative independence from everything immediately presented by [their] needs, desires, circumstances, and the like," so that they can "distinguish and distance [them]selves from what [they] happen to desire or need and from the situation in which [they] find [them]selves." PETER BENSON, JUSTICE IN TRANSACTIONS: A THEORY OF CONTRACT LAW 370 (2019).

For Benson and other Kantian and Hegelian theorists this proposition implies that independence must be understood as "higher-order" or "conceptually more basic" than self-determination (*Id.*, at 389–390, 473). But this conclusion by no means follow. Accountable agency does not, indeed cannot, imply a *permanent* state of distinction between our selves and who we actually are, that is, our higher-order projects and constitutive circumstances as well as the more concrete plans and interests we currently have.

Thus, the text tries to capture the crucial role of people's "moral power of asserting their sheer independence vis-à-vis everything particular and given" (*Id.*, at 473) without misrepresenting an intrinsic value (independence) as an ultimate one. Safeguarding exit allows people to both appreciate the constitutive role of their communities (and other contextual features) while being able to distance themselves from the standpoint of who they are and critically examine all these features.

55 *See* ANDREW MASON, COMMUNITY, SOLIDARITY AND BELONGING: LEVELS OF COMMUNITY AND THEIR NORMATIVE SIGNIFICANCE 58–59 (2000).

56 *See* Kenneth L. Karst, *The Freedom of Intimate Association*, 89 YALE L.J. 624, 632, 637 (1980). *See also* MICHAEL WALZER, SPHERES OF JUSTICE: A DEFENSE OF PLURALISM AND EQUALITY 234–39 (1983); MARILYN FRIEDMAN, WHAT ARE FRIENDS FOR? 208 (1993). Parenthood may possibly be a different matter, a context where duty should precede right. *See* Hanoch Dagan & Elizabeth S. Scott, *Reinterpreting the Status-Contract Divide: The Case of Fiduciaries*, in CONTRACT, STATUS, AND FIDUCIARY LAW 51, 62–66 (Paul B. Miller & Andrew S. Gold, eds., 2016).

57 *See* Dagan & Heller, *supra* note 42, at 574–77; *Cf.* Eduardo M. Peñalver, *Property as Entrance*, 91 VA. L. REV. 1889, 1894, 1940, 1957–58 (2005). Exit is particularly threatening to egalitarian communities since it exacerbates the challenges of brain-drain, adverse selection, and free-riding. *See* RAN ABRAMITZKY, THE MYSTERY OF THE KIBBUTZ: EGALITARIAN PRINCIPLES IN A CAPITALIST WORLD 250–51, 263 (2018). It is thus unsurprising that the typical attempts to solve the "inherent problems associated with equal sharing of resources" in such communities – especially as "members' outside options increase and their ideology declines" – involve various "lock-in mechanisms." Some of these devices take the form of prohibitive exit taxes, which inhibit exit directly. Many others take indirect forms: a "comprehensive socialization of members" to "unquestioning obedience" and severe limits of members' outside opportunities by reducing their contact with the outside world and limiting them to "commune-specific education" that is of little use elsewhere. *Id.*, at 251, 258, 266–67, 282.

58 *See* ELINOR OSTROM, GOVERNING THE COMMONS: THE EVOLUTION OF INSTITUTIONS FOR COLLECTIVE ACTION 190, 212 (1990).

59 *See* Sarah Blandy et al., *The Dynamics of Enduring Property Relationships in Land*, 81 MODERN L. REV. 85 (2018).

60 *See* ROBERT C. ELLICKSON, ORDER WITHOUT LAW: HOW NEIGHBORS SETTLE DISPUTES 60–64, 69, 76, 274 (1991).

61 *See* RUSSELL HARDIN, COLLECTIVE ACTION 186 (1982); H. L. A. HART, THE CONCEPT OF LAW 193 (1961); JEREMY WALDRON, *When Justice Replaces Affection: The Need for Rights*, in LIBERAL RIGHTS 370, 373–74, 376, 385, 387 (1993); Lisa Bernstein, *Merchant Law in a Merchant Court: Rethinking the Code's Search for Immanent Business Norms*, 144 U. PA. L. REV. 1765, 1793 (1996); Carol M. Rose, *Trust in the Mirror of Betrayal*, 75 B.U. L. REV. 531, 535, 537–38, 540–41, 546, 550 (1995).

62 *See generally* Dagan & Heller, *supra* note 42. For a response to the view that law should not promote commons property types in order to ensure that cooperators do not underinvest in screening potential cooperators and in learning how to cooperate better, see *Id.*, at 580–81.

63 For a survey of some of the pertinent literature, see GREGORY S. ALEXANDER & HANOCH DAGAN, PROPERTIES OF PROPERTY 57–70 (2012).

64 *See generally* James Griffin, Well-Being: Its Meaning, Measurement and Moral Importance ch. 8 (1986).
65 *See infra* Chapter 5 note 43 and accompanying text.
66 *But cf.* C.B. Macpherson, *Property as Means or End, in* Theories of Property: Aristotle to the Present 3, 6 (Anthony Pearl & Thomas Flanagan eds., 1979).
67 Eric A. Posner & E. Glen Weyl, *Property is Another Name for Monopoly*, 9 J. Legal Analysis 51, 52, 69 (2017). *Cf.* Lee Anne Fennell, *Fee Simple Obsolete*, 91 N.Y.U. L. Rev. 1457 (2016); Markovits & Schwartz, *supra* note 37.
68 As Katrina Wyman argues, Posner and Weyl have not empirically supported the propositions that there currently is a large-scale misallocation of resources, that it is attributable to private ownership rather than to other causes, and that the benefits of implementing their proposal will exceed the costs. *See* Katrina M. Wyman, *In Defense of the Fee Simple*, 93 Notre Dame L. Rev. 1, 25–38 (2017). *See also* Oren Bar-Gill & Nicola Persico, *Bounded Rationality and the Theory of Property*, 94 Notre Dame L. Rev. 1019 (2019).
69 *See, e.g.,* Terry L. Anderson & P.J. Hill, *The Evolution of Property Rights: A Study of the American West*, 18 J.L. & Econ. 163 (1975).
70 *See also infra* Chapter 4 text accompanying notes 66–69.
71 Rawls, *supra* note 18, at 26–27.
72 Robert Nozick, Anarchy, State, and Utopia 42 (1974).
73 *Id.*, at 43–45.
74 *Cf.* T.M. Scanlon, What We Owe to Each Other 122–23 (1998).
75 As Raz noted, "Utilitarians and others who make much turn on people's preferences as such leave out of their reckoning much essential information. They regard people's desires as opaque natural events, whereas in fact they are, in most cases, active attitudes which people hold for reasons." *See* Joseph Raz, Ethics in the public domain 132–34 (1994).
76 *See supra* text accompanying note 37.
77 *See, e.g.,* U.S. Const. art. I, § 8 ("The Congress shall have Power... *[t]o promote the Progress of Science* and useful Arts, by securing for limited Times to Authors and Inventors the exclusive Right to their respective Writings and Discoveries." [emphasis added]).
78 *See* Berne Convention for the Protection of Literary and Artistic Works art. 6*bis*(1), Sept. 9, 1886, *as revised* July 24, 1971, *and as amended* Sept. 28, 1979, S. Treaty Doc. No. 99-27 (1986). *See also, e.g.,* Study on the Moral Rights of Attribution and Integrity, 82 Fed. Reg. 7870 (U.S. Copyright Off. Jan. 23, 2017).
79 *See* Dagan *supra* note 48, at 50–52.
80 For my critique of *illiberal* commons structures, see Dagan *supra* note 48, at 66–69.

81 *Contra* Nozick, *supra* note 72, at 331.
82 *See infra* Chapter 6 text accompanying notes 123–140.
83 *Cf.* Richard H. Pildes, *Conceptions of Value in Legal Thought*, 90 Mich. L. Rev. 1520, 1557 (1992).
84 *Cf.* Eyal Zamir & Barak Medina, Law, Economics, and Morality 1–8, 79–104 (2010) (defending "threshold deontology").
85 *See* Rawls, *supra* note 18, at 542.
86 *See generally* Cass Sunstein, *Incommensurability and Valuation in Law*, 92 Mich. L. Rev. 779 (1994).
87 The discussion in the text of the subservience of the owner's right to use to her right to control explains why owners do not lose title to unused properties. Generally, for property to be autonomy-enhancing it should be up to the owner whether, when, and how to use a resource. It is not by chance that exceptions in the form of compulsory license can be found regarding purely utilitarian property types. *See* Martin J. Adelman, *Property Rights Theory and Patent-Antitrust: The Role of Compulsory Licensing*, 52 N.Y.U. L. Rev. 77 (1977).
88 As the following text clarifies, I acknowledge – indeed, emphasize – the distinction between private and public authority. Speaking of private authority, then, should not invoke Raz's familiar service conception of authority and his normal justification thesis. *See* Arthur Ripstein, *Private Authority and the Role of Rights: A Reply*, 14 Jerusalem Rev. Legal Stud. 64, 64–67 (2017).
89 Morris R. Cohen, *Property and Sovereignty*, 13 Cornell L.Q. 8, 12–13 (1927). For related claims, see Robert L. Hale, *Coercion and Distribution in a Supposedly Non-Coercive State*, 38 Pol. Sci. Q. 470 (1923); Louis L. Jaffe, *Law Making by Private Groups*, 51 Harv. L. Rev. 201 (1937).
90 Cohen, *supra* note 89, at 12.
91 *See* Avihay Dorfman, *Private Ownership and the Standing to Say So*, 64 U. Toronto L.J. 402 (2014). *Cf.* Larissa Katz, *Exclusion and Exclusivity in Property Law*, 58 U. Toronto L. J. 275 (2008).
92 *See* Dorfman, *Id.*, at 405–07.
93 The text implicitly responds to a possible concern regarding the claim that property's powers are more fundamental than its rights and liberties. This claim may seem in tension with the presupposition of certain rights and duties in Hohfeld's understanding of powers. But Cohen's and Dorfman's analysis, which I endorse, should not be understood as challenging this truism. Rather than making an analytical point, it helps us to refine both a normative and a critical lesson about property. Property's distinctive significance does not lie in the way it allocates access to resources but in the way it structures our interpersonal relationships. *See* Dorfman, *supra* note 91, at 408–18 (highlighting the practical as opposed to the merely epistemic standing that characterizes private ownership). This is why property's normative

powers stand at the center of both its contribution to people's self-determination and its legitimacy challenge.

This last point still seems debatable because, ostensibly, owners' Hohfeldian power does not pose any normative concern: by adding a favorable option, it seems to generate in nonowners an "agreeable form of liability." Wesley N. Hohfeld, *Some Fundamental Legal Conceptions as Applied in Judicial Reasoning*, 23 YALE L.J. 16, 54 n.90 (1913). But this rejoinder still misses the main point of property being, as noted, not about access but about society's authority structure.

94 Cohen, *supra* note 89, at 12.
95 *Id.*, at 11.
96 *Cf.* Joseph William Singer, *The Legal Rights Debate in Analytical Jurisprudence from Bentham to Hohfeld*, 1982 WISC. L. REV. 975 (1982); Andrei Marmor, *On the Limits of Rights*, 16 LAW & PHIL. 1 (1996).
97 For the distinction between these two meanings of power, see Christopher Essert, *Legal Powers in Private Law*, 21 LEGAL THEORY 136, 139–45 (2015).
98 Cohen, *supra* note 89, at 14.
99 *See generally* EVAN FOX-DECENT, SOVEREIGNTY'S PROMISE: THE STATE AS FIDUCIARY (2011).
100 Dorfman, *supra* note 92, at 498–501. *See also* Lisa Austin, *The Power of the Rule of Law*, *in* PRIVATE LAW AND THE RULE OF LAW 270, 283, 286 (Lisa Austin & Dennis Klimchuk eds., 2014).
101 Allen Buchanan, *Political Legitimacy and Democracy*, 112 ETHICS 689, 689–90 (2002).
102 *But cf.* David Owens, *Property and Authority*, 27 J. POL. PHIL. 271 (2019). Owens claims that whereas his thesis "need not commit itself as to the precise basis of our authority interest," it can accommodate accounts that adjust "the level" of our normative control to "why control might be valued (the ability to plan your life, self-expression, self-development, and so on)." *Id.*, at 285. But he also insists that the authority interest "applies *regardless of whether the claims, liberties, and powers in question are given to individuals to further their personal interests.*" *Id.*, at 288. This last proposition unacceptably disconnects property's architecture from its justificatory foundation.
103 Even this proposition somewhat understates the role of law in this context. *See* Hanoch Dagan & Avihay Dorfman, *Postscript to* Just Relationships: *Reply to Gardner, West, and Zipursky*, 117 COLUM. L. REV. ONLINE 261, 262–66 (2017).
104 JOSEPH RAZ, PRACTICAL REASON AND NORMS 102 (1975). As Raz has recently insisted, "normative powers exist because there is a sufficient normative case to give the power-holders the power to change certain normative situations when they choose to do so." Joseph Raz, Normative Powers, https://ssrn.com/abstract=3379368. The text aims to clarify that normative case and its limits.

105 *Cf.* BRUCE A. ACKERMAN, PRIVATE PROPERTY AND THE CONSTITUTION 71–76 (1977); JOHN RAWLS, POLITICAL LIBERALISM 298 (1993).
106 JEDEDIAH PURDY, THE MEANING OF PROPERTY: FREEDOM, COMMUNITY, AND THE LEGAL IMAGINATION 9–10 (2010). While endorsing this proposition, I disagree with Purdy's view that property "emerges as serving no master value at all," so that its only dominant feature is "the capacity to integrate [propety's] distinct values, making them mutually reinforcing" in property's "ordinary activity." *Id.*, at 18.
107 Austin, *supra* note 100, at 278–79. This dimension may explain why not only exclusion, but also use, cannot be property's fundamental building block.
108 Robert Lamb, *The Power to Bequeath*, 33 L. & PHIL. 629, 646, 652 (2014). *See also* DANIEL HALLIDAY, INHERITANCE OF WEALTH: JUSTICE, EQUALITY, AND THE RIGHT TO BEQUEATH (2018). *Cf.* Shelly Kreiczer-Levy, *Property's Immortality*, 23 CARDOZO J.L. & GENDER 107 (2016).
109 Charles R. Beitz, *Property and Time*, 27 J. POL. PHIL. 419, 427 (2018). *Cf.* ADAM J. MACLEOD, PROPERTY AND PRACTICAL REASON 1–3 (2015). *But cf.* Shmuel Nili, *The Idea of Public Property*, 129 ETHICS 344, 356 (2019).
110 *See, e.g.*, MACLEOD, *supra* note 109, at 70–71.
111 As the text implies, the fact that property is not a sine qua non condition of self-determination does not undermine its justifiability. It does, however, bolster the challenge to its legitimacy.
112 *See supra* text accompanying note 67.
113 *See* https://en.wikipedia.org/wiki/Tiny_house_movement.
114 *Cf.* Sarah E. Hamill, *Community, Property, and Human Rights: The Failure of Property as Respect*, 27 J.L. & SOC. POL. 7 (2017).
115 *See* Christopher Essert, *Property and Homelessness*, 44 PHIL. & PUB. AFF. 266, 278–81 (2016).
116 *Cf.* Avihay Dorfman, Property Beyond Exclusion (unpublished manuscript).
117 *See infra* Chapter 5 text accompanying notes 55–69.
118 *See* JEREMY WALDRON, *Homelessness and the Issue of Freedom*, *in* LIBERAL RIGHTS 309 (1993).
119 *See* Thomas W. Merrill, *Accession and Original Ownership*, 2 J. LEGAL ANALYSIS 459, 499–503 (2009).
120 *Cf.* G.A. COHEN, ON THE CURRENCY OF EGALITARIAN JUSTICE, AND OTHER ESSAYS IN POLITICAL PHILOSOPHY 151, 153, 184, 188 (2011). Like many other political philosophers, both friends and foes of property, Cohen fails to appreciate that, as a legal construct, property can be structured in ways that are, other things being equal, more – or less – autonomy-enhancing.
121 MICHAEL HARDT & ANTONIO NEGRI, ASSEMBLY: HERETICAL THOUGHT 85, 97 (2017).

122 *See* Jedediah Purdy, *Some Pluralism About Pluralism: A Comment on Hanoch Dagan's "Pluralism and Perfectionism in Private Law"*, 113 COLUM. L. REV. SIDEBAR 9 (2013).
123 Hardt and Negri add that their "conception of the common is aimed at social wealth, not individual possessions," so that "there is no need to share your toothbrush or even give others say over most things you make yourself." HARDT & NEGRI, *supra* note 121, at 98.
124 *Id.*, at 105.
125 *Cf.* Julie Dickson, *Is Bad Law Still Law? Is Bad Law Really Law?*, *in* LAW AS INSTITUTIONAL NORMATIVE ORDER 161, 169, 170, 174 (Maksymilian Del Mar & Zenon Bankowski eds. 2009).
126 *See* MICHAEL WALZER, INTERPRETATION AND SOCIAL CRITICISM 1–32 (1987).
127 *Cf.* Nicholas Blomley, *The Right to not be Excluded*, *in* RELEASING THE COMMONS 89, 95–96 (Ash Amin & Philip Howell eds., 2016).
128 *See* JOHN LOCKE, TWO TREATISES OF GOVERNMENT 303, §§ 31, 37, 46 (Peter Laslett ed., 1960) (1690).
129 For a similar analysis of the structure of Grotius's account of property, see Dennis Klimchuk, *Natural Rights and Natural Law*, *in* THE OXFORD HANDBOOK OF NEW PRIVATE LAW (Andrew Gold et al. eds., forthcoming).
130 A good example illustrating how the scope of owners' authority is tailored to its contribution to their self-determination is the doctrine of aerial trespass, which typically condemns *only* low-altitude flights. *Cf.* Dorfman, *supra* note 116.
131 *See* Hugo Bleakey, *Without Consent: Principles of Justified Acquisition and Duty-Imposing Powers*, 59 PHIL. Q. 618, 625 (2009).
132 Due to its inherent effects on others, then, the right to property is subject to internal restrictions not only if it hinders the realization of its "justificatory purpose" but also if it simply fails to serve it. *Cf.* Attila Mráz, External and Internal Restrictions of Fundamental Rights (unpublished manuscript).
133 As the text implies, the category of holdings indirectly promoting our autonomy includes not only commercial property types. There are other types of resources as well, where ownership serves purely instrumental purposes and its significance is thus typically exhausted by the resource's exchange value. (There are also specific *items* that people own, whose significance to their self-determination is remote; think, for example, of many chattels that are simply accumulated in people's basements. But a rule-of-law legal system operates, as it should, in clear predetermined categories. *See infra* Chapter 6. It thus avoids a case-by-case examination of the *actual* autonomy-enhancing service of people's particular holdings.)

The legal ownership of trust property may be a particularly interesting example here. On the one hand, the trustee usually has authority to decide how (if at all in a discretionary trust) the beneficiary's interests will be promoted. Beneficiaries have very little say (if at all) on how the property is managed and very little access (if at all) to the subject matter of the trust, and even their right to information on how the trust is managed is highly qualified. On the other hand, the trustee's private authority is qualified, full of obligations, and, most importantly, structured so as to ensure that the purpose of the trustee's actions *qua* owner is to promote someone else's interests in the property.

These aspects should not be surprising. In fact, they follow my claim that property's private authority should be carefully circumscribed to reflect its service to autonomy given that, whereas the choice to become a trustee enhances autonomy directly, the trustee's ownership of the trust property does so only *indirectly*. First, the legal ownership of trust property is functional to the settlor's and/or the beneficiary's self-determination, because it allows them to enlist the services of the trustee, and second, it is likewise strictly functional to, rather than constitutive of, the trustee's own autonomy because ownership here is a tool for potentially becoming a trustee.

134 For my purposes, the means of production include all the factors – both physical assets and IP – that a firm (or an individual) owns and which are administered on its behalf by its managers (or controlling shareholders). Another important – indeed crucial – means of production is credit. This means that the liberal theory of property developed in these pages may well call for significant reforms of the credit market, just as it does regarding the labor market. A discussion of these implications must wait for another day.

135 *See* ADOLF A. BERLE, JR. & GARDINER C. MEANS, THE MODERN CORPORATION AND PRIVATE PROPERTY 277–79 (1933).

136 *Cf.* Hanoch Dagan & Sharon Hannes, *Managing Our Money: The Law of Financial Fiduciaries as a Private Law Institution*, in PHILOSOPHICAL FOUNDATIONS OF FIDUCIARY LAW 91, 103–05, 118, 113–13, 121 (Andrew Gold & Paul Miller eds., 2014).

137 *Cf.* Nien-hê Hsieh, *Rawlsian Justice and Workplace Republicanism*, 31 SOC. THEORY & PRACTICE 115, 118–20 (2005).

138 As usual in law, there are also hard cases, on the border of the personal and the commercial, such as small family-owned businesses.

139 134 S. Ct. 2751 (2014).

140 This is not, to be sure, the only difficulty with that decision, not even from a corporate law perspective. *See* Elisabeth de Fontenay, *Individual Autonomy in Corporate Law*, 8 HARV. BUS. L. REV. 183, 199–213 (2018).

141 Molly Shaffer Van Houweling, *Authors v. Owners*, 54 HOUS. L. REV. 371, 373, 389, 401 (2016). Shaffer Van Houweling correctly notes, however, that this entitlement may not always be sufficient. She thus recommends that, when a copyright owner refuses to disseminate the author's revised version, the author would be entitled "to disseminate it herself, provided that she

shared any profits with the copyright owner under terms equivalent to those of the original transfer agreement." *Id.*, at 389.

142 Brandeis referred to *democratic* authority. *See* Michael Sandel, *Democracy's Discontent: America in Search of a Public Philosophy*, 85 Geo. L. J. 2073, 2075–76 (1996); Tim Wu, The Curse of Bigness: Antitrust in the New Gilded Age 33–44 (2018). But, as the text suggests, his insight is in fact broader.

143 *See* Hanoch Dagan, *Political Money*, 8 Elect. Law J. 349 (2009).

144 Nor concerns of intergenerational justice. *See* Beitz, *supra* note 109.

145 The text should be read as deliberately bracketing important questions as to the specific standard that should guide the liberal state's commitment to its constituents' self-determination – for example, is it enough that citizens are provided with adequate opportunities for self-determination, or must these opportunities be equal. This, and similarly significant challenges of a liberal theory of distributive justice, go beyond the ambition of a liberal theory of property. For the purposes of this book, the important proposition is that property's justifiability depends on the compliance of the state with its obligation to support its citizens' self-determination, whatever the precise content of this obligation turns out to be.

146 *See supra* text accompanying note 13.

147 Alexander, *supra* note 50, at xiv.

148 Rawls, *supra* note 18, at 293–94.

149 Alexander, *supra* note 50, at xv. For Alexander, this foundation is human flourishing rather than self-authorship. But for the purpose of the claim mentioned in the text, this otherwise significant difference between our approaches is inconsequential.

150 *Contra* Ripstein, *supra* note 1, chs. 8–9; Ernest J. Weinrib, *Poverty and Property in Kant's System of Rights*, in Corrective Justice 263, 284–89 (2012).

151 *Cf.* Elisabeth Jacobs, *Everywhere and Nowhere: Politics in Capital in the Twenty-First Century*, in After Piketty: The Agenda for Economics and Inequality 512, 515–18, 524–31 (Heather Boushey et al. eds., 2017).

152 *Cf.* Property-Owning Democracy: Rawls and Beyond (Martin O'Neil & Thad Williamson eds., 2012).

153 *See* Waldron, *supra* note 35, at 115–17, 423, 425–27, 430–39, 444–45. *See also, e.g.*, Joseph William Singer & Jack M. Beermann, *The Social Origins of Property*, 6 Can. J.L. & Juris. 217, 228, 242–45 (1993).

154 Waldron, *supra* note 35, at 444. Waldron's qualifier, which the text omits, implies that his claim is less radical, referring to "some conception" of private property. But if property can vindicate autonomy only by ascribing to each person full-blown private authority, this qualifier is misplaced. *See* Avihay

Dorfman, *The Normativity of the Private Ownership Form*, 75 MOD. L. REV. 981, 1008 (2012).

155 Recall, however, that because property is not strictly essential to self-determination, people should be able to waive their right to have property.
156 *Cf.* Essert, *supra* note 115, at 276, 290, 295.
157 MATTHEW DESMOND, EVICTED: POVERTY AND PROFIT IN THE AMERICAN CITY 5, 298–99 (2016).
158 *Id.*, at 299, 308–09, 312.
159 *See, e.g.*, Laura S. Underkuffler, *Fiduciary Theory: The Missing Piece for Positive Rights*, in FIDUCIARY GOVERNMENT 96 (Evan J. Criddle et al. eds., 2018).
160 *Cf.* ALEXANDER, *supra* note 50, at 121–33.
161 In other words, in order to evaluate the legitimacy of any existing property system, we would need to know how well it complies with the requirements discussed in the text. We would also need to develop criteria for setting up the threshold of legitimacy, given that no property system fully complies with these requirements. Both tasks are beyond the scope of this book.
162 *See* Martijn W. Hesselink, *Private Law Principles, Pluralism and Perfectionism*, in GENERAL PRINCIPLES OF EU LAW AND EUROPEAN PRIVATE LAW 21 (Ulf Bernitz & Xavier Groussot eds., 2013).
163 On this distinction, see Peter De Marneffe, *Liberalism, Liberty, and Neutrality*, 19 PHIL. & PUB. AFF. 253 (1990).
164 *See generally* BARRY SCHWARTZ, THE PARADOX OF CHOICE: WHY MORE IS LESS (2004).
165 *Cf.* Martijn W. Hesselink, *Democratic Contract Law*, 11 EUR. REV. CONTRACT L. 81 (2015).
166 *Cf.* Amnon Lehavi, *Land Law in the Age of Globalization and Land Grabbing*, in COMPARATIVE PROPERTY LAW: GLOBAL PERSPECTIVES 290 (Michele Graziadei & Lionel Smith eds., 2017).
167 As the text implies, democracy in my view is also premised on, and thus circumscribed by, the right of each individual to self-determination.
168 As the text implies, other alternatives are bound to downgrade people's right to choose their path or authorize their systemic subordination. Indeed, respecting all persons equally requires enabling all individuals to choose, or at least discover, their own life plans. *See* Leslie Green, What is Freedom For?, http://papers.ssrn.com/sol3/papers.cfm?abstract_id=2193674.
169 What follows draws on Hanoch Dagan & Avihay Dorfman, *Justice, Politics, and Interpersonal Human Rights*, 51 CORNELL INT'L L.J. ONLINE 139, 146–49 (2018).
170 *See* DUNCAN KENNEDY, A CRITIQUE OF ADJUDICATION 109–13, 147–48, 155 (1997); Gary Peller, *Reason and the Mob: The Politics of*

Representation, 2 TIKKUN 28, 92 (1987); Gary Peller, *The Metaphysics of American Law*, 73 CAL. L. REV. 1151, 1152, 1155 (1985).

171 *See* Yitzhak Benbaji, *Contract Law in a Just Society*, 20 THEORETICAL INQ. L. 411 (2019). This paragraph, where I depart from my prior claims embracing perfectionism, draws on Hanoch Dagan & Michael Heller, *Freedom, Choice, and Contract*, 20 THEORETICAL INQ. L. 595, 604–08 (2019). *See also Id.*, at 601–04.

172 The text does *not* imply that my position converges with the Kantian view. In addition to the significant differences I discuss in Chapter 5, neither the structural pluralism typifying liberal property (analyzed in Chapter 4), nor its distributive commitments (which I have already addressed) can be defended – at least not as strongly as they are within the autonomy-based understanding of property – if property's ultimate commitment, and of law more generally, is to our independence.

173 The text deliberately echoes Allan Patten's conception of "neutrality of treatment." *See* ALLAN PATTEN, THE MORAL FOUNDATION OF MINORITY RIGHTS 27–28 (2014).

174 The specific contours of property's structural pluralism, as detailed below, also resolve the concern that an autonomy-enhancing law would not be evenhanded due to infeasibility, intrusiveness, and status quo bias. *See* CLAASSEN, *supra* note 53, at 29–30.

Chapter 4

1 As the text implies, my claim is that the commitment to structural pluralism is an integral part of the liberal idea of property rather than merely a possible add-on premised on some extraneous normative ideal.

2 Interestingly, Henry Smith, whose coauthored work with Thomas Merrill is often (including in this book) considered core to the exclusion theory of property, has conveyed serious reservations about some of its central claims. *See* Henry E. Smith, *The Thing about Exclusion*, 3 BRIGHAM-KANNER PROP. RTS. CONF. J. 95 (2014). *See also* Henry E. Smith, *Exclusion Versus Governance: Two Strategies for Delineating Property Rights*, 31 J. Legal Stud. S453 (2002); Thomas W. Merrill & Henry E. Smith, *The Architecture of Property*, in RESEARCH HANDBOOK ON PRIVATE LAW THEORIES *9–10 (Hanoch Dagan & Benjamin Zipursky eds., forthcoming).

3 J.E. PENNER, THE IDEA OF PROPERTY IN LAW 5 (1997); J.E. Penner, *The "Bundle of Rights" Picture of Property*, 43 UCLA L. REV. 711, 754, 766 (1996); Thomas W. Merrill & Henry E. Smith, *The Morality of Property*, 48 WM. & MARY L. REV. 1849, 1851–52 (2007); Henry E. Smith, *Property as the Law of Things*, 125 HARV. L. REV. 1691, 1705 (2012).

4 Merrill & Smith, *supra* note 3, at 1891–92; Henry E. Smith, *Mind the Gap: The Indirect Relation Between Ends and Means in American Property Law*, 94

CORNELL L. REV. 959, 965 (2009). James Penner further argues that these exceptions can only be determined legislatively. *See* PENNER, *supra* note 3, at 100–01. I discuss – and criticize – in Chapter 6 the view that innovations in property law are solely the province of legislatures. Katrina Wyman argues that the functionalism that is supposed to guide the delineation of the exceptions makes the "new essentialist" view of property "highly malleable." *See* Katrina Wyman, *The New Essentialism in Property*, 9 J. LEGAL ANALYSIS 183 (2018). Wyman may be correct when claiming that proponents of this view are unable to provide a principled premise for setting this boundary. As the text suggests, however, this failure does not undermine the significance of the – troublesome, as I argue – effect of their claim regarding exclusion's presumptive force. For further criticism of the view that exclusion captures the essence of property, see, e.g., Avihay Dorfman, *Private Ownership*, 16 LEGAL THEORY 1 (2010); Avihay Dorfman & Assaf Jacob, *The Fault of Trespass*, 65 U. TORONTO L.J. 48 (2015); James Y. Stern, *What Is the Right to Exclude and Why Does It Matter?*, in PROPERTY THEORY: LEGAL AND POLITICAL PERSPECTIVES 38 (Michael H. Otsuka & J.E. Penner eds., 2018); Avihay Dorfman, Property Beyond Exclusion (unpublished manuscript).

5 *See* Thomas W. Merrill & Henry E. Smith, *Optimal Standardization in the Law of Property: The Numerus Clausus Principle*, 110 YALE L.J. 1, 9–24 (2000).

6 *See infra* text accompanying notes 20 and 27. For a more elaborate discussion, see HANOCH DAGAN, PROPERTY: VALUES AND INSTITUTIONS Ch. 1 (2011). Another example is the different rules governing third party effects in agency law and trust law. As Ben McFarlane and Andreas Televantos explain, the ostensible authority doctrine of agency law does not apply to trust law because the law sees beneficiaries as "the passive recipients of the fruits of assets managed by the trustees, without a 'duty of watching' over those trustees." Ben McFarlane & Andreas Televantos, *Third Party Effects in Private Law: Form and Function*, 1 OXFORD STUD. PRIVATE L. THEORY (2020).

7 Indeed, property governance refers to the way law proactively facilitates – and in some contexts even enables – people's cooperation. For Kantians, this facilitation seems to be discretionary and, in any event, not really part of property law. *Cf.* Hanoch Dagan & Michael Heller, *Autonomy for Contract, Refined*, 38 L. & PHIL. (2020).

8 Richard A. Posner, *Comment on Merrill on the Law of Waste*, 94 MARQ. L. REV. 1095 (2011).

9 *See* DUKEMINIER ET AL., PROPERTY 490 (7th ed., 2010).

10 *See, e.g., respectively* Reste Realty Corp. v. Cooper, 251 A.2d 268 (N.J. 1969); Hilder v. St. Peter, 478 A.2d 202 (Vt. 1984). For tenants, the main advantage of the latter doctrine over the former is that it allows them to stay in possession and withhold rent.

11 Gregory S. Alexander, *Governance Property*, 160 U. Pa. L. Rev. 1853, 1868 (2012).
12 *See* Robert H. Sitkoff, *An Agency Costs Theory of Trust Law*, 89 Cornell. L. Rev. 621 (2004).
13 *See* Dagan, *supra* note 6, at Pt. III.
14 This section follows Hanoch Dagan & Michael A. Heller, *Conflicts in Property*, 6 Theoretical Inq. L.197 (2005).
15 *See* Dagan, *supra* note 6, at 234.
16 *See, e.g.*, Henry Hansmann, *Condominium and Cooperative Housing: Transactional Efficiency, Tax Subsidies, and Tenure Choice*, 20 J. Legal Stud. 25 (1991).
17 *See, e.g.*, Frank H. Easterbrook & Daniel Fischel, *Close Corporations and Agency Costs*, 38 Stan. L. Rev. 271 (1986).
18 *See, e.g.*, Robert C. Ellickson, Order without Law: How Neighbors Settle Disputes 60–64, 69, 76, 274 (1991).
19 *See* Margaret A. McKean, *Success on the Commons: A Comparative Examination of Institutions for Common Property Resource Management*, 43 J. Theoretical Pol. 247, 258, 260–61 (1992).
20 *See respectively* Dagan, *supra* note 6, at 168–70; *Id.*, at 21–23.
21 Restatement (Third) of Servitudes §§ 6.4, 6.2(1) (2000).
22 *Id.* §§ 6.5–6.8.
23 *Id.* §§ 6.2(3), 6.16, 6.18.
24 *See* Dagan, *supra* note 6, at 193
25 A somewhat similar analysis applies to the tenancy by the entirety. *See id.*, at 16–17.
26 *See id.*, at 16–17 & 20–26.
27 *See, e.g.*, John P. Dwyer & Peter S. Menell, Property Law and Policy: A Comparative Institutional Perspective 218 (1998).
28 *See supra* Chapter 2 text accompanying note 23.
29 *See supra* accompanying notes 3–4.
30 For other accounts of free-standing pluralism, see John Page, Property Diversity and its Implications (2017); Anna di Robilant, *Property: A Bundle of Sticks or a Tree?*, 66 Vand. L. Rev. 869 (2013).
31 *Cf.* Stephen R. Munzer, *A Bundle Theorist Holds on to His Collection of Sticks*, 8 Econ J. Watch 265, 269 (2011).
32 Joseph Raz, The Morality of Freedom 381, 395, 398–99, 406 (1985).
33 For the limited subset of tort questions wherein structural pluralism can be autonomy-enhancing, see Hanoch Dagan, *Pluralism and Perfectionism in Private Law*, 112 Colum. L. Rev. 1409, 1428–29 (2012).
34 Charles Fried, *Contract as Promise: Lessons Learned*, 20 Theoretical Inq. L. 367, 377 (2019).
35 Note that the maxim of structural pluralism is orthogonal to the discussion on the legal recognition of same-sex marriage, which hangs on the liberal state's

obligation to make the (autonomy-enhancing) institution (or private-law-type) of marriage equally available to everyone.

36 *See* AMERICAN LAW INSTITUTE, PRINCIPLES OF THE LAW OF FAMILY DISSOLUTION: ANALYSIS AND RECOMMENDATIONS ch. 7 (2002); RESTATEMENT (THIRD) OF SERVITUDES §§ 2.1, 2.4, 2.6, 3.2 (2000).

37 *See* HANOCH DAGAN & MICHAEL A. HELLER, THE CHOICE THEORY OF CONTRACT 111–13 (2017).

38 Creative uses of property types may legitimately generate overlaps and modifications. Thus, for example, a dramatic increase in the use of tenancies in common has been recorded in the Bay Area in situations that, elsewhere, led to condominiums. *See* https://www.stimmel-law.com/en/articles/tenancy-common-ownership-san-francisco-and-bay-area-communities.

39 *See supra* Chapter 3 text accompanying notes 51–56.

40 Thus, Nozick claims that "the holdings of a person are just if he is entitled to them by the principles of justice in acquisition and transfer, or by the principle of rectification of injustice (as specified by the first two principles)." This means that "[i]f each person's holdings are just, then the total set (distribution) of holdings is just," so that any further use of the state's coercive apparatus, however attractive normatively, is an illegitimate transgression against people's rights. ROBERT NOZICK, ANARCHY, STATE, AND UTOPIA 153 (1974). These principles imply that, subject to the requirements of the principle of rectification, the role of government and of its legitimate power to tax is limited to the protection of rights to person and property. They thus denounce the use of the state's coercive apparatus for either helping the underprivileged, or even to supply goods and services that arguably improve the quality of life for everyone. *See generally* JONATHAN WOLFF, ROBERT NOZICK: PROPERTY, JUSTICE AND THE MINIMAL STATE (1991).

41 "The central core of the notion of a property right in X," Nozick writes, "is the right to determine what shall be done with X" and "to reap the [emerging] benefits" of such determination. NOZICK, *supra* note 40, at 171. The Blackstonian conception of property also underlies Nozick's famous Wilt Chamberlain fable (*Id.*, at 161) that, at least in its strong interpretation, only works if we assume that ownership must take the form of an unqualified and unconditional right. *See, e.g.*, WILL KYMLICKA, CONTEMPORARY POLITICAL PHILOSOPHY 102–03 (1990).

42 For a poignant criticism by a particularly competent commentator, see ROBERT NOZICK, THE EXAMINED LIFE: PHILOSOPHICAL MEDITATIONS 286 (1989).

43 NOZICK, *supra* note 40, at 333.

44 *Id.*, at 312, 332–33.

45 *Id.*, at 309, 320, 332–33.

46 On its face, the text overstates the conclusions of the discussion that follows because my argument refers to law *or law-like conventions*, implying that the

infrastructure required for a framework of utopias need not necessarily emanate from state law. But for non-statist sources to function like law they do have to be law-like, namely, normative coercive institutions. *Cf.* Hanoch Dagan, Reconstructing American Legal Realism & Rethinking Private Law Theory ch. 2 (2013).

47 Nozick, *supra* note 40, at 312.
48 *See, e.g.,* George Simmel, Conflict and The Web of Group Affiliations 130, 150–54 (1955); Shai Stern, Taking Community Seriously: Toward a Reform in Takings Law (unpublished manuscript).
49 Nozick, *supra* note 40, at 321.
50 *Id.,* at 329. Nozick mentions a few other difficulties in implementing his ideal of utopia in the actual world. *See Id.,* at 307.
51 *See* Thomas W. Merrill, *Property as Modularity,* 125 Harv. L. Rev. F. 151, 157–58 (2012).
52 Raz, *supra* note 32, at 162.
53 *Id.,* at 133, 265.
54 *See supra* text accompanying note 8.
55 Posner, *supra* note 8, at 1096.
56 *See supra* Chapter 3 notes 57–62 and accompanying text.
57 *See, e.g.,* Russell B. Korobkin & Thomas S. Ulen, *Law and Behavioral Science: Removing the Rationality Assumption from Law and Economics,* 88 Cal. L. Rev. 1051 (2000). On top of these transaction costs, there are certain features of cooperative endeavors – notably affirmative asset partitioning – that are (almost literally) impossible to achieve without legal intervention. *See* Henry Hansmann & Reinier Kraakman, *The Essential Role of Organizational Law,* 110 Harv. L. Rev. 387 (2000).
58 *Cf.* Hanoch Dagan & Michael A. Heller, *The Liberal Commons,* 110 Yale L.J. 549, 578–79 (2001); Ronald J. Gilson, Charles F. Sabel & Robert E. Scott, *Braiding: The Interaction of Formal and Informal Contracting in Theory, Practice, and Doctrine,* 110 Colum. L. Rev. 1137 (2010).
59 *See, e.g.,* Robert W. Gordon, *Unfreezing Legal Reality: Critical Approaches to Law,* 15 Fla. St. U. L. Rev. 195, 212–14 (1987).
60 *See, e.g.,* Ian Ayres, *Menus Matter,* 73 U. Chi. L. Rev. 3, 8 (2006).
61 Note also that choosing a type is the beginning rather than the end because people can tailor most terms within most types so that they have greater choice-making capability overall by operating within the legally facilitated range of types. Finally, whatever detrimental effects law's active facilitation may entail, they are likely to be remedied if property law addresses the prescriptions discussed in the last two sections of this chapter – to reinforce minoritarian and utopian property forms, and to structure a residual category of private arrangement.
62 I do not deny that a theoretical account of private law could start from an ideal world having no such imperfections but, at some point, these

imperfections would have to be addressed. It is actually hard to imagine how a theory of private *law* that ignored such imperfections could have practical relevance for doctrinal areas where they are not merely a peripheral concern but a *systematic* difficulty. Ignoring this difficulty would be self-defeating if a theory of law aimed to provide guidance for, or justification of, the actual legal doctrines that govern the terms of interaction among private individuals.

63 *Cf.* ROBIN WEST, NORMATIVE JURISPRUDENCE: AN INTRODUCTION 201–03 (2011).

64 Leslie Green, *The Forces of Law: Duty, Coercion, and Power*, 29 RATIO JURIS 164, 171 (2016).

65 *Cf. Id.*, at 167 ("It is a feature of our concept of law that it is *coercive if necessary*, though not necessarily coercive.").

66 Thomas Merrill's concession that property entails exclusion only vis-à-vis "strangers" – as opposed to "potential transactors," "persons within the zone of privity," and "neighbors" – does not go far enough. *See* Thomas W. Merrill, *The Property Prism*, 8 ECON J. WATCH 247, 250 (2011).

67 *See, e.g.,* BRUCE A. ACKERMAN, PRIVATE PROPERTY AND THE CONSTITUTION 71–76 (1977); JOHN RAWLS, POLITICAL LIBERALISM 298 (1993).

68 *See supra* Chapter 3 text accompanying notes 1–28.

69 *Cf.* Katrina M. Wyman, *In Defense of the Fee Simple*, 93 NOTRE DAME L. REV. 1, 39–44 (2017).

70 For this privilege and the academic controversy over its justification, see generally GREGORY S. ALEXANDER & HANOCH DAGAN, PROPERTIES OF PROPERTY 309–20 (2012).

71 *See supra* Chapter 3 text accompanying notes 133–140.

72 To give a contemporary example, consider what has happened with leaseholds. There, a single type has been largely bifurcated: the residential type is now replete with "non-waivable rights and obligations [that] may have little to do with the history of lease concepts," while the commercial leasing type lacks any such "wholesale substitution." *Compare* 1 FRIEDMAN ON LEASES § 1:2.1 (Patrick A. Randolph, Jr. ed., 5th ed., rel. 20, 2012) (describing modern approach to residential leases), *with id.* § 1:2.2 (describing commercial leasing).

73 *See generally, e.g.,* WILLIAM T. ALLEN ET AL., COMMENTARIES AND CASES ON THE LAW OF BUSINESS ORGANIZATION (3rd ed., 2009); LARRY E. RIBSTEIN, THE RISE OF UNINCORPORATION (2010); Elisabeth de Fontenay, *Individual Autonomy in Corporate Law*, 8 HARV. BUS. L. REV. 183, 193–95 (2018).

74 *See, e.g.,* FRANK H. EASTERBROOK & DANIEL R. FISCHEL, THE ECONOMIC STRUCTURE OF CORPORATE LAW 34–35 (1991).

75 Victor Li, *The End of Partnership?*, ABA J., Aug. 2015, at 48.

76 *Id.*, at 71 (quoting Robin Gibbs).

77 Ori Aronson, *The How Many Question: An Institutionalist Guide to Pluralism*, *in* INSTITUTIONALIZING RIGHTS AND RELIGION: COMPETING SUPREMACIES 147, 147 (Leora F. Batnitzky & Hanoch Dagan eds., 2017).
78 *Id.*, at 147, 162.
79 *See infra* text accompanying note 84.
80 The prevailing taxonomy in property law is not conducive to property's autonomy-enhancing *telos* either. Take, for example, the entrenched division between the system of estates in land and the question of concurrent ownership. This distinction is not arbitrary: co-owners can (and do) own a piece of property in fee simple, whereas in a condominium, for example, the unit owner owns the interior of her unit in fee simple and the condominium association (often a corporation) owns the common elements in fee simple, with the unit owner having a share in the corporation. Although this distinction has some implications, it supports a taxonomy that obscures the division of property types into spheres, which is crucial for properly addressing the requirement of intra-sphere multiplicity.
81 *See* Lawrence W. Waggoner, The American Law Institute Proposes Simplifying the Doctrine of Estates, https://ssrn.com/abstract=1612878.
82 *See* Wesley Newcomb Hohfeld, *Fundamental Legal Conceptions as Applied in Judicial Reasoning*, 26 YALE L.J. 710, 710, 720, 733–34, 746–47 (1917). As the text of this chapter clarifies, by invoking Hohfeld I do *not* implicitly invoke, let alone endorse, the dubious conception of property as bundles.
83 *See supra* Chapter 2 text accompanying notes 64–65.
84 *See* DAGAN & HELLER, *supra* note 37, at 128–30. For further political economy concerns, see Oren Bar-Gill & Clayton P. Gillette, *On the Optimal Number of Contract Types*, 20 THEORETICAL INQ. L. 487 (2019). For my response, see Hanoch Dagan & Michael Heller, *Freedom, Choice, and Contract*, 20 THEORETICAL INQ. L. 595, 615–19 (2019).
85 Another interesting example is the Creative Commons project. *See* DAGAN, *supra* note 6, at 80.
86 *See* Avital Margalit, *Commons and Legality*, *in* PROPERTY AND COMMUNITY 141 (Gregory S. Alexander & Eduardo M. Peñalver eds., 2009). *Cf.* Tsilly Dagan & Avital Margalit, *Tax, State, and Utopia*, 33 VA. TAX REV. 549 (2014).
87 *See generally* Robert J. Shiller & Allan N. Weiss, *Home Equity Insurance*, J. REAL EST. FIN. & ECON 21 (1999). *See also* Lee Anne Fennell, *Homeownership 2.0*, 102 NW. U. L. REV. 1047 (2008).
88 *See* DAGAN & HELLER, *supra* note 37, at 122–23.
89 Brett Theodos et al., Urban Institute, *Affordable Homeownership: An Evaluation of Shared Equity Programs* 3–4, 56 (2017), www.urban.org/sites/default/files/publication/88876/affordable_homeownership_0./pdf. *See also, e.g.*, Michael Diamond, *The Meaning and Nature of Property: Homeownership*

and Shared Equity in the Context of Poverty, 29 ST. LOUIS U. PUB. L. REV. 85, 88–89, 102–03 (2009).

90 *See* John E. Davis, *More than Money: What is Shared in Shared Equity Homeownership?*, J. AFFORDABLE HOUSING & COMMUNITY DEV. L., Spring/Summer 2010, at 259, 268.

91 *See* John E. Davis, *Shared Equity Homeownership*, *in* NATIONAL HOUSING INSTITUTE 75 (2006), http://www.nhi.org/pdf/SharedEquityHome.pdf; Diamond, *supra* note 89, at 87–89; Edwin Stromberg & Brian Stromberg, *The Federal Housing Administration and Long-Term Affordable Homeownership Programs*, 15(2) CITYSCAPE 247, 248–50 (2013).

92 *Cf.* Ryan Sherriff, *Shared Equity Homeownership State Policy Review*, J. AFFORDABLE HOUSING & COMMUNITY DEV. L., Spring/Summer 2010, at 279

93 *See supra* Chapter 3 text accompanying notes 145–149.

94 REPORT ON AFFORDABLE HOMEOWNERSHIP, *supra* note 89, at 45. *Cf.* Susan Saegert et al., *Longing for a Better American Dream: Homeowners in Trouble Evaluate Shared Equity Alternatives*, 96(2) SOC. SCI. Q. 297 (2015).

95 *See* California Worker Cooperative Act, ch. 192, 2015 Cal. Legis. Serv. (West); Northcounty Coop. Found., In Good Company: A Guide to Cooperative Employee Ownership 3, http://www.cccd.coop/files/worker_coop_toolbox.pdf [http://perma.cc/8BMK-PSG2].

96 *See* Priya Baskaran, *Introduction to Worker Cooperatives and Their Role in the Changing Economy*, 24 J. AFFORDABLE HOUSING & COMMUNITY DEV. L. 355, 370 (2015); *What is a Worker Cooperative?*, US Federation of Worker Cooperatives (Mar. 24, 2016), https://usworker.coop/about/what-is-a-worker-coop.

97 *See generally* David Ellerman & Peter Pitegoff, *The Democratic Corporation: The New Worker Cooperative Statute in Massachusetts*, 11 N.Y.U. REV. L. & SOC. CHANGE 441 (1982–1983).

98 Kathleen, O'Malley, AB 816 Bill Analysis at 11 (Cal. 2015), http://www.leginfo.ca.gov/pub/15-16/bill/asm/ab_0801-0850/ab_816_cfa_20150715_173239_asm_floor.html.

99 *See* Cal. Worker Coop. Pol'y Coal., Fact Sheet (June 24, 2015), https://d3n8a8pro7vhmx.cloudfront.net/theselc/pages/226/attachments/original/1439488297/AB816_Fact_Sheet_vs_3.pdf?1439488297.

100 Christina Oatfield, Governor Brown Signs California Worker Cooperative Act, AB 816, SUSTAINABLE ECONS. LAW CTR. (Aug. 12, 2015), http://www.theselc.org/governor_brown_signs_california_worker_cooperative_act [http://perma.cc/K393-3KLN].

101 *See supra* text accompanying note 26.

102 *See* DAGAN, *supra* note 6, at 223–27.

103 *See* DUKEMINIER ET AL., PROPERTY 412 (8th ed., 2014).

104 *See* DAGAN, *supra* note 6, at 16–17.

105 *See* DAGAN & HELLER, *supra* note 37, at 116–22.

106 *See supra* Chapter 2 text accompanying notes 26–28.

107 *Cf.* Martijn W. Hesselink, *Private Law Principles, Pluralism and Perfectionism*, *in* GENERAL PRINCIPLES OF EU LAW AND EUROPEAN PRIVATE LAW 21 (Ulf Bernitz & Xavier Groussot eds., 2013).

108 The qualified language of the text reflects the potential gap between what is currently termed "general" contract law, which piggybacks on the arm's length commercial contract, and a residual law of free-standing contracting, which should be shaped around the obligation to take account of idiosyncrasies. A residual contract law that can serve as a liberating device should be as open as possible to idiosyncratic choices, and thus arguably "emptier." Rather than setting up majoritarian defaults, then, it should probably be guided by an effort to set aside such conventional preconceptions and offer as many checklists as possible, thus allowing people to check an option or enter their own. *See* DAGAN & HELLER, *supra* note 37, at 84.

109 *See* Thomas W. Merrill & Henry E. Smith, *Optimal Standardization in the Law of Property: The* Numerus Clausus *Principle*, 110 YALE L.J. 1, 3 (2000).

110 *See* Michael A. Heller, *The Boundaries of Private Property*, 108 YALE L.J. 1163, 1165–66 (1999).

111 *See* Merrill & Smith, *supra* note 109, at 52–53.

112 *See Id.*, at 26–34.

113 *See* Henry Hansmann & Reinier Kraakman, *Property, Contract, and Verification: The* Numerus Clausus *Problem and the Divisibility of Rights*, 31 J. LEGAL STUD. 373, 374–75, 380–84, 416–17, 419 (2002). *See also* Glen O. Robinson, *Personal Property Servitudes*, 71 U. CHI. L. REV. 1449, 1484–88 (2004); Sarah Worthington, *The Disappearing Divide Between Property and Obligation: The Impact of Aligning Legal Analysis and Commercial Expectations*, 42 TEXAS INT'L L. REV. 917, 926 (2007).

114 *See* Merrill & Smith, *supra* note 109, at 33, 43–45.

115 Liberal property law, therefore, which focuses on the structurally pluralistic understanding of *numerus clausus* as a principle of standardization of property types seeking to offer people a stable menu of alternative frameworks of interpersonal relationships, should also strive to enable a broad realm of contractual freedom in property law. *See supra* notes 36–38 and accompanying text.

116 Henry E. Smith, *Standardization in Property Law*, *in* RESEARCH HANDBOOK ON THE ECONOMICS OF PROPERTY LAW 148, 153 (Kenneth Ayotte & Henry E. Smith eds., 2011).

117 *See* Hanoch Dagan & Irit Samet, *Express Trust as the Missing Piece in the Liberal Property Regime Jigsaw*, *in* PHILOSOPHICAL FOUNDATIONS OF TRUST LAW (Simone Degeling et al. eds., forthcoming).

118 *See, e.g.* RESTATEMENT (THIRD) OF SERVITUDES §3 (2000).

119 *See* Yun-chien Chang & Henry E. Smith, *The* Numerus Clausus *Principle, Property Customs, and the Emergence of New Property Forms*, 100 Iowa L. Rev. 2275, 2287–88 (2015).
120 This reconstruction of the *numerus clausus* principle is surely antithetical to its understanding as one of restriction, rather than reduction. *See* Avihay Dorfman, *Property and Collective Undertaking: The Principle of* Numerus Clausus 61 U. Toronto L.J. 467 (2011). But this understanding relies on a rigid, and I think indefensible, distinction between property and contract. *See infra* Chapter 6 note 28.
121 *See* Teresa Rodriguez de las Hers Ballell, Introduction to Spanish Private Law: Facing the Social and Economic Challenges 181–82 (2010); Christoph U. Schmid & Christian Hertel, Real Property Law and Procedure in the European Union: General Report 15 (2005), https://www.eui.eu/Documents/Departments Centres/Law/ResearchTeaching/ResearchThemes/EuropeanPrivateLaw/ RealPropertyProject/GeneralReport.pdf; Christian von Bar, *The* Numerus Clausus *of Property Rights: A European Principle?*, *in* English and European Perspectives on Contract and Commercial Law 441, 447 (Louise Gullifer & Stefan Vogenauer eds., 2014); Isabel V. González Pacanowska & Carlos Manuel Díez Soto, *National Report on the Transfer of Movables in Spain*, *in* 5 National Reports on the Transfer of Movables in Europe: Sweden, Norway and Denmark, Finland Spain 393, 429–31 (Wolfgang Faber & Brigitta Lurger eds., 2011); Javier Gómez Gálligo, *The Property Registry*, http://www.elra.eu (April 23, 2010), https:// www.elra.eu/spanish-property-registration-law/.

Chapter 5

1 *See* Hanoch Dagan & Avihay Dorfman, *Just Relationships*, 116 Colum. L. Rev. 1395 (2016); *Id.*, *Against Private Law Escapism: Comment on* Arthur Ripstein, *Private Wrongs*, 14 Jerusalem Rev. Legal Stud. 37 (2017); *Id.*, *The Human Right to Private Property*, 18 Theoretical Inq. L. 391 (2017); *Id.*, *Justice in Private: Beyond the Rawlsian Framework*, 36 L. & Phil. 171 (2018); *Id.*, *Postscript to* Just Relationships: *Reply to Gardner, West, and Zipursky*, 117 Colum. L. Rev. Online 261 (2017); *Id.*, *Interpersonal Human Rights* 51 Cornell Int'l L.J. 361 (2018).
2 For a survey and critique, see Dagan & Dorfman, *Just Relationships*, *supra* note 1.
3 *See* Rafeeq Hasan, *Freedom and Poverty in the Kantian State*, 26 Eur. J. Phil. 911 (2018); Rafeeq Hasan, *The Provisionality of Property Rights in Kant's Doctrine of Right*, 48 Canadian J. Phil. 850 (2018); Louis-Philippe Hodgson, *Kant on Property Rights and the State*, 15 Kantian Rev. 911 (2010).

4 Thus, Pettit's ideal of "people's undominated standing in relation to one another" – Philip Pettit, *Freedom in the Market*, 5 POL. PHIL. & ECON. 131, 147 (2006) – echoes the Kantian celebration of personal independence, which I criticize in the following pages. Both also explicitly set aside stronger claims to self-determination. *See Id.*, at 132–34.

Like the Kantians, Pettit also belittles the justificatory challenge of property by claiming that "[t]he property regime can have the aspect of an environment akin to the natural environment" (*Id.*, at 139). As noted in Chapter 3, this proposition implies that he fails to appreciate that any form of property necessarily generates *new* vulnerabilities. Pettit does acknowledge that "[t]he picture will be very different" if we recognize "the continuing role of government" in creating and sustaining "the system of property titles and property rights" (*Id.*, at 140). But he immediately dismisses this view, which I defended in Chapter 2, by "supposing" that "the property regime sprang from a history of individual adjustments" (*Id.*, at 140). Pettit neither justifies this supposition nor explains why it leads to the proposition he seeks to establish.

Finally, Pettit suggests that "public interference" is dramatically different from private interference because it "can be nonarbitrary," and thus would merely condition but would not compromise people's freedom. This proposition again shares the Kantian ideal view of the state that, as I claim below, is out of place when considering how much of people's interpersonal obligations can be legitimately delegated to the state.

5 Ernest J. Weinrib, *Poverty and Property in Kant's System of Rights*, IN CORRECTIVE JUSTICE 263, 265 (2012).
6 ARTHUR RIPSTEIN, FORCE AND FREEDOM: KANT'S LEGAL AND POLITICAL PHILOSOPHY 4, 14, 34, 45 (2009).
7 *See* WEINRIB, *supra* note 5, at 275.
8 *See* RIPSTEIN, *supra* note 6, at 91, 93.
9 Arthur Ripstein, *Kantian Perspectives on Private Law*, in THE OXFORD HANDBOOK OF NEW PRIVATE LAW (Andrew Gold et al. eds., forthcoming).
10 *See* WEINRIB, *supra* note 5, at 276–77, 283.
11 *See* RIPSTEIN, *supra* note 6, at 90. For a view in which this is also Locke's position, see Jeremy Waldron, *Nozick and Locke: Filling the Space of Rights*, SOC. PHIL. & POL'Y 81 (2005).
12 *See* Ernest J. Weinrib, *Ownership, Use, and Exclusivity: The Kantian Approach*, 31 RATIO JURIS 123, 134–35 (2018).
13 *See* RIPSTEIN, *supra* note 6, at 278.
14 The poor cannot have a right to subsistence since they cannot coerce the state that, in this view, is the ultimate repository of legitimate coercive power.
15 *See* WEINRIB, *supra* note 5, at 284–85, 288.
16 *See Id.*, at 278, 280.
17 *See* RIPSTEIN, *supra* note 6, at 192, 197–98, 279–80.

18 Lawyer-economists typically share this Kantian position for reasons of efficiency. *See, e.g.,* Louis Kaplow & Steven Shavell, *Why the Legal System Is Less Efficient than the Income Tax in Redistributing Income*, 23 J. LEGAL STUD. 667 (1994). Many have criticized this claim, but delving into this debate is unnecessary for my purposes.

19 The following text also explains why Larissa Katz misses the point when she claims that "rich public levers for public policy" can properly respond to concerns of relational justice. *See* Larissa Katz, *Legal Forms in Property Law Theory, in* PROPERTY THEORY: LEGAL AND POLITICAL PERSPECTIVES 23 (Michael H. Otsuka & J.E. Penner eds., 2018).

20 Globalization significantly exacerbates the difficulty. *See* Tsilly Dagan, *The Global Market for Tax and Legal Rules*, 21 FLORIDA TAX REV. 148 (2017).

21 *Cf.* David Enoch, *Hypothetical Consent and the Value(s) of Autonomy*, 128 ETHICS 6, 14 (2017).

22 *Cf.* David Singh Grewal, *The Laws of Capitalism*, 128 HARV. L. REV. 626, 665 (2014); Zachary Liscow, Democratic Law and Economics (unpublished manuscript).

23 Hanoch Dagan, *Political Money*, 8 ELECT. LAW J. 349, 350, 364 (2009).

24 Robert E. Goodin, *Democracy, Justice and Impartiality, in* JUSTICE AND DEMOCRACY 97, 104 (Keith Dowding et al. eds., 2004).

25 The text should not be read as an indictment of democratic lawmaking; it only echoes the truism that its products can be legitimate even if they do not fully comply with the requirements of justice.

26 *See* HANOCH DAGAN, PROPERTY: VALUES AND INSTITUTIONS ch. 6 (2011).

27 *Cf.* SAMUEL SCHEFFLER, EQUALITY AND TRADITION: QUESTIONS OF VALUE IN MORAL AND POLITICAL THEORY 135, 141–42 (2010). For a delicate account of the intricate relationship between personal and corporate responsibility for the needs of the disadvantaged, see Isadore Twersky, *Some Aspects of the Jewish Attitude Toward the Welfare State, in* A TREASURY OF TRADITION 221, 228–29, 323–33 (Norman Lamm & Walter S Wurzburger eds., 1967).

28 To make the welfare system somewhat more reliable, Kantians should have at least advocated a radical reform of it into one providing universal rather than means-tested entitlements to avoid branding anyone as dependent. Given the features and dynamics of government bureaucracies, however, even such a reform would not necessarily eliminate dependence, particularly in the Kantian utopia where the poor have no enforceable rights.

29 WEINRIB, *supra* note 5, at 288.

30 *See* RIPSTEIN, *supra* note 6, at 194.

31 *See generally* GOSTA ESPING ANDERSEN, THE THREE WORLDS OF WELFARE CAPITALISM (1990).

32 *See* David Enoch, Ideal Theory, Utopianism, and What's the Question (in Political Philosophy) (unpublished manuscript).
33 *See* Avishai Margalit, The Decent Society 222–46 (1996).
34 *Id.*, at 212–21, 236–37.
35 *See* John Rawls, Political Liberalism 268–69 (1993); John Rawls, Social Unity and Primary Goods, in John Rawls: Collected Papers 359, 371 (Samuel Freeman ed., 1999); Ronald Dworkin, Law's Empire 296, 299 (1986).
36 *See* Dagan & Dorfman, *Justice in Private*, *supra* note 1, at 178.
37 Kantians do acknowledge, as indicated, that people owe one another duties as members of the public but reiteratedly claim that our only duty as private individuals is noninterference.
38 This point epitomizes the difference between the understanding of private discrimination as relational injustice and the grounding of its wrongness on its (by definition contingent) effects on "the power relations between different social groups in our society," or the "stereotypes of the kind that result in certain people being regarded as inferior to others, or less worthy of deference." Sophia Moreau, Faces of Inequality: A Theory of Wrongful Discrimination *15 (2020). As Moreau indicates, her view implies that our legal duties as individuals not to engage in wrongful discrimination "complement public or institutional duties" and may thus diminish considerably "if the state is doing a great deal" in this regard. *Id.*, at *19, 30.
39 The case is of course reminiscent of *Masterpiece Cakeshop v. Colorado Civil Rights Commission*, 138 S. Ct. 1719 (2018), where the Supreme Court seems to agree that "while [] religious and philosophical objections are protected, it is a general rule that such objections do not allow business owners and other actors in the economy and in society to deny protected persons equal access to goods and services under a neutral and generally applicable public accommodations law." *Id.*, at 1727.
40 As Dorfman notes elsewhere, even a regime that would empower everyone with Blackstonian rights would not remedy relational injustices. In fact, such "levelling up" would only intensify the injustice of the impermissible interpersonal subjections it authorizes. *See* Avihay Dorfman, Property Beyond Exclusion *23 (unpublished manuscript).
41 *See supra* note 21 and accompanying text.
42 *See supra* Chapter 3 text accompanying notes 89–100.
43 *Cf.* Bernard Williams, *Persons, Character and Morality*, in Moral Luck 1, 12 (1981). Nothing in this argument turns on Williams' development of the concept of a ground project, including his psychological argument that the demands of impartial morality exert unreasonable pressure on the personal integrity of those who pursue such projects.
44 *See* Dagan & Dorfman, *Just Relationships*, *supra* note 1, at 1443.

45 *See* Dagan & Dorfman, *Justice in Private*, supra note 1, at 173–74, 176.
46 Arthur Ripstein, *Private Authority and the Role of Rights: A Reply*, 14 JERUSALEM REV. LEGAL STUD. 64, 80 (2017).
47 A particularly hard case is the accommodation of poverty. There is, however, a strong normative (principled) case for accommodating poverty in private law and, although it faces challenging institutional constraints, they are not necessarily overwhelming. *See* Hanoch Dagan & Avihay Dorfman, *Poverty and Private Law: Beyond Distributive Justice*, https://ssrn.com/abstract=3637034.
48 *See supra* Chapter 3 text accompanying note 19.
49 This requirement, which limits the extent of accommodative duties, does not guarantee the degree of independence that an independence-based private law regime would secure. Yet, this arrangement is justified because ensuring one party's independence in these cases implies that the other party to the interaction would be denied both equal power to determine the terms of interactions and substantive freedom to act as a self-determining agent.
50 *See, e.g.*, MOREAU, *supra* note 38, at *22.
51 *See infra* Chapter 6 text accompanying note 22. *See generally* Hanoch Dagan & Roy Kreitner, *The Other Half of Regulatory Theory*, 52 CONN. L. REV. 605 (2020).
52 For the recent debate on this front, see GREGORY S. ALEXANDER & HANOCH DAGAN, PROPERTIES OF PROPERTY 309–20 (2012). As the text implies, while the selection criterion (significance to personhood) for identifying the type of resources that are the object of robust authority is universal, the specific identification of resources that comply with it (e.g., homes) is, to some extent, a convention. *See infra* Chapter 2 text accompanying note 54.
53 Felix S. Cohen, *Dialogue on Private Property*, 9 RUTGERS L. REV. 357, 370–74, 379 (1954).
54 *See respectively* Gregory S. Alexander, *The Social-Obligation Norm in American Property Law*, 94 CORNELL L. REV. 745, 801–10 (2009); John A. Lovett, *Progressive Property in Action: The Land Reform (Scotland) Act 2003*, 89 NEB. L. REV. 301 (2011); Paula A. Franzese et al., *The Implied Warranty of Habitability Lives: Making Real the Promise of Landlord-Tenant Reform*, 69 RUTGERS U.L. REV. 1 (2016); DAGAN, *supra* note 26, at 50–52.
55 Kevin Gray & Susan Francis Gray, *Civil Rights, Civil Wrongs and Quasi-Public Space*, 1 EUR. HUM. RIGHTS L. REV. 46, 83–84 (1999).
56 Joseph W. Singer, *No Right to Exclude: Public Accommodations and Private Property*, 90 NW. U.L. REV. 1283, 1298–1300 (1996).
57 *See Id.*, at 1290–91.
58 Gray & Gray, *supra* note 55, at 99–100.
59 *Cf. Marsh v. Alabama*, 326 U.S. 501, 506 (1946) ("The more an owner, for his advantage, opens up his property for use by the public in general, the

more do his rights become circumscribed by the statutory and constitutional rights of those who use it.").

60 *Cf.* Kevin Gray, *Equitable Property*, 47(2) CUR. LEGAL PROBS. 157, 173–74, 209 (1994).

61 Recognizing community as an intrinsic property value does not lessen the disrespect conveyed by exclusion from public accommodations. Our entire civic body is also a human community, so that preserving open boundaries between sub-communities also serves the community value of property. This prescription explains and justifies noteworthy property rules that govern classical socialization venues, such as parks and beaches. It is also relevant to other venues, notably businesses of the type discussed here, because they constitute spheres of social life that should be open to universal participation (where boundaries serve no legitimate community value). *See* Singer, *supra* note 56, at 1448, 1476.

62 The text is deliberately cautious, anticipating hard cases such as people renting out their apartment for a limited time on Airbnb.

63 Margaret J. Radin, *Property and Personhood*, 34 STAN. L. REV. 957, 1011 (1982).

64 As the text implies, the gap between giving reasons and motivating is not a conceptual truth about law but a normative requirement that the law governing liberal societies must comply with. This limitation on the enforcement of motives reflects both substantive considerations, such as those pertaining to the distinction between political and personal morality of right and virtue, and instrumental ones, notably the unverifiability of persons' internal mental states.

65 *See* Avihay Dorfman, *Private Ownership and the Standing to Say So*, 64 U. TORONTO L.J. 402, 413 nn. 26 and 36 (2014).

66 *See* Avihay Dorfman, Toleration in Law (unpublished manuscript).

67 *Id.*

68 *See supra* note 65 and accompanying text.

69 The practical implications of these two lines of analysis are often likely to converge, but not always. Consider, for example, a provision in a will stating that the testator's children will only inherit if they marry a Jewish partner. *See, e.g., Shapira v. Union National Bank*, 39 Ohio Misc. 28 (1974). Dorfman's account seems to support the majority position, which validates such a condition. In my approach, this condition is just as offensive to the devisee's self-determination as a forfeiture condition that penalizes marriage (e.g., "to *A* for life, but if *A* marries, then to *B*"), which is usually deemed invalid. *See* DUKEMINIER ET AL., PROPERTY 272 (8th ed., 2014).

70 Dorfman, *supra* note 40, at *13.

71 *See* RIPSTEIN, *supra* note 6, at 292.

72 The argument is not that a state of dependence cannot ever arise out of private owners' discriminatory attitudes but that it cannot arise in any

systematic manner as long as the state, acting on its duty to support the poor, provides – directly or via incentives – housing alternatives that sustain equality of opportunity for all nonowners. *See* James Penner, *The State Duty to Support the Poor in Kant's Doctrine of Right*, 12 BRITISH J. POL. & INT'L RELATIONS 88 (2010).

73 *See* Arthur Ripstein, The Division of Responsibility 2.0 (unpublished manuscript). *Cf.* Evan Fox-Decent, *The Constitution of Equity*, in PHILOSOPHICAL FOUNDATIONS OF THE LAW OF EQUITY 116 (Dennis Klimchuk et al. eds., 2020); Shmuel Nili, *The Idea of Public Property*, 129 ETHICS 344, 359 (2019).

74 *Cf.* Aravind Ganesh, *Wirtbarkeit: Cosmopolitan Right and Innkeeping*, 24 LEGAL THEORY 159, 166–69 (2018).

75 *Cf.* JOHN EEKELAAR, FAMILY LAW AND PERSONAL LIFE 167–68 (2nd ed., 2017). ("Statements suggesting that people should act first according to their responsibilities rather than in response to the rights of others" should be "subject to particularly close scrutiny," given their tendency "to advance sectional interests (think of patriarchal structures and forced marriage) or religious or political ideologies even of a populist nature.")

76 *See generally* ELIZABETH ANDERSON, THE IMPERATIVE OF INTEGRATION chs. 6–7 (2010) (defending the democratic egalitarian case for racial integration in various social domains, including housing).

77 Arguably, discrimination is often an artifact of perception and can be harmful to people who are not, in fact, members of the class of persons the discriminator has been targeting.

78 Some of the adverse consequences (or costs) mentioned are the upshot of the owner's sheer biases, but they may also be associated with the economic value of the property. In any event, the duty to accommodate includes the accommodation of both kinds of adverse consequences, for it does not turn on whether or not it is economically rational to discriminate.

79 *See, e.g.,* Fair Housing Act, 42 U.S.C. §§ 3601–3619 (2012).

80 In addition, contextual concerns can also shape the contents of the accommodation required for the terms of the interaction between the relevant participants to count as relationally just. Thus, the duty to accommodate need not affect the right of landlords to determine tenants' maintenance obligations or similar leasing terms.

81 42 U.S.C. § 3603(b)(1)–(2) (2012). There may be good policy reasons for these exceptions, but such exceptions are inconsistent with the demands of relational justice.

82 334 U.S. 1 (1948).

83 *See* RICHARD R. W. BROOKS & CAROL M. ROSE, SAVING THE NEIGHBORHOOD: RACIALLY RESTRICTIVE COVENANTS, LAW, AND SOCIAL NORMS 173–74 (2013).

84 *Cf.* H.L.A. HART, THE CONCEPT OF LAW 82, 87–88 (1961).

85 *See* Nicholas O. Stephanopoulos, *Civil Rights in Desegregating Americas*, 83 U. Chi. L. Rev. 1329, 1339–1374 (2016).
86 Although integration may be underway, according to a recent HUD survey, "hundreds of thousands of FHA violations [still] take place" each year, which means that "[t]he struggle against discrimination has not yet been won." Stephanopoulos, *supra* note 85, at 1375–76.
87 *See* Tony Honoré, *Ownership*, *in* Making Law Bind: Chapters Legal and Philosophical 161, 165–66 (1987).
88 The text hints at the understanding of land use law and environmental law as regulatory means for meeting interpersonal obligations in complex and interconnected settings. There is some truth to this proposition, but the aggregative underpinnings of these doctrines are undeniable. Like other subsets of the modern regulatory apparatus, they are probably best characterized in hybrid terms as having significant elements of public *and* private law. *See* Dagan & Kreitner, *supra* note 51.
89 *See* Gregory S. Alexander, *Takings and the Post-Modern Dialectic of Property*, 9 Const. Commentary 259, 263, 267–69, 272–73, 275 (1992).
90 Arthur Ripstein, Private Wrongs 50 (2016).
91 *See, e.g., Id.*, at 53–80, 288–95; Peter Benson, *Misfeasance as an Organizing Normative Idea in Private Law*, 60 U. Toronto L.J. 731 (2010).
92 *See, e.g.*, Thomas W. Merrill, *Property as Modularity*, 125 Harv. L. Rev. F. 151, 157 (2012).
93 *See, e.g.*, Robert L. Hale, *Prima Facie Torts, Combination, and Non-Feasance*, 46 Colum. L. Rev. 196, 214 (1946).
94 *See respectively, e.g.*, Douglas J. Den Uyl, *The Right to Welfare and the Virtue of Charity*, *in* Altruism 192, 192–93, 197, 205, 222–23 (Ellen Frankel Paul et al. eds., 1993); Saul Levmore, *Waiting for Rescue: An Essay on the Evolution and Incentive Structure of the Law of Affirmative Obligations*, 72 Va. L. Rev. 879 (1986).
95 *See similarly* Sandy Steel, *Rationalising Omissions Liability in Negligence*, 135 L. Q. Rev. 484, 493–95 (2019).
96 *See, e.g.*, Restatement (Second) of Contracts § 161(b) (1981); *Obde v. Schlemeyer*, 353 P.2d 672 (1960); Hanoch Dagan & Avihay Dorfman, *Justice for Contracts*, https://ssrn.com/abstract=3435781.
97 *See, e.g.*, Robert Stevens, Torts and Rights 205–06 (2007).
98 *See* Avihay Dorfman & Assaf Jacob, *The Fault of Trespass*, 65 U. Toronto L.J. 48, 75 (2015); Dagan, *supra* note 26, at 18–26. For analogous doctrines in copyright, see Molly Shaffer Van Houweling, *Equitable Estoppel and Information Costs in Contemporary Copyright*, 23 Lewis & Clark L. Rev. 553 (2019). For a particularly problematic exception to this otherwise coherent set of rules, see *District of Columbia v. Wesby*, 138 S. Ct. 577 (2018). For a powerful critique, see Timothy M. Mulvaney, *A World of Distrust*, Colum. L. Rev. Forum (forthcoming), https://ssrn.com/abstract=3479239.

99 *See* Adam J. MacLeod, Trespass and Intention: Three Forms (unpublished manuscript).
100 SUSAN MOLLER OKIN, JUSTICE, GENDER, AND THE FAMILY 136 (1989).
101 *See* CLARE CHAMBERS, AGAINST MARRIAGE: AN EGALITARIAN DEFENSE OF THE MARRIAGE-FREE STATE (2017).
102 *See* Amy L. Wax, *Bargaining in the Shadow of the Market: Is There a Future for Egalitarian Marriage?*, 84 VA. L. REV. 509, 636–37 (1998).
103 ELIZABETH ANDERSON, VALUE IN ETHICS AND ECONOMICS 151 (1993).
104 *See* DAGAN, *supra* note 26, at Ch.9.
105 *See, e.g.,* EVAN MCKENZIE, PRIVATOPIA 122–23, 125–128, 140–42, 144–145, 146 (1994).
106 *See, e.g.,* Susan F. French, *The Constitution of a Private Residential Government Should Include a Bill of Rights*, 27 WAKE FOREST L. REV. 345, 350 (1992). The application of these prescriptions to indigenous communities that have an historic claim to self-government raises further complications that exceed the scope of this book. *See* Angela R. Riley, *(Tribal) Sovereignty and Illiberalism*, 95 CAL. L. REV. 799 (2007).
107 *See, e.g.,* LENORE J. WEITZMAN, THE DIVORCE REVOLUTION: THE UNEXPECTED SOCIAL AND ECONOMIC CONSEQUENCES FOR WOMEN AND CHILDREN IN AMERICA 323–56 (1985).
108 *See* MOLLER OKIN, *supra* note 100, at 147.
109 *See* Martha L. Fineman, *Implementing Equality: Ideology, Contradiction and Social Change*, 1983 WISC. L. REV. 789, 827–30.
110 For a critique of other attempts to explain rehabilitative alimony, see DAGAN, *supra* note 26, at 220–21.
111 *See* John C. Williams, Annotation, *Propriety in Divorce Proceedings of Awarding Rehabilitative Alimony*, 97 A.L.R.3d 740, 743–44 (1980).
112 Admittedly, this is an imperfect solution, which becomes increasingly unsatisfying insofar as the state renounces its responsibilities to address dependence and vulnerability. *See* Emily J. Stolzenberg, *The New Family Freedom*, 59 B.C.L. REV. 1983 (2018).

Chapter 6

1 *See* Thomas W. Merrill & Henry E. Smith, *Optimal Standardization in the Law of Property: The Numerus Clausus Principle*, 110 YALE L.J. 1, 26–34, 56–68 (2000). Long ago, the English legal historian W. S. Holdsworth noted that "the Legislature has had a larger share in shaping the land law than it has had in shaping any other branch of private law." W.S. HOLDSWORTH, AN HISTORICAL INTRODUCTION TO THE LAND LAW 325 (1927). Recently, the dominance of legislation seems as apparent regarding property's frontiers: the law of intellectual property. *See* Shyamkrishna Balganesh, *The Pragmatic Incrementalism of Common Law Intellectual Property*, 63 VAND. L. REV. 1543,

1544 (2010). But these descriptive propositions should be treated cautiously. Reliance on Holdsworth's statement must be of limited value in this context given that his book was published shortly after the massive statutory revision of land law in England. Nor is it at all clear that legislation dominated American property law (particularly in comparison to contract law, given the predominant status of the Uniform Commercial Code). *See, e.g.,* GREGORY S. ALEXANDER, COMMODITY & PROPRIETY: COMPETING VISIONS OF PROPERTY IN AMERICAN LEGAL THOUGHT 1776–1970, at ch. 4 (1997). On the courts' continued activity in developing intellectual property law despite the significant expansion of statutory law, see, e.g., Balganesh, *Id.*

2 Merrill and Smith mention six characteristics, but I note two because: (1) The ambiguity resulting from the limited binding effect of decisional rules issued by intermediate courts of appeal and the lack of a federal common law jurisdiction are of limited significance since they do not argue against decisional rules prescribed by a State Supreme Court. (2) Their discussion of the stability of legislation adds little to that of comprehensiveness and, therefore, I combine both into one category. (3) The features of prospectivity and implicit compensation are, as Merrill and Smith admit, far less relevant to information costs. More significantly, the possible disruption of the common law traditional retroactive application and the ability of legislatures to provide implicit compensation as part of a comprehensive statute are by no means, even on their face, peculiar to property. I thus discuss these features below.

3 *See* supra Chapter 4 text accompanying notes 112–114.

4 *See* ADRIAN VERMEULE, JUDGING UNDER UNCERTAINTY: AN INSTITUTIONAL THEORY OF LEGAL INTERPRETATION 10 (2006).

5 *See, respectively,* RICHARD A. POSNER, HOW JUDGES THINK 11–12, 60–61, 371 (2008); LAWRENCE BAUM, JUDGES AND THEIR AUDIENCES: A PERSPECTIVE ON JUDICIAL BEHAVIOR 16–21, 90, 106 (2006). As the text implies, the effects of judges' role morality is at least partly dependent on their training and recruitment, and – more generally – on the conception of law ingrained in legal education. *See* HANOCH DAGAN, RECONSTRUCTING AMERICAN LEGAL REALISM & RETHINKING PRIVATE LAW THEORY 83 (2013).

6 OLIVER W. HOLMES, *The Path of the Law, in* COLLECTED LEGAL PAPERS 167, 187 (1920).

7 *See* TIMOTHY A.O. ENDICOTT, *The Impossibility of the Rule of Law, in* VAGUENESS IN LAW 185, 193 (2000). *See also* MATTHEW H. KRAMER, OBJECTIVITY AND THE RULE OF LAW 114 (2007).

8 *See, e.g.,* DUKEMINIER ET AL., PROPERTY 200–01 (7th ed. 2010).

9 For significant developments in landlord–tenant law, see, for example, the Fair Housing Act, 42 U.S.C. 3601–3619, 3631 (2002) (limiting landlords' discretion in selecting tenants); *Myers v. E. Ohio Gas Co.*, 464 N.E.2d 1369,

1373 (Ohio 1977) (loosening the rigid forms of leasehold estates); *Hilder v. St. Peter*, 478 A.2d 202 (Vt. 1984) (implying an unwaivable warranty of habitability). *See generally* Edward H. Rabin, *The Revolution in Residential Landlord-Tenant Law: Causes and Consequences*, 69 CORNELL L. REV. 517 (1984).

10 The most important developments here are the rise of no-fault divorce, the entrenchment of the norm of equal division, and the expansion of the scope of the marital property estate. *See generally* HANOCH DAGAN, PROPERTY: VALUES AND INSTITUTIONS ch. 9 (2011).

11 *See* RESTATEMENT (THIRD) OF SERVITUDES (2000).

12 KARL L. LLEWELLYN, THE COMMON LAW TRADITION: DECIDING APPEALS 37–38 (1960). My reliance on this account in order to present an attractive ideal of adjudication does not imply involvement in the historical debate about the original nature of common law adjudication. For competing views on this matter, see DAVID LOBBAN, THE COMMON LAW AND ENGLISH JURISPRUDENCE 1760–1850 at 12–16 (1991); WILLIAM CORNISH, *Sources of Law*, *in* 11 THE OXFORD HISTORY OF THE LAWS OF ENGLAND 41, 45 (2010); Gerald J. Postema, *Classical Common Law Jurisprudence (Part I)*, 2 OXFORD U. COMMONWEALTH L.J. 155 (2002); Gerald J. Postema, *Classical Common Law Jurisprudence (Part II)*, 3 OXFORD U. COMMONWEALTH L.J. 1 (2003); A.W.B. SIMPSON, *The Common Law and Legal Theory*, *in* 1 FOLK LAW: ESSAYS IN THE THEORY AND PRACTICE OF LEX NON SCRIPTA 119 (Alison Renteln & Alan Dundes eds., 1994).

13 *See* K. N. Llewellyn, *The Normative, the Legal, and the Law-Jobs: The Problem of Juristic Method*, 49 YALE L.J. 1355, 1385 (1940). The discussion of adjudication draws on my account of the legacy of legal realism, which is all too often misunderstood and at times even distorted. *See* DAGAN, *supra* note 5, at ch. 2; Hanoch Dagan, *The Real Legacy of American Legal Realism*, 38 OXFORD J. LEGAL STUD. 123 (2018).

14 *See supra* Chapter 2 text accompanying notes 64–65.

15 LLEWELLYN, *supra* note 12, at 36, 38, 190–91, 217, 222–23; Llewellyn, *supra* note 13, at 1385.

16 FELIX S. COHEN, *Field Theory and Judicial Logic*, *in* THE LEGAL CONSCIENCE: SELECTED PAPERS OF FELIX S. COHEN 121, 125–26 (Lucy Kramer Cohen ed., 1960). *See also, e.g.,* LLEWELLYN, *supra* note 12, at 46–47, 132; KARL L. LLEWELLYN, *American Common Law Tradition and American Democracy*, *in* JURISPRUDENCE: REALISM IN THEORY AND IN PRACTICE 282, 308–10 (1962).

17 Herman Oliphant, *A Return to Stare Decisis*, 14 A.B.A. J. 71, 73–74, 159 (1928). *See also, e.g.,* LLEWELLYN, *A Realistic Jurisprudence: The Next Step*, *in* JURISPRUDENCE, *supra* note 16, at 3, 27–28, 32; Walter Wheeler Cook,

Scientific Method and the Law, in AMERICAN LEGAL REALISM 242, 246 (William W. Fisher III et al. eds., 1993).

18 According to Frederick Schauer, the concrete examples that judges face distort rather than illuminate their judgment because they systematically trigger certain cognitive biases. *See* Frederick Schaue, *Do Cases Make Bad Law?* 73 U. CHI. L. REV. 883 (2006). *See also* LARRY ALEXANDER & EMILY SHERWIN, DEMYSTIFYING LEGAL REASONING 111–14 (2008). But as Jeffrey Rachlinski shows, beside the cognitive weaknesses of adjudication, courts have several cognitive advantages over legislatures that may facilitate superior lawmaking. *See* Jeffrey J. Rachlinski, *Bottom-Up Versus Top-Down Lawmaking*, 73 U. CHI. L. REV. 933, 950–61 (2006).

19 LLEWELLYN, *The Current Recapture of the Grand Tradition*, in JURISPRUDENCE, *supra* note 16, at 215, 217, 219–220. *See also* Postema, Part I, *supra* note 12, at 167, 175, 177–80. Joseph Raz's analysis of the phenomenon of distinguishing cases brings home a similar point. *See* JOSEPH RAZ, THE AUTHORITY OF LAW 183–97 (1979). For a careful account of the process by which a given case is taken as an example, see Gerald J. Postema, A Similibus ad Similia *Analogical Thinking in Law*, in COMMON LAW THEORY 122–24 (Douglas E. Edlin ed. 2007).

20 *Cf.* Balganesh, *supra* note 1, at 1549.

21 *See, e.g.*, Thomas W. Merrill, *Faithful Agent, Integrative, and Welfarist Interpretation*, 14 LEWIS & CLARK L. REV. 1565, 1578 (2011). *But see* OWEN FISS, *The Forms of Justice*, in THE LAW AS IT COULD BE 1 (2003).

22 *See* http://portal.hud.gov/hudportal/HUD?src=/program_offices/fair_housing_equal_opp/aboutfhe. *See generally* Hanoch Dagan & Roy Kreitner, *The Other Half of Regulatory Theory*, 52 CONN. L. REV. 605 (2020).

23 *See, e.g.*, NEIL K. KOMESAR, IMPERFECT ALTERNATIVES: CHOOSING INSTITUTIONS IN LAW, ECONOMICS, AND PUBLIC POLICY 139–40 (1991); Margaret H. Lemos, *Interpretive Methodology and Delegation to Courts: Are "Common Law Statues" Different?*, in INTELLECTUAL PROPERTY AND THE COMMON LAW 89 (Shyamkrishna Balganesh ed., 2013).

24 *Cf.* Hanoch Dagan & Avihay Dorfman, *Justice for Contracts*, https://ssrn.com/abstract=3435781.

25 Recall that Merrill and Smith mention this feature when making their case for property exceptionalism. *See supra* note 2. As the text implies, however, not only is this feature not unique to property but does not even apply across the board of property law.

26 *See* Hanoch Dagan, *Restitution and Slavery: On Incomplete Commodification, Intergenerational Justice, and Legal Transitions*, 84 B.U. L. REV. 1139 (2004).

27 *Cf.* Christopher Serkin, *Existing Uses and the Limits of Land Use Regulations*, 84 N.Y.U. L. REV. 1222, 1224 (2009).

28 Avihay Dorfman argues that because our property types "represent society's *shared acknowledgement* of the basic terms of interactions for private individuals seeking to trade property rights," *only* the legislature should be authorized to create or modify new forms. See Avihay Dorfman, *Property and Collective Undertaking: The Principle of* Numerus Clausus 61 U. TORONTO L.J. 467, 510–513 (2011). The following discussion explains why such a strong a priori case against judicial activism in property fails. For a fuller response, see Hanoch Dagan, *Judges and Property*, in INTELLECTUAL PROPERTY AND THE COMMON LAW, *supra* note 23, at 17. Dorfman also claims that "the move from contract to property transforms the brute claims placed by [a promisee] on third parties into pronouncements of right." Avihay Dorfman, *The Society of Property*, 62 U. TORONTO L.J. 563, 588 (2012). But a simple conveyance of *A* to *A* and *B* as joint tenants, for example, which obviously does not necessitate a private innovation of a property form, generates a parallel additional normative burden.

29 *See* Balganesh, *supra* note 1, at 1592.

30 *See* ANDREI MARMOR, *Legislative Intent and the Authority of Law*, in INTERPRETATION AND LEGAL THEORY 155 (1992). *See also* WILLIAM N. ESKRIDGE JR., DYNAMIC STATUTORY INTERPRETATION (1994).

31 *Cf.* SCOTT J. SHAPIRO, LEGALISM 351, 358 (2011).

32 *See, e.g.*, AMY GUTMAN & DENNIS F. THOMPSON, DEMOCRACY AND DISAGREEMENT (1996); HENRY S. RICHARDSON, DEMOCRATIC AUTONOMY: PUBLIC REASONING ABOUT THE ENDS OF POLICY (2002).

33 *See, e.g.*, RICHARD A. POSNER, LAW, PRAGMATISM, AND DEMOCRACY 108–09, 132–43 (2003).

34 Note that I do not claim for judicial supremacy, as in judicial review. My sole focus is on the legitimacy of judicial rule-making where legislatures are silent.

35 Even if one insists that such an axiom is justified in the discussion of democracy-based legitimacy, it is out of place in the discussion of legitimacy in a democracy. The latter, broader type of legitimacy that concerns me here accommodates differing types of citizens' participation and of decision-makers' accountability.

36 Another reason relates to comparative costs: voters "often face a far less expensive road [than litigants] to registering their needs ... in the political process." *See* KOMESAR, *supra* note 23, at 127.

37 *Cf.* Merrill & Smith, *supra* note 1, at 67. When the stakes in adjudication are large, the parties' representation tends to be imbalanced as well. But many mundane property cases come up when the stakes are not particularly high. Moreover, to preempt another possible objection, I may add that the notion that judicial passivity can upset the marginality of these topics within our public discourse does not seem particularly plausible.

38 *See generally* JESSICA LITMAN, DIGITAL COPYRIGHT (2001).

39 *See supra* text accompanying notes 16–20. *See also* Matthew Steilen, *The Democratic Common Law* 2011 THE JOURNAL OF JURISPRUDENCE 437. *Cf.*

Alon Harel & Tsvi Kahana, *The Easy Core Case for Judicial Review*, 2 J. Legal Analysis 1 (2010).
40 *See* Komesar, *supra* note 23, at 135–36.
41 Llewellyn, *supra* note 12, at 48, 132; Llewellyn, *American Common Law Tradition*, *supra* note 16, at 309–10.
42 *See supra* note 5 and accompanying text.
43 *See supra* Chapter 4 text accompanying notes 37–38.
44 Consider, for example, cases where the plaintiff argues for some degree of protection against appropriation of a resource she holds, where the preexisting law perceives this type of resource as part of the public domain.
45 A subset of these types of property development may involve, however, significant redistributive effects that, in turn, may serve as an independent justification for judicial passivity. *See supra* text accompanying notes 25–26.
46 Here again, there may be cases in between these categories where judges may legitimately begin a process of law reform that would benefit from a further legislative intervention able to solidify that reform in a comprehensive scheme of rules. This may well be the full story of common-interest communities.
47 Henry E. Smith, *Property Is Not Just a Bundle of Rights*, 8 Econ. J. Watch 279, 287 (2011); Henry E. Smith, *Property as the Law of Things*, 125 Harv. L. Rev. 1691, 1705–06 (2012).
48 Smith, *The Law of Things*, *supra* note 47, at 1719.
49 *See* Arthur Ripstein, *Private Authority and the Role of Rights: A Reply*, 14 Jerusalem Rev. Legal Stud. 64, 85, 88 (2017). For parallel criticism of my autonomy-based conception of contract, see Arthur Ripstein, *The Contracting Theory of Choices*, 38 Law & Phil. (2020); Daniel Markovits & Alan Schwartz, *Plural Values in Contract Law: Theory and Implementation*, 20 Theoretical Inq. L. 571 (2019). For my responses, see, respectively, Hanoch Dagan & Michael Heller, *Autonomy for Contract, Refined*, 38 L. & Phil. (2020); Hanoch Dagan & Michael Heller, *Freedom, Choice, and Contract*, 20 Theoretical Inq. L. 595, 622–35 (2019).
50 Smith, *The Law of Things*, *supra* note 47, at 1705–06.
51 Henry E. Smith, *On the Economy of Concepts in Property*, 160 U. Pa. L. Rev. 2097, 2100, 2102, 2105, 2113, 2116, 2128 (2012).
52 In this respect, I join Martin Krygier's meta-claim whereby, in order to understand the rule of law, we must begin with its *telos*. *See* Martin Krygier, *Four Puzzles about the Rule of Law: Why, What, Where? and Who Cares?*, *in* NOMOS L: Getting to the Rule of Law 64, 67–73 (2011).
53 While conformity with the rule of law is an inherent value of law, my understanding of the rule of law implies that Joseph Raz is correct when insisting that (1) it is a matter of degree and (2) it may conflict with other values, so that less conformity may at times be preferable because it helps to realize these values. *See* Joseph Raz, *The Rule of Law and Its Virtues*, *in* The Authority of Law: Essays on Law and Morality 210, 222, 225,

228–29 (1979). *See also, e.g.,* JOHN GARDNER, LAW AS A LEAP OF FAITH: ESSAYS ON LAW IN GENERAL 33, 192, 195–96 (2012). *But see* Ernest J. Weinrib, *The Intelligibility of The Rule of Law, in* THE RULE OF LAW: IDEAL OR IDEOLOGY 59 (Allan Hutchinson & Patrick Monahan eds., 1987). For a critique of Weinrib's conception of the rule of law, see Hanoch Dagan, *Private Law Pluralism and the Rule of Law, in* PRIVATE LAW AND THE RULE OF LAW 158, 177–79 (Lisa Austin & Dennis Klimchuk eds., 2014).

54 *See* RAZ, *supra* note 53, at 213, 218. Whereas the requirement of law's guidance is important because of law's coercive power, the emphasis here is not on limiting this power and thus its potential abuse, but rather on circumscribing its detrimental effects on people's self-authorship. This is also why the desirability of predictability to autonomy may be disputed in more benevolent authority settings, such as parenthood.

55 *See, e.g.,* LON L. FULLER, THE MORALITY OF LAW 39 (rev'd ed. 1964).

56 F.A. HAYEK, THE ROAD TO SERFDOM 54 (1944). In general, Hayek's account of the rule of law is more amenable to the constraint conception. *See* T.R.S. Allan, *The Rule of Law as Private Law, in* PRIVATE LAW AND THE RULE OF LAW, *supra* note 53, at 41. Furthermore, relying on Hayek for the conception that founds the rule of law on our commitment to self-authorship is somewhat ironic. Hayek ascribes no significance to nongovernment factors, which can deprive people of control over their life in ways as debilitating as those implemented by governments. His views are also alien to the notion that government is responsible for actively ensuring a range of choices.

57 John Tasioulas, *The Rule of Law, in* THE CAMBRIDGE COMPANION TO THE PHILOSOPHY OF LAW (John Tasioulas ed., 2020). As Tasioulas explains, the rule of law does not simply require that "the law's intervention into our lives be predictable, but that it be predictable in a certain way, i.e. one that exemplifies the respect for our rational nature shown by adherence to its formal-procedural requirements." Indeed, "predictions of the legal consequences of acting on our decisions, made on the basis of the law's compliance with the rule of law," require that "officials act on the basis of their rational apprehension of legal rules," so that "ordinary citizens are able to anticipate how officials are liable to impinge upon their activities by means of a comparable grasp of those same rules."

58 RAZ, *supra* note 53, at 220, 222. *Cf.* David Dyzenhaus, *Liberty and Legal Form,* PRIVATE LAW AND THE RULE OF LAW, *supra* note 53, at 92.

59 Joseph Raz, *The Law's Own Virtue,* 39 OXFORD J. LEGAL STUD. 1, 2 (2019).

60 *See* Antonin Scalia, *The Rule of Law as a Law of Rules,* 56 U. CHI. L. REV. 1175 (1989).

61 Emily Sherwin, *Rule-Oriented Realism,* 103 MICH. L. REV. 1578, 1589, 1590, 1591 (2005). *See also, e.g.,* Richard H. Fallon, Jr., *"The Rule of Law" as a Concept in Constitutional Discourse,* 97 COLUM. L. REV. 1, 14–15 (1997).

62 *See generally* Larry Alexander & Emily Sherwin, The Rule of Rules (2001).
63 Frederick Schauer, *Is the Common Law Law?*, 77 Calif. L. Rev. 455, 455–56, 464, 467 (1989). *See also, e.g.*, Pierre Legrand, *European Legal Systems Are Not Converging*, 45 Int'l & Comp. L.Q. 52, 68–70 (1996).
64 *See supra* Chapter 2 text accompanying notes 64–65.
65 15 N.E.2d 793 (N.Y. 1938).
66 *See* Dukeminier et al., Property 872 (7th ed. 2010).
67 *Neponsit*, 15 N.E.2d at 795.
68 *Id.*, at 795–96.
69 *See supra* Chapter 2 text accompanying notes 64–65. *See also* Dagan, *supra* note 13, at 128, 131.
70 *Neponsit*, 15 N.E.2d at 796
71 *Id.*, at 797.
72 *Id.*, at 797–98.
73 Later cases indeed show that *Neponsit* is standing for such rules. *See, e.g.*, *Riverton Cmty. Ass'n v. Myers*, 142 A.D.2d 984, 985 (N.Y. App. Div. 1992); *Lincolnshire Civic Ass'n v. Beach*, 64 N.Y.S.2d 248 (N.Y. App. Div. 1975).
74 *See* Sherwin, *supra* note 61, at 1591–94.
75 *Cf.* Joseph William Singer, *Property as the Law of Democracy*, 63 Duke L.J. 1288, 1306–07 (2014).
76 *See* Hanoch Dagan, *Doctrinal Categories, Legal Realism, and the Rule of Law*, 164 U. Pa. L. Rev. 1889, 1910, 1907–08 (2015).
77 *See* Christopher Essert, *The Office of Ownership*, 63 U. Toronto L.J. 1 (2013).
78 This process culminated in the Restatement of Servitudes, which replaces the touch and concern requirement with a list of "public policy" issues that justify invalidating servitudes and substitutes the privity test with rules that accommodate the verification interest of third parties. *See* Restatement (Third) of Servitudes §§ 3, 5 (2000).
79 *See* Timothy Endicott, *The Value of Vagueness*, *in* Philosophical Foundations of Language in the Law 14, 23, 28, 30 (Andrei Marmor & Scott Soames eds., 2011); Richard A. Posner, The Problems of Jurisprudence 48 (1990); John Braithwaite, *Rules and Principles: A Theory of Legal Certainty*, 27 Australian J. Legal Phil. 47 (2002).
80 *See* Hanoch Dagan, *Lawmaking for Legal Realists*, 1 The Theory and Practice of Legislation 112, 118–19 (2013).
81 *See* Jeremy Waldron, *Vagueness and the Guidance of Action*, *in* Philosophical Foundations of Language in the Law, *supra* note 79, at 58, 65–66, 69.
82 *See* Hanoch Dagan, The Law and Ethics of Restitution 12–18 (2004). There may be one exception to this rule: when broad social agreement prevails on the pertinent matter. *See also* Fuller, *supra* note 55, at 50,

92; Fallon, *supra* note 61, at 49–50; John Gardner, *Rationality and the Rule of Law in Offences against the Person*, 53 CAMBRIDGE L.J. 502, 513, 515–17 (1994). In contemporary societies, however, this condition applies to very few issues.
83 *See* Carol M. Rose, *Crystals and Mud in Property Law*, 40 STAN. L. REV. 577 (1988).
84 This does not mean that such guidance is always effective. Thus, even the New York Court of Appeals failed at times to rely on and properly apply *Neponsit*'s reformulation of the animating principle of covenant law. *See, e.g., Eagle Enters. v. Gross*, 349 N.E.2d 816 (N.Y. 1976).
85 Smith acknowledges that "[o]ptimal concepts [] have a medium level of generality" – Smith, *supra* note 51, at 2105 – but nothing in his critique supports the assertion that the correct level of abstraction is that of the broad and heterogeneous property law.
86 *Cf.* Dagan & Heller, *Autonomy for Contract, supra* note 49.
87 *See* Dagan, *supra* note 13.
88 *See* Frederick Schauer, *Editor's Introduction*, in KARL N. LLEWELLYN, THE THEORY OF RULES 1, 5, 7–8, 18, 20–24 (Frederick Schauer ed., 2011). *See also* Fallon, *supra* note 61, at 16–17; Margaret Jane Radin, *Reconsidering the Rule of Law*, 69 B.U. L. REV. 781, 803 (1989).
89 This focus on the government is important because it affects people.
90 A.V. DICEY, INTRODUCTION TO THE STUDY OF THE LAW OF THE CONSTITUTION 188, 196 (10th ed. 1959). *See also, e.g.*, RONALD A. CASS, THE RULE OF LAW IN AMERICA 3, 17–18 (2001); Raz, *supra* note 59, at 15.
91 *See* Krygier, *supra* note 52, at 79–80.
92 E.P. THOMPSON, WHIGS AND HUNTERS: THE ORIGIN OF THE BLACK ACT 266 (1975).
93 Jeremy Waldron, *The Concept and the Rule of Law*, 43 GA. L. REV. 1, 11, 32 (2008).
94 Jeremy Waldron, *Is the Rule of Law an Essentially Contested Concept (in Florida)?*, 21 L. & PHIL. 137, 159 (2002).
95 Waldron, *supra* note 93, at 6, 31. *See also, e.g.*, Krygier, *supra* note 52, at 75–76, 78, 82, 88. *Cf.* David Dyzenhaus, *Recrafting the Rule of Law*, in RECRAFTING THE RULE OF LAW: THE LIMITS OF LEGAL ORDER 1, 7, 9 (David Dyzenhaus ed., 1999).
96 *See* Jeremy Waldron, *Stare Decisis and the Rule of Law: A Layered Approach*, 111 MICH. L. REV. 1, 14–21 (2012). *Cf.* William Lucy, *Abstraction and the Rule of Law*, 29 OXFORD J. LEGAL STUD. 481 (2009).
97 *Cf.* Lisa Austin, *Pluralism, Context and the Internal Life of Property: A Response to Hanoch Dagan*, 63 U. TORONTO L.J. 22 (2013).
98 Duncan Kennedy claims that this worry is bogus because "juristic work intended to inflect the law in the judge's (or jurist's) preferred ideological direction" is legitimate, adding that to think otherwise is to adhere to a

"fetishized or reified belief in the rule of law." But this proposition is far from comforting, because – as Kennedy admits – it implies that the jurist's "role constraint is no more than 'do your best under all the circumstances to do something politically good.'" DUNCAN KENNEDY, LEGAL REASONING: COLLECTED ESSAYS 6–8, 163, 165, 168 (2007).

99 BRIAN Z. TAMAHANA, ON THE RULE OF LAW: HISTORY, POLITICS, THEORY 125 (2004); Brian Z. Tamahana, *How an Instrumental View of Law Corrodes The Rule of Law*, 56 DEPAUL L. REV. 469, 493 (2006).

100 *See* Waldron, *supra* note 94, at 142–43; Frederick Schauer, *The Failure of the Common Law*, 36 ARIZ. ST. L.J. 765, 781–82 (2004). *See also, e.g.*, Robert S. Summers, *A Formal Theory of the Rule of Law*, 6 RATIO JURIS 127, 134, 137–38 (1993).

101 *See* DAGAN, *supra* note 13, at ch. 2; Dagan, *supra* note 13.

102 *Shelley v. Kraemer*, 344 US 1 (1948).

103 *See supra* Chapter 5 text accompanying note 83.

104 Carol Rose, *Shelley v. Kraemer*, *in* PROPERTY STORIES 189, 192 (Gerald Korngold & Andrew P. Morriss eds., 2nd ed. 2009). *Cf.* Mark D. Rosen, *Was Shelley v. Kraemer, Incorrectly Decided? Some New Answers*, 95 CAL. L. REV. 451 (2007).

105 Rose suggests that this puzzle can be solved by reference to the welfarist commitment of property law to minimize negative externalities on third parties who may not share the preferences of the existing transactors. But, as Rose herself admits, making the protection of third parties from the idiosyncratic preferences of current transactors the core of property raises difficult questions for cases such as *Shelley*, where third parties are likely to share these current preferences. Rose, *supra* note 104, at 216–17.

106 *Id.*, at 220.

107 *Noble v. Alley* [1951] S.C.R. 64 (Can.).

108 A more difficult case involves exclusion by law of cultural minority groups. *See supra* Chapter 5 text following note 112.

109 *Cf. supra* Chapter 3 text accompanying notes 58–62.

110 *Contra* Lior Jacob Strahilevitz, *Information Asymmetries and the Rights to Exclude*, 104 MICH. L. REV. 1835, 1848 (2006).

111 *See, e.g.*, MICHAEL MARTIN, LEGAL REALISM: AMERICAN AND SCANDINAVIAN 39–40, 76 (1997); Joseph William Singer, *Normative Methods for Lawyers*, 56 UCLA L. REV. 899 (2009).

112 *Cf.* RONALD DWORKIN, LAW'S EMPIRE 76–86 (1986).

113 *See* Austin, *supra* note 97.

114 *See supra* Chapter 4 text accompanying note 64–65.

115 *See supra* Chapter 2 text accompanying note 1.

116 The text implicitly assumes that the authority of the state is not fundamental but derivative of its contribution to personal and collective self-determination. State sovereignty is thus based on its function as a fiduciary,

which means that human rights are constitutive of its legitimacy. *See* Eyal Benvenisti, *Sovereigns as Trustees of Humanity: On the Accountability of States to Foreign Stakeholders*, 107 Am. J. Int'l L. 295, 302 (2013); Evan Fox-Decent & Evan Criddle, *The Fiduciary Constitution of Human Rights*, 15 Legal Theory 301, 302, 304–05, 310, 315–18, 320–21 (2009).

117 *See* Hanoch Dagan & Avihay Dorfman, *The Human Right to Private Property*, 18 Theoretical Inq. L. 391 (2017), on which this section relies. *See also* Id., *Justice in Private: Beyond the Rawlsian Framework*, 36 L. & Phil. 171 (2017).

118 *See* Robert Nozick, Anarchy, State, and Utopia (1974).

119 Alan Brudner with Jennifer M. Nadler, The Unity of the Common Law 353 (2013).

120 *See* Julian Arato, *Corporations as Lawmakers*, 56 Harv. Int'l L.J. 229, 261–71 (2015), who discusses the predominance of the Blackstonian conception of property in contemporary international investment law. This might have been expected, given the crucial (though quiet) contribution of this conception of property to the development of a practice that Martii Koskenniemi terms "informal empire," namely, "a horizontal structure of horizontal relationships between holders of subjective rights of *dominium* – a structure of human relationships that we have accustomed to label 'capitalism.'" Martii Koskenniemi, *Empire and International Law: The Real Spanish Contribution*, 61 U. Toronto L.J. 1, 32 (2011).

121 *Cf.* Hanoch Dagan & Michael A. Heller, The Choice Theory of Contract ch. 3 (2017).

122 As the text implies, I neither need to nor do take a position on whether this convention arises by deliberate design, incremental adaptation, or spontaneously, possibly reflecting "a general sense of common interest." David Hume, A Treatise of Human Nature 490, bk. 3, pt. 2, § 2 (1965) (1739–1740). *Cf.* James E. Krier, *Evolutionary Theory and the Origin of Property Rights*, 95 Cornell L. Rev. 139 (2009).

123 *Cf.* Seana Valentine Shiffrin, *Promising, Intimate Relationships, and Conventionalism*, 117 Phil. Rev. 481, 520 (2008). *Contra* Shmuel Nili, *The Idea of Public Property*, 129 Ethics 344, 355 (2019). Implicitly, the text contends with Alan Brudner's challenge, stating that only the Hegelian doctrine of embedded atomism makes sense of a conception of property that is not subordinate to the sovereignty of a public authority. *See* Alan Brudner, *How Are Private Wrongs Possible?*, in Research Handbook on Private Law Theories (Hanoch Dagan & Benjamin Zipursky eds., forthcoming).

124 Joseph Raz, *Why the State?*, *in*, In Pursuit of Pluralist Jurisprudence 136 (Nicole Roughan & Andrew Halpin eds., 2017). In line with the discussion that follows, Raz claims that the significance of state law does not justify

concentrating exclusively on state law or neglecting other law-like phenomena. *Id.*
125 *See supra* Chapter 5 text accompanying note 11.
126 For the most forceful articulation of the statist position, stating that demands of distributive justice stop at the border because only within the state – the "collectively imposed collective authority" – can each member play a dual role "both as one of society's subjects and as one in whose name its authority is exercised," see Thomas Nagel, *The Problem of Global Justice*, 33 Phil. & Pub. Aff. 114 (2005).
127 *See respectively* Joshua Cohen & Charles Sabel, *Extra Rempublicam Nilla Justitia?*, 34 Phil. & Pub. Aff. 147 (2006); Iris Marion Young, *Responsibility and Global Justice: A Social Connection Model*, 23 Soc. Phil. & Pol´y 102 (2006).
128 *See* Hanoch Dagan & Avihay Dorfman, *Interpersonal Human Rights*, 51 Cornell Int´l L.J. 361 (2018); Hanoch Dagan & Avihay Dorfman, *Justice, Politics, and Interpersonal Human Rights*, 51 Cornell Int´l L.J. Online 139 (2018).
129 *See* Ward Anseeuw et al., Transnational Land Deals for Agriculture in the Global South: Analytical Report Based on the Land Matrix Database 39, 41 (2012).
130 *See, e.g.*, Peter Hay et al., Conflict of Laws 1231 (5th ed. 2010).
131 *See Oppenheimer v. Cattermole*, [1976] AC 249 (HL). *See also* Leif Wenar, Blood Oil: Tyrants, Violence, and the Rules that Run the World 102 (2016) (criticizing the sparse use of this exception).
132 I acknowledge that structural reform may be more difficult to implement, also because it would require an institutional and procedural framework. (To fully understand *legal* rights, one must attend to their institutional instantiations.) But even if it is unlikely to develop, a revision of the choice-of-law exception along the lines of a substantive reform can serve as a "second-best" solution. *See* Dagan & Dorfman, *Interpersonal Human Rights*, *supra* note 128; Dagan & Dorfman, *Justice and Politics*, *supra* note 128, at 151–55.
133 *See* Olivier DeSchutter, *The Green Rush: The Global Race for Farmland and the Rights of Land Users*, 52 Harv. Int´l L.J. 504, 528 (2011).
134 *See* Hanoch Dagan, *Property Theory, Essential Resources, and the Global Land Rush*, *in* Governing Access to Essential Resources 81 (Olivier DeSchutter & Katharina Pistor eds., 2015).
135 *See* Food & Agric. Org. of the United Nations, Voluntary Guidelines on the Responsible Governance of Tenure of Land, Fisheries and Forests in the Context of National Food Security §§ 7.1, 7.3, 10.1, 16.1–.2, 16.8–.9 (2012).
136 Future investigations may need to address further issues as well, such as prohibitions or restrictions that some legal systems impose on property purchases of non-citizens.

Chapter 7

1 *See* Robert L. Hale, *Coercion and Distribution in a Supposedly Non-Coercive State*, 38 POL. SCI. Q. 470 (1923); Hugh Collins et al., *Introduction: Does Labour Law Need Philosophical Foundations?*, in PHILOSOPHICAL FOUNDATIONS OF LABOUR LAW 1, 5, 9 (Hugh Collins et al. eds., 2018). *See also, e.g.,* G.A. COHEN, SELF-OWNERSHIP, FREEDOM, AND EQUALITY 34 (1995); C.B. MACPHERSON, THE POLITICAL THEORY OF POSSESSIVE INDIVIDUALISM: HOBBES TO LOCKE 55–56 (1962). *Cf.* GOSTA ESPING ANDERSEN, THE THREE WORLDS OF WELFARE CAPITALISM 16, 21 (1990).
2 Collins et al., *supra* note 1, at 26.
3 Hugh Collins, *Is the Contract of Employment Illiberal?*, in PHILOSOPHICAL FOUNDATIONS OF LABOUR LAW, *supra* note 1, at 48, 52, 63.
4 Recall that this book does not engage in the separate, albeit related, task of delineating the proper domains of the market and the state.
5 *Cf.* CHRISTOPHER MCMAHON, AUTHORITY AND DEMOCRACY: A GENERAL THEORY OF GOVERNMENT AND MANAGEMENT 17 (1994) ("property rights in productive resources cannot provide a moral basis for managerial authority, understood as the authority to tell employees what to do, as opposed to what to refrain from doing").
6 *See* HANOCH DAGAN & MICHAEL A. HELLER, THE CHOICE THEORY OF CONTRACTS (2017) as well as further articles to which I refer below.
7 Thus, I do not consider here the possibility of substituting the current default, where workers have no share in the production's surplus value. Even more fundamentally, I do not offer an autonomy-based account of incorporated persons that transcends their economic function, which is urgently needed in private law theory.
8 *But cf.* Collins, *supra* note 3.
9 Thus, this chapter offers a preliminary answer to the concerns of the early critics of "free labor." *See* AMY DRU STANLEY, FROM BONDAGE TO CONTRACT: WAGE LABOR, MARRIAGE, AND THE MARKET IN THE AGE OF EMANCIPATION 61–97 (1998).
10 *See* ALBERT O. HIRSCHMAN, RIVAL VIEWS OF MARKET SOCIETY AND OTHER RECENT ESSAYS 105–24 (1986).
11 *See, e.g.,* FRANK H. KNIGHT, RISK, UNCERTAINTY, AND PROFIT 76–77, 79 (1921); George J. Stigler, *Perfect Competition, Historically Contemplated,* 65 J. POL. ECON. 1, 14 (1957).
12 *See, e.g.,* NATHAN B. OMAN, THE DIGNITY OF COMMERCE: MARKETS AND THE MORAL FOUNDATIONS OF CONTRACT LAW 23–30 (2016).
13 JOHN O'NEILL, THE MARKET: ETHICS, KNOWLEDGE AND POLITICS 4 (1998). I think that my addition of "services" does not deviate from the thrust of this definition and is required in order to properly cover all market

activities. For a somewhat similar definition, see Geoffrey Hodgson, Economics and Institutions: A manifesto for a Modern Institutional Economics 174 (1988).
14 Cf. Oman, *supra* note 12, at 34–35.
15 *See generally* Katharina Pistor, The Code of Capital: How the Law Creates Wealth and Inequality (2019). Law's treatment of mandatory arbitration and no-class-action clauses can also have important effects on the performance of the market in terms of human empowerment. *See* Hanoch Dagan & Michael Heller, *Why Autonomy Must Be Contract's Ultimate Value*, 20 Jerusalem Rev. Legal Stud. 148, 162 (2019).
16 *See* Hanoch Dagan et al., *The Law of the Market*, 83 L. & Contemp. Probs. i (2020).
17 William A. Jackson, *On the Social Structure of Markets*, 31 Cambridge J. Econ. 235, 236 (2007).
18 Debra Satz, Why Some Things Should Not Be for Sale: The Moral Limits of Markets 22 (2010).
19 Elizabeth Anderson, Value in Ethics and Economics 151 (1993).
20 Nathan Oman suggests that voluntariness need not be "an attribute of well-functioning markets." Oman, *supra* note 12, at 27. Part of his argument relies on the familiar difficulties inherent in defining consent, and thus voluntariness, which are real but cannot imply the detachment of markets from voluntary transactions. Another premise of this purported disconnection is the suggestion that consumer transactions cannot plausibly be understood as premised on contractual consent. *Id.*, at 29. But a proper understanding of consumer contracts implies, as I argue elsewhere, that voluntariness is secured in this context by ensuring that the non-bargained terms correspond to (or exceed) consumers' typical expectations, so that attributing consent to the consumer is no more objectionable than attributing consent to a buyer of a car who lacks knowledge of its mechanical features. *See* Dagan & Heller, *supra* note 6, at 83.
21 O'Neill, *supra* note 13, at 12.
22 Anderson, *supra* note 19, at 144–45.
23 Jackson, *supra* note 17, at 236–37, 239, 241. O'Neill recognizes the heterogeneity of markets but, nonetheless, insists on the impersonality of market relations by relegating the personal bonds of the less impersonal market formations to the status of "accidental features," which are "eroded" as trading transcends historic small-knit communities. O'Neill, *supra* note 13, at 12. As the text suggests, relational contracts are far from being marginal or declining in modern, developed markets economies, and the relational setting in which these contracts are situated affects their structure and content. *See* Robert E. Scott, *The Promise and the Peril of Relational Contract Theory, in* Revisiting the Contract Scholarship of

STEWART MACAULAY: ON THE EMPIRICAL AND THE LYRICAL 105, 108 (Jean Braucher et al. eds. 2013).
24 LISA HERZOG, INVENTING THE MARKET: SMITH, HEGEL, AND POLITICAL THEORY 160–62 (2013). In other words, not only must "[t]he value of the market instrument" be assessed, as Amartya Sen argues, by "more fundamental values" – Amartya Sen, *The Moral Standing of the Market*, 2(2) SOC. PHIL. & POL´Y 1, 8 (1985) – but these values, chiefly people's right to self-determination, should determine the content and implication of the market's legal building blocks.
25 Or at least used to believe so. For his more recent position, see J.E. Penner, *Property, in* THE OXFORD HANDBOOK OF NEW PRIVATE LAW (Andrew Gold et al. eds., forthcoming).
26 J.E. PENNER, THE IDEA OF PROPERTY IN LAW 13, 88–90 (1997).
27 *Id.*, at 71. *Cf.* Christopher Essert, *Property and Homelessness*, 44 PHIL. & PUB. AFF. 266, 292 (2016).
28 Anthropologists argue, of course, that gifts are also a matter of reciprocal exchange. *See* MARCEL MAUSS, THE GIFT (Ian Cunnison trans., 1967); Carol M. Rose, *Giving, Trading, Thieving, and Trusting: How and Why Gifts Become Exchanges, and (More Importantly) Vice Versa*, 44 FLA. L. REV. 295 (1992).
29 PENNER, *supra* note 3, at 180
30 *See* A.M. Honoré, *Ownership, in* OXFORD ESSAYS IN JURISPRUDENCE: A COLLABORATIVE WORK 107, 107, 118 (A.G. Guest ed., 1961). *See also, e.g.,* GRANT NELSON ET AL, CONTEMPORARY PROPERTY 5 (3rd ed. 2008); JON BRUCE & JAMES ELY JR., CASES AND MATERIALS ON MODERN PROPERTY LAW 1 (6th ed. 2003); SHELDON KURTZ & HERBERT HOVENKAMP, CASES AND MATERIALS ON AMERICAN PROPERTY LAW 2 (5th ed. 1993).
31 Penner himself seems to have accepted it eventually. *See* Penner, *supra* note 25.
32 A. JAMES CASNER ET AL., CASES AND TEXT ON PROPERTY 627 (5th ed. 2004).
33 *See* UNIFORM COMMERCIAL CODE 2-102 (2002) (chattels); 35 U. S. C. § 261 (Lexis 2018) (patents); 17 U. S. C. § 201 (d)(1) (Lexis 2018) (copyright); 15 USCS § 1060 (a)(1) (Lexis 2018) (trademarks); 12 OKL. ST. § 1448 (B) (Lexis 2018) (publicity); 19 G. C. § 31403 (Lexis 2018) (goodwill); CAL REV & TAX CODE § 3692 (b) (Lexis 2018) (oil, gas, and minerals); TEX STAT. § 55.193 (Lexis 2018) (water); N.C. GEN. STAT. § 146–47 (Lexis 2018) (timber).
34 *See Moore v. Regents of University of California*, 51 Cal. 3d 120, 166 (Cal. 1990) (Mosk, J. dissenting) (licenses and prescription drugs). *See also, e.g.,* Susan Rose-Ackerman, *Inalienability and the Theory of Property Rights*, 85 COLUM. L. REV. 931, 931 (1985) (endangered species).

35 *See* Cal Fish & G. Code, §§ 3039, 7121 (Lexis 1990) (fish or wild game caught pursuant to license).
36 *See, e.g.,* John Dwyer & Peter Menell, Property Law and Policy: A Comparative Institutional Perspective 2 (1998); Margaret Jane Radin, *Market-Inalienability*, 100 Harv. L. Rev. 1849, 1854 (1987).
37 Claire Priest, *Creating an American Property Law: Alienability and Its Limits in American History*, 120 Harv. L. Rev. 385, 392 (2006). Priest does show in some detail that the historical progression is far more complicated.
38 *But cf.* Jeremy Waldron, The Right to Private Property 53–55, 431–34 (1988).
39 Peter G. Stillman, *Hegel's Analysis of Property in the* Philosophy of Right, 10 Cardozo L. Rev. 1031, 1042 (1989). The power to *unilaterally* disengage from one's property through its abandonment or destruction may also seem a clear manifestation of an owner's autonomy and, to some extent, it indeed is. *See* Lior Jacob Strahilevitz, *The Right to Abandon*, 158 U. Pa. L. Rev. 355 (2010); *Id., The Right to Destroy*, 114 Yale L.J. 781, 823 (2005). But both abandonment and destruction entail various external effects, which property law rightly addresses. *See* Eduardo M. Peñalver, *The Illusory Right to Abandon*, 109 Mich. L. Rev. 191 (2010); Gregory S. Alexander, *Of Buildings, Statues, Art, and Sperm: The Right to Destroy and the Duty to Preserve*, 28 Cornell J.L. & Pub. Pol´y 619 (2018).
40 Eric A. Posner & E. Glen Weyl, Radical Markets: Uprooting Capitalism and Democracy for a Just Society 278–83, 285–86 (2018).
41 *See supra* Chapter 3 text accompanying notes 67–73.
42 Posner & Weyl, *supra* note 40, at 277, 286–87, 289–90, 292.
43 *See supra* Chapter 3 text accompanying notes 71–73.
44 Economists and mainstream utilitarians, therefore, are correct when attending to preference satisfaction rather than to a (particularly reductive) hedonistic accounting of pleasure and pain that leaves no room for choice and agency and, as such, is not specific to human beings. For utilitarians, see, e.g., R. M. Hare, Moral Thinking: Its Levels, Method, and Point 143 (1981); Daniel M. Hausman, *Hedonism and Welfare Economics*, 26 Econ. & Phil. 321, 321 (2010). For economists, see, e.g., Lionel Robbins, An Essay on the Nature and Significance of Economic Science 86 (1932); J. R. Hicks, *The Foundations of Welfare Economics*, 49 Econ. J. 696, 698 (1939).
45 *See* Cass Sunstein, Free Markets and Social Justice 5 (1998). *See also, e.g.,* Andrew Sayer, Radical Political Economy: Critique and Reformulation 93 (1995).
46 *See supra* text accompanying notes 13–14.
47 *See* David Harvey, A Brief History of Neoliberalism 2 (2005); David Singh Grewal & Jedediah Purdy, *Law and Neoliberalism*, 77(4) L. & Contemp. Probs. 1, 6 (2014).

48 HERZOG, *supra* note 24, at 160, 162. Similarly, David Grewal argues that the "ultimate requirement for the invention of the economy" is an "account of the value (more broadly, the ethical import) of market exchange," and that this process is "never ending" since it implies "a marshaling and limiting of necessary political will under the aegis of a constructive ethical account." DAVID SINGH GREWAL, THE INVENTION OF THE ECONOMY (forthcoming).
49 *See supra* Chapter 3 text accompanying notes 128–159.
50 They also diverge from any plausible notion of desert, on which claims as to the justice of the market are often premised. *See* HERZOG, *supra* note 24, at 84–111.
51 As Frank Knight noted, markets are games of ability, effort, and luck – and luck is probably the foremost one of the three. *See* Frank H. Knight, *The Ethics of Competition*, 37 Q. J. ECON. 579, 607–12 (1923). *See also* Andrew Lister, *Markets, Desert, and Reciprocity*, 16 POL. PHIL. & ECON. 47, 48, 50–52 (2017).
52 *See supra* Chapter 3 text accompanying note 10.
53 *See* ELIZABETH ANDERSON, PRIVATE GOVERNMENT: HOW EMPLOYERS RULE OUR LIVES (AND WHY WE DON'T TALK ABOUT IT) 4, 17–22 (2017); O'NEILL, *supra* note 13, at 71, 77–78; JEDEDIAH PURDY, THE MEANING OF PROPERTY: FREEDOM, COMMUNITY, AND THE LEGAL IMAGINATION 16–17 (2010); SATZ, *supra* note 18, at 24–25, 41–42. This argument is related to, but nonetheless distinct from, the celebration of the market as a regime of polycentric governance. *See* MILTON FRIEDMAN, CAPITALISM AND FREEDOM 7–21 (1962); RANDY BARNETT, THE STRUCTURE OF LIBERTY: JUSTICE AND THE RULE OF LAW 139–42, 238 (1998).
54 O'NEILL, *supra* note 13, at 75–77, 79–80, 82–83.
55 *See supra* text accompanying note 23.
56 *See* DAGAN & HELLER, *supra* note 6, at 58–63.
57 *Cf.* HANOCH DAGAN, PROPERTY: VALUES AND INSTITUTIONS 69 (2011).
58 Another example of an indirect contribution of market behavior to autonomy comes up in the context of investment decisions in pension funds that transcend pure preference satisfaction and involve investors' pursuit of non-financial goals. *See* Roy Kreitner, *Money Talks: Institutional Investors and Voice in Contract*, 20 THEORETICAL INQ. L. 511 (2019).
59 *See* DAGAN & HELLER, *supra* note 6, at 73, 81–82. This virtue of consumer contracts need not absolve consumers from moral responsibility where the seller's use of contract undermines the autonomy of third parties. *See* Avihay Dorfman, *Against Market Insularity: Market, Responsibility, and Law*, 28 CORNELL J.L. & PUB. POL'Y 553 (2018); Lisa Maria Herzog, *Who Should Prevent Sweatshops? Duties, Excuses, and The Division of Moral Labour in The Global Economy*, *in* MARKETS AND MORALITY (Hans-Christoph Schmidt et al. eds., forthcoming).

60 *See* Shelly Kreiczer-Levy, Destabilized Property: Property Law in the Access Economy (2019).
61 Charles Fried, *The Ambitions of* Contract as Promise, *in* Philosophical Foundations of Contract 17, 20 (Gregory Klass et al. eds., 2014).
62 2 F.A. Hayek, Law, Legislation, and Liberty: The Mirage of Social Justice 109 (1982).
63 Satz, *supra* note 18, at 8. For the market to entail this liberating function, law should also facilitate the possibility of at least partially exiting the money-based valuation of the market itself. *See infra* text accompanying note 66.
64 John Gray, The Moral Foundations of Market Institutions 25 (1992).
65 *Cf.* Posner & Weyl, *supra* note 40, at 19, 286.
66 *See* Rashmi Dyal-Chand, Collaborative Capitalism in American Cities: Reforming Urban Market Regulations (2018). Dyal-Chand contrasts these formations with "liberal market economy." As the text clarifies, I claim that their facilitation is in fact *required* by liberalism, properly interpreted. *See also, e.g.,* Eva Vriens et al., Mutuals on the Move: Exclusion Processes in the Welfare State and the Rediscovery of Mutualism (unpublished manuscript). *Cf.* Gar Alperovitz, *The Pluralist Commonwealth and Property-Owning Democracy, in* Property-Owning Democracy: Rawls and Beyond 266 (Martin O'Neil & Thad Williamson eds., 2012).
67 *See supra* Chapter 4 text accompanying note 84.
68 *See generally* Alan Manning, Monopsony in Motion 3–10 & tbl.1.1 (2003).
69 *See* OECD, OECD Employment Outlook 2019: The Future of Work ch. 4 (2019), https://doi.org/10.1787/9ee00155-en.
70 *See Id.*, at 56.
71 As opposed to job-sharing programs, which are voluntary agreements designed to accommodate reduced working hours, work-sharing programs provide an alternative to unemployment during economic downturns. Work-sharing programs allow an employer to forego layoffs by reducing the working hours and wages of all employees. Instead of paying unemployment benefits to newly laid-off workers, the government subsidizes the wages paid to these reduced-hour workers. *See* Megan Felter, *Short-Time Compensation: Is Germany's Success With Kurzarbeit an Answer to U.S. Unemployment?*, 35 B.C. Int'l & Comp. L. Rev. 481, 487 (2012); William B. Gould IV, *A Century and Half Century of Advance and Retreat: The Ebbs and Flows of Workplace Democracy*, 86 St. John's L. Rev. 431, 441 (2012).
72 For a general overview of flexible work arrangements, discussion of pros and cons, and a rich selection of secondary sources, see Christine Avery & Diane Zabel, The Flexible Workplace: A Sourcebook of Information and Research 37–80 (2001).

73 Joan C. Williams et al., *Better on Balance? The Corporate Work/Life Report*, 10 WM. & MARY J. WOMEN & L. 367, 410–11 (2004) (noting "island" type, whereby two attorneys share one position but maintain separate caseloads and "twins" type in which two attorneys act as one and share a single caseload).
74 Marion Crain, *"Where Have All the Cowboys Gone?" Marriage and Breadwinning in Postindustrial Society*, 60 OHIO ST. L.J. 1877, 1952 (1999).
75 For an outline of the government's job-sharing policies, see U.S. OFFICE OF PERSONAL MANAGEMENT, http://www.opm.gov/employment _and_benefits/worklife/officialdocuments/handbooksguides/pt_employ_jobsharing/pt08.asp.
76 *See* Robert C. Bird, *Why Don't More Employers Adopt Flexible Working Time?*, 118 W. VA. L. REV. 327, 341–42 (2015).
77 *See* Erika C. Collins, *Labor and Employment Developments From Around the World*, 38 INT'L LAW. 149, 169 (2004).
78 *See* RESTATEMENT (THIRD) OF EMPLOYMENT LAW § 2.01 cmt. b (2015); Barry D. Roseman, *Just Cause in Montana: Did the Big Sky Fall?*, American Constitution Soc'y, Sept. 2008, https://secure.acslaw.org/files/roseman%20issue%20brief_0.pdf.
79 One could go a step further. States vary in how they define "at will" along three major dimensions: Is there a public policy exception? Is there an implied contract exception? And is a covenant of good faith and fair dealing implied? Some states recognize all three, putting them closer to the "for cause" type; most states are in the middle, and some recognize none. *See* Charles J. Muhl, *The Employment-at-Will Doctrine: Three Major Exceptions*, MONTHLY LABOR REV. 3 (2001). Currently, one state-chosen combination is available to employees, but a state could define and offer an additional "at will" type involving a distinct cluster of exceptions matching a different normative balance.
80 *See* Jesse Rudy, *What They Don't Know Won't Hurt Them: Defending Employment-at-Will in Light of Findings That Employees Believe They Possess Just Cause Protection*, 23 BERKELEY J. EMP. & LAB. L. 307, 309–10 (2002).
81 *Cf.* Aditi Bagchi, *The Employment Relationship as an Object of Employment Law*, in THE OXFORD HANDBOOK OF NEW PRIVATE LAW (Andrew Gold et al. eds., forthcoming).
82 More expansive interpretations would require affirmative duties of inclusion such as, for example, a demand from big developers to offer at least some units to the less well-off and from big employers to provide professional training to those who were not lucky enough to benefit from a proper education. For a discussion of limits on exclusion generated by poverty, see Hanoch Dagan & Avihay Dorfman, *Poverty and Private Law: Beyond Distributive Justice*, https://ssrn.com/abstract=3637034.

83 *See* Hanoch Dagan, *Between Regulatory and Autonomy-Based Private Law*, 22 European L.J. 644, 657 (2016); Hanoch Dagan & Avihay Dorfman, *Against Private Law Escapism: Comment on Arthur Ripstein*, Private Wrongs, 14 Jerusalem Rev. Legal Stud. 37, 51 (2017). *Cf.* Gray, *supra* note 64, at 29.

84 Collins, *supra* note 3, at 53–54.

85 *See supra* text accompanying note 53.

86 The text raises one of the complicated interfaces between relational justice and distributive justice. *Cf.* Sophia Moreau, Faces of Inequality: A Theory of Wrongful Discrimination *18–19 (2020).

87 Collins et al., *supra* note 1, at 7.

88 National Labor Relations Act, 29 U.S.C § 151 (1935).

89 Claus Offe, Disorganized Capitalism: Contemporary Transformations of Work and Politics 177–78 (1985).

90 Unionization, like any other type of collective action, creates internal difficulties of its own. A specific problem relates to the unions' compliance with relational justice, ensuring that they do not end up serving the interests of the relatively strong workers at the expense of the weaker ones. These concerns, similar to those facing commons property types, exceed the scope of this book.

91 *See* Mark Barenberg, *The Political Economy of the Wagner Act: Power, Symbol, and Workplace Cooperation*, 106 Harv. L. Rev. 1379, 1423 (1993). For the predominant – independence-based – view of contract that shaped much of the discourse on employment and labor law for both friends and foes of its features, see Dru Stanley, *supra* note 9, at 61–97.

92 *Cf.* Roberto Mangabeira Unger, *The Critical Legal Studies Movement*, 96 Harv. L. Rev. 561, 629–30 (1983).

93 *Cf.* Kate Andrias, *The New Labor Law*, 126 Yale L.J. 2 (2016).

94 *See* Paul Weiler & Guy Mundlak, *New Direction for the Law of the Workplace*, 102 Yale L.J. 1907, 1911 (1993). *Cf.* Guy Mundlak, The Two Logics of Labour's Collective Action: Organizing and Membership in Hybrid Regimes ch.7 (forthcoming).

95 *See* Weiler & Mundlak, *supra* note 94, at 1912–13. For labor law to support relational justice for both union and nonunion employees, unions should be able to negotiate so-called agency shop contracts requiring employees to pay union dues as a condition of employment. To the extent that "right to work" laws in some states now prohibit agency shop, these laws *limit* the contractual freedom of both union and nonunion employees. More importantly, agency shop does not meaningfully reduce individual autonomy. It results in an ex ante reduction in the amount of money belonging to an employee who has to pay dues in return for higher wages and benefits and better working conditions. Even assuming that some employees are unwilling third-party beneficiaries to agency shop provisions, a sufficient multiplicity of contract types ought to empower employees to seek out employers with desirable union

agreements. Mandatory rules are particularly justified where needed to sustain the viability of intra-sphere multiplicity. *See* DAGAN & HELLER, *supra* note 6, at 87–88. *But see* Janus v. Am. Fed'n of State, Cty., & Mun. Emps., Council 31, 138 S. Ct. 2448 (2018) (holding that union fees for nonunion members in public sector unions violates those non-members' free speech rights).

96 Sabine Tsuruda, *Working as Equal Moral Agents*, https://ssrn.com/abstract=3594512.
97 *See* Hanoch Dagan & Roy Kreitner, *The Other Half of Regulatory Theory*, 52 CONN. L. REV. 605, 631–37 (2020); Dagan & Dorfman, *supra* note 82, at 1442–45.
98 *See* Collins, *supra* note 3, at 65 ("The ECtHR has insisted that employers cannot lawfully interfere disproportionately with an employee's manifestation of religion at work, or dismiss someone simply for membership of a political party"). *See also* Tsuruda, *supra* note 96 (discussing needed reform regarding workers' "expression of reactive attitudes, such as indignation of being morally wronged, and [of their] character development").
99 *See* ANDERSON, *supra* note 53, at 39–40, 48–54, 60, 62–64, 67–69. *See also* Carole Pateman, *Self-Ownership and Property in the Person: Democratization and a Tale of Two Concepts*, 10 J. POL. PHIL. 20, 33, 48, 47 (2002); Nien-hê Hsieh, *Rawlsian Justice and Workplace Republicanism*, 31 SOC. THEORY & PRACTICE 115, 121–26 (2005).
100 *See Bărbulescu v. Romania*, App. No. 61496/08, Eur. Ct. H.R. (Grand Chamber, 2017), http://hudoc.echr.coe.int/eng?i=001- 177082.
101 *State v. Shack*, 277 A.2d 369, 369, 374 (1971).
102 *Lechmere, Inc. v. NLRB*, 502 U.S. 527, 537-38 (1992).
103 *See, e.g.,* Jeffrey M. Hirsch, *Taking State Property Rights Out of Federal Labor Law*, 47 B.C.L. REV. 891 (2006).
104 *Cf.* Cynthia L Estlund, *Labor, Property, and Sovereignty After* Lechmere, 46 STAN. L. REV. 305 (1994).
105 *See* Joseph William Singer, *The Reliance Interest in Property*, 40 STAN. L. REV. 611 (1988).
106 As the text implies, my account converges with Singer's, though I do not subscribe to the view that these workers' rights are premised on reliance or to the view of property rights as shifting rights, insofar as it legitimates an a posteriori approach to entitlement prescription. *See* DAGAN, *supra* note 57, at 28.
107 *Cf.* SATZ, *supra* note 18, at 42–43, 95, 99.
108 *Id.*, at 94, 97.
109 *See supra* Chapter 3 text accompanying note 10.
110 Michael E. Bratman, TIME, RATIONALITY, AND SELF-GOVERNANCE, 22 PHIL. ISSUES 73, 74 (2012).

111 *Id.*, at 82.
112 *See, e.g.*, Rose-Ackerman, *supra* note 34, at 937–41. For an early account of these reasons, see JOHN STUART MILL, PRINCIPLES OF POLITICAL ECONOMY AND CHAPTERS ON SOCIALISM 345–46 (JONATHAN RILEY ED., 2008). Regarding land, see Michael Heller, *The Boundaries of Private Property*, 108 YALE L.J. 1163 (1999).
113 *See* Hanoch Dagan & Michael Heller, *Autonomy for Contract, Refined*, 38 L. & PHIL. (2020). As Aditi Bagchi notes, "[t]he same ideal of moral agency that makes promise valuable makes the power to revise and reject commitments valuable as well ... [so that] our interest in moral agency demands both fidelity and rebellion against [our] former self." Aditi Bagchi, *Contract and the Problem of Fickle People*, 53 WAKE FOREST L. REV. 1, 3 (2018). Bagchi argues that this ideal competes with the promissory principle, which she conceives as uncompromising, and that contract's accommodation of revision is the epitome of the justified divergence of contract and promise. *Id.*, at 35. As I argue elsewhere, the purported dogmatism of the promissory principle relies on the misguided transfer theory of promise. Once it is set aside, we see that the contract-promise purported divergence is unnecessary: both can – indeed should – accommodate revision, and thus must not be overly dogmatic. *See* DAGAN & HELLER, *supra* note 6, at 30–32.
114 *See* Hanoch Dagan & Ohad Somech, *When Contract's Basic Assumptions Fail: From Rose 2d to COVID-19*, https://ssrn.com/abstract=3605411. *Cf.* Dori Kimel, *Promise, Contract, Personal Autonomy, and the Freedom to Change One's Mind*, *in* PHILOSOPHICAL FOUNDATIONS OF CONTRACT, *supra* note 61, at 96, 101–03.
115 *See, e.g.*, Deborah A. DeMott, *The Fiduciary Character of Agency and the Interpretation of Instructions*, *in* PHILOSOPHICAL FOUNDATIONS OF FIDUCIARY LAW 321, 333–36 (Andrew Gold & Paul Miller eds., 2014).
116 *See* Ronald J. Gilson, *The Legal Infrastructure of High Technology Industrial Districts: Silicon Valley, Route 128, and Covenants Not to Compete*, 74 N.Y.U. L. REV. 575, 594–619 (1999); *see also* ANDERSON, *supra* note 53, at 66.
117 *See* THE WHITE HOUSE, NON-COMPETE AGREEMENTS: ANALYSIS OF THE USAGE, POTENTIAL ISSUES, AND STATE RESPONSES 3 (2016).
118 *See, e.g.*, Shu-Yi Oei & Diane Ring, *Human Equity? Regulating the New Income Share Agreements*, 68 VAND. L. REV. 681 (2015).
119 *See* Dagan & Heller, *supra* note 113; Dagan & Somech, *supra* note 114; Hanoch Dagan & Michael Heller, *Specific Performance*, https://ssrn.com/abstract=3647336; Bagchi, *supra* note 113.
120 RESTATEMENT (SECOND) OF CONTRACTS § 359(1).
121 For the common law, see, e.g., RESTATEMENT (SECOND) OF CONTRACTS § 367(1). For the civil law, see, e.g., Charles Szladits, *The Concept of Specific Performance in Civil Law*, 4. AM. J. COMP. L. 208, 226 (1955).

122 *Contra* Arthur Ripstein, *The Contracting Theory of Choices*, 38 L. & Phil. (2020); Robert Stevens, Contract, Rights and the Morality of Promising (unpublished manuscript).
123 *See supra* Chapter 3 text accompanying notes 83–86.
124 *See* Michael J. Sandel, What Money Can't Buy: The Moral Limits of Markets 9 (2012). As the text implies, the pertinent risk I discuss need not, although it often does, involve violations of the parties' relational justice as well. For a famous example, see Ronald Dworkin, *Is Wealth a Value?*, 9 J. Legal Stud. 191, 209–12 (1980) (discussing the case of the enlightened slave owner).
125 Lyn K.L. Tjon Soei Len, Minimum Contract Justice: A Capabilities Perspective on Sweatshops and Consumer Contracts 23 (2017). *See also, e.g.*, China Labor Watch, Tragedies of Globalization: The Truth Behind Electronics Sweatshops (2011); Marisa Anne Pagnattaro, *Labor Rights Are Human Rights: Direct Action Is Critical in Supply Chains and Trade Policy*, 10 S.C. J. Int'l L. & Bus. 1 (2013); Alexandra Rose Caleca, *The Effects of Globalization on Bangladesh's Ready-Made Garment Industry: The High Cost of Cheap Clothing*, 40 Brook. J. Int'l L. 279 (2014).
126 *See* Deirdre McCann & Judy Fudge, *Unacceptable Forms of Work: A Multidimensional Model*, 156 Int'l Labour Rev. 147 (2017).
127 Notice that this anti-commodification rationale is immune from the critique targeting other "corruption" arguments that may violate the injunction of equal concern and respect. *See* Lyn K.L. Tjon Soei Len, *Equal Respect, Capabilities and the Moral Limits of Market Exchange*, 2017 Transnational Legal Theory 1, 115–16.
128 For a helpful synthesis of pertinent accounts, see McCann & Fudge, *supra* note 126.
129 *See* Cynthia Estlund, *What Should We Do After Work? Automation and Employment Law*, 128 Yale L. J. 254 (2018).
130 *Cf.* Nien-hê Hsieh, *Work, Ownership, and Productive Enfranchisement*, in Property-Owning Democracy, *supra* note 66, at 149, 153.
131 Jürgen Habermas, Between Facts and Norms: Contributions to a Discourse Theory of Law and Democracy 413, 416 (1996).
132 The most normalizing feature of modern states and economies does indeed lie elsewhere: without work in the market, only the most enterprising can find ways to eat.
133 The multiple-floors strategy confronts operational challenges as well. I cannot delve into them here but just imagine a regime compelling employers to offer – *in addition* to the current floor – a couple of other alternatives from a list of acceptable nonconventional floors. Employees would then be constricted to the alternative they chose, though they could probably shift, with proper notice, to the majoritarian floor.

134 *See* MARGARET JANE RADIN, CONTESTED COMMODITIES 103–10 (1996). Radin treats the adjectives "noncommodified" and "non-market" as interchangeable. As is by now clear, I disagree, but this disagreement has no bearing on the current claim. *See also* Tsilly Dagan & Talia Fisher, *The State and the Market – A Parable: On the State's Commodifying Effects*, 3(2) PUBLIC REASON 44 (2011).

135 *See supra* text accompanying notes 22–23. *See generally* Roy Kreitner, *Voicing the Market: Extending the Ambition of Contract Theory*, 69 U. TORONTO L.J. 295, 326 (2019) ("[M]arkets potentially provide extensive room for discussion of the reasons to value a product, a service, or an investment. Contracting in markets can be a site of reasoned discussion about what the market should achieve rather than exclusively a single-minded means to maximize returns.").

136 RADIN, *supra* note 134, at 106.

137 McCann & Fudge, *supra* note 126, at 156–57.

138 *See* ANDERSON, *supra* note 53, at 128–30.

139 *Cf.* ANDERSON, *supra* note 19, at 146.

140 *See* RADIN, *supra* note 134, at 110; ANDERSON, *supra* note 53, at 69–70. At least on its face, the German model of codetermination seems a particularly inviting starting point for rethinking the workplace along these lines. *See* Klaus J. Hopt, *Labor Representation on Corporate Boards: Impacts and Problems for Corporate Governance and Economic Integration in Europe*, 14 INT'L REV. L. & ECON. 203 (1994); Katharina Pistor, *Codetermination in Germany: A Socio-Political Model with Governance Externalities*, in EMPLOYEES AND CORPORATE GOVERNANCE 163 (Margaret Blair & Mark Roe eds. 1999). *See also* ISABELLE FERRERAS & MIRANDA RICHMOND MOUILLOT, FIRMS AS POLITICAL ENTITIES: SAVING DEMOCRACY THROUGH ECONOMIC BICAMERALISM (2017).

141 HERZOG, *supra* note 24, at 69–73.

142 The term "ground project" in this context should not be equated with career but with (at least minimally) meaningful work. Without some such measure, selling one's labor – promising to comply with the employer's directives – is tantamount to a consensual subordination to another's authority. *Cf.* Collins, *supra* note 3, at 53–54.

143 *See supra* Chapter 5 note 43 and accompanying text.

144 HERZOG, *supra* note 24, at 75, 78.

Chapter 8

1 *Cf.* JEREMY WALDRON, THE RIGHT TO PRIVATE PROPERTY 438 (1988).

2 *See supra* Chapter 3 text accompanying note 111–112.

3 *See Stop the Beach Renourishment, Inc. v. Fla. Dep't of Envtl. Prot.*, 560 U.S. 702, 708–09 (2010).

4 *See supra* Chapter 6 text accompanying note 7.
5 *See* Charles R. Beitz, *Property and Time*, 27 J. POL. PHIL. 419, 428 (2018). *Cf.* Shmuel Nili, *The Idea of Public Property*, 129 ETHICS 344, 356 (2019).
6 *Contra* Laura S. Underkuffler, *Property and Change: The Constitutional Conundrum*, 91 TEXAS L. REV. 2015, 2016–17, 2034–35 (2013).
7 Christopher Serkin claims, along similar lines, that "What property *does* is protect reasonable reliance by constraining the pace of change." Dynamism and change are "inherent in property," but property, at the same time, "ensures that rules and expectations shift incrementally, and that people are given time to adapt to those changes." Christopher Serkin, What Property Does *5, 17 (unpublished manuscript). Serkin justifies this feature of property by reference to owners' reliance, which he understands as "a psychological phenomenon more than a legal one" and as evolutionary, rather than static. *Id.*, at *8–9, 14. Thus, while descriptively our accounts converge, conceptually and normatively they are very different.
8 *See infra* text accompanying note 44.
9 505 U.S. 1003 (1992).
10 *Id.*, at 1027–28.
11 *Id.*, at 1029–31.
12 *Id.*, at 1036–61 (Blackmun, J., dissenting).
13 *See* Richard A. Epstein, *Lucas v. South Carolina Coastal Council: A Tangled Web of Expectations*, 45 STAN. L. REV. 1369, 1377–78 (1993).
14 *Lucas*, 505 U.S. at 1025–26. For the current purpose, it is not important whether these Coasean propositions are necessarily correct. The point of the text is more limited: given Scalia's endorsement of this position, it seems remarkable to invoke nuisance law as the secure premise of the property pact.
15 *Id.*, at 1055 (Blackmun, J., dissenting). *See also* John F. Hart, *Colonial Land Use Law and Its Significance for Modern Takings Doctrine*, 109 HARV. L. REV. 1252, 1297–98 (1996). Unsurprisingly (albeit somewhat grudgingly), in addition to the references to the common law, Scalia also invokes the State's "complementary power to abate nuisances that affect the public generally, or otherwise." *Lucas*, 505 U.S. at 1029.
16 *Stop the Beach*, 560 U.S. at 715 (emphasis omitted).
17 *Id.*, at 727.
18 *Lucas*, 505 U.S. at 1027.
19 *Id.*, at 1058 (Blackmun, J., dissenting).
20 *See* Hart, *supra* note 15, at 1297–98.
21 *See, e.g.*, HANOCH DAGAN, PROPERTY: VALUES AND INSTITUTIONS 28 (2011).
22 1 F.A. HAYEK, LAW, LEGISLATION, AND LIBERTY 102 (1982).
23 *See* Gerald J. Postema, *On the Moral Presence of Our Past*, 36 MCGILL L.J. 1153, 1168 (1991).
24 *Cf. Stop the Beach*, 560 U.S. at 727–28; RONALD DWORKIN, TAKING RIGHTS SERIOUSLY 86 (1977).

25 Louis Kaplow, *Transition Policy: A Conceptual Framework*, 13 J. Contemp. Legal Issues 161, 170 (2003). *See also, e.g.*, Michael J. Graetz, *Legal Transitions: The Case of Retroactivity in Income Tax Revision*, 126 U. Pa. L. Rev. 47, 49–63 (1977).
26 H.L.A. Hart, The Concept of Law 92 (1961).
27 *Id.*
28 At first glance, rules of eminent domain law and of regulatory takings law may seem primary rather than secondary rules because they refer to rights of the state over people's property. On reflection, however, all are in fact rules about the state's *power* to affect people's property and, as such, are squarely within Hart's definition of secondary rules.
29 364 U.S. 40, 49 (1960).
30 I do not contest Nestor Davidson's observation that "it is clear that, over time, a set of regulatory constraints, even if challenged initially, can so deeply settle into the law of property that no owner would be reasonable in challenging it." Nestor Davidson, *Resetting the Baseline of Ownership: Takings and Investor Expectations after the Bailouts*, 75 Md. L. Rev. 722, 726–27 (2016). But this proposition does not purport to resolve the circularity critique that applies exactly to the period before the law restabilizes, namely, at the crucial moment of legal transition.
31 *Lucas*, 505 U.S. at 1031.
32 *Id.* Justice Rehnquist seems to offer a similar interpretation in his dissenting opinion in *Lake Tahoe*, where he distinguishes "a moratorium prohibiting all economic use for the period of six years" from "typical moratoria," which "prohibit only certain categories of development" that are part of "the long-standing, implied limitations of state property law." *See Tahoe-Sierra Pres. Council, Inc. v. Tahoe Reg'l Planning Agency*, 535 U.S. 302, 352 (Rehnquist, C.J., dissenting, joined by Scalia & Thomas, JJ.).
33 Another reading would qualify the text by understanding Scalia's propositions in conjunction with the *Penn Central* tests that may refine it.
34 *See* Richard A. Epstein, Takings: Private Property and the Power of Eminent Domain 5, 204–09 (1985); Richard A. Epstein, *Takings, Exclusivity and Speech: The Legacy of* PruneYard v. Robins, 64 U. Chi. L. Rev. 21, 27–28 (1997).
35 *Lucas*, 505 U.S. at 1069 (Stevens, J., dissenting).
36 *Id.*
37 *Id.*, at 1070.
38 *Pa. Coal Co. v. Mahon*, 260 U.S. 393, 422 (1922) (Brandeis, J., dissenting).
39 *See* Frank Michelman, *The Common Law Baseline and Restitution for the Lost Commons*, 64 U. Chi. L. Rev. 57, 69 (1997).
40 Joseph William Singer, *Justifying Regulatory Takings*, 41 Ohio N. U. L. Rev. 601, 608, 659 (2015).

41 C. Edwin Baker, *Property and Its Relation to Constitutionally Protected Liberty*, 134 U. PA. L. REV. 741, 765 (1986).
42 The following summary draws on the literature analysis in DAGAN, *supra* note 21, at 90–95.
43 As Nozick forcefully argued in his sounding retreat from "the libertarian position [he] once propounded," that position fails in part because it neglects to give any "official political" expression to our "joint goals" and thus threatens "to truncate the reality of our social solidarity and concern for others." *See* ROBERT NOZICK, *The Zigzags of Politics, in* THE EXAMINED LIFE: PHILOSOPHICAL MEDIATIONS 286, 286–88 (1989).
44 *See supra* Chapter 3 text accompanying notes 147–149.
45 *See supra* Chapter 5 text accompanying notes 30–32.
46 *See* DAGAN, *supra* note 21, at 128–31, 142–44.
47 *Cf. Kelo v. City of New London, Conn.*, 545 U.S. 469, 505 (2005) (O'Connor, J., dissenting).
48 *Cf. Id.*, at 505 (Thomas, J., dissenting).
49 Jean Hampton, *Selflessness and the Loss of Self, in* ALTRUISM 135, 136, 148, 161 (Ellen Frankel Paul et al. eds., 1993).
50 Eminent domain law has become a somewhat controversial subject in recent years, but the rule whereby owners whose land is taken for public use are generally entitled to compensation seems indisputable. This rule emerges from the language of the Fifth Amendment, but is far from unique to American constitutional property law. Many jurisdictions require full (fair market value) compensation, and even those that acknowledge the possibility of partial or even no compensation, view these as justified exceptions limited to specific categories of cases. *See* T. ALLEN, THE RIGHT TO PROPERTY IN COMMONWEALTH CONSTITUTIONS 223–224, 240 (2000); A.J. VAN DER WALT, CONSTITUTIONAL PROPERTY LAW 506, 510–511 (3rd ed. 2011).
51 *Penn Central Transportation Co. v New York*, 438 U.S. 104 (1978).
52 Daniel A. Farber, *Murr v. Wisconsin and the Future of Takings Law*, 2017 SUP. CT. REV. 115, 163–64.
53 *Id.*, at 164.
54 There is still a gap between the following propositions that summarize the *principles* the liberal pact implies and a takings jurisprudence that properly complies with the rule of law. For my suggestion on a rule-of-law abiding doctrine, see Hanoch Dagan, *Expropriatory Compensation, The Rule of Law, and Distributive Justice, in* RETHINKING EXPROPRIATION LAW I: PUBLIC INTEREST IN EXPROPRIATION 349 (Björn Hoops et al. eds., 2015).
55 *Cf. PruneYard Shopping Center v. Robins*, 447 U.S. 74, 93 (1980) (Marshal, J., concurring) (whereas "common-law rights [are not] immune from revision by State or Federal Government," they are also not "defined solely by

state law"; property has "a normative dimension as well, establishing a sphere of private autonomy which government is bound to respect.").
56 *Lucas*, 505 U.S. at 1034–35 (Kennedy, J., concurring).
57 *Id.*, at 1030.
58 *See* Andrew Burrows, *Common Law Retrospectivity, in* JUDGE AND JURIST 543, 545 (Andrew Burrows et al. eds. 2013).
59 *See Id.*, at 550.
60 KARL N. LLEWELLYN, THE COMMON LAW TRADITION: DECIDING APPEALS 36 (1960); KARL N. LLEWELLYN, JURISPRUDENCE: REALISM IN THEORY AND IN PRACTICE 361–62 (1962). *See also, e.g.*, John Dewey, *My Philosophy of Law, in* MY PHILOSOPHY OF LAW: CREDOS OF SIXTEEN AMERICAN SCHOLARS 73, 77 (1941, 1987); GERALD J. POSTEMA, *Justice Holmes: A New Path for American Jurisprudence, in* LEGAL PHILOSOPHY IN THE TWENTIETH CENTURY: THE COMMON LAW WORLD 43, 64–70 (2011).
61 LLEWELLYN, COMMON LAW TRADITION, *supra* note 60, at 190–91, 222–33; KARL N. LLEWELLYN, THE CASE LAW SYSTEM IN AMERICA 77 (1933) (Paul Gewirtz ed. Michael Alsandi trans. 1933, 1989). *See also, e.g.*, HAYEK, *supra* note 22, at 120. This requirement of fitness is, for Llewellyn, not a global imperative but a far more localized injunction. *See* LLEWELLYN, COMMON LAW TRADITION, *supra* note 60, at 194; *see also id.*, at 44.
62 BENJAMIN N. CARDOZO, THE NATURE OF THE JUDICIAL PROCESS 179 (1921).
63 *See* OLIVER W. HOLMES, *The Path of the Law, in* COLLECTED LEGAL PAPERS 167, 181 (1920); LLEWELLYN, JURISPRUDENCE, *supra* note 60, at 211–12; Hessel E. Yntema, *Jurisprudence on Parade*, 39 MICH. L. REV. 1154, 1169 (1941).
64 LLEWELLYN, COMMON LAW TRADITION, *supra* note 60, at 36, 38, 190, 217.
65 Thomas Nagel, *The Problem of Global Justice*, 33 PHIL. & PUB. AFF. 114, 128 (2005).
66 *Stop the Beach*, 560 U.S. at 738 (Kennedy, J., concurring). Justice O'Connor's concurring opinion in *Palazzolo v. Rhode Island*, 533 U.S. 606 (2001) can be interpreted along similar lines: although in that case petitioner's claim was not barred by the fact that title was acquired after the regulation's effective date, O'Connor insisted, "the timing of the regulation's enactment relative to the acquisition of title" remains material "to the *Penn Central* analysis" of investment-based expectations. *Id.*, at 633 (O'Connor, J., concurring). By contrast, in *Stop the Beach* itself, Scalia vehemently opposes Kennedy's characterization of the common law tradition. *See id.*, at 722. But his objections stand only if the property rights at hand there are conceptually severed from the bundle to which they belong. Conceptual severance, if

widely applied, obviously renders the notion of incremental modifications of the law unintelligible. Fortunately, this strategy has been firmly rejected. *See infra* text accompanying note 105.
67 *See, e.g., Reste Realty Corp. v. Cooper*, 251 A.2d 268 (N.J. 1969).
68 *See, e.g., Willard v. 1st Church of Christ, Scientist*, 498 P.2d 987, 991 (Cal. 1972).
69 Eyal Benvenisti, *The Origins of the Concept of Belligerent Occupation*, 26 L. & History Rev. 621, 621–23, 628, 633 (2008). For an example of an outright violation of these principles, see Yael Ronen & Yuval Shany, *Israel's Settlement Regulation Bill Violates International Law*, JUST SECURITY (December 20, 2016), https://www.justsecurity.org/35743/israels-settlement-regulation-bill-violates-international-law/.
70 *See supra* text accompanying notes 62–64.
71 *Cf.* Larry Alexander, *Introduction to the Conference on Legal Transitions*, 13 J. CONTEMP. LEGAL ISSUES 1, 3 (2003).
72 Indeed, the liberal pact inculcates a sense of modesty regarding our current conception of justice and a healthy expectation of law and from law that it should work itself pure by constantly inviting criticism and moral challenges. Unlike denials of the legality of particularly pernicious rules at the time of their inception, retroactive application avoids "the illusion that injustice is always already in the past" and the attendant risk of moral complacency and blindness to present injustice. *Cf.* Audrey Macklin, *Can We Do Wrong to Strangers, in* CALLING POWER TO ACCOUNT: LAW, REPARATIONS, AND THE CHINESE CANADIAN HEAD TAX 60 (David Dyzenhaus & Mayo Moran eds., 2005).
73 *In re* African-Am. Slave Descendants Litig., 304 F. Supp. 2d 1027, 1035 (N.D. Ill. 2004). The following paragraphs draw on my extensive discussion of the African-American lawsuits for restitution of gains from slave labor. *See* Hanoch Dagan, *Restitution and Slavery: On Incomplete Commodification, Intergenerational Justice, and Legal Transitions*, 84 B.U. L. REV. 1139, 1164–74 (2004).
74 *Lucas*, 505 U.S. at 1069 (Stevens, J., dissenting).
75 Carol M. Rose, *Property and Expropriation: Themes and Variations in American Law*, 2000 UTAH L. REV. 1, 24–28 (2000).
76 Morris R. Cohen, *Property and Sovereignty*, 13 CORNELL L.Q. 8, 24 (1927). James Madison, apparently, had a different view. *See* Michael Treanor, *The Original Understanding of the Takings Clause and the Political Process*, 95 COLUM. L. REV. 782, 839 (1995). For further references to the claim that slave owners might have deserved compensation, see Kaimipono David Wenger, *Slavery as a Takings Clause Violation*, 53 AM. U. L. REV. 191, 196–97 n.18 (2003).
77 Likewise, a liberal law of contract should have refused to respect agreements for the sale of slaves entered into prior to emancipation. Embarrassingly, this

was not the case. *See* Andrew Kull, *The Enforceability After Emancipation of Debts Contracted for the Purchase of Slaves*, 70 CHI.-KENT L. REV. 493 (1994). Kull refers to the concern of unsettling expectations in this area as "a social cost" and to the retrospective annulment of these contracts as an instance of "political justice." Kull, *Id.*, at 531–32. Both descriptions are wrong, because the practice of contract, like that of property, can be justified if, but only if, it is premised on people's ultimate right to self-determination. *See* HANOCH DAGAN & MICHAEL A. HELLER, THE CHOICE THEORY OF CONTRACTS 41–47 (2017); Hanoch Dagan & Michael Heller, *Autonomy for Contract, Refined*, 38 L. & PHIL. (2020); Hanoch Dagan & Michael Heller, *Why Autonomy Must Be Contract's Ultimate Value*, 20 JERUSALEM REV. LEGAL STUD. 148, 149–64 (2019).

78 CONSTITUTION OF THE REPUBLIC OF SOUTH AFRICA § 25 (3)(4) (1996).
79 *Heart of Atlanta Motel, Inc. v. United States*, 379 U.S. 241, 258, 260 (1964).
80 *Kirchberg v. Feenstra*, 450 U.S. 455, 456–57, 460–61 (1981).
81 Cohen, *supra* note 76, at 26.
82 The *locus classicus* is Louis Kaplow, *An Economic Analysis of Legal Transitions*, 99 HARV. L. REV. 509 (1986).
83 *See Verizon Communications v. FCC*, 535 U.S. 467, 497–523 (2002); *Ala. Power Co. v. FCC*, 311 F.3d 1357, 1369–72 (2002). Incumbents are often granted a generous return on their historic investments.
84 *See Illinois Transportation Trade Association v. City of Chicago*, 839 F.3d 594 (7th Cir. 2016). *See also* William J. Baumol & Thomas W. Merrill, *Deregulatory Takings, Breach of the Regulatory Contract, and the Telecommunications Act of 1996*, 72 N.Y.U. L. REV. 1037, 1066 (1997). *Contra* J. Gregory Sidak & Daniel F. Spulber, *Deregulatory Takings and Breach of the Regulatory Contract*, 71 N.Y.U. L. REV. 851, 860–61, 863–64 (1996). Even devoted libertarians have little sympathy for transitory victims of deregulation. *See* Richard A. Epstein, *Beware of Legal Transitions: A Presumptive Vote for the Reliance Interest*, 13 J. CONTEMP. LEGAL ISSUES 69, 71 (2003).
85 *See* Kyle D. Logue, *Tax Transitions, Opportunistic Retroactivity, and the Benefits of Government Precommitment*, 94 MICH. L. REV. 1129, 1149 (1996).
86 Compensation would be inappropriate in such cases because the incumbent would already have captured enough countervailing regulatory benefits prior to deregulation. *Cf.* Baumol & Merrill, *supra* note 84, at 1057–67.
87 *Lucas*, 505 U.S. at 1068.
88 Indeed, putative protection against such legal avulsion would have provided these actors a perverse competitive advantage vis-à-vis other actors who refused to engage in such activities. Even if managers of such potential future defendants are likely to ignore these consequences at the outset, sophisticated competitors who avoid the pertinent practice are likely to remind investors of the risks they are taking, thus indirectly forcing their internalization.

89 *See, e.g.,* Underkuffler, *supra* note 6, at 2016–27.
90 *See* Hanoch Dagan & Michael Heller, America's Property Pact (unpublished manuscript).
91 *Stop the Beach,* 560 U.S. at 715.
92 *Compare, e.g.,* Barton H. Thompson, Jr., *Judicial Takings,* 76 Va. L. Rev. 1449 (1990) *with* Eduardo M. Peñalver & Lior Jacob Strahilevitz, *Judicial Takings or Due Process?,* 97 Cornell L. Rev. 305 (2012); Laura S. Underkuffler, *Judicial Takings: A Medley of Misconceptions,* 61 Syracuse L. Rev. 203 (2011).
93 *See supra* text accompanying notes 67–68.
94 *Contra* Frederic Bloom & Christopher Serkin, *Suing Courts,* 79 U. Chi. L. Rev. 553 (2012).
95 Elsewhere, I argued that eminent domain law should follow those jurisdictions, such as Germany and South Africa, where certain expropriation cases should trigger only partial compensation. *See* Hanoch Dagan, *Eminent Domain and Regulatory Takings: Towards a Unified Theory,* Rethinking Expropriation Law III: Compensation for Expropriation 21, 32–33 (Björn Hoops et al. eds., 2018).
96 458 U.S. 419, 426, 434 (1982).
97 *Id.,* at 442–56 (Blackmun, J., dissenting).
98 For a charitable interpretation of *Loretto* as an attempt (albeit not a very successful one) to carve out a bright-line rule that protects against extreme physical invasions of a private owner's resources (such as a home) that are constitutive of one's identity and should, therefore, *always* be deemed legal avulsions, see Dagan, *supra* note 95, at 29–30.
99 The term "average reciprocity of advantage" was coined by Justice Oliver Wendell Holmes in *Jackman v. Rosenbaum Co.,* 260 U.S. 22, 30 (1922), and *Pennsylvania Coal Co. v. Mahon,* 260 U.S. 393, 415 (1922).
100 *See supra* text accompanying note 38.
101 *Compare, e.g., Florida Rock Indus. v. United States,* 18 F.3d 1560, 1571 (Fed. Cir. 1994), cert. denied, 513 U.S. 1109 (1995) with *Keystone Bituminous Coal Ass'n v. DeBenedictis,* 480 U.S. 470, 491 (1987).
102 Dagan, *supra* note 21, at 103.
103 *See Id.,* at 115–19.
104 Margaret Jane Radin, *The Liberal Conception of Property: Crosscurrents in the Jurisprudence of Takings,* in Reinterpreting Property 120, 126–30 (1993).
105 *Murr v. Wisconsin,* 137 S.Ct. 1933, 1944, 1949 (2017). In fact, it may require to look at the claimant's total holdings in the same surroundings. *See* Dagan, *supra* note 21, at 88, 119. The *Murr* majority also seemed open to this suggestion. *Id.,* at 1943–49.
106 Farber, *supra* note 52, at 146, 165.

107 Singer, *supra* note 40, at 606, 635–36 . Indeed, as the text implies, only a few types of cases may trigger compensation in Singer's account: "(a) uncompensated *destruction* or *occupation* of property without adequate reason; (b) uncompensated, unjustified permanent *physical invasions*; (c) uncompensated deprivation of certain *core property rights* without sufficient cause; and (d) laws that impose *unfair burdens* on owners that should, in fairness and justice, be shared by the public as a whole." *Id.*, at 642.

108 The meaning of "public use," which delimits the legitimate scope of the power of eminent domain, has been the subject of some controversy in recent years. Be that as it may, it is hardly ever questioned that a certain threshold of "publicness" should be a prior condition to the exercise of the power of eminent domain, and it is just as uncontroversial that once this – high or low – threshold is crossed and we turn to the question of compensation, the relative significance or even urgency of the pertinent public purpose makes no difference.

109 *See supra,* text accompanying notes 87–88.

110 *Hadacheck v. Sebastian,* 239 U.S. 394, 410 (1915).

111 *See supra* note 14 and accompanying text.

112 RESTATEMENT (SECOND) OF TORTS § 840D & Cmt. b. (AM. LAW INST. 1979).

113 *Cf.* Serkin, *supra* note 7, at *50.

INDEX

accession, innocent, 141
accountability, 157–158
accountable agency, 260n54
accretions, 229–230
Ackerman, Bruce, 32
ad hocery, 227–228
adjudication, 149
   legitimacy of, 155–158
   limits of, 154–155
   performance of, 151–155
   v. legislation, 216
advantage, reciprocity of, 238–239
adverse possession, 141
Airbnb, 284n62
Alexander, Gregory, 72, 83
alienability, 184
alimony, rehabilitative, 145
American Law Institute, 105
Anderson, Elizabeth, 182
anti-discrimination laws, 133, 196
antitrust policy, 71
Armstrong v. United States, 219
Aronson, Ori, 103
authority over things, 63–65
authority, private, 4–6, 144–146
   autonomy and, 41–42
   carefully delineated, 69–70
   owners-employers' private authority, 199–200, 210–211
   relationally just, 128–131
authority, service conception of, 263n88
authors' rights, 70
autonomy, 1–4
   and distribution, 71–75
   as market's *telos*, 188–189
   and multiplicity, 89–93
   owners', 211
   and private authority, 41–42
   promotion of, 44–46

property as instrumental to, 55–56
   as self-determination, 42–44
   as side constraint, 58–59
   as ultimate value, 36
   without perfectionism, 77–78
autonomy-based markets, 185
autonomy-based pluralism, 36–38, 89
avulsions, 212, 232–235

Bagchi, Aditi, 308n113
Beitz, Charles, 64
Bentham, Jeremy, 13
Benvenisti, Eyal, 232
bequest, power to, 66
Berlin, Isaiah, 47
Black, Hugo, 219
Blackmun, Harry, 215, 217
Blackstone, William, 9, 42
   property theory of, 79–81, 100–102
Brandeis, Louis, 71, 222, 238
Bratman, Michael, 200
Brudner, Alan, 29–30, 44, 297n123
Buchanan, Allen, 62
bundle of sticks, 33
Burwell v. Hobby Lobby Store, 70
buying or leasing, 135–136

Cardozo, Benjamin, 230
categories of deciding, 23
categories of thinking, 23–25
change
   life plans, 200–203
   property transitions, 242
   rule of, 217–220
   and stability, 211–212
choice
   employment at will/for choice, 195
   expanded, 191–192
   individual, 90–91

319

citizenship, 250n7
co-authorship, 156–157
Cohen, Felix, 130, 153
Cohen, G.A., 265n120
Cohen, Morris, 60, 233
co-housing, 138
collectivist property types, 58
commercial property types, 102
commodification, incomplete, 206
common law, 150, 152–154, 229
common-interest communities, 86–87, 163–165
commons property, 84–89
  liberal commons, 54–55
  utilitarian v. social, 85–86
communication costs, 111, 149
community, 51–55
  common-interest, 86–87, 163–165
  intrinsic value of, 51–53
  liberal value of, 53
community property, 87, 109, 234–235, *see also* property
community property types, 110
conceptual severance, 239
concurrent ownership, 110
concurrent property rights, 84
Constitution, 233
  Equal Protection Clause, 139
  Takings Clause, 215, 229
consumer contracts, 191
contract law, 97, 278n108
contract(s)
  consumer, 191
  freedom of, 92–93
  long-term, 202
  property and, 25–26
  right to terminate, 202
  social, 117–118
cooperative property types, 97
copyright law, 58
corrective justice, 8
costs
  communication, 111, 149
  information, 97
  transaction, 97
  verification, 111
courts, 158–159
cultural effects
  of Kantian property, 120–121
  of property, 97–99

Davidson, Nestor, 312n30
Δ question, 103–104
democracy, 76, 120
dependent contractors, 194
deregulation, 235, 316n84
design, market, 192–193
Desmond, Matthew, 73
Dicey, Albert Venn, 169
diminution of value, 239–240
discrimination
  anti-discrimination laws, 133, 196
  convoluted explanations and, 137
  non-discrimination, 195–197
  refusals to sell or lease, 135–136
distribution
  autonomy and, 71–75
  property for all, 73–74
distributive justice, 124
doctrinalism, property, 34
domination, 197
Dorfman, Avihay, 60–62, 114, 134–135, 291n28
Dworkin, Ronald, 122

Eagle Enters. v. Gross, 295n84
easy cases, 158
easy rescue, 141–142
economic analysis, 223
Emancipation, 234
eminent domain, 237–238, 313n50
employment
  at will/for choice, 195–196
  dependent contractors, 194
  owners-employers' private authority, 199–200
environmental law, 286n88
Epstein, Richard, 221
equal protection, 139
equality, 38
equitable division, 110
Essert, Christopher, 66
European Court of Human Rights, 199
eviction, 73
exchange, voluntary, 182
exclusion theory, 184
exit, 36, 43, 54, 59, 97
expanded choice, 191–192
expectations, 217–218, 220, 228, 230, 238

Index

fair housing, xii, 131, 135–139
Fair Housing Act, 138, 234
fair use doctrine, 58
family life, 109–110
Farber, Daniel, 227
fee-simple-absolute property type, 23
feudalism, 8
free markets, 188
free tenures, 8
freedom of contract, 92–93
freedom of exit, 54
freedom of speech, 135
Fugitive Slave Act, 233
future self, 200–202

global land rush, 176–178
governance, participatory, 87
governance, property, 82–84
Grewal, David, 303n48
ground projects, 127
guidance, 161–163

Habermas, Jürgen, 205
Hadacheck v. Sebastian, 241
Hague Regulations, 232
Hampton, Jean, 226
hard cases, 133–134, 146, 235–236, 267n138
Hardt, Michael, 67
Hart, H. L. A., 45, 128, 218
Hayek, Friedrich, 186, 218, 293n56
Hegel, Georg Wilhelm Friedrich, 29–30, 73, 207
Heller, Michael, 25, 54, 84, 110, 214
Herzog, Lisa, 183, 207
Hirschman, Albert, 181
Hohfeld, Wesley, 26–27, 30
Holdsworth, W. S., 287n1
Holmes, Oliver Wendell, 317n99
home equity insurance, 108
homeownership, shared equity, 107–109
Honoré, Tony, 140, 184
housing
　co-housing, 138
　fair housing, xii, 131, 135–139
　as human right, 74
human capital, 207
human right to property, 173–176, *see also* property rights

in personam, 27
in rem, 27
inclusion, 195–197
incommensurability, 59
incomplete commodification, 206
independence, 42–44
　irreducible value of, 46–47
　Kant's conception of, 115–116
independent contractors, 194
indigenous communities, 287n106
individual choice, 90–91
individual sacrifice, 226–227
information costs, 97
informative standards, 166–168
institutional question, 149–151
interdependence, 123
interest groups, 120, 226
interpretive theory, 16–19
intimacy, 109–110

Jackson, William, 183
job-sharing, 194–195
judges, 158–159, 229–230
judicial activism, 155–158
judicial takings doctrine, 237
judiciary system, 151–155
just markets, 179–180
justice
　background regime, 72–73
　and politics, 120
　private responsibility for, 124–125
　unjust property types, 142–146
justice, corrective, 8
justice, distributive, 124
justice, relational, 7–9, 71, 124, 126–128, 195–200
　inherent limits, 129
　property's, 113
　property's legitimacy and, 125–126
　relationally just private authority, 128–131
　three limitations on, 129–130

Kant, Immanuel, 9, 42
Kantian property, 115–118
　ambiguities of, 118–120
　cultural effects of, 120–121
　mission impossible, 118–122
　mission undesirable, 122–126
Katz, Larissa, 281n19

Kennedy, Anthony, 228–230
Kennedy, Duncan, 295n98
Knight, Frank, 303n51
Komesar, Neil, 157
Korsgaard, Christine, 258n25
Koskenniemi, Martii, 297n120
Krygier, Martin, 292n52
Kuhn, Thomas 256n64

labor
  division of, 122–124
  markets and, 207–209
  worker cooperatives, 109
  workers' inalienable rights, 198–199
  workers' voice, 206–207
labor law, 197–198
labor markets, 207–209
labor unions, 306n90
land ownership
  global land rush, 176–178
  limitations on, 215–216
  shoreline, 212–214
land use law, 286n88
landlord-tenant law, 83, 288n9
law(s). *see also* common law, property law
  markets and, 181–182
  material and cultural effects of, 97–99
  nature of, 129
  property and, 13–14
  role of, 96–100
  rule of, 129, 159–163, 168–170, 172–173
  second-order rules, 218–219
  for utopia, 96–100
leaseholds, 275n72
leasing, 135–136
Lechmere Inc. v. NLRB, 199
legal reform, internal, 104–106
legal theory, 14–15
  interpretive, 16–19
  property theory as, 13–16
legislation, 149, *see also* law(s)
  adjudication v., 216
  and common law, 152–154
  performance of, 151–155
legislatures, 155–159
legitimacy
  concept of, 291n35
  of judge-made law, 155–158
  of property, 125–126, 210–212
liberal commons, 54–55
liberal market economy, 304n66

liberal markets, 200
liberal polity, 35–40
liberal property
  and equality, 38
  and rule of law, 172–173
liberal property law, 1, 10
  afterword, 244
  challenge to conventional views, 9–10
  three pillars of, 4, 10, 146, 174
liberal property pact, 214, 227–231
  boundaries to, 231–236
  in practice, 228
liberal theory
  critique of welfare foundationalism, 57–58
  as interpretive theory, 16–19
liberalism, xi, 77–78
libertarian pact, 221–225
libertarian theory, 93
liberty, negative, 187–188
LLCs, 102
Llewellyn, Karl, 152, 229
LLPs, 102
Locke, John, 1, 30, 69, 73
long-term contracts, 202
Loretto v. Teleprompter Manhattan, 238
Lucas v. S.C. Coastal Council, 214–217, 221–222, 228, 236

Madison, James, 315n76
marital property, 109, 143–144
markets, 180–183, 310n135
  autonomy-based, 185
  autonomy-enhancing, 200
  design of, 192–193
  free, 188
  heterogeneity of, 182–183
  just, 179–180
  and labor, 207–209
  and law, 181–182
  mobility of, 189–191
  for negative liberty, 187–188
  pre-theoretical definition of, 180–181
  property and, 183–185
  roles of, 189
  telos, 188–189
  for welfare, 186–187
marriage, 52, 110, 273n35
Marx, Karl, 190
Masterpiece Cakeshop v. Colorado Civil Rights Commission, 282n39
McFarlane, Ben, 271n6

Index

means of production, 5, 42, 69
Merrill, Thomas, 149, 251n8, 270n2, 275n66
Mill, John Stuart, 190
Mises, Ludwig von, 186
misfeasance-nonfeasance distinction, 140–141
mobility, 189–191
monism, property, 19–20
monistic theory, 21–22
moral rights, 58
Moreau, Sophia, 282n38
multiplicity
  and autonomy, 89–93
  intra-sphere, 92
  layers of, in Nozick's utopias, 95–96
Murr v. Wisconsin, 239

N question, 103–104
negative liberty, 187–188
Negri, Antonio, 67
Neponsit Property Owners' Ass'n v. Emigrant Industrial Savings Bank, 163–166, 294n73
neutrality, 75–78
Noble v. Alley, 171
non-citizens, 232
non-compensable avulsions, 211–235
non-compete agreements, 202
non-discrimination, 195–197
non-owners, 211
nonproperty, 67
normal science, 34–35
normalization, 204–206
Nozick, Robert, 45, 57
  libertarian theory, 93
  theory of utopia, 93–96
nuisance law, 215–216
nuisance test, 242
numerus clausus, 110–113, 149–151

O'Connor, Sandra Day, 314n66
O'Neill, John, 181
Offe, Claus, 197
Office of Fair Housing and Equal Opportunity, 154
Oliphant, Herman, 153
Oman, Nathan, 300n20
Ostrom, Elinor, 54
Owens, David, 264n102
owners' responsibilities, 139–142, 144–146
owners-employers' private authority, 199–200, 210–211
ownership
  Blackstonian, 100–102
  concurrent, 110
  Kantian, 117
  limitations on, 215–216
  of shoreline land, 212–214
  vulnerability and stability across time, 210–212

Palazzolo v. Rhode Island, 314n66
panglossianism, 67–68
paradigm shifts, 34–35, 153
participatory governance, 87
Patten, Allan, 270n173
Penn Central test, 227–228, 238, 240
Penn Coal. v. Mahon, 222
Penner, James, 184
Pettit, Philip, 280n4
perfectionist liberalism, 77–78
permanent physical occupation, 238
personhood, 31, 50–51
plans
  changing, 200–203
  self-determination, 200–203
pluralism
  autonomy-based, 36–38, 89
  freestanding, 89
  profound, 87–88
  structural, xi, 6–7, 22–23, 79–113, 130–131, 165–166, 193
  value, 36–38
politics, 120
Posner, Eric, 56, 186
poverty, 116–117, 283n47
power
  to commit, 202–203
  conferring institution, 63
  as influence, 61, 66, 100
  interest group, 226
  interpersonal, 5
  normative, 2, 13, 41, 60–61, 63, 201–202
  of property, 59–62, 68–71
private authority
  autonomy and, 41–42
  carefully delineated, 4–6, 69–70
  owners-employers' private authority, 199–200, 210–211
  relationally just, 128–131
  temporally extended, 144–146

private law, 39
private responsibility, 124–125
privatization, 58
progressive pact, 222–223, 225–227
progressive school, 32
property
  accretion of, 229–230
  afterword, 243–247
  for all, 73–74
  for autonomy, 1–4, 58–59
  as category of thinking, 23–25
  commons, 84–89
  community, 87, 109, 234–235
  community value of, 51–55
  and contract, 26
  core of, 149–151
  cultural effects of, 97–99, 120–121
  design of, 15–16
  distribution of, 71–75
  dominion conception of, 9–10, 38, 123
  and easy rescue, 141–142
  form and substance of, 31–35
  governance of, 82–84
  heterogeneity of, 81–82
  instrumental value of, 49–50, 55–56
  intrinsic value of, 49–50
  justification for, 15–16, 62–67
  and law, 13–14
  legitimacy of, 125–126, 210–212
  liberal theory of, 1, 12
  limitations of, xi, 68–71
  lumpiness of, 28
  marital, 109, 143–144
  and markets, 183–185
  multiplicity of, 89–93
  owners' responsibilities, 139–142
  physicalist view of, 27
  as power-conferring, 63
  powers of, 59–62, 68–71
  private, 120
  private authority, 4–6
  and promotion of autonomy, 44–46
  relational justice, 113
  and rule of law, 159–161
  stability of, 151–152, 211–212
  temporally-extended authority over things, 63–65
  third party effects, 253n27, 271n6
  and time, 210
  trust, 266n133
  utility of, 55–58
  variety of, 79–82
  welfare foundationalist view of, 56–57
property doctrinalism, 34
property law. *see also* liberal property law
  co-authorship, 156–157
  growth of, 152
  internal critique and reform, 104–106
  making of, 147
  paradigm shifts, 34–35, 153
  structural pluralism of, xi, 6–7, 22–23, 79–113, 130–131, 165–166, 193
    autonomy-based, 89
    profound, 87–88
property monism, 19–20
property pacts, 219
  liberal pact, 214, 227–236
  libertarian pact, 221–225
  Lucas' compact, 214–217
  progressive pact, 222–223, 225–227
  as rule of change, 219–220
  unacceptable, 220–223
property rights, 1, 36, 184, 209
  concurrent, 84
  Hohfeldian, 26–27
  as human rights, 173–176
  successive, 84
  universalist foundation, 173–174
property theory
  architectural approach to, 251n8
  Blackstonian, 79–81, 100–102
  Hegelian, 29–30
  Kantian, 115–126
  as legal theory, 13–16
  libertarian, 93
  limits of, 74–75
  Lockean, 1, 69, 73, 249n1
  personhood, 31, 50–51
  utilitarian, 45, 85–86
property transitions, 242
property types, 6–7, 19–23
  adequate range of, 102–106
  collectivist, 58
  commercial, 102
  community, 110
  cooperative, 97
  fee-simple-absolute, 23
  missing, 106–110
  partial functional substitutes, 102–103
  reconsideration of, 142–143
  reform guidelines, 246
  residual, 112–113

Index

rich mosaic of, 89–93
social, 86
substance and form, 34
unjust, 142–146
variety of, 79–82
veteran, 131–132
when and what to add, 106–107
proprietary estoppel, 141
public accommodations, 131–135
    relational justice, 132–133
    veteran property type, 131–132
public concerns, 144–146
public domain, 28, 292n44
public interest, 240
public use, 318n108

racial covenants, 138
Radin, Margaret Jane, 50, 206
Rawls, John, 42, 45, 57, 122
Raz, Joseph, 44, 90, 161, 263n88, 290n19, 292n53
reciprocity of advantage, 238–239
refusals to sell or lease, 135–136
regulation
    deregulation, 235, 316n84
    eminent domain, 237–238, 313n50
    legitimate regulations, 240
rehabilitative alimony, 145
Rehnquist, William, 312n32
relational justice, 7–9, 71, 124, 126–128, 195–200
    inherent limits of, 129
    property's, 113
    property's legitimacy and, 125–126
    three limitations on, 129–130
relationally just private authority, 128–131
rescue, easy, 141–142
residual category of property, 112–113
resources, 26–31
responsibility
    owners' responsibilities, 139–142, 144–146
    private responsibility for justice, 124–125
Restatement (Fourth) of Property, 105
Restatement of Servitudes, 152, 294n78
rights. *see also* property rights
    authors', 70
    to exclude, 36
    to exit, 43, 54, 59
    moral, 58
    to terminate long-term contracts, 202
    workers' inalienable rights, 198–199

Ripstein, Arthur, 115
Rose, Carol, 170
rule of change, 217–220
rule of law, 129
    as constraint, 168–170
    as guidance, 161–163
    liberal property and, 172–173
    property and, 159–161
rule(s)
    second-order, 218–219
    structural pluralism and, 165–166

sacrifice, individual, 226–227
Scalia, Antonin, 214–217, 219–220
Schauer, Frederick, 162
science, normal, 34–35
Scientific Policymaker, 32
second-order rules, 218–219
self-authorship, 43
self-determination, xii, 2, 39, 45
    autonomy as, 42–44
    future self, 200–202
    from independence to, 42–44
    as intertemporal, 64
selling or leasing, 135–136
Sen, Amartya, 301n24
Serkin, Christopher, 311n7
Shaffer Van Houweling, Molly, 70, 267n141
Shapira v. Union National Bank, 284n69
sharing, 51
    job-sharing, 194–195
    marital property, 109, 143–144
    second-order consent, 82
    work-sharing, 304n71
Shelley v. Kraemer, 138, 170–172
shoreline land, 212–214
Singer, Joseph, 131, 199
slavery, 233–234
Smith, Adam, 190, 196, 207
Smith, Henry, 27–29, 149, 159, 251n8, 270n2
social commons, 85–86
social contract, 117–118
social property types, 86
specific performance, 203
speech, freedom of, 135
stability, 151–152
    change and, 211–212
    across time, 210–212
stagnation, 151–152
standardization, 110–111

standards, informative, 166–168
stare decisis, 219
State v. Shack, 199
statism, 121
Stevens, John Paul, 222
Stop the Beach Renourishment, Inc. v. Fla. Dep't of Envtl. Prot., 216–217, 230–231, 237

Takings Clause, 215, 229
Tahoe-Sierra Pres. Coouncil, Inc. v. Tahoe Reg'l Planning Agency, 312n32
takings law, 238
    deregulation and, 235
    diminution of value, 239–240
    economic analysis of, 223
    eminent domain v. regulation, 237–238
    judicial takings, 237
    liberal, 242
    nuisance test, 242
    Penn Central balancing test, 227–228, 238, 240
    and public interest, 240
    reciprocity of advantage, 238–239
Taylor, Charles, 260n52
Televantos, Andreas, 271n6
things
    property's temporally-extended authority over, 63–65
    Smith on, 27–29
third party effects, 253n27, 271n6
time, 63–65, 210
transaction costs, 97
transindividualism, 259n47
transitions, property, 242
trust law, 83
trust property, 266n133

Uber, 51, 194
universalism, 173–174
utilitarian commons, 85–86

utilitarianism, 45
utility, 55–58
utility surplus, 203–204
utopia
    laws for, 99–100
    Nozick's theory of, 93–96

values
    autonomy as the ultimate value, 35–36
    autonomy-based value pluralism, 36–38
    neither ultimate nor instrumental, 47–48
    ultimate, intrinsic, and instrumental, 46–50
verification costs, 111
voice, workers', 206–207
voluntariness, 300n20
voluntary exchange, 182
vulnerability, 210–212

Wagner Act, 197
Waldron, Jeremy, 50, 169
waste law, 82–83, 96
Weinrib, Ernest, 115
welfare
    aggregate, 56
    dependence on, 121–122
    markets for, 186–187
welfare foundationalism, 56–58, 187
welfare state, 115, 122
Weyl, Glen, 56, 186
Williams, Bernard, 282n43
work sphere, 109–110
worker cooperatives, 109
workers' inalienable rights, 198–199
workers' voice, 206–207
work-sharing, 304n71
Wyman, Katrina, 262n68, 271n4

Zipcar, 51
zoning laws, 240